D0079981

By Leo Hansen

Second Edition

Culture and Architecture:

AN INTEGRATED HISTORY

Bassim Hamadeh, CEO and Publisher
Kassie Graves, Director of Acquisitions
Jamie Giganti, Senior Managing Editor
John Remington, Senior Field Acquisitions Editor
Monika Dziamka, Project Editor
Brian Fahey, Licensing Specialist
Miguel Macias, Graphic Designer
Kaela Martin and Berenice Quirino, Associate Editors
Kat Ragudos, Interior Designer

Printed in the United States of America

ISBN: 978-1-5165-1082-5 (pbk) / 978-1-5165-1083-2 (br)

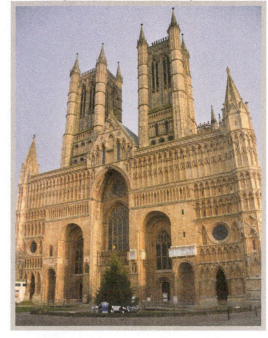

Contents

Preface

This book is divided into seven parts. After Part One, which is introductory, the remainder of the text is separated into six general eras or ages of cultural and architectural history: Prehistoric, Ancient, Late Antiquity, Medieval, Pre-Modern, and Modern. Chapters within each era describe the most significant styles and periods of each.

Some Notes by the Author on the Conventions of Dates and Measures

The terms *BC, Before Christ*, and *AD* for, *Anno Domini (in the year of the Lord)*, have been replaced in some recent academic works by BCE, *Before Common Era*, and CE, *Common Era*. This has raised the ire of some, who consider the removal of the reference to Christ after more than a thousand years to be just as insensitive as its inclusion. Removing the term *Anno Domini* will not change the basic fact that the birth date of Jesus Christ is the indelible demarcation line separating "positive" years from "negative" years. The non-existent year 0 has to be established at some point, and the present 0 used by the Gregorian, or Western calendar (whose adoption is universal with only a few exceptions) is unlikely to be changed any time soon. The days of the week and months of the years also have religious connotations, but there is little controversy over these, because they are named after gods whose adherents have long been silent.

That noted, in this textbook year dates after the year 0 do not have any designation, neither the traditional, *A.D.* or *AD*, nor the *C.E.* or *CE*. Years before 0 are noted with the designation BCE, which is an abbreviation of both *Before Christian Era* and *Before Common Era*. The author is hopeful that, because *BCE* is similar to the traditional *B.C.*, or *BC, Before Christ,* there will be little confusion. It is commonly believed that the birth of Christ actually took place in 4 BCE or 5 BCE, and thus, by being less specific, *Before Christian Era* is a more accurate term than *Before Christ*.

The notation of *c.* before a date (an abbreviation of the Latin *circa)* denotes that there is an uncertainty about the exact year. The notation of *c.* after the date is an abbreviation for century. The notation *b.* before a date indicates the year given is that in which an individual was born. The notation *r.* before a date indicates the years are those the individual reigned. The metric system is used for nearly all measurements of distances. The table below will help readers convert between the metric system and the English system. Historically, various systems of measurement have been used. The earliest measurement of length is the *cubit,* which was based upon the length of the human forearm. The Egyptian royal cubit, or *mahe*, was further divided into *palms* and *digits* and was approximately 52.3 centimeters in length. A Roman *cubitus* was 44.4 centimeters, or about 1.5 feet (a foot and one-half). A Roman foot, called a *pes*, was about 29.3 centimeters.

A Roman *digit* was one-sixteenth (0.016) of a pes. A Roman *palm* was one-fourth (0.25) of a pes. A *stadium* was 625 *pedes*. The metric system was first adopted by the French in 1799, and is now universal, with the exception, currently, of the United States and Myanmar (Burma).

METRIC UNIT	SYMBOL	APPROXIMATION	FACTOR	UNIT
1 millimeter	m	× 0.04	0.039370	inches
1 centimeter	cm	× 0.4	0.393700787	inches
1 meter	M	× 3.3	3.280839895	feet
1 kilometer	km	× 0.6	0.62137119	miles
1 kilometer	kKm	× 3280	3280.8399	feet

PART

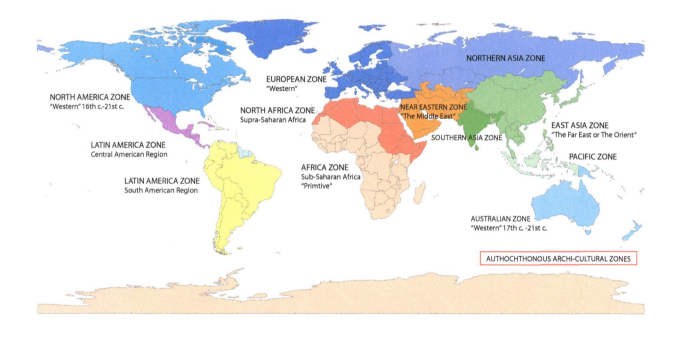

NORTH AMERICA ZONE
"Western" 16th c.-21st c.

EUROPEAN ZONE
"Western"

NORTHERN ASIA ZONE

NORTH AFRICA ZONE
Supra-Saharan Africa

NEAR EASTERN ZONE
"The Middle East"

EAST ASIA ZONE
"The Far East or The Orient"

LATIN AMERICA ZONE
Central American Region

SOUTHERN ASIA ZONE

PACIFIC ZONE

LATIN AMERICA ZONE
South American Region

AFRICA ZONE
Sub-Saharan Africa
"Primtive"

AUSTRALIAN ZONE
"Western" 17th c. -21st c.

AUTHOCHTHONOUS ARCHI-CULTURAL ZONES

ONE

Introduction

Architecture is the most easily observable of all art forms and the most visible remnant of past civilizations. Artifacts such as pottery, tools, or literature can be more valuable in helping to recreate the religious beliefs, socioeconomic structures, or ways of life of populations, but it is the monuments these groups leave behind that provide the most distinctive images—the pyramids of ancient Egypt, the temples of ancient Greece, the cathedrals of Medieval Europe. Although some works of architecture have been removed from their original sites and placed in museums (for example, the Pergamonmuseum in Berlin contains several whole ancient structures), works of architecture are freely found in civic and pastoral environments on every continent.

To properly study a work of architecture, it is important to view it within its cultural context; otherwise it loses much of its meaning, and thus, its value as an art form. If you take away a building's situation, its history, its mythology, the social mores of its builders, and the stories of its construction and occupation, then it becomes merely brick, stone, concrete, metal, or glass. With all of these factors included, a building becomes alive.

Even in ruins, the magnificence of the great monuments of history is scarcely diminished. For some, ruins elicit a nostalgic mourning for civilizations that have perished or otherwise been lost. The stone walls of the citadel at Mycenae in Greece call to mind Homer and the *Iliad*. The Roman Forum calls to mind Shakespeare's *Julius Caesar*. For others, it is the ruins themselves that are admired and become objects of the paeans of writers and poets:

> *For Time hath not rebuilt them, but uprear'd*
> *Barbaric dwellings on their shatter'd site,*
> *Which only make more mourn'd and more endear'd*
> *The last few rays of their far-scatter'd light*
> *And their crush'd relics of their vanish'd might.*

— from *Childe Harold's Pilgrimage*, Lord Byron (George Gordon) (1788–1824), about the ruins of Corinth, Greece

All cultural aspects, such as artifacts, art, literature, etc., are categorized to help historians examine these elements in their proper contexts, which in turn, allows for the identification of patterns of ideas and thought, cross-cultural comparisons of these patterns and ideas, the chronological development of methods and artistic trends, and the influences of or upon other aspects of culture. The most common classification of cultural artifacts is by period or style. The terms *period* and *style* are often used conjunctively in broad discussions of cultural history. The online Art and Architecture Thesaurus (AAT) sponsored by the Getty Research Institute classifies works of art and architecture using the single category consisting of "any named, defined style, historical or artistic period, movement, group, or school."

In art, *style* is simply a one-word description of a work's cultural and historical situation. Some works of art fit neatly into categories, and others do not. The works of Frank Lloyd Wright, perhaps in testament to his comportment or disposition, defy compartmentalization. Familiar terms, such as *Medieval* and *Renaissance*, were not products of their own ages, but rather labels applied long after their time period. The Middle Ages referred to the period between the ancient world and the modern world, but the passage of time has shifted what is considered to be modern. Gothic architecture was once considered "modern." The term "Renaissance" was scarcely used until 1860, when Jakob Burckhardt published the work *The Civilization of the Renaissance in Italy*. Some buildings—especially monumental works like churches—took centuries to complete from start to finish. Some, such as the Köln (Cologne) Cathedral in Germany, maintained its original style, even though the prevailing styles had changed several times during its construction process. Other buildings or building groups have an amalgam of styles, as subsequent generations of builders and architects reacted to changes in social, economic, technological, and aesthetic values.

There is a fluidity inherent in styles and periods, both in place and time. However, the communication of ideas from one community to another was considerably slower previously than it is today. In the fifteenth century, the Flamboyant Gothic style was prevalent in France at the same time that the Renaissance prevailed in neighboring Italy. The German architectural theorist Paul Frankl wrote that "the development of a style is an intellectual process overriding national characteristics and individual artists." Nonetheless, there are exceptions. Some styles are uniquely nationalistic, such as English Tudor. Some are individualistic: Andrea Palladio (Palladian) and Henry Richardson (Richardsonian) are among several individuals who have styles named after them. Eugène-Emmanuel Viollet-Le-Duc (1814–1879), the French theorist, wrote a ten-volume Descriptive Dictionary of French Architecture. In it, he defined style as "the manifestation of an ideal based upon a principle." Style belongs to mankind; it is independent of the object.

A *period*, or *era*, is a particular length of time defined by a unique social, political, or natural condition or circumstance. A period may contain several styles that have enough differences to warrant their independence from one another but have enough similarities to support their affiliation within a single period. There is not always universal agreement by historians on the names of periods and styles. The term "Late Antiquity" has emerged relatively recently as a distinct period in cultural history, its styles previously seen as either Ancient or Medieval. In the twentieth and twenty-first centuries, new styles have emerged at unprecedented rate. If critical history can offer any guidance, it is likely that the final nomenclatures and divisions of what we presently call the Modern Era will not be settled until sometime in the distant future.

CHAPTER ONE

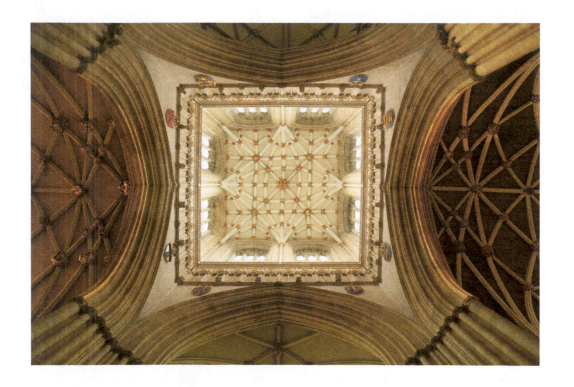

The Beauty of Architecture

Architecture is the art which so disposes and adorns the edifices raised by man for whatsoever uses, that the sight of them contributes to his mental health, power and pleasure.

It is very necessary, in the outset of all inquiry, to distinguish carefully between Architecture and Building.

To build, literally to confirm, is by common understanding to put together and adjust the several pieces of any edifice or receptacle of a considerable size. Thus we have church building, house building, ship building, and coach building. That one edifice stands, another floats, and another is suspended on iron springs, makes no difference in the nature of the art, if so it may be called, of building or edification. The persons who profess that art, are severally builders, ecclesiastical, naval, or of whatever other name their work may justify; but building does not become architecture merely by the stability of what it erects; and it is no more architecture which raises a church, or which fits it to receive and contain with comfort a required number of persons occupied in certain religious offices, than it is architecture which makes a carriage commodious or a ship swift. I do not, of course, mean that the word is not often, or even may not be legitimately, applied in such a sense (as we speak of naval architecture); but in that sense architecture ceases to be one of the fine arts, and it is therefore better not to run the risk, by loose nomenclature, of the confusion which would arise, and has often arisen, from extending principles which belong altogether to building, into the sphere of architecture proper.[1]

—from *The Seven Lamps of Architecture* by John Ruskin.

Art is a means of self-expression; it is the expression of an idea and satisfaction derived from its exploration, both by the artist and the person experiencing the art.

However, art is more than just an idea. It has substance. It must speak a universal—not a personal—language. It must have clarity and integrity, and it should be harmonious. It should be a complete entity within itself, so that nothing could be added or taken away without affecting

[1] Ruskin, John. The Seven Lamps of Architecture. http://www.gutenberg.org/files/35898/35898.txt

its value. Art speaks symbolically, not directly. It is food for thought. It must be sincere, and it must be truthful. If the end purpose of a work is praise or fame or profit, then it is self-conscious, and therefore, it is art, not Art.

These thoughts are a select few of many in the history of human thought that have proposed well-reasoned responses to the question "What is Art?" The inquirers have been philosophers, artists, writers, critics, and the merely inquisitive. Providing a definition of art is a relatively straightforward task. To define Art, however, is more elusive; it is a journey with no certain end. Some have proposed that any analysis of art is completely subjective, while others have seen a potential for objectivity. A child's schoolhouse drawing hung on the door of a refrigerator is art, yet the deceptively simplistic abstract works of art by Paul Klee—the Swiss artist who once mused that "art does not reproduce the visible, it makes visible"—are called Art. It seems reasonable enough to assume that a child's crayon drawing should not be given the same consideration as a drawing by Leonardo da Vinci, but what are the tools of rational thought that give credibility to this assumption? The innumerable objects that are, in the broad spectrum, in between the ordinary and the magnificent are the heart of the matter and are the subject of the debate: At what point does the criticism become subjective?

If you enter any museum or gallery filled with late twentieth century and twenty-first century works or installations, you may be apt to come away with the belief that anything is art. But if anything is art, then nothing is art. That is simply how language works: a word limits and confines an object—it is this or this, but not that or that. When Marcel Duchamp submitted a porcelain urinal for an exhibition of the Society of Independent Artists in New York in 1917 and called it "Fountain," the society rejected the work, and Duchamp resigned from the group. However, since then, the concept of what constitutes Art expanded exponentially, and today, there is a general acceptance of the notion that if an object is placed in a museum or gallery, it is Art. Not everyone, of course, agrees with this assessment. The ongoing debate over this and other issues dealing with the principles of art and beauty is the crux of the area of philosophical inquiry called *aesthetics*. The Modernist movement of aesthetics focused on the experience of art and smiled-upon avant-garde experimentalism, such as Duchamp's "Fountain." The Postmodernists expanded the "art world" even further by embracing popular arts and works, by accepting a greater degree of self-consciousness, and by diminishing the role of the object of the art and placing more emphasis upon its context.

James Joyce (1882–1941), in a notebook entry from 1903, defined art simply as the "human disposition of sensible or intelligible matter for an aesthetic end." He explained further that objects that are considered to be utilitarian, like "houses, clothes, and furniture" can be works of art if they are "disposed for an aesthetic end." This distinction is appreciably helpful when considering the notion of whether architecture is or is not art. Although there are some dissenters, the most common resolution of such queries is yes, it is an art, and its functionality is the most important quality that separates it from the other arts.

Georg Wilhelm Friedrich Hegel (1770–1831), in his work *Aesthetic* (1835), regarded the pyramid as the paradigm of architecture, since its function is a symbolic one. The symbolic potential of architecture is seen clearly in the pyramid. The Great Pyramid of Giza, the largest of all pyramids ever built, was built around 4,500 years ago. It was built by Khnum-Khufwy, or Khufu, as a tomb, but also as an emblem of his apotheosis as a god-king. The pharaohs had many names, and Khufu had included a reference to the god Horus among his titles. The Eye of Horus, originally a hieroglyph, is a sign not only of royal authority, but of protection. In the Middle Ages, the eye became a symbol of the trinity, of God watching over humanity. There is a pyramid and an "Eye of Providence" on the reverse side of the Great Seal of the United States, which is reproduced on every one-dollar bill. The symbolic value of the pyramid and the eye together is clear: God is protecting the nation and its people. The symbolic value of architecture is key to understanding its place among painting, sculpture, music, etc.

The most nonpareil characteristic of architecture, relative to the other arts, is its monumentality. Great works of architecture are generally described as being majestic, prodigious, or awe-inspiring. Even the most diminutive buildings, such as the Maison Carrée in Nîmes, France, are of a much grander scale than other works of art. There is potential for such scale in an epic novel, with help from the imagination of the reader, but the physical stature of literature is inconsequential. Architecture is the most visible and the most comprehensive of all the arts. It is sculpture, mathematics, physics, spirituality, faith, discovery, invention, intuition, history, and philosophy—all in one. The great monuments of architecture are conspicuous testaments to human imagination and achievement.

The vast majority of buildings constructed have no ambitions to become art, and thus, there is both architecture and Architecture. There are several objective means we can use to elevate certain works of architecture, at least to the point where subjective discussion is possible. Any object, made by nature or man, that is considered to be of such excellence, grandeur, or beauty as to inspire great admiration or awe, is said to be sublime. The best modern buildings, like the great buildings of antiquity, remind us that the puissance of architecture is its ability to create a beauty that is mild enough to contribute to, and not detract from, its immediate milieu, and strong enough to demonstrate those qualities that make it exceptional. Works of architecture become public from the moment of their creation. Architecture, like all the arts, has the power to create a cathartic beauty. But unlike the other arts, it can do so *en passant*—because it is an indispensable part of our daily existence.

There are many factors that contribute to the sublimity of a work of architecture. If one looks at all the buildings in an encyclopedia of architectural history such as *A History of Architecture on the Comparative Method* (1905) by Bannister Fletcher (1866–1953), almost all of the buildings that are cited reflect a consciousness of design—an intent to create an object of beauty on the part of the architect or builder. While a composer of music, an artist, or a writer may claim the purest intentions that the art they create has been done for art's sake, it is more difficult for an architect to make that claim. An architect builds structures that will no doubt be seen, no doubt be subject to critical opinion, and no doubt will affect the environment in which lives the entirety of the world's population.

An understatement, as well as an overstatement, can lead to sublimity in any work of art. It is reticence, not the promulgation of form, that is the tour de force of Frank Lloyd Wright's Fallingwater residence in Southwest Pennsylvania. Conversely, it is the richness of texture that gives a Baroque work, either in music or architecture, its artistic value. An understated design succeeds in one instance, but not in others, for reasons of context, scale, proportion, and similar aspects of design. In other words, the simplicity that marks the memorable passages in Beethoven's symphonic masterpieces would not be as effective if the context of the entire symphony, or the realm of contemporaneous music, was of like construction. Self-conscious statements in themselves do not necessarily create masterpieces. A Rolls-Royce medallion and front piece applied to a Volkswagen Beetle is not sublime, it is kitsch. A pediment gratuitously applied to the facade of a small residence or a branch bank is not grand, it is frivolous. Another condition of the sublime in an architectural work of art is that is must be "suprafunctional"—that is, it must consider the non-utilitarian aspects of its placement. While this may be construed as a prima facie exclusion of Modernism, it is not necessarily so. If the expression of its function, or its structure, or both, is integral to the design, then such a statement goes beyond function. The English art critic John Ruskin (1819–1900) believed there are two virtues of buildings. The first is that they do "their practical duty well," and the second is that "they be graceful and pleasing in doing it."

Works that are considered to be sublime likely possess an eccentricity—innovation, novelty, and distinction. If art is an imperfect reproduction of nature, then it is the imprecision of art that makes it sublime. Francis Bacon (1561–1626) noted in his essay "Of Beauty" that "there is no excellent beauty that hath not some strangeness in the proportion." When we see the perfunctory recapitulation of designs in a "chain" restaurant or cookie-cutter housing development, the language is not only familiar, it is vulgar. It has no dignity.

The first known treatise on architecture, and the only one to survive from antiquity, was written by the Roman architect Marcus Vitruvius Pollio (c. 85–c. 20 BCE), more widely known simply as Vitruvius. His work,

De Architectura (also known as *The Ten Books on Architecture*, or simply *On Architecture*) addressed the layout of cities, the proper use of building materials, the design of temples, the orders, public buildings, private buildings, finish materials and methods, water, sundials and clocks, and machines. Its discovery in the early fifteenth century was an important event that helped instruct architects of the Renaissance. In its most noted passage, Vitruvius states that the three objectives for buildings should be durability, convenience, and beauty, famously translated by Henry Wotten in 1624 as "firmness, commodity, and delight."

Vitruvius saw in the human body, with its precise proportions and symmetry, a guide for designing a temple, the archetypal structure of Greek and Roman architecture. In *Book 1, The Fundamental Principles of Architecture*, he described the most important elements of Architecture: Order, a measured consideration of building components as their own entities and as parts of the whole; Arrangement, putting things in their proper places; Eurythmy, beauty derived from the proportions of components; Symmetry, an agreement between the components and their placement in the whole; Propriety, adherence to approved principles, the maintenance of principles throughout both the exterior and interior, and attentiveness to the issues that affect a building or its site that are derived from nature; and Economy, a balance of cost and common sense.

The Roman philosopher Plotinus (204–269) took the Classical idea of the correlation between "whole" and "part" a step further. He wrote that "only a compound can be beautiful." The parts do not have a beauty in themselves, but as contributing parts of the whole.

Although there are no architectural texts prior to Vitruvius, Plato's influential discussion of form, coincidently or not, provides a platform for the nature of architecture in Classical Greece. Plato (c. 427 or c. 423–c. 347 BCE) argued that the consideration of εἶδος, or form, is far more constructive than a consideration of the object, because it is closer to being real; it is eternal and never changing. An object may be imperfect, and it may be immature or it may age. The form of Greek temple changed little for centuries. Greek architects sought not to invent new forms of the temple, but to achieve, in their material object, the closest proximity to the perfection of that form. Johann Joachim Winckelman (1717–1768), in his essay "Reflections on the Imitation of Greek Works in Painting and Sculpture" (1755), citing Plato, wrote that ideal forms of beauty "come from images created by the mind alone."

The philosopher Thomas Aquinas (1225–1274) wrote in his eminent work *Summa Theologiae* that there are three requirements for beauty: *integritas sive perfectio*, *proportio sive consonantia*, and *claritas* (integrity or perfection, proportion or consonance, and clarity). When Aquinas was a student in Cologne, he studied Aristotle, but this work is not just a reiteration of ancient Greek philosophy. For Aquinas, beauty is also a personal or human experience. Beauty is transcendental—a ray of light penetrating through clouds in a sky possesses the quality of beauty as much as it possesses luminosity. However, it is our experience of the object that completes the relationship—the interaction between the viewer and the object. The qualities of integrity and consonance are validated by our perception of them.

A building's integrity comes from its faithful adherence to its design intentions, eschewing the wanton use of architectural languages, the forced application of harmony at the expense of utility, the capricious use of styles, the abnegation of meaning, the inhibition of substance, and reliance on repetition alone to create pattern and rhythm. Ruskin hoped, at the conclusion of *The Stones of Venice*, that architects would design more structures like "Giotto's campanile." Little did Ruskin know that there eventually would be a building just like the campanile in Las Vegas. When a building is copied or repeated, brick for brick, then its value is undermined, just as a copy of a Renoir painting, no matter how finely crafted, also lacks integrity.

A mathematical basis for proportional harmony has been known since at least the time of the Greek mathematician and philosopher Pythagoras (570–495 BCE). He compared the sounds made by plucking two strings of a lyre at proportional lengths: 1:1, 1:2, 2:3, and 3:4 and found each of them to be in harmony. The 1:1 (the same length and the same sound) is called the *unison*; the

1:2 the *diapason* (the modern octave); the 2:3 *the diapente* (the modern fifth); the 3:4 the *diatessaron* (the modern fourth). The geometrical equivalents of these proportions are 1:1, a single point; 1:2, the golden rectangle (Figure A); 2:3 the sides of the triangles of a pentagram (Figure B); and 3:4, the 3:4:5 ratio of the triangles of a pentagram (Figure C). Though it should be noted, the actual ratio of the golden rectangle is 0.618, not quite 2/3.

The *golden section* is the division of a line in such a manner that the ration of the greater part to the whole is equal to the ratio of the smaller part is to the greater part. The unique mathematical elegance of the golden section can be seen in the equations $1 \div 1.618 = 0.618$, $1.618 \times 1.618 = 2.618$, $1/\Phi = \Phi - 1$ (Φ is the golden section ratio), and $\Phi \times \Phi = 1 + \Phi$. Numerous studies have demonstrated that Φ is found abundantly in the designs of nature, most famously the nautilus shell. The golden section can be found in ancient structures by precise or intuitive planning. For instance, at the Great Pyramid of Khufu (twenty-sixth century BCE) at Giza, the distance of half the base of the pyramid and the apothem, the line drawn from its center (its top) to its side (the end of the base) forms a golden section ratio. Pyramids are not complicated structures, but they require a sophisticated understanding of mathematical and geometric principles. There is evidence that Egyptian builders may have been aware of a mathematical foundation for visual harmony two millennia before Pythagoras.

The mathematical relationship between music and architecture has fascinated architects and architectural theorists throughout history. René Ouvrard (1624–1694) wrote in *Architecture harmonique* (1677) that a building cannot be perfect "if it does not follow the same rules as composition or the harmonizing of musical chords."

The concept of comprehensible order was first developed in the Classical period. While the order of a temple from Ancient Greece is relatively easy to discern, the order of Frank Gehry's Bilbao Museum is not. Yet the apparent disorder of Bilbao can ultimately be seen as just another type of order, one that uses more complicated geometries than traditional buildings. An architect defines the order of a building by reference to a style, by establishing a new style, or by combining aspects of the

FIGURE 1.2

The Greek astronomer Euclid. Hexagonal Pabel from the Florence Cathedral. Nino Pisano (c.1349–1368). Museo del Duomo, Florence, Italy.

old and new. Within the parameters of its own rules, the architectural style of a building, a design may succeed or fail, depending upon the ability of its designer to grasp, and then to re-evaluate, its expected order. The celebrated "arms" of St. Peter's Cathedral in Rome have intentions that are clear: they welcome all into the church.

Ibn al-Haytham (c. 965–1039), was a scholar of science and mathematics who translated Greek texts into Arabic. In his book *Kitab al manazir*, or *Book of Optics* (c. 1027), he expanded upon the Platonic notion of form, incorporating the process of the vision and its effect upon how we evaluate an object. He noted there are two ways of seeing, by glancing and by contemplation. In glancing at an object, a person sees only its "manifest features." If a person contemplates all its parts, it can know the form of the object. The Classical conception of the fundamental association of the parts of an object and its whole is taken a step further: the beholder of an object cannot ascertain it completely without knowing its parts. Later aesthetic philosophers would argue the point even further: all necessary contemplation of an object is affected by culture.

Medieval architects attribute their inspiration not from Nature, but from God himself. Abbot Suger (1081–1151), who is credited with facilitating, at least, the rise of the Gothic style in France, quoted what was obviously a well-known expression of his time in his book *The Book of Suger: Abbot of St.-Denis, On What Was Done Under His Administration* (1144–1149): "For other foundation can no man lay that that is laid, which is Jesus Christ." Of the sumptuousness of the exuberant Gothic detailing, he wrote, "Our sufficiency is our God."

Leon Battista Alberti (1404–1472) was an Italian who was an embodiment of a Renaissance man; he was an architect, writer, poet, artist, and philosopher. During the Renaissance, architects and artists sought a return to Classical ideals, so it is not surprising that Alberti's treatise on the art of building *De re aedificatoria* (1452) was modeled after Vitruvius's work, of which he was both admirer and critic. Alberti reiterated the Classical notion that "Nature must be imitated" in the design of buildings. He cited three basic components of beauty: number, outline, and position. A fourth, *concinnitas*, an elegant or skillful arrangement of objects, is created when these components are composed and connected appropriately. The principles of beauty in architecture are the same as those for beauty in art and in nature. Everything that is created by nature is achieved by the laws of *concinnitas*. "Beauty," he wrote in his treatise on painting, *De Pictura* (1435), "is the adjustment of all parts proportionately so that one cannot add or subtract or change without impairing the harmony of the whole."

Andrea Palladio (1508–1580) was the most influential architect of the Renaissance, and one of the most influential in all of history. His treatise *I Quattro Libri dell'Architettura*, or *The Four Books of Architecture* (1570) provided in-depth details and drawings of the classical orders and the decorative language of architecture; his own villa and townhouse projects; his own public building projects; and reconstructions of the temples of ancient Rome. Like Alberti, Palladio's formula for beauty evoked the attitudes of the Classical world: there is a proper place and situation for all buildings and their components "neither above or below its dignity and use." Like Alberti and the architects of ancient Greece and Rome, he thought the parts should each to each other and each to the whole.

Vicenzo Scamozzi (1548–1616), the architect of Salzburg Cathedral and the building that forms the southern facade of Piazza San Marco in Venice, published *L'idea della architettura universal* in 1615. He also believed in a strong role for mathematics in architecture. For him, architecture is a science; beauty is gained by careful and rational attention to the same mathematical principles used by God to create the perfections of Nature, the quintessential specimen of which is the human body.

Beginning in the medieval period, and continuing on through and after the Renaissance, Christian architects have been fascinated with the design of the temples of the Old Testament—Solomon's Temple, the First Temple, destroyed by the Neo-Babylonians in 587 BCE; the Second Temple, destroyed by the Romans in 70, and Ezekiel's Temple, from the *Book of Ezekiel* 40–42. Juan Bautista Villalpando (1552–1608), in his *Ezekiel Commentaries* (1604) linked the design of the Old Testament temples to Vitruvius and suggested that, for an object to be considered beautiful, it must be capable of being divided into three parts "that are so contrary to each other they cannot be reduced to a single fabric." This is, as a matter of course, a concept first posited by Aristotle (384–322 BCE) in *Poetics* (335 BCE), in which he wrote about the tripartite nature of tragedy.

The reverence of architects for the role of symmetry in architectural aesthetics faltered little until the Modern period. Eteinne-Louis Boullée (1728–1799), an artist and architect, wrote a treatise on architecture in the last decade of the eighteenth century entitled *Architecture, Essai sur l'art*, in which we wondered what humans would think of someone whose nose was not centered, whose eyes were not equally placed from the center line of the face, and whose limbs were of different lengths. He refused to accept even "the slightest disorder" in a composition. Variety, grandeur, and grace were other qualities that contribute to an object's beauty.

The British architect Sir John Soane (1753–1837), whose residence (now museum) in London is teeming with curios from the ancient world, wrote that buildings should have a distinctness of character and be "comfortable to the uses it is intended for" in a lecture to the Royal Academy sometime between 1812 and 1815. Soane's remarks prefigured those made almost a century later by the American Louis Sullivan (1856–1924), who famously thought that a building's form should follow its function. The French architect Eugéne-Emmanuel Viollet-le-Duc (1814–1879) also declared, in a lecture in 1859, a similar notion: "There is no style but that which is appropriate to the object." Viollet-le-Duc called upon architects to invent an "architecture of our own times," using the acquired knowledge of history, rather than reusing the styles of the past, "An architecture is created only by a rigorous inflexible compliance with modern requirements." He called upon a wholesale rejection of architectural schemes that do not consider the building's structure.

In the early nineteenth century, architects still adhered to the idea of unity. Claude-Nicolas Ledoux (1736–1806) wrote that "the relationship of the masses to details or ornaments," and unity is the form of all beauty, words uttered by Augustine of Hippo (354–430) more than 1400 years earlier (*omnis porro pulchritudinis forma unitas est*).

The German philosopher Immanuel Kant (1724–1804) is generally considered the most influential philosopher since antiquity, and his work *The Critique of Aesthetic Judgment* is widely considered the most important discussion of aesthetics, especially in its relation with the modern era. Kant described the judgment of aesthetics as having four "moments," and he offered a definition of beauty at the end of each of these spheres of thought. Beauty is an object of a delight or aversion that is apart from any interest; that which is universally pleasing; the form of the purposiveness of an object, so far as this is perceived in it without any representation of purpose; and that which, apart from a concept, is recognized as an object of necessary delight. It is the third of these, regarding purpose, that is important in a discussion about architecture. The plastic arts—sculpture and architecture—are kinds of formative arts—those created for the senses. Unlike sculpture, architecture presents concepts that are possible only through art. Its form is

not derived from nature, but an arbitrary purpose. Kant wrote this long before sculptors created abstract works from steel beams, but the distinction is still clear—unlike the other arts, is a product of the "elective will."

Many of Kant's aesthetic concepts were harbingers of the modern attitude toward art. For instance, in *The Critique of Aesthetic Judgment*, he wrote that there can be no objective rule for the judgment of beauty, which is affected and limited by experience. Sublimity does not exist in nature, only in our minds. On the other hand, aesthetic judgments can be universal if they are rational and disinterested—that is, if one removes a posteriori knowledge, that which is based upon experience or empirical evidence.

Kant's differentiation of architecture as an introspective, rather than an allusive, creation was reiterated by fellow German philosopher Arthur Schopenhauer (1788–1860) in *The World as Will and Idea* (1818, 1844). "It does not give us a copy," he wrote, "but the thing itself." The architect has the power not just to repeat an idea, as the other arts do. His or her object is the idea. What of symmetry, which has been paramount to the idea of beauty since the ancient world? It is not necessary. Ruins are beautiful, and they quite often have lost their symmetry.

By the second half of the nineteenth century, an intellectual crusade among philosophers, artists, and architects to untether the dependence of aesthetic thought from Classical ideals began to gain some traction. In his essay "In the Cause of Architecture" (1908) Frank Lloyd Wright (1867–1959) wrote that "the uniformity of type" that had permeated architectural history from the beginning, would never return; traditionalism was yielding to individualism. His vision was an architecture that was simpler, more expressive but with fewer lines and fewer forms, more articulate with less labor, more fluent, more plastic, more coherent, and more organic. Unlike many other modernists, Wright saw a role for ornament. Adolf Loos (1870–1933) was a Moravian who worked and lived most of his life in Vienna. His essay "Ornament and Crime," also written in 1908, expressed the belief that ornament in architecture was "no longer an expression of our culture."

Charles-Eduord Jeanneret, known as Le Corbusier (1887–1966), recognized the need for significant adjustments in architectural design in response to the industrial and mechanical ages of the nineteenth and twentieth centuries, the most significant of which was a greater focus on "utility, comfort, and practical arrangement." Nonetheless, he saw that architecture is alone among the arts in achieving a "platonic grandeur." The aim of architecture, he wrote in *Vers une architecture*, often translated at *Toward a New Architecture* (1923), is to create a "perception of the harmony which lies in emotional relationships." This can be achieved through mathematical order, speculation, and the aforementioned platonic grandeur—the use of ideal forms.

The rejection of Classicism was not based on the notion that Classical thought was no longer valid, but rather that it was no longer timely. The German philosopher Martin Heidegger (1889–1976) believed that the essences of varied aspects of a particular culture, such as poetry and the other arts, are rooted in their own historical era. The Greek temple, for example, by its very nature has more significance to the ancient Greek than it does to those living in the modern era. Art opens the eyes of the beholder, but these revelations occupy moments of a specific place and time. When art can no longer perform this function, it loses it worth.

Walter Gropius (1883–1969), the founder of the Bauhaus school, presented one of the most concise manifestos of Modernism in his book produced for an exhibition in Dessau in 1925 entitled *International Architecture*. The aim of architecture is to "design our surrounding buildings from an inner law without lies and ornamentation, to represent functionally their meaning and purpose through the tension of their building masses, and to reject everything superfluous that masks their absolute form." The interrelationship of form and beauty is a particularly modern concept and the most important ideas of architectural aesthetics today. Louis Kahn (1901–1974), in his essay "Order and Form" (1955) said that form "emerges from the structural elements inherent in the form." Le Corbusier wrote that architecture is "the play of forms … correct, wise and magnificent."

FIGURE 1.3

Human Scale: Le Corbusier's Modulor Man. Unité d'habitation. Marseilles, France

An interest in the purity of form, which reached a peak in the middle of the twentieth century, had lost its steam in the latter decades of the century. One of the most influential books of architectural theory from this period was *Complexity and Contradiction in Architecture* (1966) by Robert Venturi (b. 1925), with its famous retort to Mies van der Rohe's earlier bon mot "Less is more," "Less is not more. Less is a bore." In essence, richness of meaning is to be favored over clarity of meaning. Venturi's book is often cited as the opening salvo in the war against modernism. Its antithesis, Postmodernism, began in earnest in the 1970s and lasted a few decades.

As a philosophy and theory, Postmodernism rejected absolutism in favor of relativism and pluralism. There is no truth that has not been affected by context, whether political, social, or historical. Post-modernist theories of architecture, on the contrary, embraced history. "Traditional post-modernists," according to Robert Stern, in his essay "The Doubles of Post-Modern" (1981), "reject the anti-historical biases of modernism." Historical influences should not be seen as "constraints on … artistic excellence." Michael Graves, the architect of one of the icons of Postmodernism, The Portland Municipal Services Building (1982), wrote in his essay "A Case for Figurative Architecture" that a "significant architecture must incorporate both internal and external expression."

Two academic labels of the late twentieth century, whose origins were tied to philosophy and literary criticism—Poststructuralism and Deconstructivism—were also associated with architectural trends of the late twentieth and early twenty-first centuries. Poststructuralism argued against the model of using structures to evaluate human culture. In architecture, this meant a complete disregard and denial of formal "rules" of design. Deconstruction is a theory or critical analysis that denies the existence of a single meaning of signs and symbols; therefore, no object of discussion can be independent or self-sufficient. Deconstructivist architecture promotes the rejection of familiar or traditional forms as being historically derivative in favor of forms that are distorted or dislocated. It aims to provoke, not nurture, the senses; ideals of harmony and coherence are replaced by discomfort and disquietude.

In addition to form, much discussion in the later years of the twentieth century focused on functionality—both its veneration and denigration. In "Building Dwelling Thinking" from *Poetry, Language, Thought* (1971) Heidegger wrote "only if we are capable of dwelling (which is the basic character of Being), only then can we build." The British architect and critic Kenneth Frampton bemoaned in the 1974 essay "On Reading Heidegger" a tendency of architects to build "monuments" in situations that simply demanded "buildings," a cry heard even more often some 40 years on. On the other hand, Peter Eisenman (b. 1932) in his essay "Post-Functionalism" suggested "theoretical assumptions of functionalism are in fact cultural rather than universal." In the absence of functionalism, there are the positive alternatives, ones in which consciousness of the object itself is raised to higher levels than ever known before.

For Further Discussion

What is Art? Establish your own criteria and methods for the evaluation of art and for the inclusion of various art forms in general aesthetic discussions. Use examples to clarify and amplify your positions.

CHAPTER TWO

Culture and Architecture

…Glaucus now came before the Temple of Fortune, the jutting portico of that beautiful fane (which is supposed to have been built by one of the family of Cicero, perhaps by the orator himself) (and) imparted a dignified and venerable feature to a scene otherwise more brilliant than lofty in its character. That temple was one of the most graceful specimens of Roman architecture. It was raised on a somewhat lofty podium; and between two flights of steps ascending to a platform stood the altar of the goddess. From this platform another flight of broad stairs led to the portico, from the height of whose fluted columns hung festoons of the richest flowers. On either side the extremities of the temple were placed statues of Grecian workmanship; and at a little distance from the temple rose the triumphal arch crowned with an equestrian statue of Caligula, which was flanked by trophies of bronze. In the space before the temple a lively throng were assembled—some seated on benches and discussing the politics of the empire, some conversing on the approaching spectacle of the amphitheatre. One knot of young men were lauding a new beauty, another discussing the merits of the last play; a third group, more stricken in age, were speculating on the chance of the trade with Alexandria, and amidst these were many merchants in the Eastern costume, whose loose and peculiar robes, painted and gemmed slippers, and composed and serious countenances, formed a striking contrast to the tunicked forms and animated gestures of the Italians. For that impatient and lively people had, as now, a language distinct from speech—a language of signs and motions, inexpressibly significant and vivacious: their descendants retain it, and the learned Jorio hath written a most entertaining work upon that species of hieroglyphical gesticulation.[1]

—from *The Last Days of Pompeii* by Edward George Bulwer-Lytton (1803–1873)

On the twenty-fourth of August in the year 79, Pompeii and Herculaneum, Roman cities near the Amalfi coast in present-day Italy, were destroyed by the volcanic eruption of Mount Vesuvius. The lava flow and ash from the volcano buried the city and its people as if they were time capsules deliberately left in place for a distant generation to find. Plaster casts made by archaeologists of the voids left in the hardened volcanic rock after the bodies of victims had decayed over time, show stop-action images of the horror of the last hours of minutes in the cities. Bulwer-Lytton's historical novel tries to imagine the lives of the people that lived in the doomed city of Pompeii, but the above passage speaks of something more important—the fundamental interrelationship between culture and architecture, universal in place and unbroken in time. The novel's characters are immersed in the city's architecture, as we are in our own architecture of today. Architecture serves an important function in our lives, but at the same time, it also can enrich our lives culturally, even spiritually.

Culture is the single most distinctive quality separating humans from other beings. It is the most visible barometer of the enduring attainments of civilizations. The annals of history often focus on political and social upheaval, the foundation and growth of empires, the rise and fall of power and grandeur. Individuals have gained fame

---

1   Bulwer-Lytton and Edward George, The Last Days of Pompeii, pp. 62. Copyright in the Public Domain.

FIGURE 2.2

Temple of Vespasian. Pompeii, Italy.

by bragging of their conquests, while others gave gained their notoriety in the failure to satisfy their aggressive ambitions. Yet the lands and riches gained and lost, as a matter of course, are not maintained forever. "Human happiness," wrote Herodotus, "the Father of History," "never remains long in the same place." Culture, however, survives and becomes an eternal testament to the people who forge and fashion the crests and emblems of the trials and triumphs of human existence. The assessment of a civilization, nation, or social group is largely based on an analysis of its intellectual and cultural achievements.

While a precise definition of culture may be as elusive as a precise definition of art, for the sake of this text, culture is defined as the art, artifacts, tools, social practices, beliefs, and habitats of a distinct or particular social group. In essence, it is the aggregate of every aspect of a society, each aspect affecting the other and becoming a complex matrix of activities and thoughts. A group's culture acquires a personality in much the same manner

as an individual, and these characteristic traits are passed on from generation to generation. A society accumulates a body of collective knowledge, which in turn affects an individual's thought processes, moral values, aesthetic ideals, and religious beliefs. Areas or regions can be linked culturally, but not politically. Ancient Greek culture prior to Alexander was shared by sovereign and independent city-states throughout the Central Mediterranean.

The diffusion of culture is accomplished through dissemination, the dispersal of ideas or culture by means of communication or direct contact, and through genetic transmission passed on from generation to generation. The most common facilitator of the dissemination of ideas is trade. Cultural exchange is a useful byproduct of the essential process of the exchange of goods, services, and capital. Trade was a major factor in the development of Egyptian, Mesopotamian, and Greek civilizations, with the Nile River, the Tigris and Euphrates, and the Aegean and Mediterranean seas serving as their respective conduits. War is another facilitator, sometimes beneficial to both the victor and the vanquished. It is believed that the ogive arch, of Gothic architecture, was brought back to Europe by the Crusaders when they returned from the Holy Land. The conquest of Northern Africa, Europe, and Western Asia by the Roman Empire spread Roman culture to those areas and, later, helped to spread Christianity. In addition to trade, travel and tourism also facilitates the exchange of cultural ideas and practices.

The expansion or migration of a population is yet another method of cultural diversion. In general, when a cultural idea emanates from a source, its influence diminishes, both in intensity and in number, as the distance from the source increases. At the periphery, when two adjacent populations meet, there is an opportunity for the co-mingling of ideas and, thus, for potential changes to the mores of each population. Gothic architecture is considerably uniform in its practice in France, where it was born, but in Italy and in Eastern Europe, more variations of the style are visible.

Colonization allows for cultures to affect new or repopulated areas, often at remote distances from their origins. The Greeks exported their culture to Southern

Italy and Sicily, an area called Magna Graecia, beginning in the eighth century BCE although they were not technically true "colonies." Colonial architecture, in the Americas, in Coastal and Southern Africa, and in Southern Asia, distributed European culture across the planet between the late fifteenth century and the early twentieth century.

Literature has also been a catalyst throughout history for the widespread spread of culture. In the twelfth century, the romance became a popular source of entertainment in Europe. At first written in verse, then later in prose, romance literature created stories of love, adventure, and mysticism that were, in part, based upon the classics, either from antiquity or the Early Middle Ages. Writers, such as Chrétien de Troyes, became famous. One such writer, Rustichello da Pisa, met a Venetian named Marco Polo (c. 1254–c. 1324) while they were both imprisoned in Genoa. Polo told Rustichello of a trip to and from Cathay (Northern China) and his 20-year stay as one of the semu ren (foreign-born officials or, literally, "people with blue eyes") in the court of the Kublai Khan. Around 1300, Rustichello gathered these stories told to him by Polo into a book entitled *Livres des merveilles du monde*, or *Books of the Marvels of the World*. Later, that book became known as *The Travels of Marco Polo*.

Polo's journey, still fascinating and intriguing, was not particularly unique or new, but its influence was undeniable. Christopher Columbus had a copy of a subsequent publication of the book in which he had made marginal notes, and this was certainly inspirational—his voyage in 1492 was a journey to the East. Polo's book prompted an invigorated interest in the Orient by Europeans. Yet, the most telling aspect of the story is the reaction of the Europeans to Polo's stories: disbelief. The book was nicknamed "Il Milione," in one part referring to Polo's use of the name Emilione and, in the other, mocking the book for its telling of "millions" of lies. The Silk Road, a network of trade routes between the Mediterranean and China, had existed for over 1,500 years, but Polo's work helped to promote a cultural exchange in both directions, because it inspired others to make the same voyage and to find better, quicker, and easier routes between the East and West.

Another example is the rise of interest in ancient Egyptian art and architecture after the publications of *Description de l'Égypte*, a collaborative work of the scholars and scientists who accompanied Napoleon during his expedition to Egypt between 1798 and 1801, and *The Discovery of the Tomb of Tutankhamen* (1923) by the archaeologist Howard Carter. Grauman's Egyptian Theatre in Los Angeles, California, is one of the more famous examples of Egyptian Revival architecture.

In the modern age, a proliferation of communication inventions, from the telegraph to the Internet, has exponentially increased both the quantity of information exchanged between cultures and the rapidity in which the information the exchanges take place. A byproduct of the Information Age is that the lines that demark the boundaries between cultures have become blurrier, and the multifarious cultures, some of which have existed for centuries, have merged—or are merging into—a single World Culture.

Prior to the modern age, the dissemination of ideas among cultures was limited by geographic distances and boundaries. The landmasses of the earth are physically separated into distinct zones of cultural isolation: Western civilization, consisting of Europe, North America, and Australia; Eastern, or Oriental, Civilization, consisting of Eastern and Southern Asia; Northern Asia; Supra-Saharan Africa; Sub-Saharan Africa; the Pacific Islands; Central America; and South America. The term *primitive* is used to describe Sub-Saharan African, Pacific Island, Indigenous Australian, and Native American or Pre-Columbian cultures or to describe cultures that have a subordinate technological culture.

Some aspects of culture are universal, shared by populations so remote from one another that it is unlikely that there would have been any contact between them. For example, the progression of the development of communities—from small tribal villages, to larger agrarian towns, then to cities and city-states—is a patterned model seen in all the habitable continents. Other common characteristics are the basic structure of a militarized state, whether for expansive or defensive purposes; the patriarchal autocracy or oligarchy as the form of government; the central, and often domineering, role of religion; the establishment of a writing system; the use of slave labor; the division of labor; the distinction of gender roles; the establishment of social classes; trade networks; and the creation of monumental architecture. These similarities suggest that there are common characteristics in the development of any civilization.

If two remote cultures share a specific feature of culture, such as the same belief system, the same aesthetic tendencies, or the same methods of construction, this can be attributed to one of two different factors (or a combination thereof): *dissemination* and *simultaneous discovery*, a theory that a new idea, thought, or cultural means of expression can be developed by one or more disconnected sources. The building of pyramid structures, for example, is common to ancient Mesopotamian civilizations, ancient Egypt, the Mayans of Central America, and the Khmer civilization in Southeast Asia. In spite of some attempts to suggest that there was communication between these remote peoples, archaeological evidence suggests that the idea of building a religious structure that resembles a mountain is something that should be considered as altogether unique. In all such cases, save for the Egyptians, the notion that the gods live in the heavens seems a likely common inspiration.

In human history, there have been several catalytic inventions and discoveries that proved to be great stimuli to the progress of civilization. Many of these corresponded to a breakthrough in communication, information gathering, or information retention. They include the development of speech and language; the development of writing; the invention of the printing press; the inventions of the Industrial Revolution of the nineteenth century, such as the railroad, the steamship, and electricity; the inventions of the Second Industrial Revolution of the twentieth century, such as the automobile and airplane; and the inventions of the Digital Age, the computer and the internet.

The evidence for the development of language is based upon paleoanthropological studies of the skeletons of hominids. For obvious reasons, the pinpointing of even a broad range for dating the origins of speech is debated by scholars and scientists. However, it seems unlikely that the development of language and the development of culture can be separated. The most important event in this process is the development of syntax, a system of rules developed by a population group that establishes the uses and meanings of vocalizations. The earliest date for the origins of culture coincides with the appearance of "modern" humans, about 200,000 years ago. The latest date suggested is approximately 35,000 years ago. This latter date corresponds to the earliest known works of art—cave paintings and portable sculpture.

The first writing systems, in Mesopotamia and in Egypt, which were responses to the need for keeping track of food products and other goods traded and stored in small communities, were key factors in the growth and expansion of both cultures. The advent of literature followed not long thereafter. In Egypt, variations of the Book of the Dead, which were guides to the afterlife for Egyptian ruling class, were integral elements in the creation of the tombs of pharaohs and nobles, either in written documents placed with the body or in art decorating the walls of tomb structures. Prior to a culture's developmeint of writing, it is said to be pre-historic. If a writing system is not quite fully developed, then it is said to be proto-historic; once it is developed, then it is said to be part of the historic period.

The invention of the printing press in 1440 by Johannes Gutenberg, a resident of Mainz in what was then the Holy Roman Empire, was a major contributing factor to the scientific and industrial revolutions that would follow in the next few centuries. It contributed to the spread of the Reformation. Both of these events conceptually changed European town planning. Medieval towns and cities were dominated by the ecclesiastical and political elites. In the centuries that followed the Middle Ages, these groups shared their prominence with commerce and the growing presence of both a noble class and a commercial class.

The last two centuries—the nineteenth and the twentieth—substantially changed the way people live. The inventions of the elevator in the mid-nineteenth century and the invention of air-conditioning in the twentieth century, as well as the development of structural steel and the reinforcing steel used in concrete, collectively had the most visual effect upon cities—they allowed humans to building tall buildings, and tall buildings completely transformed how cities look and how they function. In the late twentieth and early twenty-first centuries, the process of accumulating and sharing information increased exponentially; the task of understanding all the implications and benefits thereof is still a work in process.

In addition to language, the common characteristics shared by most cultures are tools, artifacts, social traditions, the creation of habitats, a system of teaching and learning, a form of government, art, recreation, food and clothing, and religion. Each contributes, in varying degrees, to the identity of cultures—those characteristics and traits that distinguish one culture from another. With many historical and some contemporary cultures, the most instrumental of these characteristics was a religious belief system shared by an overwhelming majority of its citizens. Until the twentieth century, the most significant structures in most cities and communities were religious in nature—temples, cathedrals, churches, mosques, etc. The image of a cathedral spire, pagoda, or minaret towering over the surrounding structures is archetypal prior to the twentieth century. These structures could be seen from surrounding farmlands from miles away.

The nuclei of European cities (as well as the occasional town whose antiquity has been preserved in entirety) are evidences of culture and architecture enjoined in a uniform display. What is seen—the architecture and the urban fabric—and what is unseen—the rituals and experiences of daily life prior to the industrial revolution—focuses on the Church, which was more than just the spiritual center of the community. It was also the social center, and its formidable presence influenced both politics and economics. Open spaces adjacent to cathedrals were centers of diverse activities, such as commerce and public celebrations. Groups of peoples of varied social classes and occupations were united by a single purpose. In Eastern Asia, the Hindu or Buddhist temple had a similar relationship. In Northern Africa and in Western Asia, the mosque performed a similar function. In addition to the great temples, cathedrals, and mosques that occupied the most visible and most important locations in an urban center, larger towns and cities had neighborhood religious centers, with architectural works that sometimes rivaled their more important parents, albeit of a smaller scale.

The myths, stories, and beliefs of a particular culture, civilization, or religious group are collectively called *mythology*. The belief in a particular deity or deities, or the common rituals and practices of its participants related to a belief system, is called *religion*. To refer to the practices or beliefs of a person or group as mythology is generally regarded as disrespectful or condescending, although from a scholarly perspective, there is a significant amount of interchangeability in their uses. A potential result of the interactions of two cultural groups coming into contact with one another, whether benign or combative, is *syncretism*, the unification or consolidation of religions, cultures, or ideas. A well-known example of syncretism is the pairing by the Romans of their own gods with Greek gods who had similar aspects, such as Zeus and Jupiter, Aphrodite and Venus, Herakles and Hercules. Both mythology and religion can play important roles in the design and decoration of non-religious buildings as well as religious buildings, especially in theocratic systems of government or in communities and cultures where a single religion is predominant.

A community leader, someone who has ascended to a position of authority through heritage, popularity or esteem, or brute force, is the next most significant facet of a particular culture. Those who are remembered in history as being the most effective, prodigious, or notorious have often bestowed on their publics their own personalities, principles and beliefs. In the ancient world, the residences of these leaders are often described as palaces. The word palace comes from the name of the hill in ancient Rome, the Palatine, where the wealthy citizens of the city, including civic and imperial leaders, resided. In some cases, a palace was used as a governmental center in addition to being the residence of the sovereign and his or her entourage of family and close friends and advisors. In ancient Egypt, the word pharaoh became a title for the king of Egypt beginning in the fifteenth century BCE. Prior to this time, the word was a descriptive for the house in which the king lived, the "Great House." The origin of the hieroglyph was a house with columns, a design presumably reserved for the ruling class.

A *castle* is a fortified royal or aristocratic residence. In Germany, where there are many extant castles, such as the ones that perch on rocky promontories above the Rhine River, the word for castle is *schloss*, a word which is also used to describe a city palace or country estate house. Unlike palaces, which are typically found in urban centers, manor houses, estates, chateaux, and villas are large country residences for wealthy landowners. In France, royal and aristocratic residences are called *chateâux* (singular *chateâu*). In England, and elsewhere, this type of residence is called a *manor house*; in Italy, it is called a *villa*. In republics and democracies, or in any political system whose power does not rest with a single authority, the affairs of the community are administered in a town hall, known as the *hôtel de ville* in France, the *Rathaus* in Germany, and the *palazzo del comune* in Italy.

Literature is another enduring aspect of culture. Italo Calvino (1923–1985), the Italian journalist and novelist, wrote that a classic work of literature never finishes "saying what it has to say." In this respect, works of literature are born in a specific place and time but have the potential to transcend both. They are universal; they can speak to anyone at any time. The Greeks invention of Drama gave rise for the need for a new architectural form—the theater, which the Greeks created by carving the *theatron*, the seating area, out of hillsides. The Romans later created a structure for the theatron, and also created an amphitheater for the gladiatorial games, which was a theater mirrored along its longer axis.

The first works of literature were written on clay tablets. Later, a paper-like material made from the papyrus plant was first used in Egypt in the third millennium BCE, and then exported to Greece. The **Ancient Library of Alexandria** (third century BCE) was established during the Ptolemaic dynasty and housed a large number of scrolls, books rolled from papyri, as well as meeting rooms and lecture halls. It is one of the most important of many great works of architecture from antiquity that did not survive. The loss of its contents is one of the greatest tragedies in cultural history, if not the greatest. The Roman writer Plutarch (46–120), in his *Life of Caesar*, wrote that the library was destroyed when Julius Caesar set fire to his own ships during a naval battle, and the fire spread to docks and then the mainland of Alexandria.

Art is never considered to be the most vital aspect of a civilization, but it is often the most memorable. In addition to individual paintings and sculptural works found in museums and private collections all over the world, many works of art were created specifically for use in or for the decoration of buildings. Some of these works are *in situ*, while others have been moved to museums for protection from the elements and from thieves. Until the late nineteenth century and early twentieth century, the integration of art into works of architecture was, in effect, preconditioned. Architects assumed that wall paintings, sculpture, mosaics, and other decorative objects would be part of any significant building program, from temples and churches to bridges, civic monuments, and houses. In the Renaissance, the artist and the architect were often the same person. In the twentieth century attitudes about art in architecture changed. Currently, art is rarely attached to a public or private building; it is placed. It is more peripheral. In1989, Prince Charles, at the time the heir to the British throne, lamented in an essay written for *Architectural Design* entitled "The Ten Commandments of Architecture" that architects and artists "used to work together naturally; today, they are worlds apart."

Since the civilizations of ancient Egypt and ancient Mesopotamia—thus, for approximately 5,000 years—public art in both religious and secular buildings provided the best cultural opportunity for people of all economic and social classes in both Western and Eastern civilizations until the modern era. Those who could not understand the written words of a religious text could see the images in temples and cathedrals. The tenets of a faith could be expressed in a universal language that required little education—the language of visual representation. Although not all the interior spaces in these religious buildings were accessible to the public—some were intended for the literati, the priests and administrators—the use of religious icons and symbols was an important tool in affecting the general population, who had less stake in the proselytization of the religious beliefs adopted by those members of the political, religious, and social classes that directly influenced cultural traditions.

For centuries, the posterity of the collective body of knowledge, both spiritual and secular, was held safe within the enclaves of faith—the monasteries of Christianity, the madrasas of Islam, and the learning centers within temple complexes of Hinduism and Buddhism. Samarkand, an ancient Silk Road city located in Uzbekistan, was an important center for Islamic studies, but also was instrumental in the preservation of cultural traditions, and for a brief period in the fifteenth century, it was the site of an astronomical observatory. The Registan, a large public square, is flanked by three madrasas, Islamic centers of education: the Ulugh Beg Madrasah (1417–1420), the Tilya-Kori Madrasah (1646–1660) and the Sher-Dor Madrasah (1619–1636). The House of Wisdom (ninth century; destroyed thirteenth century) in Baghdad was a center for the study of the sciences and humanities, both for the preservation of ancient literature and for the generation of new ideas, built during the so-called Islamic Golden Age.

Beginning in Late Antiquity, some devout Christians sought a complete immersion into their faith. Some lived in isolation, others in communities whose common goal was a life of piety and commitment to chastity and virtuousness. These monasteries grew substantially in number and in stature for centuries. Lay persons would bestow gifts of land and wealth upon them, with the idea that by giving to those who were closest to God's favor, their own souls would be rewarded. In addition to tending to spiritual needs, monasteries in Western Europe delivered social services that were no longer provided by the Roman Empire after its collapse, such as taking care of the sick and the poor and providing lodging for travelers and pilgrims. Monks copied works of ancient literature and, thus, prevented cherished texts or Greek and Roman writers and philosophers from being lost forever. Monasteries were indefatigable patrons of the arts—the visual arts (architecture, painting, and sculpture), as well as music. The walls of cathedrals and churches are de facto museums of art, and like the temples of Rome, Greece, Egypt, and Mesopotamia, they are culture and architecture merged into one.

Some works of architecture have become cultural icons, of their city, their people, or their nation. The great pyramids come to mind immediately when Egypt is discussed; as is the Colosseum at the mention of Rome or

FIGURE 2.3
Elizabeth Tower with Big Ben clock. London, England.

FIGURE 2.4
Eiffel Tower. Paris, France.

the Roman Empire. **The Eifel Tower** (1889) was hated by many Parisians when it was first built. The French writer Guy de Maupassant despised it so much, he ate often at the restaurant at the base of the tower, because it was one of the few places in Paris that he did not have to look at it. Yet, in time, the tower became a symbol of Paris, and of France, its form ubiquitously displayed on travel posters, as souvenirs and jewelry, in books and in films. Other buildings throughout the world that have become familiar emblems include the **Sydney Opera House** (1957–1973) in Sydney Australia; the **Guggenheim Museum** (1997) in Bilbao, Spain; the **Gateway Arch** (1965) in St. Louis, Missouri; **Elizabeth Tower** (1859), commonly known as Big Ben, in London; **La Sagrada Familia** (1882–est. 2026) in Barcelona, Spain; and an assemblage of buildings in the Art Deco style in Miami Beach, Florida. They are reminders of one of the most important values of art, which is symbolism, which in turn reinforces the idea that not only is architecture an art, but it is the most visible of all the arts.

For Further Discussion

Select a particular architectural building type (such as temples, museums, theaters, etc.), and then, examine the relationship between the characteristic features of its design and the cultural form for which purpose it serves. For example, how were the designs of Greek theaters affected by how Greek drama was structured and staged? It may be helpful to focus upon a particular period or style of architecture.

CHAPTER THREE

Colloquial Architecture

There the form stood, motionless as the hill beneath. Above the plain rose the hill, above the hill rose the barrow, and above the barrow rose the figure. Above the figure was nothing that could be mapped elsewhere than on a celestial globe.

Such a perfect, delicate, and necessary finish did the figure give to the dark pile of hills that it seemed to be the only obvious justification of their outline. Without it, there was the dome without the lantern; with it the architectural demands of the mass were satisfied. The scene was strangely homogeneous, in that the vale, the upland, the barrow, and the figure above it amounted only to unity. Looking at this or that member of the group was not observing a complete thing, but a fraction of a thing.

The form was so much like an organic part of the entire motionless structure that to see it move would have impressed the mind as a strange phenomenon.[1]

− From *The Return of the Native* by Thomas Hardy (1840–1928)

The above description of a hilltop by Thomas Hardy (1840–1928), which is set in a fictionalized area in Southwest England he called Wessex, is a literary portrait of a simple pastoral scene. That the scene that is presented assumes a form that could be described as architectural should not surprise. Hardy apprenticed as an architect before advancing on his writing career. However, there is no doubt that, in the opening paragraphs of his novel, he is imparting on his readers a sketch of beauty—not an edifice with Classical proportions or an epic painting of a moment in the life of Christ, but an unassuming vignette—somewhat, but not completely accidental. It makes the point that beauty exists even when it has not been carefully organized and detailed in advance.

In *Gestalt* psychology, which was developed in Berlin beginning in 1890, the whole of an object is not equal to but greater than the sum of its parts. Applied to the scene from *The Return of the Native*, the hill, the barrow, and the figure create a separate object. According to the theory of the *gestalt effect*, the human mind is capable of envisioning a distinct and whole form, not just a collection of objects that may or may not have a relationship with one another. In his seminal book *Art and Visual Perception: A Psychology of the Creative Eye* (197 4) Rudolf Arnheim (1904–2007) used the fundamental principles of Gestalt Theory to analyze and understand visual experiences, which would then result in an enhanced comprehension of the visual arts—paintings, sculpture, and architecture. He used Michelangelo's dome at St. Peter's Basilica in Rome to illustrate the point that "visual expression resides in any articulately shaped object or event." Hardy's hilltop scene, like the dome of St. Peter's, is composed of form that fit naturally one atop the other. The human eye grasps that the assemblage of forms achieves a balance in both cases, because the mind has used a conceptual awareness of weight and shape and other facets (such as color, light, space, movement, etc.) make its judgment.

---

1   Thomas Hardy, The Return of the Native. Copyright in the Public Domain.

The articulation of form is, therefore, something that is achieved by architects, whose creations involve the arrangement, consolidation, and manipulation of shapes. They are conscious efforts to create beauty. Forms found in nature can also appear to have been a form of expression. It is the sublimity of some elements of the natural world that are used in teleological arguments for the existence of God; that is, something that is so profoundly magnificent must have been designed by an entity of supreme intelligence. Such objects found in nature have, in turn, become sources of inspiration for architects.

Structures that are less prescribed, fabricated by builders with little formal training, or found in less-traveled areas of town and country, can also be widely admired. These achievements are often collective, in the sense that one structure works with other structures to create a homogeneous communal composition. The most commonly used term for such works is *vernacular*, meaning having domestic or functional qualities; being of a particular country, culture, or region; or lacking a particular style. Another similar term—*indigenous*, refers to something uniquely associated with a certain people, culture, or location—something that is innate. *Authochthonous* simply describes something that is derived from local sources, materials, or methods or is related to a non-migrant, non-colonial culture. For the sake of simplicity, all of these terms will be used interchangeably for the purpose of this chapter, and collectively called *colloquial architecture.*

Frank Lloyd Wright, writing of his own works, which he called *Organic Architecture*, thought that architecture should be of "human scale" and of proper and consistent proportion. He believed that a building's form should be determined "by way of the nature of materials." No one would consider Wright's works to be vernacular, but his statement clearly demonstrates a common objective. In Organic architecture, Wright explained in *A Testament* (1957), "environment and building are one." In the same book, he enumerated the principles of organic design as follows: kinship of building to ground; decentralization; appropriate "character;" the organic interpretation of building materials; spatial depth; the expression of space; the integrity of form; livability of shelter; the use of

materials according to their nature; and style developed from *within*, with *cultural integrity*. Wright stressed that his principles were based upon "the simple laws of common sense," as opposed to those of his contemporaries, which he thought were sometimes elitist and academic.

Many of Wright's principles can be found in colloquial architecture. The primary objective of colloquial architecture is to facilitate the practical use and purpose of a building; in other words it is to satisfy its *function*. While function is an important aspect of formal architecture, it is sometimes sacrificed for the sake of symbolism, adherence to the imperatives of style or historical precedent, or to preconceived designs concepts of the architect.

Whereas ornamentation is applied as an entity unto itself to formal buildings for both symbolic and decorative purposes, the ornamentation of colloquial buildings is often achieved through a necessary, functional element, such as a door, balcony railing, or chimney. Color is another aesthetic device often used, either to highlight a particular aspect or component, or to distinguish one building from another. The pastel-colored houses of Key West, Florida, are one example. The primary colors used in villages in Scandinavia and Great Britain are another. A popular image of the city of Copenhagen is the row of colloquial houses painted in primary colors, sited along a quay in the Nyhavn district.

Another aspect of colloquial architecture that is analogous to Wright's Organic architecture is the prodigious

FIGURE 3.2
Sant'Antine Nurage. Sardinia, Italy.

use of materials. On the Island of Sardinia there are 8,000 surviving stone constructions from the Bronze Age called *nuraghe*. The stones used are considerably smaller than those used in the Megalithic period. The people that built them are called the Nuraghic Civilization. A common feature of the nuraghe was a central tower. The exact purpose of the structures is unknown, but possible uses are a temple, royal residence, warehouse, meeting hall, fortress for defensive purposes, or some combination thereof. The **Palmavera Nuraghe** (c. 1500–c. 800 BCE), near Alghero, Sardinia, was built with limestone and sandstone. Its main tower is roughly 9 meters in diameter and 8 meters tall, and is surrounded by a *bastion*, a projecting mass as a fortification wall. The **Nuraghe of Santine**, also known locally as the *House of the King* (c. 1500–c. 500 BCE) near Torralba, Sardinia, is the tallest nuraghe, as well as the tallest prehistoric structure in the Mediterranean. Its stone walls were originally 21 meters high, of which 17.5 meters remain.

The relatively recent farm community **Village des Bories** (late eighteenth century) was built in the Provencal region of France of stone huts using what is called a "dry stone" technique, without mortar. Most of the buildings have a similar form, the keel of a boat turned upside down. They were used for residences, keeping of animals, grain storage, and other agricultural purposes. In County Kerry, Ireland, a similar technique was used to create what has been described as a small chapel. It is called the **Oratory of Gallarus** (date unknown).

Informal, or casual, architecture is often constructed with only a nominal use of drawings, typically a *plan*, and rudimentary *sections and elevations.* Formal works of architecture would include all of these, shown in greater detail and with more complete dimensions and, perhaps, a physical *model*. That being said, producing a set of detailed architectural drawings is a relatively recent practice. In ancient Greece, architects described the important aspects of a building to be constructed with documents called *syngraphai*, which relied mostly on the written word rather than diagrams. It was not until the Renaissance that the use of more sophisticated drawings came into use.

Prodigious works of colloquial architecture seek a common rather than a refined beauty, an implied rather than an expressed order and a perceived balance as opposed to mathematical equilibrium or pure symmetry. They are less self-conscious; that is, they are designed for communities, not individuals. They may not be solely functional, but they would never forsake function in favor of singularity or expression. In general, they seek the familiar not the exotic, whether in reference to materials or form. They respond to topographical and climatic site conditions. They are traditional more often than adventurous.

Although symbolism is a term usually associated only with formal architecture and seen lacking in informal architecture, that is not always the case. For example, in the twelfth and thirteenth centuries, wealthy landowners in the town of San Gimignano, in Tuscany, Italy, built scores of stone towers, ostensibly for fortification purposes, but generally as displays of wealth and power. The 13 towers that still exist make the town look like

Oratory of Gallarus. County Kerry, Ireland.

San Gimignano, Italy

FIGURE 3.5
St. Coloman Church. Bavaria, Germany.

FIGURE 3.6
Gol Stave Church, Norway.

a miniature, medieval Manhattan from a distance. The towers are simple stone structures that mostly lack even the minimal decorative features common in castle and town gates from the Middle Ages. Similar motives prompted the building of the small town of Vatheia, on the Mani Peninsula, at the very southern end of the Peloponnese in Greece.

The straightforwardness of colloquial architecture can often be explained simply by the fact that these builders have fewer resources—of capital or manpower or both. Small chapels and neighborhood or country churches often have little or simple ornamentation but can nonetheless exhibit proportional or creative skills worthy of attention. In smaller or less-wealthy communities, ambitions of grandeur are not practical, and a modesty of design sometimes requires a more instinctual perception of architectural beauty. One such anonymous church inspired one of the more familiar poems of the English language, Thomas Gray's "Elegy Written in a Country Churchyard," which is a paean to those not famous, whose names are not Milton or Cromwell, legendary figures of English literature and history, respectfully. Gray compares them to the unnoticed splendors of nature:

Full many a flower is born to blush unseen,
And waste its sweetness on the desert air.

The *stave* church, constructed of timber posts and beams, with steep roofs to quickly cast off snow, was common in Northern Europe, and many have survived to today in Norway, although some have been rebuilt. A *stave* is a timber post. The **Borgund Stave Church** (1180–1250) has a basilica plan, a secular form created by the Romans that was adapted as the prototypical church of Christianity.

The most common forms of colloquial architecture are those used for *human habitat*, a constructed or adopted environment used to shelter persons, or simply, a *home*. There are numerous varieties of homes, past and present, from basic shelter types similar to those developed in the Paleolithic era (see Chapter 4) to clustered houses that share common walls and roofs. Because the design of indigenous houses is often responsive to local climate conditions, local customs and social practices, the availability of construction materials, and the political and economic conditions, certain type of housing are identifiable with certain areas or populations. While there is no doubt that in the twentieth and twenty-first centuries, architecture has become more global and, thus, more unvaried, native and ethnic diversity still exists, even if in a diminished capacity. The next few paragraphs describe a sampling of unique forms of human habitat.

In Africa, villages composed of traditional huts are still common. In Southern Africa, the *rondavel* is basically the same type of shelter first developed by the ancestors of humans hundreds of thousands of years ago. It is circular, with *wattle and daub* walls, interwoven branches and twigs covered with mud or clay, and conical roofs made from wood and covered with *thatch*, straw, reeds, palm fronds, and other similar material.

In Inner Mongolia, a region of Northern China, the Mongols, who have a longstanding tradition of being *nomadic*, having no permanent place of settlement, use portable tent-like structures called *yurts*, which have a collapsible frame. They are circular, and the side walls are often made of animal skins or felts. Like the rondavel, its origins are prehistoric. The Bedouin of the Arabia and the Near East are herders that move with their animals using tents made of camel hair.

Another example of a prehistoric housing technique that has endured until the modern era is the *trullo*, a small hut-like dwelling made from stacking rough limestone boulders found in Apulia, in Southern Italy. The roofs of trulli are made of rough stone boulders that are corbelled to create a cone or dome. Some trulli walls are covered with stucco, which is then whitewashed. The tips of conical roofs are often decorated. A similar design is found in the beehive houses near Aleppo in Syria.

There was much diversity in the autochthonous architecture of North America, those traditions that existed prior to the arrival of the Europeans and the cultural upheaval that ensued. Native Americans used the indigenous materials that were available to them, from using ice and snow in the extreme northern climates, to grasses and palm fronds in the southern regions. Technologically, they were more sophisticated than Paleolithic-style huts; however, from an archetypal point of view, they were very similar.

FIGURE 3.7
Trulli. Alberobello, Italy.

In the Northeast and in the Great Lakes region, the *wigwam* was common. It was either round or oblong, and used flexible poles stuck into the ground, leaving a hole in the top for the smoke to escape. The outer covering was reed, grass, sheets of birch, elm, or chestnut bark. In the Midwest, if the tribe moved from one seasonal location to another, they built a frame at both locations, and carried the outer covering with them. They also built summer houses, which provided shade in the day and an open sleeping space at night. A conical-shaped wigwam was used by tribes along the Northern Atlantic coast, where winter conditions were more severe.

A *longhouse*, used by the Iroquois in upstate New York, could be up to 120 meters long. It had no windows, just doors at either end, which were covered by a flat porch. The *chickee* hut was used by the Seminole and Miccosukee Indians in Southern Florida. It had a raised platform for sleeping, and was covered by thatch material from the sabal palm. The *tipi* was erected, using three or four poles that were crossed at the top and tied together. It was a simple but clever construction that used only the wood poles, stakes, pins, animal skins, and ropes. The region where it was used was the Upper Plains—Montana, Idaho, Wyoming, Nebraska, and the Dakotas.

An *earthlodge* was used in the Great Plains. The roof of the structure was made from earth or sod placed on a radiating wood frame, with posts in the center. The Pawnee tribe, located in present-day Nebraska and Kansas, associated each of their villages with a particular god-star. The layout of the earthlodge also had mythological significance. There was a sacred altar at one end. In front of the altar was the *skararu*, a square hole in the ground, which represented the throne of *Tirawa*, the main god of the Pawnees. In front of the skararu was a sacred place, called a *wiharu*. A firepit was in the center, and beds were placed in a circle inside the outer wall. The entrance always faced east, toward the morning star. This is where the young women slept. The altar was at the western end, toward the evening star. Older women slept at this end. The presence of Tirawa was visible when the sunlight penetrated through the hole in the center of the roof above the fireplace.

Taos Pueblo (c. 1000–1450), near Taos New Mexico, is the largest and most famous example of a *pueblo*, a multi-storied adobe residential complex of the Southwestern United States. *Adobe* is sun-dried clay, sometimes mixed with organic material, formed into bricks or placed monolithically in a wall. Families share walls and ceilings with neighbors and enter their unit from above via wooden ladders. The design, with few windows and no traditional doors, helps to keep the living units cool in summer and warm in winter. Taos Pueblo is similar in concept to an ancient site in Turkey, Catal Huyuk, discussed in Chapter 4.

In Southeast Asia, traditional houses made of hardwood or bamboo are built on stilts for several reasons, the most immediate of which is the frequent flooding that occurs in the region. High pitched gable and curved gable roofs efficiently shed rainwater to keep interiors

dry. *Khlongs* are stilt houses built on the water. Some are built on rafts, so that during high water periods they can float.

The *siheyuan* is a traditional courtyard house found in Northern China, especially in Beijing, the entrance to a siheyuan is through a gate at its southeastern corner. The entry leads to a courtyard, which is surrounded by living space on all sides, an extended family may live in one siheyuan, with the eldest members having the most important space, across from the entry. Several siheyuan are typically arranged in a row, accessed via an alley, called a *hutong*. In the late twentieth and twenty-first centuries, many hutong were demolished and replaced by tall buildings, however there has been a more recent movement to preserve those that remain.

A building's function can be an integral part of its beauty. Windmills are popular subjects of art and destination places for tourists. Part of their allure is that, simply, they are, in essence, buildings with moving parts. However, the blades or sails that are affected by the winds have a unique tectonic form—an object that is symmetrical but not quite in equilibrium. The **Kinderdijk Mill Network** (c. 1740) in the Netherlands is a United Nations Educational, Scientific and Cultural Organization (UNESCO) world heritage site and has one of the largest concentrations of historic windmills at one site.

At the narrowest point of the Arno River in Florence, there has been a bridge since the Roman period. At some point in its history, merchants built small shops out of

A stilt house in Cambodia.

Kinderdijk Mill Network. Netherlands.

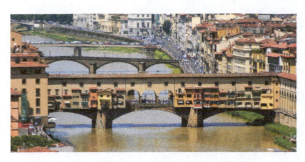

FIGURE 3.10
Ponte Vecchio, Florence, Italy.

wood. By the thirteenth century, these had become so well-established that the city organized a special agency for the bridge's management. After a flood destroyed the bridge in 1333, a replacement bridge, the **Ponte Vecchio** (1345) was constructed, and stalls for the merchants were built into its redesign, made from stone, not wood. Although its basic structure is formal, with a center arched span and two equal side arches, the *ad hoc* character of subsequent remodeling and additions of shops give it a colloquial aspect. It was not uncommon in the Medieval period for bridges to support merchant stalls. The **Rialto Bridge** (1591) in Venice and the **Pulteney Bridge** (1774) in Bath, England, are two other examples. In the mid-span of the **Pont Saint-Bénézet** (1177–1185), in Avignon, there is a small chapel built in the twelfth and thirteenth century. The famous **London Bridge** (1176–1209) once supported 200 buildings, many of which were three and four stories tall. However, due to the great fire risk they triggered, all the buildings were torn down by the late eighteenth century. In 1967, the city sold the bridge, and it was carefully demolished and reconstructed in Lake Havasu City, Arizona.

Although not commonplace, bridges are sometimes regarded as works of architecture as well as works of engineering, whether or not an architect, per se, is involved in the design. The **Stari Most** (sixteenth century) or Old Bridge in Mostar, Bosnia and Herzegovina, was designed by an Ottoman Empire architect. It is a pedestrian bridge that spans the Neretva River with a single, graceful pointed arch, and built with the local *tenelija* stone. For hundreds of years it was considered one of the region's architectural treasures. In 1993, during the civil war that took place in the area, the bridge was destroyed, an event that became symbolic of the tragedy of that war to its participants, and of war in general to the rest of the world. It was rebuilt, with international assistance, in 2004.

The design of colloquial architecture is achieved through the shared knowledge of local or regional methods and practices. Of great importance is the fact that these structures are typically built by native craftsmen who are aware of the availability and purposefulness of local materials, climate conditions, and local and technological expertise. In small towns and villages, this practice is repeated, creating a homogenous distribution of like forms and materials. When congregated, this assemblage can obtain the characteristics of a singular epic work of architecture, achieving the same qualities used to judge individual works—eccentricity, order, balance, hierarchy, integrity, grandness of scale, unity, complexity, harmony, and rhythm, and others—a singular work may lack, such as human scale. The individual units that formulate this composition may lack these qualities on their own, but collected together, they become monumental.

In the Andalusia region of Spain, in the provinces of Càdiz and Malaga, there exist some homogenous villages and towns collectively called the *Pueblos Blancos*, or White Towns. All the structures in these villages have whitewashed walls and terra cotta roofs. The bright white walls are visible from great distances, in vivid contrast with the darker natural colors of the terrain. White stucco villages and towns are common in Greece, such as on the islands of Santorini and Myknonos. In Greece, the roofs are also painted. Churches in these towns are often painted a sky blue. Color is added by brightly painted doors and shutters.

The most impressive colloquial communities are those that are autochthonous responses to their particular natural circumstances. The most common type of these is called a *hilltown*, a town or village built on the side and summit of a hill, adopting its general shape. Frank Lloyd Wright once opined that "No house should ever be on a hill or on anything. It should be of the hill. Belonging to it. Hill and house should live together each the happier for the other." That is exactly the idea of many hilltowns.

FIGURE 3.11
Trevi, Italy.

The idea of occupying the hillside and, thus, preserving the valley for farming is as old as the Neolithic era. The Etruscans, who occupied Central Italy before the Roman period, adopted this practice. They may have learned it from the Greeks, who occupied Southern Italy and Sicily. Today, hilltowns, generally from the medieval period, are scattered throughout the country. The regions of Tuscany and Umbria have well-known hilltowns such as Montepulciano, Cortona, Montalcino, Orvieto, and Trevi. There are five villages that constitute the Cinque Terre ("Five Lands"), an area along the Liguria coastline in Northwest Italy, which is a UNESCO world heritage site.

FIGURE 3.12
Matera, Italy.

The town of Matera, located in the province of Basilicata in Southern Italy, is located on a hilltop that overlooks a ravine that has been preserved in its natural state, the site has been occupied since the Paleolithic era and permanently settled since the Neolithic era. Until recently, many residents of the town lived in rock caves, thus giving the town its nicknames "la Città Sotterranea," or the Subterranean City and the town of *sassi*, or stones. Structures are built both on top of and into the natural rock outcropping that abuts the ravine. The stone used for all its buildings—houses, shops, churches, etc.—was quarried locally and, thus, the human-made form blends nearly seamlessly with the natural form.

The novelist and poet Edgar Allen Poe (1809–1849) once observed that "there is no exquisite beauty … without some strangeness in the proportion." Most vernacular buildings, such as the "cookie-cutter" houses of suburbia, merit little notice, in part because they offer no strangeness, no peculiarity of style. On the other hand, some vernacular structures have a greater grasp of the basic concepts of beauty than many formal buildings designed by architects with grand objectives. The attractiveness of these colloquial works is not unintentional, but in relation to the great formal works of architecture, the process is more intuitive, more reliant on a subconscious understanding of what is beauty.

It is the strangeness, or uniqueness, of a region called Cappadocia, in Turkey, that makes it an object of much admiration. It is an area of volcanic rock formations,

FIGURE 3.13

Monastery. Meteora, Greece.

some of which resembled tectonic sculptures, which the local people nicknamed "fairy chimneys." The area has been populated since the Neolithic Age. The area contains many dwellings and churches that are built into the ground. Originally built during the years of the Christian persecution in the first centuries of Christianity, the tradition of cave houses continued until the modern era. The use of natural caves for habitation is described as being *troglodytic* or *rupestrian*.

A similar spectacular geological setting, also a UNESCO world heritage site, is the Metéora, an area in Central Greece where there are massive natural pillars, mostly sandstone, rise from the Thessalian plain, creating what is described as a "forest of stone." Beginning in the fourteenth century, monks began building monasteries atop these pillars, the highest of which is more than one-half kilometer above the adjacent grade level. They were built using pulleys, ropes, and ladders, and once in place, access was via these extremely long ladders, nets, and baskets.

For Further Discussion

Find an example of indigenous or colloquial architecture from your local community. Identify local or regional materials or methods of construction, and discover why they were used. Are these materials and methods still used today? If not, why not?

PART

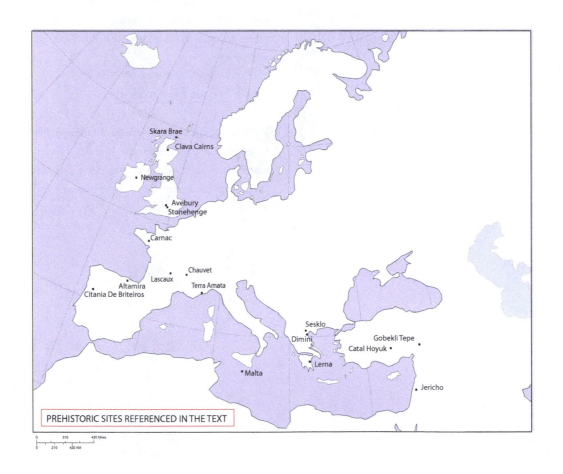

Skara Brae
Clava Cairns
Newgrange
Avebury
Stonehenge
Carnac
Chauvet
Lascaux
Altamira   Terra Amata
Citania De Briteiros
Sesklo
Dimini   Gobekli Tepe
Catal Hoyuk
Lerna
Malta
Jericho

PREHISTORIC SITES REFERENCED IN THE TEXT

0   210   420 Miles
0   210   420 KM

TWO

Prehistory

One of the fundamental challenges for historians and archaeologists reads like an algebraic curve turned upside down: the further you go back in history, the less information is available, and this difficulty of increases exponentially relative to time. There are many types of archeological finds that an archaeologist can use to try and piece together a civilization from its residue, but the most helpful are cultural artifacts, such and tools and art; architecture, in various states of ruin; and literature. A civilization or culture that is *prehistoric* is one without a writing system, without literature of any kind. Art, artifacts, and architecture tell the *what* about a particular population; literature often explains *why*. Working without the explanations, archaeologists, historians, anthropologists, and paleoanthropologists often have to qualify their conclusions and statements. However, it is precisely this challenge that draws the interest of many into this field.

CHAPTER FOUR

Origins of Culture and Architecture

The men of old were born like the wild beasts, in woods, caves, and groves, and lived on savage fare. … It was the discovery of fire that originally gave rise to the coming together of men, to the deliberative assembly, and to social intercourse, And so, as they kept coming together in greater numbers into one place, finding themselves naturally gifted beyond the other animals in not being obliged to walk with faces to the ground, but upright and gazing upon the splendor of the starry firmament, and also in being able to do with ease whatever they chose with their hands and fingers, they began in that first assembly to construct shelters. Some made them of green boughs, others dug caves on mountain sides, and some, in imitation of the nests of swallows and the way they built, made places of refuge out of mud and twigs. Next, by observing the shelters of others and adding new details to their own inceptions, they constructed better and better kinds of huts as time went on.[1]

— from *De Architectura, or Ten Books of Architecture,* by Marcus Vitruvius Pollio

At what point did human cultural history begin? Was it when self-awareness in humans had evolved to a level that triggered the creation of art? Was it when humans began to live in shelters or in communities of shelters? Or did it begin with history, when humans first learned to use written languages? To place this important threshold in its proper perspective, it is necessary to first grasp a broad history of the human experience on earth.

Single-celled organisms appeared on earth approximately 700 million years after the earth was formed, and for the next 3.5 billion years, they were the only forms of life on the planet. Around 600 million years ago, multi-celled organisms appeared. *Hominids*—primates that walk upright—appeared around 7 million years ago. The first hominids that made tools—*Homo habilis*—appeared about 2.3 million years ago. *Homo ergaster,* which appeared 1.8 million years ago, created more sophisticated tools and were probably the first hominids to create shelters, at least 400,000 years ago. The first humans—*Homo sapiens*—first appeared in Africa about 250,000 years ago. If the entire history of the earth were represented by a single day, then humans have existed only for the last 36 seconds, and have lived in organized communities for *only the last fraction of a second.*

The "Out of Africa" theory of human evolution contends that until 100,000 years ago, humans occupied only the African continent. At that point, a very slow process of migration began, first at the land bridge between Africa and Asia, then to Europe and East Asia, and to the Americas, via a land bridge present during the ice age's global recession of shorelines. By 10,000 years ago, every continent except Antarctica was occupied by humans. There had been earlier migrations out of Africa by earlier hominids, but the last great migration of humans during the *Paleolithic,* or the Old Stone Age, was the most extensive. It required, in some cases, traversing bodies of water, and it required adaptations to colder environments.

The Paleolithic era began with the first use of stone tools by *H. habilis* some two million years ago and continued until about 10,000 years ago. It accounts for roughly 96 percent of all of human history. In the last 2.5 million

---

1   Marcus Vitruvius Pollio, The Ten Books on Architecture, trans. Morris Hicky Morgan. Copyright in the Public Domain.

years, there have been 50 periods when the average surface temperature of earth became cooler and 50 periods where the temperature became warmer. These periods are not consistent, neither in magnitude nor duration. A period of cooling is called a *glacial*, or ice age, and a period of relative warming is called *interglacial*. There are further cycles within glacials called *stadials*, colder periods, and *interstadials*, which are warmer. When temperatures are lower, slowly moving masses of ice called glaciers expand toward the equator; in warmer periods, they recede toward the poles.

The glaciers of the *Wurm* glacial, the last ice age, began to melt around 14,450 years ago (give or take 200 years). Around 11,550 years ago (give or take 70 years), the temperatures began to increase more rapidly. Around 8,000 years ago, the glaciers reached their present location. This interglacial that we currently experience is called the *Holocene*.

As the glaciers retreated, forests and fields of grasses, such as barley and wheat, populated the once-forbidding landscape. Groups of nomadic peoples, who had previously survived by hunting wild animals and gathering fruits and berries from plants, became the first farmers. Farming allowed these people to settle into the first villages. It was a gradual process that lasted over 5,000 years, between 11,000 and 6,000 BC. This period is one of the great milestones of human history and accounts for the sudden acceleration of the pace of cultural development, which has increased exponentially since.

The first villages arose in what is called the Fertile Crescent (modern Iraq, Jordan, Syria, Israel, and Lebanon), around 6000 BC. Around 4500 BC, denser populations shifted to the great river valleys of the ancient world—the Tigris and Euphrates, the Indus, and the Nile. This shift was the result of, or resulted in, development of more sophisticated farming tools, and the domestication of oxen.

Farming allowed for greater concentrations of people. The need for storage of grain and other farming products begat the development of ceramics for storage, to keep the ever-increasing yields from crops free from rats, mice, and insects. It also precipitated the development of non-domestic structures, for storage and administration. There

is evidence also, that there was a religious center in many of these villages, a condition that would be common to communities, large and small, for thousands of years.

By 6000 BC, the majority of people living on earth lived in agrarian societies—that is, agricultural communities, rather than with foraging, nomadic tribes. Agriculture is more efficient than foraging—it can support a greater population in a smaller area. Nonetheless, the concentration of people into permanent communities, and the ensuing increases in populations brought about different kinds of difficulties, the spread of disease being the most menacing. As these communities grew, several fundamental properties of civilizations were slowly established: power structures that were typically patriarchal and familial; religious practices that influenced many aspects of daily life; conflict between adjoining tribes and communities; and the establishment of military practices for expansion or for defense. All of these elements would persist well into the modern era.

Studies of chimpanzees in the Gombe Stream Chimpanzee Reserve in Tanzania in the early 1960s, described in *In the Shadow of Man* (1971) by Jane Goodall (b. 1934), described various methods of communication used by the chimpanzees. For instance, when a chimpanzee has discovered a food source, he will bark loudly to communicate the location of his discovery to other chimps. If he becomes alarmed, then he calls out a *wraaa* sound to summon support. Similar studies, before and since, have discovered that communication skills are far more sophisticated in the animal world than previously thought. However, no other species besides humans has the capacity for language, and this ability, more than any other distinction, has propelled the human species to its place as the dominant species on earth.

Language is an essential ingredient of culture. Communication of knowledge expands capabilities from a single individual to multiple individuals and, eventually, to an entire culture. The offspring of those individuals can pass this and other information along to future generations. However, there is a limit to the amount of information that can be transferred. If the knowledge can be written down, then this amount can dramatically increase. This entire process is called *collective learning*, a critical ingredient in the development of culture and civilization. Other species communicate, but only humans can communicate via a language system. The most important component of language is syntax, the rules used to transfer thoughts into a recognizable vocabulary.

By studying the behavior of chimpanzees—the closest relatives to humans—and by examining the archaeological evidence, paleoanthropologists have reconstructed the physiological characteristics of early humans at various stages in history. It is a fluid process. New archaeological finds can significantly affect previous theories and suppositions. What remains unchanged, however, is the broad picture of the process of human evolution, from the time when the communication skills of humans were limited, to ones similar to those exhibited by the chimps at Gombe, to the current state of human development, as lasting for several million years.

In startling contrast to this slow, plodding advancement, there have been four catalytic events that proved to be great stimulants to the progress of civilization in recent human history. Each of these corresponded to a breakthrough in collective learning. The first such event was the development of written language by the river valley civilizations of the Nile and the Tigris-Euphrates rivers around 5,000 years ago. These writing systems, Sumerian cuneiform and hieroglyphics, respectively, led to the great monumental works of art and architecture in Mesopotamia and Egypt. The second event occurred in the middle of the fifteenth century with the invention of the printing press, which allowed for collective knowledge to be accessible to a substantially greater percentage of the population. This event, combined with the explorations of the late fifteenth and sixteenth centuries that opened communication between zones of the world that had previously been isolated, contributed to the accelerated spread of technology during the Industrial Revolution. The invention of the telegraph and telephone in the late nineteenth century was a third event propelling the rapid developments of culture and civilization in the twentieth century. The latest event was the simultaneous development and expansion of the personal computer and the Internet in the last two decades of the twentieth century. The process of accumulating and sharing information increased exponentially, and we are currently still in the process of understanding the implications and benefits thereof.

Architectural history is an integral part of sociocultural history, both as being influenced by, and having an influence upon, society and culture. The structural remnants, both monumental and fundamental, of each civilization tell us much about the people who built them.

The preliminary roots of architecture began with the establishment, by early humans, of a home base. The first home base sites were essentially transient camp sites without fire, and clearly not places of refuge, or even a constant sleeping place. They were places of fixed resources, where they could find an abundance of stone for tools, nuts for foraging, or carcasses for scavenging. They were transient, because the resources they offered were either finite or itinerant. Still, this was the first step in the development of human structure building—the coalescence of separate resources—the materials to make tools to acquire and prepare food, and the food itself.

There are several models for development of home base sites by early hominids, all of them derived from evidence at archeological sites where there is a distinct

FIGURE 4.2

African Round Thatched Huts. Botswana.

clustering of animals bones, combined with evidence of stone tools. In one model, tools were brought to a foraging area, left there after use, and gradually accumulated over time. The presence of the accumulated tools attracted repeated use of the same site, further increasing the accumulation of tools at the site, and further increasing its popularity.

A second model, central place foraging, suggests that home bases are a social development, and implies food-sharing, division of labor, communication skills, and cooperation among members of a group. Mary Leakey's studies of Olduvai living floors led her to conclude that at the home bases there were signs of a "new type of social stability."

Paleoanthropologists in the twentieth century were able to study several "Stone Age" societies, such as the San in Southern Africa (also known as the Bushmen), who lived in the harsh, dry climate of the Kalahari Desert in Botswana. Because the Bushmen were nomadic, the shelters they built, called *scherms*, were temporary. They were made of branches covered with grass and were dome-like in shape. The grass was not placed with great precision, and a gust of wind would blow it away. It is this structural type—the domed hut—that is the archetype for primitive shelter building. The circular form of the structure is evident in present-day residential structures all over Africa.

When the Bushman did not build a hut, he placed a stick in the ground upright, then arranged his possessions around it, and slept next to it. In this manner, the Bushman created a sense of place, identifying himself, on a temporary basis, with a particular portion of the landscape, however temporary.

Shelter-building is a skill that is not limited to humans. The beaver's water lodge, which has considerable similarities to early human shelters, surpasses the archetypal human hut in both engineering (durability in a challenging environment) and innovation (secret entrances and waterproofing). For humans, the process of shelter-buildings is an adaptive behavior, rather than an instinctual behavior, requiring an advanced ability for abstract thought, advanced tool making, and for multiple occupancy shelters, at least a rudimentary means of communication. Without innate skills of nest-building,

the capability for abstract thinking had to precipitate these acts of creation, specifically an intrinsic awareness of the concept of structure. Primates, with the exception of human beings, are not sophisticated nest-builders. As demonstrated in studies by Goodall and others, chimpanzees and gorillas make temporary foliage "'seats'" or nightly nests in forest habitats for comfort, but these are abandoned after each use.

In the late 1950s, Mary Leakey, digging in the Great Rift Valley in Africa, discovered circumstantial evidence of a primitive hut. This circular cluster of stones may denote a circular shelter or wind break; it is the earliest circumstantial—but not conclusive—evidence of structure found among animal bones and debris at Site DK in Olduvai Gorge Bed I, Tanzania. The site has been dated by radioactive techniques to about 1.8 mya (million years ago). If Leakey's interpretation is correct, then the first shelters were probably built by *Homo habilis*, an ancestor of humans who lived from 2.5 to 1.7 mya. If not, then it is likely that early *Homo sapiens* were the first hominid species to build shelters. These early humans are sometimes designated as a separate species called *Homo ergaster* by some paleoanthropologists, and African-European *Homo erectus* by others.

The *Acheulean Tradition* is a term that describes a phase of early human technology that began in Africa around 1.7 or 1.6 mya. Acheulean tools are more sophisticated (e.g., bifacial rather than unifacial) and are more specialized than the previous tradition of tool-making, the *Oldowan* tradition. Acheulean hand axes show evidence that they were designed. Evidence for shelters is understandably sparse and difficult to interpret, but there is no doubt there was a very, very gradual progression from early humans merely establishing a home base to the creation of seasonal temporary structures, to seasonal permanent structures, and finally, to permanent structures. If the finds at Olduvai are an early indication of shelter building, then the process lasted almost two million years. Even if Olduvai is discounted, then the time period for the early development of shelters lasted hundreds of thousands of years.

The archetype structure for all Paleolithic shelters consists of a *foundation*, stones that act as weights or

FIGURE 4.3

Terra Amata shelter archaeological reconstruction. Terra Amata Museum, Nice, France.

FIGURE 4.5

Archaeological site reconstruction of Terra Amata shelter. Terra Amata Museum, Nice, France.

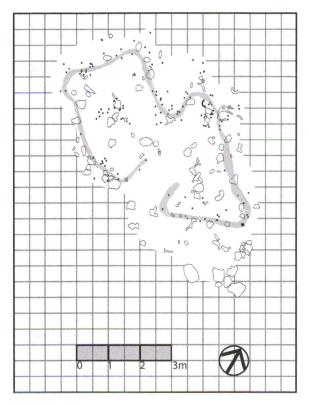

0   1   2   3m

FIGURE 4.4

Plan of Terra Amata

receptors, a *skeleton* or framework, and a tent-like *skin*. In some constructions, the framework was built tightly, so that the outer skin was not used. The foundation consists of stones set directly upon the ground, or partially buried. If branches are set up to create an inverted "'V'" or a pointed arch, there is a tendency for the arch to spread apart at the bottom, just as there is a tendency for the focal point of the arch to push together. Foundation stones placed outside of the branches would resist the force at the bottom. Stones placed on the inside of the branches reduce potential movement due to a lever reaction at the focal point. If the branches are wedged in several piled stones, then some resistance against an uplift force by a strong wind is realized.

The framework can be made of wood branches or animal bones, and was either a tent-like inverted "V" or parabolic shape or a single lean-to sloped roof with walls dug out of, or naturally recessed into, the earth. The skin provided additional weather proofing against precipitation and temperature. Possible materials for the skin are animal hides and furs, grasses, and mud. The use of mud and branch walls anticipated the long-standing practice (until the late twentieth century) of wood lath and plaster.

Beyond the Rift Valley in Africa, the earliest evidence of a human shelter is at **Terra Amata** (c. 400,000–380,000 BCE) in present day Nice, France, which was occupied on a seasonal basis. The significance of the date is compounded by the fact that the huts are familial, if not communal, which would represent a substantial advance from temporary shelters, which would have logically preceded these. There are several huts measuring 4 to 6 meters wide by 7 to 15 meters long. The floors of the huts

Origins of Culture and Architecture   41

had hearths, and there is also evidence of a wind screen made out of piled stones, which would have protected the entrances to the huts. Acheulean tools, such as choppers, scrapers, and hatchets, were found at the site. According to the excavator, Henri de Lumley, the huts were constructed by burying saplings a few inches in diameter into the ground. They were presumably crossed at the top like tepees, intertwined by the extensions of small branches from the end of the poles, or tied at the top by some other method. The presumed removal of branches to make poles is a subtle, but important step in structure building, requiring an "abstraction" of a simple branch into a building material of another shape.

Ohalo II, a year-round campsite in Israel's Jordan Valley is, at present, the best *in situ* locale of prehistoric architecture. It was situated on the banks of the Sea of Galilee and was discovered only after the water level dropped at least 23 meters during a drought in 1989. The site is 212.5 meters below sea level, and has been radiometrically dated to 19,400 years ago. Three brush huts, a grave, a stone installation, hearths, and a garbage heap were found. Each hut is 3 to 5 meters long, with the hearths located outside. Flints, animal bones, bird bones, and the charred remains of fruits, grains, nuts, and seeds of a hundred different plant species were found on the floor of the huts. Because seeds of fruits that ripen in three separate seasons (spring, summer, and autumn) were found, it is apparent the site was occupied for the majority or the entirety of the year.

Neanderthal man—*Homo neanderthalensis* or *Homo sapiens neanderthalensis*—evolved from *Homo heidelbergensis* around 200,000 years ago, and lived simultaneously with *Homo sapiens* for 170,000 years, until around 30,000 years ago. They lived in complex social groups, knew how to make fire, and lived in caves and in shelters that employed branches and small tree limbs as a basic structure, with branches or animal hides as a skin. In 2010, paleoanthropologists confirmed that Neanderthals interbred with *H. sapiens*.

The origins of art—and implicitly, the origins of culture—date to the Upper Paleolithic period, or between 45,000 and 10,000 years ago. At Sungir, in Russia, a burial site from as much as 32,000 years ago,

there is evidence that the people who lived at the site decorated themselves with jewelry, which is a portable form of art. The earliest sculptural objects were made by the Gravettians, the name given to a people who lived in Eastern and Central Europe in this period. The Venus of Willendorf and the Venus of Laussel are the most famous of small female figurines carved out of stone, ivory, clay or bone with similar characteristics—emphasized thighs, buttocks, breasts, and bellies.

Parietal artwork, figures or objects painted on walls, has been found in caves and in sheltered rock formations all over Western Europe, primarily in Southwestern France, Spain, and Portugal. Parietal artwork dates from c. 30,000 years ago to c. 10,000 years ago, during the last of the Pleistocene glaciations, the Wurm glacial—commonly known as the Ice Age. The greatest collection of art is at Lascaux, in the Dordogne area of France. There are 600 paintings of deer, aurochs, horses, and abstract figures, as well as 1,500 engravings, mostly of horses. The series of caves has seven main sections: The Hall of the Bulls, The Axial Gallery, The Passage, The Apse, The Shaft, The Nave, and the Diverticule of the Felines. The Hall of the Bulls contains the largest painted figures of Pleistocene art.

The pigments used in cave art are either iron oxide (red), manganese (black), or charcoal (black). Cave water, animal oils, or plant oils were used to bind the pigments to the wall surfaces. The use of more than one pigment for a single figure is rare. In general, there were three distinct subjects for cave art: animals, humans, and signs (abstractions). There are few sites with scenes—representations of more than one animal.

The interpretation of prehistoric art is an inquiry that cannot ever result in unequivocal resolutions. The two most common theories are *l'art pour l'art* (art for art's sake) and sympathetic magic—they were used as part of a ritual to aid in the hunting of the animals, which represent the greater majority of all the figures. These caves are certainly important in the history of culture and art, but there are several good reasons for inclusion in an architectural history. First, if the ultimate goal of architecture is the creation of space, then the selection and adoption of a ready-made space, in the absence of true design, is nevertheless a creative process of discovery, in which an environment and a function are linked together to form a previously unfound relationship. Second, there seems to be a hierarchy of spaces in some of the larger caves, such as at Lascaux, according to David Lewis-Williams in his book *The Mind in the Cave*. Lascaux has seven distinct areas, and Williams suggests that different rituals were performed in each one.

The temporary and seasonal huts that served as shelters for humans for tens of thousands of years, gradually gave way in the later Paleolithic and Mesolithic periods to more sophisticated and more permanent structures. For the next 20,000 years or so, humans who were capable of creating the works of art found at Altamira and Lascaux lived in primitive huts or in caves. The next phase of human history, which began when the first farming villages were built, would ultimately result in the first major threshold in the ascent to civilization—the invention of writing.

The birth of cultural architecture—structures constructed by communities for religious, political, or social purposes, and structures with art and other symbolic decoration—is now dated to around 10,000 to 12,000 years ago, some 7,000 to 9,000 years or so earlier than previously believed, since the discovery (in 1983), and excavations (which began in 2007) of an important archaeological site in Southeastern Anatolia, Göbekli Tepe, (c. 9600 BCE). At this site, located near Şanlıurfa, Turkey, the population constructed at least 20 circles, each formed by the erection of ten, more or less, standing stones, some of which were 6 meters tall. There were two t-shaped stones in the center of circle. Most of the pillars were decorated with bas-relief images—animals generally, but some abstractions.

The purpose of the structures is not known; it possibly could be the world's oldest extant religious monument. The builders of Göbekli Tepe had not yet discovered the use of metal tools, they had not invented the wheel, and they did not use animals such as oxen to move the stones, some of which weighed 16 tons. Whatever their motivations, their commonality of purpose and resolve is a notable achievement at such an early stage of human progress.

Two landmark events of the Neolithic Age—the birth of agriculture and the domestication of animals—led to the development of villages, which appeared throughout the populated world. Some structures were no doubt made of wood, but, understandably, evidence of this is elusive. The archaeological evidence that is available is from villages that were made of more permanent materials. Some of these were complex structures that housed larger family groups and groups of families. The birth of agriculture gave rise to a division of labor within communal groups, which, in turn, meant that more time and effort could be devoted to the construction of these villages. The first structures built for purposes other than shelter, the use of stone for structures, and the use of more permanent materials for shelter building were all developments of the Neolithic Age. Two distinct types of Neolithic communities were: a *hilltop fortress*, a collection of structures, either attached or free-standing, within a perimeter wall, and located on a hilltop for defensive visibility; and a *cluster community*, a grouping of houses that share common walls.

Most of the extant evidence we have for these early cluster communities comes from the Near East, from the Dead Sea north to what is now Eastern Turkey, and from Mesopotamia, culminating at the Persian Gulf. The most famous of these are **Jericho** (c. 8300–7300 BCE), in modern Israel north of the Dead Sea, and **Catal Huyuk** (c. 7400 BCE) in modern Turkey. Catal Huyuk is a complex of houses whose walls were made of mud bricks, and whose flat roofs were made with timbers. They were spaced closely together and covered with mud. There were no streets, nor was there a central common space, elements that would define the design of cities for thousands of years. Each house, however, had an area that was used as a shrine to honor the dead. The wall of the shrine was decorated with a bull or bull horns, as well as the bones of the deceased. The entrance to the individual houses was by a ladder through a hole in the roof, which also served as a vent for smoke from a hearth. The walls of the houses were shared with the walls of neighboring houses, so that the city itself became one large structure.

There are several Neolithic sites in Greece. Two impressive sites in Thessaly, Greece—Sesklo and

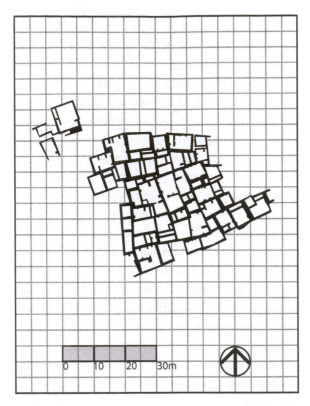

FIGURE 4.6
Catal Hoyuk Plan.

today, but archaeologists have found small clay models of houses, from which they have derived reconstructions of the villages. Pottery found at houses in Sesklo were decorated with geometric designs of four different colors: white, black, red, and yellow.

The most spectacular Neolithic village site—due to both its setting and the comprehensibility of its ruins—is **Skara Brae** (c. 3000 BCE), located in the Orkney Islands off the north coast of Scotland. There are ten surviving houses, most of which were built atop an earlier village. The houses have similar designs. The exterior wall is a *cavity wall*, a wall formed by two layers of masonry with a space in between. The inner and outer layers are *dry stone walls*, masonry walls built without mortar; the interior space is filled with *midden*—waste material, such as animal bones, potsherds, small stones, and sea shells. The design is not dissimilar from some insulated structures built today and would have protected the houses from the severe weather of the region. The midden served as both insulation and waterproofing.

In the middle of each house was a fire pit. The roof structure is unknown, but could have been constructed from wood or from whale bones. One of the most remarkable features of the houses is the presence of built-in furniture. There are beds, with possible canopies, dressers, and storage boxes. Short walls were built as low partitions to divide the spaces.

There are extant examples of Neolithic-style villages and fortifications in both the Bronze Age and Iron Age. **Maiden Castle** (c. 600–450 BCE), located in Dorset

Dimini—date from 5000 to 4000 BCE. Another site at Lerna, in the Peloponnese, dates from 5500 to 2500 BCE. They were also made from mud bricks, but instead of flat roofs, they had sloping, thatched roofs, with holes to allow smoke to escape. Some houses had two floors. The walls were painted white, but the openings around windows and doors were decorated in bright colors. The stone foundations are all that is left at these sites

FIGURE 4.7
Skara Brae, Orkney Islands, Scotland.

FIGURE 4.8
Skara Brae, Orkney Islands, Scotland.

county in England, is an example of an *oppidum*, or *hill-fort*, a fortified village with earthen defensive walls. At **Citânia De Briteiros** (first century) in Portugal, round stone houses made of dry stone masonry were covered with conical roofs.

For Further Discussion

How would you create a shelter today using only Stone Age tools and only the resources from the natural environment of your area? What elements would be similar to a modern house? What elements would be different, apart from technological advances?

CHAPTER FIVE

The Megalith Builders

They had proceeded thus gropingly two or three miles further when on a sudden Clare became conscious of some vast erection close in his front, rising sheer from the grass. They had almost struck themselves against it.

"What monstrous place is this?" said Angel.

"It hums," said she. "Hearken!"

He listened. The wind, playing upon the edifice, produced a booming tune, like the note of some gigantic one-stringed harp. No other sound came from it, and lifting his hand and advancing a step or two, Clare felt the vertical surface of the structure. It seemed to be of solid stone, without joint or moulding.

Carrying his fingers onward he found that what he had come in contact with was a colossal rectangular pillar; by stretching out his left hand he could feel a similar one adjoining. At an indefinite height overhead something made the black sky blacker, which had the semblance of a vast architrave uniting the pillars horizontally. They carefully entered beneath and between; the surfaces echoed their soft rustle; but they seemed to be still out of doors. The place was roofless. Tess drew her breath fearfully, and Angel, perplexed, said—

"What can it be?"

Feeling sideways they encountered another tower-like pillar, square and uncompromising as the first; beyond it another and another. The place was all doors and pillars, some connected above by continuous architraves.

"A very Temple of the Winds," he said.

The next pillar was isolated; others composed a trilithon; others were prostrate, their flanks forming a causeway wide enough for a carriage and it was soon obvious that they made up a forest of monoliths grouped upon the grassy expanse of the plain. The couple advanced further into this pavilion of the night till they stood in its midst.

"It is Stonehenge!" said Clare.

"The heathen temple, you mean?"

"Yes. Older than the centuries; older than the d'Urbervilles![1]

— from *Tess of the D'Urbervilles* by Thomas Hardy (1891)

It is not altogether surprising that Thomas Hardy would use Stonehenge as the setting for the final scene of *Tess of the D'Urbervilles*, his nineteenth century masterwork. Hardy trained as an architect before he became a poet and novelist. Near the end of the novel, Tess and her husband Angel Clare are running from the authorities after she killed a man who had assaulted her when she was young. After leaving a train at Salisbury, they find temporary refuge among the large monoliths, which had lain unmolested in the pastoral Wiltshire countryside for more than two millennia (only recently was the site enclosed by a security fence). Stonehenge was at the time, and still is, the most well-known prehistoric monument

---

1   Thomas Hardy, Tess of the d'Urbervilles: A Pure Woman Faithfully Presented. Copyright in the Public Domain.

in the world. It is located less than 90 miles southwest of London, and in the daylight, it is visible from miles around. Its mysterious origin has fascinated humankind for centuries.

In medieval times, the site was known as *Chorea gigantum*, a Latin term meaning "Giants Dance." Influenced by the *Historia Regum Britanniae*, or *The History of the Kings of Britain* (c. 1136), a work of historical fiction (mostly fiction), a legend endured for much of the first half of the second millennium that the stones originally came from Africa, and that they were transported to Ireland by giants. With the help of Merlin, the legendary wizard who was a friend to King Arthur, the stones were brought to Wiltshire by Utherpendragon, the brother of the British King Aurelius Ambrosius. The story was retold in *The Faerie Queene*, an epic poem by Edmund Spenser (c. 1552–1599), with the victorious Aurelius being buried at Stonehenge. Fascination with the site eventually led to more technical observations, including that of John Aubrey, who conducted a detailed survey of the site beginning in 1663.

Megalithic monuments, the conspicuous ruins of the Neolithic Age, have been found in all four of the world's major geographical zones, in locations that are geographically and culturally remote from each other. Archaeologists have investigated the artifacts found near the stones and determined the age of the constructions, and they have studied and recorded the shapes, sizes, and origins of the stones. Unfortunately, however, the most common characteristic of the monuments from this period in prehistory is that little is known about the people who built them. Although it is tempting to link these sites together as a common culture, there is no evidence that exists that justifies doing so. Nonetheless, there are common features and construction methods which suggest an exchange of ideas to some extent.

The simplest freestanding monument is a *menhir* (from Breton *maen-hir)*, or standing stone, a linear stone turned upright. In Portugal, there are *pedras talhas*, or hewn stones, near Evora (c. 5000 BCE). In Scandinavia, small standing stones are called *bautasten* or *rune* stones, named after the writing carved into the stone. If a large standing stone is used in a construction, it is called an

FIGURE 5.2

Menhir. Carnac, France.

orthostat. A *trilith* is a construction of three stones, two vertical and one horizontal. A *capstone* is laid horizontally, supported by two orthostats.

A *dolmen* is a table-shaped tomb, composed of two or three vertical stones and a capstone. It was typically covered with earth, but in many cases the stones are partially or completely visible due to weathering. They have been found in such diverse locations as Sardinia and China. The builders—or more correctly erectors—of dolmens used the most intuitive concept of building technology, called *post and beam*, comprised of a horizontal member, the *beam*, supported by two vertical posts, or *columns*. A *passage grave* is a circular chamber made of stones, and covered under a mound of earth. A gallery grave is an elongated passage grave, such as the *Tombe di Gigante*, or Giant's Tombs, at Arzachena in Sardinia.

FIGURE 5.3
Linear Menhir Formations. Carnac, France.

The Carnac Alignments (c. 3300 BCE) in Brittany are linear arrangements of menhirs in parallel rows, 100 to 1,000 meters in length. There are three sections visible today, Kermario, Menec, and Kerlescan, but these may have originally been a single grouping. The largest stones are at the head of the lines, and some are 3 meters tall. The stones were taken from nearby outcroppings. The eastern part of the Kermario alignment is superimposed over a previous burial mound dating from 4500 BCE. There are other dolmens and single menhirs in the area. The Grand Menhir, also near Carnac, was 20 meters long and weighed 280 tons. It rests in four broken pieces on the ground.

The oldest freestanding stone structures on Earth are the megalithic temples on the islands of Malta in the Mediterranean, which date from 3600–2500 BCE. They are generally called "prehistoric," because they belong to a culture that left no evidence that they had a formal writing system. These people had originally come from Sicily at the end of the fifth millennium BCE, using open boats to cross the Mediterranean Sea, a distance of 93 kilometers. Humans were capable of sailing such distances in the Mediterranean by at least 8000 BCE. There is no evidence of any human occupation of the islands before the arrival of these people, who probably made the venture because of population pressures in Sicily.

The Maltese archipelago consists of three main inhabitable islands: Malta, Gozo, and Comino. The most important megalithic temple sites are at Hagar Qim, Mnajdra, and Tarxien on Malta and Ggantija on Gozo. Archaeological scholars in Malta have created a special, separate period called the "Temple Period," inserted between the "Neolithic" and "Bronze and Iron" periods in Maltese timetables (c. 3000 BCE to c. 1800 BCE).

FIGURE 5.4
Entrance Portal. Hagar Qim Temple. Malata.

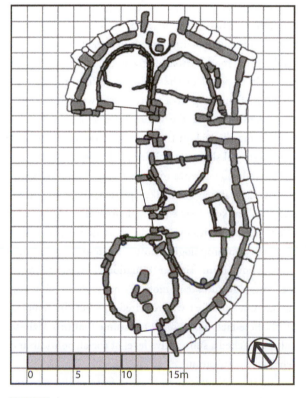

FIGURE 5.5
Hagar Qim Temple Plan.

This period was previously referred to as the Copper Age in Malta, in an attempt to link the ages of neighboring civilizations together, although there is no evidence of the use of any metals on the islands until much later. This is of no slight significance, since the stones used for constructing the Maltese temples were *dressed*, which means they were trimmed and made smooth. Stonehenge is the only other megalithic site where this occurred.

There are more than two dozen Maltese sites. A typical temple is composed of D-shaped chambers, or apses, arranged about a central axis behind a main facade. A temple could have two to six of these apses. The walls of the facade and the apses were made of rough orthostats. There is a central doorway, composed of a pair of smooth orthostats arranged in a trilithon, and there are additional doorways at the apse entrances. The floors are paving stones, or *torba*, a plaster-like material made from limestone.

This style or period in architectural history is frequently called *Megalithic*, because of the characteristic assemblage of large stones to create distinguishable monuments that have survived to this day. However, this term implies a common culture, which is considered unlikely by most scholars, given the chronology and the wide dispersal of the sites. These first attempts by humans of building at a grand scale were among the most demanding in the entire history of architecture, considering the lack of technology, communication, and organizational skills the builders had at their disposal.

There is no evidence to support any conjecture about the rituals that may have taken place at the temple sites, and it is unlikely that such evidence will ever come to light. Thus, any attempt to do so is mere speculation, although anthropologists often extrapolate cultural information from similar situations. However, there are design features common to many at the site, and the communal effort was required to erect the temples. With these facts alone, one can assume that this Maltese culture reached a substantive level of social, political, and religious organization.

There is an outer open court in front of the entrance to the temple, and evidence suggests this may have been a ceremonial area with a fire pit. That it was a gathering

FIGURE 5.6

Statue of a woman with a pleated skirt found at Tarxien Temple, Malta (copy).

area of some sort is a reasonably safe assumption. Based upon the archaeological evidence, it is likely that animal sacrifices were performed inside the temple complex. Some of the altars had a perforated stone at the base, which could have been used for tethering the animals. At Tarxien, figures of animals were incised into a stone. Knives made out of flint were found at some sites. There is no evidence of human sacrifice.

Hagar Qim Temple (c. 3600–3200 BCE) is located on a hilltop site. The stone used at this site was Globigerina limestone, which is more vulnerable to weathering from the salt spray from the nearby Mediterranean Sea. It has four apses and two entrances; the second entrance in the rear is a feature unique among the Maltese temples. The remains of a second, older temple lie 30 meters to the north.

Tarxien Temple (c. 3600–c. 2800 BCE) is actually a complex of three or four separate temples that are connected. Inside the doorway of the south temple is an altar with a spiral decoration, a motif found not only at other Neolithic sites in Europe, but at other prehistoric or ancient sites throughout the world.

Ggantija Temple (c. 3500–c. 3200 BCE), is located on the island of *Gozo*, which is about one-fourth the size of the main island, called Malta. It has two adjacent temples, one with five apses and one with four apses, and a small niche at the opposite end of the main axis. Both temples are situated within an enclosure wall. The stones are well weathered, but there is evidence that they were once plastered and painted with red ocher.

There are roughly 400 stone circles in Britain, Ireland, and Brittany, the most famous of which is **Stonehenge** (c. 3150–1500 BCE) on Salisbury Plain, near Avesbury, England. It had several phases of construction. The first phase occurred around 3000 BCE, and consisted of an earthen henge, or ring, almost 2 meters high, with a single pole at the center of the circle and an entranceway flanked with stones. This first alignment marked the northernmost moon rise each month. The final ring, named the Sarcen, marked the midwinter sunset.

The *Sarcen Circle* (c. 2600 BCE) consists of 30 uprights and 15 interlocking lintels. Inside the circle are five trilithons. This is the arrangement dominating the site today. The circle is c. 33 meters in diameter. It mimics the earlier timber-and-earth construction, even in the detailing. The stones have been dressed (made smooth), and were placed together like the original wood members, with mortise-and-tenon and tongue-and-groove joints. Instead of relatively light wood members, however, the workers were using these techniques on large boulders that could weigh several tons each, and they brought them from a location that was at least 27 kilometers away. The so-called blue stones, an earlier interior ring of stones which weighed approximately 5 tons apiece, were transported from the Preseli Mountains in present-day Pembrokeshire, Wales, a distance of 207 kilometers.

The area around Stonehenge was a burial ground in the middle of a site that was active in the late Neolithic and Bronze ages. Many of the skeletons found in *barrows*, or burial mounds, were buried in fetal positions, suggesting a burial ritual of some sort. Some of the barrows are shaped like inverted bowls, and others are elongated. A connection between the burial sites and Stonehenge has been proposed, but, in the absence of written historical evidence, the exact purposes and uses of the site remain a mystery.

Avebury Stone Circle (c. 2800–2400 BCE), also in Wiltshire, England, has a collection of monuments, including the largest stone circle in Western Europe.

FIGURE 5.7
Avebury Stone Circle. England.

Among the other notable stone circles are **Callanish Stone Circle**, Isle of Lewis, Scotland; **Castlerigg**, in Cumbria, England; the **Ring of Brodgar**, Orkney Isles, Scotland; and the Drombeg Circle (also known as the Druid's Altar) (c. 870–710 BCE) in County Cork in Ireland. An alignment with the winter solstice, similar to Stonehenge, is apparent at many of these sites. The alignment is not as precise as Stonehenge, but the winter solstice has clearly been marked. It was thought in the nineteenth century that Stonehenge and other stone circles were connected to the Druids. Before that, there was a legend that the circles were attributed to the magical powers of Merlin, of the Arthurian legends. At present, the culture responsible for building them is unknown.

FIGURE 5.8
Ring of Brodgar. Orkney Islands, Scotland.

FIGURE 5.9

Newgrange prehistoric monument. County Meath, Ireland.

Megalithic building ended in the middle of the second millennium BCE. In Bronze Age Greece (c. 3000–1100 BCE), structures were sometimes built on foundations and the vestiges of older construction. In many cases, these older foundations were composed of large boulder-like stones, which were set into place without mortar. The Greeks called these Cyclopean walls, because they believed they had been built by the race of Cyclops, a primordial race of giants that had a single eye in the middle of the forehead. Later on (c. 500 BCE), the stone was cut into polygonal-shaped boulders, a method used by the Incans in South America, centuries and thousands of miles removed.

At Brúna Bóinne, or the Palace of the Boyne, in Ireland, there are three large *tumuli*, ancient burial mounds. The largest, and most famous, is **Newgrange** (c. 2800–2400 BCE), which is generally believed to be both a *passage grave*, an underground burial chamber made of stone accessed through a corridor, and a *cairn*, a human-made mound of stones used as a burial memorial or monument, or else a temple of the yet-to-be-interpreted religion of the inhabitants of Neolithic England. The cairn is 80 meters in diameter, and its appearance is of a perfectly formed hill.

The entrance to the tumulus is on the south side. Situated in front of the entrance is what is called the horizontal *Threshold Stone*, which is carved with spiral and diamond shaped figures. There is a flat rectangular

FIGURE 5.10

Carrved Stone @ Entrance to Newgrange.

opening above the entrance. Once a year, at the winter solstice, the first rays of morning sunlight enter the interior chamber through this opening. The chamber is shaped like a beehive, with the stones corbelled from all around until a central peak is reached.

Balnuaran of Clava, or Clava Cairns (c. 2500–2000 BCE), in Northern Scotland is a site that consists of three cairns, each surrounded by a stone circle. Because the entrances of all three face the southwest, the same preoccupation with the winter solstice seen earlier at Newgrange may have existed here, as well. Although the roof structure is no longer in place, it is likely that a beehive-shaped corbelled structure was also used at Clava.

In 1836, C. J. Thomsen (1788–1865) published *A Guide to Northern Antiquities*, which was a guidebook to the National Museum of Copenhagen. He proposed the Three-Age System to classify and display prehistoric artifacts. The system uses three basic categories of technological "advancement" based on the tools that were used by a particular group of people: the Stone Age, the Bronze Age, and the Iron Age. A fourth, the Chacolithic, or Copper Age, which precedes the Bronze Age, is used for some cultures. The Stone Age has subsequently been divided in three subdivisions: the Paleolithic, the Mesolithic, and the Neolithic (the Old Stone Age, the Middle Stone Age, and the New Stone Age, respectively).

For Further Discussion

Compare the megaliths of England and Northern France with those of Malta. Suppose you see a broadcast on public television in which an historian postulates that one of the two groups borrowed the idea of megalith building from the other, would you support or challenge this theory? Why?

PART

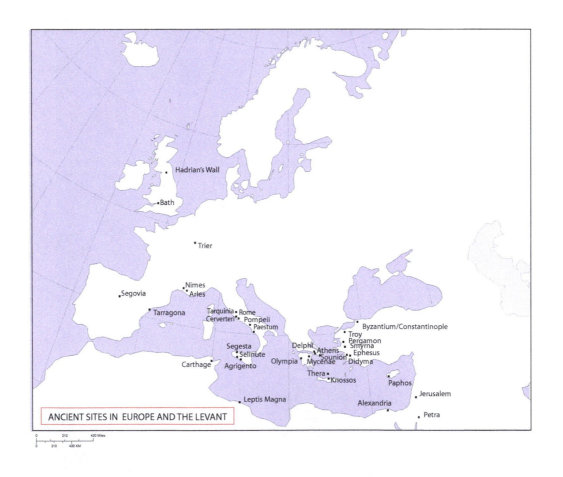

ANCIENT SITES IN EUROPE AND THE LEVANT

THREE

The Ancient World

The predominant civilizations of the ancient era are those in Western Asia, which included the Sumerians, Akkadians, Hittites, Babylonians, Assyrians, Kassites, Neo-Babylonians, Neo-Assyrians, and Persians; in Egypt, a single civilization divided into the Old, Middle, and New Kingdoms and the later Ptolemaic period; in Europe and the Mediterranean, the Minoans, Mycenaeans, Greeks, Etrurians, and Romans; the ancient Asian civilization of India, Southeast Asia, and China; the Olmecs, Toltec, Mayans, Incans, and Aztecs of Central and South America; and finally, the Native American populations of Eastern and Western North America. The progress of civilizations varied across the different geographical zones; thus, the cultural periods are not synchronous.

CHAPTER SIX

The First Civilizations

He who the heart of all matters hath proven let him teach the nation,

He who all knowledge possesseth, therein shall he school all the people,

He shall his wisdom impart and so shall they share it together.

Gilgamish—he was the Master of wisdom, with knowledge of all things,

He it was discovered the secret concealed …

… handed down the tradition relating to things prediluvian,

Went on a journey afar, all aweary and worn with his toiling,

Engraved on a table of stone all the travail.

Of Erech, the high-wall'd,

He it was built up the ramparts; he it was clamped the foundation,

Like unto brass, of Eanna, the sacred, the treasury hallowed,

Strengthened its base to grant wayleave to no one . …

Two-thirds of him are divine, and one-third of him human …[1]

— from *The Epic of Gilgamesh*

Mesopotamia

The Epic of Gilgamesh is one of the oldest surviving works of literature. It is believed to be a collection of stories first written down c. 2100 BCE. Gilgamesh is believed to be a real-life Sumerian king of Uruk that ruled around 2700 BC. The epic begins and ends with a description of the ancient city of Uruk in present-day Iraq and refers to the city as being unequaled by any other in the world. The brief prologue refers to the Eanna Temple, which is one of the better preserved of early Sumerian temples, which Gilgamesh helped to preserve. Today, there are remains of several temples connected with a portico of circular columns. These relatively well-preserved structures were among the first monumental structures in history.

Like all epics, the *Epic of Gilgamesh* is a story of a journey or quest. The hero embarks on a series of travels and returns. In a sense, the epic attempts to explain all of human history to that point, and as such, it becomes not only the world's first work of literature, it becomes the world's first literary masterpiece. Like all great works of art, revelations about the human condition—what it means to be human—are interwoven with the narrative. This epic tells of how one man, Gilgamesh, learns how to behave and to rule in a civil manner, and it tells how humans can learn to look within themselves to do the same. Moreover, it tells the story of how Enkidu, who is untamed and animal like, becomes civilized, but it also tells the story of how humanity became civilized, as well.

In the beginning of the narrative, Gilgamesh is portrayed as a tyrant who oppresses his people, "trampling them like a wild bull." The people plead to the god Anu

---

1   The Epic of Gilgamish, trans. R. Campbell Thompson. Copyright in the Public Domain.

for help, who directs the mother goddess, Aruru, to create a foil for Gilgamesh, a man of equal strength and courage, but who will create a balance to offset the inappropriate behavior of Gilgamesh. This is Enkidu, a man of the wild who drinks with the animals at a watering hole. It is a woman that tames Enkidu, and she does so with the use of "love-arts," with the help of Ishtar, the goddess of love, and one of Ishtar's priestesses, Shamhat. They make love for seven days and nights. Then she gives him clothing, and teaches him to eat like a human rather than an animal.

Whereas Enkidu is innocent, Gilgamesh is overbearing. Enkidu is nonviolent, Gilgamesh is aggressive. After a first skirmish that basically ends in a draw, the two become close friends. Afterward, Enkidu becomes more like Gilgamesh, and vice versa. Partly in response to Enkidu's prodding, Gilgamesh kills Humbaba, a monster in the cedar forest, an act that displeases the gods. Next, Gilgamesh slanders and refuses the advances of Ishtar, who pleads to Anu to send the giant Bull of Heaven to punish the hero. Gilgamesh and Enkidu kill the bull, further enraging Ishtar. After Enkidu curses those who helped make him civilized, he becomes ill and dies. Despondent, Gilgamesh embarks on a quest to find the secret of life and immortality.

He encounters Utnapishtim, the legendary survivor of the Great Flood who attained immortality. The story of the flood, which had existed in previous poetic works, is told in flashback by Utnapishtim. Utnapishtim explains to Gilgamesh that there is no immortality for humans, and that mortality is really not so bad. Utnapishtim's wife tells Gilgamesh of a place in the waters of the Great Deep, the sea under the earth's surface, where there is a magical plant that will restore youth. Gilgamesh retrieves the plant and begins the journey home but carelessly loses the plant, which is taken by a serpent. But when he returns to Uruk, he is full of wisdom, and becomes a good leader for the rest of his time on earth.

Historians believe that Gilgamesh was a real king who reigned sometime near the middle of the third millennium BCE in Sumer, in present-day Southern Iraq and the center of the region called Mesopotamia, often considered the birthplace of history. The Sumerian civilization consisted of individual city-states united by a common culture and language, until Sargon of Akkad (c. 2334–2279 BCE) conquered Sumer and other territories, from the Mediterranean to the Persian Gulf. This Akkadian empire lasted for about 100 years.

Ur Nammu, a native Sumerian who reigned from 2112–2095 BCE, reestablished the empire (called the Neo-Sumerian Empire). This period is also known as the third dynasty of Ur, named after the most important city of the period. Among the accomplishments of Ur Nammu and his son, Shulgi, who reigned from 2094 to 2047, was the establishment of the first legal codes, the further development and standardization of the cuneiform writing system, and the construction of ziggurats, temple structures built as stepped pyramids.

Near the beginning of the fourth millennium BCE, Neolithic villages, which had existed in the river valleys of the Tigris and Euphrates, Nile, and Indus rivers since around 6000 BCE, developed into early cities and city-states. These areas are the so-called "cradles of civilization;" all played dominant roles in the development of culture and architecture. The common characteristic of the three is the presence of great flood plains, which allow for high crop yields, which in turn, allow for greater population densities. The control of the flooding of the rivers via irrigation canals demanded a higher level of social organization than existed in other villages located away from the river valleys. These conditions led to the birth of organized trade, cities, writing, and ultimately, civilization.

The Tigris and Euphrates river system has its source in the mountains of Anatolia (present-day Eastern Turkey), and flows through Iraq into the Persian Gulf. In

FIGURE 6.2
Reconstruction of Ziggurat at Ur.

the fourth millennium, the people who lived in villages along the rivers began to build irrigation canals and dikes to control floods, which were frequent, unpredictable, and sometimes devastating. In the southern part of this region, which is called Mesopotamia (from the Greek meaning "between two rivers"), considerable effort was required to prepare marshes into suitable farmland. The domestication of oxen played a significant role in achieving these objectives.

By 3100 BCE, these villages had evolved into small towns and at least 20 city-states. These were the most populated communities to that point in human history. The cities were organized around a central temple, an early archetype that would persist in urban planning up until the modern era. We call these people the Sumerians; they called themselves "the black-headed people."

The greatest achievement of Sumerian civilization was the invention of a writing system, which was initially devised for the purpose of inventory of agricultural products and goods involved in increasingly sophisticated trade. It began with the use of *pictograms* or *pictographs*, pictorial representations of objects, and a corresponding base-10 quantity (10 oxen, for example). Eventually, pictograms were used to represent ideas (ideograms) and sounds (phonograms). A stylus was used to make incisions in wet clay tablets that were shaped like a wedge, and thus the system of writing is called *cuneiform*, which means "wedge-shaped." By 2800 BCE, the Sumerian written language had become completely synchronized with the spoken language.

Tablets discovered in the nineteenth and twentieth centuries revealed a remarkable array of subject matter. There is a tablet written by a farmer addressed to his son that is essentially a "farmer's almanac," itemizing what needs to be done at different times of the year. There are tablets that record history. There is a tablet that created a system of moral values. There are others that deal with law, love, the stars and planets, and taxes.

The Sumerians created the world's first literature. There are hundreds of literary tablets in existence today, and many more probably existed in that time. What is remarkable about the tablets is the wide range of literary subjects and themes. There are animal myths, theological myths, proverbs, epic tales, hymns, and lamentations.

Notwithstanding the political situation in Iraq in recent history, the greatest difficulties in understanding the architectural monuments of the Sumerians are threefold. First, the structures were made from mud-brick, and have a high degree of fragility. Second, as a result of this first condition, and of the effects of man-made destruction, there are often multiple layers of structures on one site. Third, simply put, they are very old.

Temples and temple areas were the focal point of the Sumerian cities. Eridu, considered by the Sumerians to be the world's first city, had a small temple from its inception, around 5500–5000 BCE. Later, a larger temple, built on a platform, was built around 4200 BCE and another around 4000 BCE. Uruk, owing in part to its Biblical reputation as the City of Erech, and as the city of the epic hero-king Gilgamesh, is perhaps the best-known Sumerian city. By around 2700 BCE, it had a population of around 20,000 inhabitants. The ziggurat of Anu (god of the heavens), also known as the **White Temple at Uruk**, was built on a platform in the center of the city, more than 13 meters high. The platform was built from the rubble of previous structures, and had an outer revetment wall of alternating undulations and buttresses made from mud brick. The temple also had walls built in the same way, and this feature is characteristic of Mesopotamian architecture. The interior of the temple had a long central space, with smaller chapels flanking each side.

The Sumerian civilization was not a single political entity. Each city-state was independent, although it shared a common culture and language. The Sumerian writing system spread beyond the Mesopotamian region into city-states like Ebla, in present-day Syria; Elam, in present-day Iran; and Akkad, to the north. As the cities grew, disputes arose over their borders. The Akkadians gradually adopted the Sumerian writing system as their own language, and the Akkadian language eventually became the most predominant in the region. In 2340 BCE, an Akkadian king, Sargon the Great, overran the Sumerian city-states and created the first empire in history. In 2230 BCE, this empire fell, and a Sumerian ruler, Ur-nammu, regained control of the Sumerian cities.

Ur-nammu created what is known as the Third Dynasty of Ur, or the Neo-Sumerian Empire. It is during this period that the greatest monuments of Mesopotamia were built. The **Ziggurat at Ur** measured approximately 60 meters by 45 meters. It contains three platforms. The interior core is solid, filled with rough bricks. The walls lean slightly inward. Like the Egyptian pyramids, the walls were built in alignment with the four cardinal directions.

The Amorites were from the region of the Amurru (present-day Syria), and they migrated into Mesopotamia beginning around 2000 BCE. Hammurabi, an Amorite prince, founded the great city of Babylon and the Babylonian Empire. This rise to prominence benefited from an act of nature—the Euphrates River changed its course. Suddenly, several cities that had prospered during the Sumerian period lost their prominence. Babylon was transformed, almost overnight, into an important center of commerce and trade. This first Babylonian Empire lasted for a few hundred years. The Hittites sacked Babylon around 1595 BCE, and a group of people called the Kassites, who had previously lived at the northern edge of Mesopotamia, created an empire called Babylonia, which lasted until the middle of the twelfth century BCE.

The surviving architectural monuments of the Bronze Age in the Near East (c. 3000–1100 BCE), are located in the great cities of the civilizations that rose and fell during the period, such as Assur, Nineveh, Khorsabad, Nimrud, Persepolis, and Babylon. Cities like Babylon, whose ruins are in present-day Iraq, were born and reborn. Babylon is best remembered for its ruler, Hammurabi, and his code of law, which was influential throughout the civilized world for its idea alone, if not for its contents. It introduced the concept of like punishment, *lex talionis*, which is best remembered as an "eye for an eye, tooth for a tooth," but the law code is more extensive than just that. Tribal feuds were common in small villages. Reprisals for offensive acts prolonged conflicts. Hammurabi's code set standards for punishment that intended to diminish the intensity and duration of these feuds. The elimination or reduction of the hostilities between families and tribes

FIGURE 6.3

Lamassu at Nimrud. One of two that flanked the royal palace of Ashurnasirpal II. British Museum, London.

FIGURE 6.4

Lion Gate. Hattusa, Turkey.

would be an important process in creating a united, larger, more efficient, and more powerful state.

The Hittites, or Hatti, established an empire in Anatolia, modern-day Turkey, during the Late Bronze Age. The capital of the Hittite empire was at Hattusa, a city located in what is now North-Central Turkey, where ruins of royal palaces, temples, and fortifications exist today. **The Lion Gate at Hattusa** (c. 1400 BCE) was one of five gateways in the city walls, which also had more than 100 towers. The lions are carved into monolithic slabs that protect each side of the entrance. A great temple, Temple 1, was surrounded by storerooms.

Assur, in Northern Mesopotamia, was the central city of the Assyrian civilization, which lasted longer than any other in the Near East. The origins of the Assyrians as a people are from the middle of the third millennium, but their history is one of alternating, relatively brief periods of ascension and decline until the end of the tenth century BCE. In the eighth and seventh centuries, it became the first empire to dominate the entirety of the Near East, but the severity and brutality of its rule, the constant threat of enemies that surrounded it on all sides, and the overextension of its resources all contributed to the unsettled nature of its glory. The empire ended abruptly in the last decade of the seventh century.

Old Kingdom Egypt

To say: O Great Ennead, who are in Heliopolis, make N. (Neferkarē') endure;
make this pyramid of N. endure, and this his temple, for ever and ever,
as the name of Atum, chief of the Great Ennead, endures.
As the name of Shu, lord of the upper mnś.t in Heliopolis, endures,
so may the name of N. endure,
so may this his pyramid endure, and this his temple, likewise, for ever and ever.
As the name of Tefnut, lady of the lower mnś.t in Heliopolis, is established,
so may the name of N. be established,

FIGURE 6.5

Mastaba of Mereruka, vizier to Teti (c.2345 BCE). Saqqarah, Egypt.

so may this pyramid be established, likewise, for ever and ever.
As the name of Geb, even the soul of the earth, endures,
so may the name of N. endure,
so may this pyramid of N. endure,
so may this his temple endure, likewise, even for ever and ever.
As the name of Nut, in the encircled mansion in Heliopolis, endures,
so may the name of N. endure,
so may this his pyramid endure,
so may this his temple endure, likewise, for ever and ever.
As the name of Osiris, in Abydos, endures,
so may the name of N. endure,
so may this pyramid of N. endure,
so may this his temple endure, likewise, even for ever and ever.
As the name of Osiris, as First of the Westerners, endures,
so may the name of N. endure,

so may this pyramid of N. endure,
so may this his temple endure, likewise, for ever
and ever… [2]

– from *The Pyramid Texts*

The Pyramid Texts were found in a pyramid built at Saqqara in the twenty-fourth century BCE for the pharaoh Unas. Written in hieroglyphics, the texts were carved on the walls of the chambers below the pyramid. The incantations were instructions for the resurrection of the pharaoh after his death, describing the steps, procedures, and pathways to the next life. The pyramids are deceptively simple forms that belie their grandiosity in spite of their reputation. Their plain, monolithic appearance belies the complexity of how they were constructed, the art and artifacts that were once buried inside them, and in general, the cultural sophistication of their builders.

Egypt was the most durable of all the ancient civilizations, lasting from c. 3150 BCE, with the unification of prehistoric and protohistoric peoples from the North and from the South, to 30 BCE. It was a culture that was recognized, even in antiquity, as the fountainhead for all civilization. The great pyramid at Giza was already more than a thousand years old when the temples at Luxor and Karnak were built, and these great temples were a thousand years old when the Parthenon and the great monuments of classical Greece appeared. In fact, hundreds of years after the Parthenon, another wave of ambitious building projects took place in Egypt, this time widely influenced by Greek architecture.

Herodotus, the Greek historian, toured Egypt in the fifth century BCE and famously dubbed it "the gift of the Nile." Since the Paleolithic Age, early humans had survived all along the Nile Valley by hunting, fishing, and gathering food. They lived in huts with roofs made out of reeds or palm fronds. Sometime around 7,500 years ago, agricultural communities appeared. Eventually, two distinct "kingdoms" emerged, called the Lower Kingdom in the North, and the Upper Kingdom in the South (the

Nile flows north). Around 3150 BCE, Narmer, the first king of Egypt, unified the two kingdoms. This is recorded in a stone, called the Narmer Palette, which is on display in the Egyptian Museum in Cairo.

Until the two Aswan dams were built in the twentieth century, rains from the mountainous regions in Central Africa would swell the tributaries of the Nile. When, in midsummer, this excess water flowed downstream past what is currently Rwanda, Uganda, and Sudan and into Egypt, the river rose above its banks and flooded the adjacent valley. The floodwaters carried silt, a natural fertilizer, which remained on top of the soil after the flood receded. As a rule, this happened every year. Some years, however, were drier in Central Africa, the floods would not come, and the soil would not get fertilized. Crops suffered, and famine was possible. If it rained too much, the flooding overwhelmed the villages and farms along the Nile. Narmer instigated and directed the building of irrigation canals (which are still in existence), which mitigated the potential flood damage by dispersing the water, but it also increased the fertilized area, literally turning desert into farmland. The extra food production created a surplus that could be sold to neighboring states. The wealth created by the exporting of the surplus was then used to establish a professional army, thereby increasing security and power in the region for Egypt.

Egyptian history is divided into the Old Kingdom (3100–2200 BCE), the Middle Kingdom (2100–1800 BCE), and the New Kingdom (c. 1570–1050 BCE). The gaps in between are known as Intermediate Periods, periods when the central authority broke down. After the Second Intermediate Period, and after the expelling of the Hyksos, invaders from the Levant who established a brief dynasty, Egypt became more aggressive in its relations with neighbors. For more than a thousand years, it had remained in relative isolation from other civilizations, but it became more imperial in the New Kingdom, establishing control over lands in the Levant.

Egyptian civilization has captivated scholars, artists, and travelers ever since. Architecturally, there are four notable phases of Ancient Egypt: the Old Kingdom phase, the age of the pyramids; the New Kingdom phase, the age of the great Egyptian temple; the Nubian phase,

---

2   The Pyramid Texts, trans. Samuel A. B. Mercer. Copyright in the Public Domain.

FIGURE 6.6

Stepped Pyramid of Djoser. Saqqarah, Egypt.

FIGURE 6.7

Mortuary Temple of Djoser. Saqqarah, Egypt.

an age of pyramid revival on a smaller scale; and finally, the Ptolemaic phase, the Greek-influenced temples of the fourth to the first centuries. The great monuments of Egypt are state temples, mortuary temples, and tombs. The temple was called a *pr-ntr*, meaning "house of the god," or *hwt-htr*, meaning "castle of the god."

The Egyptians buried the bodies of their important individuals in the desert. In order to prevent exposure of the body to wind erosion; a small rectangular, flat-roofed structure called a *mastaba* was placed on the surface above the burial pit. The structure resembled a bench, from which the name is derived. A doorway, which was sometimes emphasized by an architectural feature, led to an interior chamber where the body was placed at the bottom of a shaft. The chamber was often elaborately decorated with sculptural and painted images. A second chamber, called a *serdab*, was used for a statue of the deceased.

For the next several hundred years, the mastaba form remained unchanged, except for gradual increases in the size and depth of the lower burial chamber. However, during the reign of the second king of the Third Dynasty, King Djoser (sometimes spelled Zoser), there was a major adaptation that became the largest structure to that point in building history, the **Step Pyramid of Djoser** (c. 2630 BCE) at Saqqara.

At first, the tomb was just a simple mastaba made of limestone (63 meters by 63 meters by 8 meters high), constructed on top of a square shaft that descended 28 meters into the sand and rock. Imhotep, the chief of works (he is sometimes referred to as history's first known

architect), added 3 meters on all sides, then elongated the bench-like structure by adding 9 meters on the east side. On this base, a series of increasingly smaller mastabas were placed on top of the first, until the ziggurat was created, a six-layer stepped pyramid, some 60 meters tall.

The pyramid (the Egyptian word was *mer*) was the main building in a complex enclosed by a rectangular wall that measured 545 by 277 meters, and more than 10 meters tall. One approached the complex through a gate (there was one real gate and 13 false gates), and a covered walkway led into the central area. A series of unique structures called the House of the North, the House of the South, and the Heb Sed Court, with fluted columns and pilasters, filled the entire eastern side of the inner court.

Another pilaster at Saqqara resembles the head and stalk of a papyrus plant. Later on, in the fifth Dynasty, capitals were constructed that resembled the lotus flower.

FIGURE 6.8

Bent Pyramid. Dahshur, Egypt.

Thus, at Saqqara, there is evidence of three of the four forms that would dominate Egyptian architecture for the next 2,500 years: the underground tomb, the papyrus column and capital; and the pyramid.

After Djoser, there is little information about the next three kings until Sneferu, the first king of the Fourth Dynasty. Sneferu began construction on a second large ziggurat, **Meidum Pyramid** (c. 2600 BCE). Although during construction the sides were filled in with stone to create a true pyramid, the method of attaching these stones to the stepped pyramid proved to be unsound, and they fell. There is a pile of rubble at the base of it even today. After the collapse—or perhaps before—it was abandoned. Sneferu was never buried there.

Fifteen miles away from Meidum, at Dahshur, Sneferu tried again, this time planning a true pyramid from the beginning. Again, there was a problem during construction, and again, a major alteration took place. Yet again, Sneferu was not buried in the monumental tomb that was built. Two of the corners of the pyramid were on solid bedrock, but two others were not. During construction, the whole pyramid moved, causing cracks in the burial chamber. As at Meidum, the burial chamber was not located in the customary chamber located deep below the surface. Instead, it was placed inside the pyramid. After the decision to abandon the tomb, the angle of the pyramid was changed, presumably so that it could be finished quickly; then, efforts could be channeled to yet

another pyramid. This pyramid is referred to as the **Bent Pyramid** (c. 2600 BCE).

Finally, Sneferu constructed what is called the **Red Pyramid** (c. 2600 BCE), also at Dahshur. The angle of the sides of the pyramid was less steep than at the previous two. The Red Pyramid is the first real pyramid ever constructed. Although some scholars believe it became the resting place for Sneferu, it remains a possibility that he is buried in the Bent Pyramid.

Sneferu's reign ended c. 2589 BCE. His son and successor, Khufu (also written as Cheops), built what is known as the **Great Pyramid at Giza**, or the **Pyramid of Khufu** (early- to mid-twenty-sixth century BCE), the largest pyramid ever constructed. The vizier, the "overseer of the king's work," for this project was Hemiunu, the son of Nefermaat, the vizier for Sneferu. The site was a plateau, which meant the pyramids would be raised above the flood plain, and there would be a good foundation underneath the structure. It also had outcroppings of limestone, which could be used for the construction.

The angle of the pyramid is 51° 52", with all sides being, in essence, equilateral triangles. The burial chamber is near the center of the pyramid (there is also a subterranean chamber, but it was never used). On the north face is an entrance that is roughly 16 meters aboveground that leads to a narrow ascending passageway, and then to an ascending "Grand Gallery" to the King's Chamber, and another relatively level passageway to the "Queen's Chamber." There are small air shafts that connect the King's Chamber with the exterior.

FIGURE 6.9
Red Pyramid, Dahshur, Egypt.

FIGURE 6.10
Facing Stone at top of pyramid of Khafre. Giza, Egypt.

Like at Dahshur and Saqqara, the pyramid was part of a complex. Three smaller pyramids to the southeast were built for Khufu's queens and a second pyramid of Khufu, symbolic of the fact that the kings of Egypt controlled the two old north and south kingdoms. There are mastabas for his relatives and the high-ranking officials to the east and west. There is also evidence of two temples and a causeway decorated with reliefs. At the western edge of the floodplain, underneath the modern suburb of Nazlet el-Samman, are the remains of Khufu's palace and a small community of mud-brick houses.

Two other pyramid complexes were built at Giza—the **Pyramid of Khafre** (mid-twenty-sixth century BCE), whose pyramid is slightly smaller than the one built by Khufu, and the **Pyramid of Menkaure**, (mid-twenty-sixth century BCE), whose pyramid is the smallest of the three. The Khufu and Khafre pyramids originally had a casing of white limestone quarried from Tura, on the opposite bank of the Nile and to the south, but only Khafre's pyramid still retains some of the limestone near the top, as some of the limestone was removed in antiquity, with the rest removed during the ninth century for buildings in Cairo. The Menkaure Pyramid had a casing of granite near the base, but it was never finished. The **Great Sphinx** (c. twenty-sixth century), carved out of the limestone bedrock at Giza, is the oldest and largest monumental statue in the world. It has the body of a lion and the head of a pharaoh, believed to be Khafre.

The square base of a pyramid was typically oriented to the four cardinal directions. The Great Pyramid at Giza is the most accurate, being rotated only a fraction of a degree off from perfect alignment. At the beginning of construction, a great groundbreaking ceremony took place called the "stretching of the cord." Its significance of the involvement of Egypt's population cannot be overstated. Even though the ultimate purpose of the temple complex was a tomb for the king, his wife, his relatives, and the controlling elite, it was perceived by the average Egyptian as a public project. How was this presented? The average citizen had to believe that the fortunes of the king were critical to their own fortunes. That is, if the king became a god, then the whole country would prosper.

Some workers on the pyramids worked year round. Poorer farmers worked during the periods of the annual flooding, the *akhet*. Wealthier families donated food and materials. During the time of the building of the Giza pyramids (some 67 years), the town of Giza would have been a boomtown, producing construction materials and food for the laborers. The exact construction methods of the pyramids are unknown, and probably always will be, but there are many theories. There seems to be a consensus about two main points: the construction was done in courses, or layers; and earthen ramps were used, perhaps outside the structure, perhaps inside, or perhaps both.

The previously mentioned cord that the Egyptians used for layout out buildings is a rope knotted thirteen times, dividing it into 12 equal one-cubit sections. (An Egyptian cubit was .05236 meters, or 1.72 feet.) If one forms a triangle with that rope, with three lengths on one side and four lengths on the other, then the hypotenuse will be five lengths, what we know as the Pythagorean Triangle. If one then extends the vertical leg by two more units, and then mirrors the triangle about this axis, an isosceles triangle is formed, with the ratio of 5:8. This is called the golden triangle, and it is what the French architect Viollet-le-Duc called the Egyptian triangle.

What happened to the pyramid-building fixation? The successor to Menkaure, King Shepseskaf, ruled for only 4 years, which may be the reason why he did not undertake such a grand-scale project. Instead, he built a large mastaba 100 meters by 72 meters by 18 meters, high shaped like a sarcophagus with an arched roof. For his wife, Khentkawes, a similar structure was built at Giza.

FIGURE 6.11
The Sphinx. Giza, Egypt.

LEFT PAGE!!   RIGHT PAGE!!

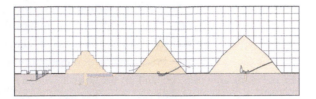

FIGURE 6.12

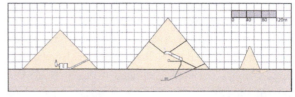

FIGURE 6.13

Comparative Sizes of Ancient Egyptian pyramids (from left to right): Mastaba; Step Pyramid of Djoser, Saqqara; Meidum Pyramid; Bent Pyramid; Red Pyramid; Great Pyramid at Giza; Nubian Pyramid.

This marked the end of the Fourth Dynasty. Commencing with the Fifth Dynasty, the royal court was moved to Abusir. Beginning with King Userkaf, the first king of the Fifth Dynasty, pyramid tombs were constructed for the kings, but they were no longer the all-consuming state projects they had once been. The cults associated with the kings lost their status. The tombs were plundered. The pyramids were used as quarry for later building projects. The era of great pyramids lasted for about 150 years, and the lesser pyramids, for almost another thousand years after that, although not continuously. The last king of the Fifth Dynasty, King Unas, built a small pyramid complex near Djoser's pyramid at Saqqara. The outer casing of the pyramid has disappeared, but its form is still visible. What is interesting is a small fragment of stone from the causeway leading to the pyramid, showing Unas smiting his enemies: a motif that will become prominent in the wave of construction in the New Kingdom. The pyramid built for King Ahmose at Abydos, c. 1525 BCE in the eighteenth Dynasty (the first dynasty of the New Kingdom), was the last pyramid built by the traditional rulers of Egypt.

During the twenty-fifth, or Nubian, Dynasty (c. 770–656 BCE), the practice of building pyramids, already around 2,000 years old, was revived by rulers from the southern region of Nubia (present-day Sudan), who took control of Egypt in the eighth century BCE. Today, there are more pyramids in the Sudan than there are in Egypt. The Nubian pyramids are smaller and steeper than the earlier ones. They were purely symbolic, as the actual tomb of the ruler was located away from the pyramid.

For Further Discussion

Explore the differences between Mesopotamian ziggurats and Egyptian pyramids. What geographical, political, and theological influences affected their design and construction; how did these differ?

CHAPTER SEVEN

68   Culture and Architecture: An Integrated History

Egypt in the New Kingdom

The following shall be said when one cometh to the FIRST PYLON. The Osiris the scribe Ani, whose word is truth, saith: "Lady of tremblings, high-walled, the sovereign lady, the lady of destruction, who uttereth the words which drive back the destroyers, who delivereth from destruction him that cometh." The name of her Doorkeeper is Neruit.

The following shall be said when one cometh to the SECOND PYLON. The Osiris the scribe Ani, whose word is truth, saith: "Lady of heaven, Mistress of the Two Lands, devourer by fire, Lady of mortals, who art infinitely greater than any human being." The name of her Doorkeeper is Mes-Ptah.

The following shall be said when one cometh to the THIRD PYLON. The Osiris the scribe Ani, whose word is truth, saith: "Lady of the Altar, the mighty lady to whom offerings are made, greatly beloved one of every god sailing up the river to Abydos." The name of her Doorkeeper is Sebqa.[1]

— from *The Book of the Dead (c. 240 BCE)*

Beyond the narrow flood plain of the western bank of the Nile River and beyond the vast desert that begins immediately at the edge of the natural and man-made limits of the greening river banks, the sun sets daily on the western horizon. There, the ancient Egyptians believed, lay the Field of Hetep, a field of offerings in the land of Osiris, the ruler of the dead in the afterlife. It was a land of luscious vegetation, abundant water, fruit trees, and fields of golden wheat and barley. Tombs discovered from the late sixth century show evidence that people placed ordinary tools, equipment, and weapons into their graves, presumably for use in the next life. When social stratification occurred in the time of the pharaohs at the end of the fourth millennium, the process for the preparation for the afterlife for the wealthy ruling class developed into an elaborate obsession that dominated Egyptian art and architecture.

The promise of an afterlife existed for the poor and the wealthy, but the wealthy had the means and resources for the great rituals associated with the burial process, including mummification. The Egyptians believed in rebirth, not reincarnation, thus preserving the body was a necessity. Burials in the hot, dry desert naturally preserved the bodies, because bacteria that decay human or animal remains thrive better in a moist environment. More elaborate chambers, with the presence of wood, linens, and other objects made from organic sources, demanded more complex means of preserving the body.

The Egyptians believed in a second entity, more like a twin-in-waiting than a soul, called one's *ka*, sometimes translated as a life-force, whose birth and death attended the individual's actual birth and death. The ka would be the recipient for the equipment, food, drink, and other items buried with the deceased. The hieroglyph for ka was a pair of raised arms. The *ba*, a bird with a human head, was a person's nonphysical qualities, as well as the individual's communication between the tomb and the outside world. One's *akh* was a third entity, which embodied brightness, symbolizing life itself. Its hieroglyph was a bald ibis.

---

1   The Book of the Dead: The Papyrus of Ani, trans. E. A. Wallis Budge. Copyright in the Public Domain.

There is no doubt that the practices and belief systems existed before the historical period in Egypt, and the development of the cultural milieu in the late fourth millennium was the first evidentiary material that survived. Valuable sources for our understanding of the rituals and beliefs of the Egyptians are the three different types of funerary texts used in Ancient Egypt: pyramid texts, coffin texts, and *The Book of the Dead*. These were blueprints for the afterlife, and they included spells and recitations, as well as procedures and rituals. The largest collection of pyramid texts is associated with the last pharaoh of the Old Kingdom, Pepi II. In the Middle Kingdom, these texts were placed inside of tomb walls and coffins of the government administrators, thus the name "coffin texts." The book the Egyptians called *Formulae for Going Forth by Day*, now commonly called *The Book of the Dead*, was a collection of spells or instructions that could be used by anyone who could afford them. The most common form used was a collection of papyrus rolls that were placed in the sarcophagus or coffin of the deceased, but *The Book of the Dead* has also been found on tomb walls and portable objects, as well.

In some texts, the journey from death through the underworld to resurrection in the next world is through a series of pylons, each sacred to a particular god and each protected by a "doorkeeper." A *pylon* in Egyptian architecture is a monumental gateway consisting of a portal flanked on either side by towers that are rectangular in plan but taper inward from the bottom. Egyptian temples are located in precincts, or sanctuaries, and pylons were placed at the main entrances to the temple proper. As the temple complexes expanded, additional pylons were placed to create segmental areas, with a pylon at the entrance to that area. Pylons were decorated with sunken relief or incised relief painted sculpture, generally of the pharaoh's successful, militaristic encounters with enemies of the kingdom.

The image of Osiris is one of the most ubiquitous figures in Egyptian art. He is often depicted with green skin, which acknowledges his roles in the fruitfulness and the annual regeneration of the Nile River Valley. He holds a crook and flail, symbols of authority and rule. According to legend, his jealous brother Seth drowned him and distributed parts of his dismembered body up and down the Nile. Isis, his sister and wife, collected all the pieces and put them together anew. Their coupling produced the falcon god Horus.

The Weighing of the Heart is one of the most well-known of the ancient Egyptian burial rites. In this ritual, the deceased stands before Osiris. The person's heart is placed on one of a pair of balancing scales, with *ma'at*—truth and justice—on the other scale. If the heart was heavy with evil or misdeeds, then Ammit, a beast with the head of a crocodile, the front body of a lion, and the back body of a hippopotamus, would devour the heart. If it was balanced or lighter, then the deceased would be allowed passage on to the Fields of Hetep. Anubis, the jackal-headed god associated with the embalming process, assisted in this ritual. Additional spells followed, which made sure that the deceased person's heart was returned to his body. The Opening of the Mouth

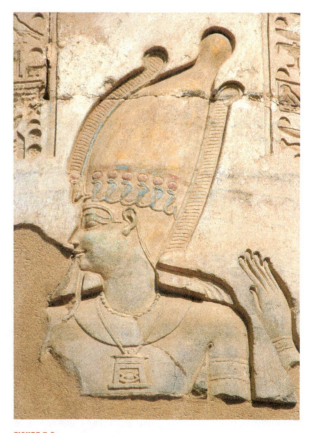

FIGURE 7.2

Osiris. From Temple of Sobek and Horus. Kom Ombo, Egypt.

ceremony was the last rite before the body was placed in the sarcophagus or coffin. Instruments were used to open the mouth of the deceased, to give life to the ka.

With few exceptions, burials took place on the west bank of the Nile. The eastern bank, where the sun rises, is associated with rebirth, and the western bank, where the sun sets, is associated with death. The pyramids were concentrated near the original administrative center of the unified Egypt at Memphis, which is located about 24 kilometers south of modern Cairo. In the Middle Kingdom, the administration center was moved to Thebes, in Southern Egypt.

Beginning with the eighteenth Dynasty, in the New Kingdom, a new burial ground emerged at Thebes, which is now called the Valley of the Kings (actually the name for two valleys located on the west bank of the Nile River). The site of the Valley of the Kings was chosen by Tuthmosis I, because it was uninhabited and secluded. There was only one entrance into the valley, so it could be guarded easily against tomb raiders. The pyramids, which were great works of architecture and engineering and are the symbols of Egyptian civilization even today, were ultimately ineffective. By the end of Intermediate Period, nearly all the tombs of those buried in the pyramids had been defiled and robbed. They had advertised their wealth too effectively.

Tuthmosis's daughter, Hatshepsut, ruled as a female pharaoh from 1498–1483 BCE. The **Funerary Temple**

of Hatshepsut (c. 1490 BCE), at Deir el-Bahari near the Valley of the Kings, is one of the more singular buildings in all of antiquity. Its style captures the simplicity and straightforwardness of the Old Kingdom. The building's architect was Senenmut. Although he was not from a royal family, there is circumstantial evidence that he and Hatshepsut were lovers. There is a graffito in a nearby cave showing a man that could be Senenmut having intercourse with a woman who is wearing a pharaoh's crown. Senenmut is buried in a tomb near the queen.

FIGURE 7.4

Funerary Temple of Hatchepsut, Deir-El-Bahari, Egypt.

FIGURE 7.3

Rock cut tombs with false doors along the Nile River for regional provincial rulers called nomarchs. Middle Kingdom or New Kingdom.

FIGURE 7.5

Hatchept Statues. Funerary Temple of Hatchepsut, Deir-el-Bahari, Egypt.

FIGURE 7.6

Colonnade. Funerary Temple of Hatchepsut, Deir-El-Bahari, Egypt.

Upon the death of Hatshepsut, her nephew Tuthmosis III became pharaoh, and under his rule Egypt prospered well. He was succeeded by his son Amenhotep IV, who changed his name to Akhenaten, to honor Aten, who had previously been a minor sun god. He instituted a monotheistic religion, often regarded as the first in history, and a significant, albeit temporary interruption of Egyptian culture. He reigned for 17 years, and upon his death, Tutankaten inherited his father's thrown. He reinstated the traditional polytheistic religion and changed his name Tutankhamen, who by circumstance alone, is the most famous pharaoh today of all of Egyptian history.

When Howard Carter and George Herbert, the fifth earl of Carnarvon, opened the **Tomb of Tutankhamen** (c. 1323 BCE) in 1922, it was the first time that a cache of richly decorated art and artifacts—enough to fill a small museum—had been seen in over 3,200 years. Many of the objects were put on display in the Egyptian Museum in Cairo, and some have traveled the world, on loan to other museums. We consider the find to be one of the greatest archaeological discoveries ever, one that allowed Egyptologists to learn more about ancient Egyptian culture, and one that has fascinated the general public for decades. However, the artists who made the works of art and the individuals who worked for the royal family, never intended for them to be seen again, as they would have been used by Tutankhamen in his next life. While some works of Egyptian art were clearly intended for public viewing (such as scenes from a pharaoh's military or political triumphs), a significant portion was created for the afterlife, located somewhere in the sky, the domain of the sun. The walls, columns, and beams of Egyptian temples and tombs of ancient Egypt were canvases for art. Inside the architectural spaces were portrait statues of kings and princes, their wives, and other members of the aristocratic class.

The temples at Luxor and Karnak, built in the imperial period, are the most famous in Egypt. The **Temple of Luxor** (fourteenth–thirteenth centuries BCE), *opet-resyt*, or "southern harem" in ancient Egyptian, was begun in the Middle Kingdom, but what is visible today is from the dynasty of Amenhotep III (c. 1390–c. 1352 BCE). The temple was dedicated to the god Amun, especially the aspect of his association with fertility, his wife Mut, and the moon god, Khonsu. The name Amun, which is also written as Amen or Amon (as there are no vowels, only consonants in the hieroglyphic language of the Ancient Egyptians), means "hidden." The sacred animals associated with Amun are the ram and the goose.

The layout of the temple corresponds to the rituals of a month-long festival; whose purpose was to ceremoniously reaffirm that the powers of the pharaoh were divinely sanctioned. A procession was held from the Karnak temple to Luxor, which included the king's entourage, musicians, members of the public, and sacred

FIGURE 7.7

Hypostyle Hall. Temple of Luxor.

FIGURE 7.8

Papyrus Bud Columns. Hypostyle Hall. Temple of Luxor.

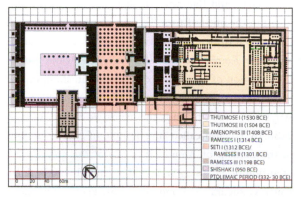

FIGURE 7.9

Temple of Luxor Plan.

barks, or boats, that carried images of the gods. The design was fluid; that is, the form of the building that we see today is the result of several additions and alterations that were made after the reign of Amenhotep III.

An avenue of sphinxes leads to an entrance pylon that was built by Ramesses II. Originally, there were two seated and four standing statues of Ramesses II, and two obelisks were in front. But only the two seated and one standing statue, as well as one obelisk, remain. The pylon is decorated with scenes from the battle of Kadesh incised in the masonry. This battle with the Hittites, which took place in 1274 BCE, was by most accounts a draw, although Ramesses II portrays the battle in a triumphant manner. This was because securing even the draw at Kadesh was a significant achievement, and because the ultimate outcome of this, and later skirmishes with the Hittites, was a needed peace treaty. Flags with cult images on top of the pylons were placed on long poles, which were visible from a distance.

The procession then passed through the peristyle court, also by Ramesses II, and then a colonnade, originally built by Amenhotep but altered by Tutankhamen (c. 1336–c. 1327) and Horemheb (c. 1323–c. 1295). Tutankhamen is shown offering gifts to the gods. The Court of Amenhotep III follows, and then a hypostyle hall. Several successive chambers lead to the sanctuary itself.

Within the vast temple complex of the **Great Temple of Amun** (nineteenth–twelfth centuries BCE) at Karnak are temples dedicated to Amun, Mut, Khonsu, Ptah, Opet, and Ramesses II. There are two axes, as opposed to the one at Luxor. The complex began as a small shrine built by Senusret (c. 1965–c. 1920), and continued until the Roman period. There are ten pylons, six in the direction of the main axis, each diminishing in size one after the other, and four in the perpendicular axis. After the second pylon is the hypostyle hall (c. 1295–c. 1186 BCE), also called "the Temple of Seti is glorious in the domain of Amun." It is one of the great spaces of antiquity, enclosing an area that could house both St. Paul's Cathedral in London and St. Peter's Basilica in Rome. The hall has 134 sandstone columns, with the 12 flanking the processional way being higher to allow for

FIGURE 7.10

Open Papyrus Style Column Capitals. Hypostyle Hall. Great Temple of Amun. Karnak, Egypt.

the construction of clerestory windows, the only source of light in the space.

Ramesses II (c. 1279–c. 1213 BCE) built two rock-cut temples, one for himself and one his queen Nefertari at the **Temple of Ramesses II** (thirteenth century BCE), at Abu Simbel in Southern Egypt, near the present-day border with Sudan. The façade of the Temple of Ramesses II is dominated by four colossal statues of Ramesses II, wearing the double crown representing Upper and Lower Egypt, and smaller statues of his family at his feet. A doorway leads to the chambers carved into the stone. A frieze of baboons decorates the uppermost part of the facade. In February and October, the rising sun penetrates into the sanctuary and illuminates the wall and statues of four gods inside the chamber: Ptah, the creator god of Memphis; Amun; the deified Ramesses II; and Harakhte.

The adjacent image has three standing colossal figures, two of Ramesses II on either side of the queen in the center, with smaller statues of their children at their feet. The temple is dedicated to Hathor, the cow-headed goddess, and the deified Nefertari. The two temples were moved from their original site between 1964 and 1968, when rising waters from man-made Lake Nasser threatened the sites.

Monumental construction projects were planned by the pharaoh, with assistance from his viziers, architects and work overseers and Seshat, the goddess of art, writing, and architecture. Egyptian temples and other monuments were built with limestone, which was quarried from outcroppings along the Nile from Cairo to Esna, and sandstone, which was available from Esna to the south, and pink and gray granites found at Aswan. Occasionally, alabaster was used as a flooring material.

The stone columns used in tombs and temples would have undoubtedly served as models studied by Greeks when their architectural style was being contrived in the seventh century. There are two kinds of column styles, rectangular and decorative. The decorative columns were reproductions in stone of previous primitive building techniques, and included columns with plain shafts and palm capitals, columns shaped like lotus buds, columns shaped like bundled papyrus, and papyrus with an open blossom. The goddess Hathor also appears as a figure on a column.

Unlike much of the artwork that decorated the Egyptian architecture from the Old Kingdom, painting and sculpture in New Kingdom works of architecture were intended for public viewing. The use of large sculptures depicting the pharaohs were developed from earlier, smaller likenesses placed near or inside tombs. The Colossi

FIGURE 7.11

Temple of Queen Nefertari. Abu Simbel, Egypt.

of Memnon, though isolated today, were once part of a temple of Amenhotep III. Standing figures are shown walking, with one step forward. Seated figures show the pharaoh, with or without his wife, with his hands on his knees, as at Abu Simbel. *Reliefs*, sculptures in which the figures or designs project from a background, are an integral part of the decoration of temples. Both the practice of *bas-relief*, which had minimal depth, and was used extensively in the Old Kingdom, and *sunken relief*, in which the figures are carved into the surface, were used in the New Kingdom. The sculptures were normally painted. In the Old Kingdom, wall paintings were placed upon mud plaster. In the New Kingdom, paintings were placed on lime or gypsum plaster.

The most common subjects for Egyptian art are funerary texts, depictions of historical events, scenes from daily life, flora and fauna, mythological events, and portraits of the pharaohs and deities. Pharaohs and deities can be identified by their distinctive headdresses, which include a white crown for Upper Egypt, a red crown for Lower Egypt, or a double crown indicating the unification of the two.

CHAPTER EIGHT

Aegean Civilizations of the Bronze Age

When he reached Crete on his voyage, most historians and poets tell us that he got from Ariadne, who had fallen in love with him, the famous thread, and that having been instructed by her how to make his way through the intricacies of the Labyrinth, he slew the Minotaur and sailed off with Ariadne and the youths. And Pherecydes says that Theseus also staved in the bottoms of the Cretan ships, thus depriving them of the power to pursue. And Demon says also that Taurus, the general of Minos, was killed in a naval battle in the harbor as Theseus was sailing out. But as Philochorus tells the story, Minos was holding the funeral games, and Taurus was expected to conquer all his competitors in them, as he had done before, and was grudged his success. For his disposition made his power hateful, and he was accused of too great intimacy with Pasiphae. Therefore when Theseus asked the privilege of entering the lists, it was granted him by Minos. And since it was the custom in Crete for women to view the games, Ariadne was present, and was smitten with the appearance of Theseus, as well as filled with admiration for his athletic prowess, when he conquered all his opponents. Minos also was delighted with him, especially because he conquered Taurus in wrestling and disgraced him, and therefore gave back the youths to Theseus, besides remitting its tribute to the city.[1]

— from *Parallel Lives* by Plutarch

The story of Theseus and the Minotaur is one of the more famous tales of Greek mythology. Theseus was the son of the king of Athens, Aigeus, and his wife Aithra, or the consequence of the rape of Aithra by the god Poseidon. Athens had been obliged by Minos, the king of Crete, to pay a tribute of seven young men and seven young women who would be fed to the Minotaur, a half-bull and half-human monster that is quartered in the Labyrinth. Theseus slays the Minotaur, and with the help of Minos's daughter, Ariadne, finds his way out of the Labyrinth. Minos was probably an actual king, or the name of many kings in Crete's archaic past. In Greek legend, he was the son of Zeus and Europa. In retribution for having failed to offer a bull as a sacrifice to Poseidon, the god caused his wife Pasiphae to be aroused by the bull, and the Minotaur is the result of the union of Pasiphae and the bull.

Daedalus (DED'l-lus), a legendary craftsman, designed the Labyrinth. Daedelus was held captive by

FIGURE 8.2

Thesues Mosaic from House of Theseus. Paphos, Cyprus. Theseus (c.). Clockwise from upper left: Ariadne, Crete, Minotaur, Labyrinth.

---

1   Plutarch, Plutarch's Lives, Volume One, trans. Bernadotte Perri. Copyright in the Public Domain.

FIGURE 8.3

Bull Head. Heraklion Archaeological Museum, Crete.

was not an archaeologist. The field of archaeology, in the modern sense of the term, did not exist then. Evans was more of a wealthy adventurer than a scholar. After hearing of the discovery of some clay tablets containing an unknown language at Herakleion, he bought the land and started digging. He found a palace—the palace of King Minos—and below it, evidence of a Neolithic settlement from at least 6000 BCE. At his own expense, he reconstructed much of Minos's palace. The accuracy of this reconstruction is often the subject of criticism by scholars, but the vividness of Evans's recreation is unparalleled. There were other Minoan sites that subsequently were discovered elsewhere in Crete, notably at Gournia, Phaestos, Agia Triada, and Malia, and in neighboring islands, such as Akrotiri on the nearby island of Santorini.

The excavations showed that the nucleus of Minoan daily life was a palace that served as a residence for the king and other higher ranking officials, a distribution and storage center for agricultural goods, a ceremonial center, a religious center, and an administrative center. These rooms and areas of the palaces were arranged around a central court area. The excavations also indicate that Minoan culture was sophisticated in almost every aspect; the architecture and artwork that they left behind both demonstrate an aesthetic awareness and appreciation. Their language, called Linear A by scholars, has yet to be deciphered. If it is ever deciphered, we may learn more about their culture and mythology.

The palaces had many entrances and were unfortified, unlike almost all other Bronze Age civilizations of the

Minos, until he escaped to Sicily with the help of the famous wings he had invented, made of feathers and wax. Deadalus's son, Icarus, despite warnings from his father, flew too close to the sun, and fell to his death. Minos went to Sicily to retrieve Daedalus, but was killed. According to Herodotus, the *Pythia* at Delphi, speaking on the behalf of Apollo, advised Crete not to assist the Greeks in their war with Persia, because the Greeks had failed to help Crete in avenging the death of Minos, a great king. The Greeks refused to help, even though Crete had helped Menelaus, whose "woman," Helen, had been abducted by a barbarian (foreigner).

When Sir Arthur Evans discovered the ruins of Knossos in 1899, he named the people of the civilization there "Minoans," after the legendary king Minos. Evans

FIGURE 8.4

Model of Akrotiri. Museum of Prehistoric Thera. Fira (Santorini), Greece.

Mediterranean and the Near East. Initially, archaeologists speculated that the eruption of the volcano at Thera caused the destruction of the palaces on Crete in the first half of the fifteenth century BCE, but recent evidence has proven that the palaces had survived the eruption, which is now placed around 1627 BCE. After 1400 BCE, Linear A is no longer used, and Linear B, the language of the later Mycenaean civilization of mainland Greece, came into use. This points to either a peaceful immersion of one society into the other, or the conquest of the Minoan culture by the Mycenaeans. Knossos was the only Cretan city rebuilt after the destructions of early fifteenth century, and this rebirth lasted for 75 years. Akrotiri, a Bronze Age site on the island of Santorini, was destroyed during the seventeenth century eruption.

At first, the palace at Knossos seems labyrinthine in its composition, although it is actually functionally well-organized. The spaces arranged around the central court are designed with movement, not symmetry, in mind. Spatial relationships vary at every turn. A full porch is adjacent to another that employs a single corner column. Sometimes the porches are L-shaped. There are spaces that were used as light wells. Despite the concentration of walls, the openness of the surrounding countryside never seems more than a step or a turn away. There is little that is repeated; an architectural surprise is more common than one that is expected. If you get used to the interpenetration of spaces—spaces that naturally become part of other spaces—you suddenly confront a solid wall, such as at the western section of the palace, which was reserved for the magazines. Above all else, it is a three-dimensional experience, which, due to the extensive restoration, is easier to appreciate than at other sites.

The Mycenaeans were the second Bronze Age culture of the Mediterranean. Like the Minoans, the Mycenaeans had a palatial society, perhaps because they modeled after the palaces in Crete. These sites were true, fortified citadels, with surrounding protective walls and a singular entrance. Mycenae, in the Argolid area of the Peloponnese in Greece, was built in the fourteenth and thirteenth centuries. Homer described the city in the *Iliad* as "well built" and "rich in gold." Heinrich Schliemann, a German businessman riding the wave of renewed interest in the "lost" sites of the ancient world, traveled to Greece in 1868, with the intention of finding the lost cities of Homer. Five years later, he had discovered—or helped to discover—both Troy and Mycenae.

The **Lion Gate** at **Citadel of Mycenae** (c. 1250 BCE) is one of the iconic images of the pre-Classical world. The approach to the gate is past the *Cyclopean* walls, named after the Cyclopes, the one-eyed giants who were sons of the god Uranus. The flanking walls of the gate are an example of *ashlar* stone masonry—dressed rectangular blocks laid in even rows, or *courses*. Two male or female lions stand perched on their hindquarters, with a single column in the middle. The column tapers from top to

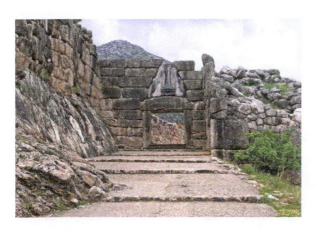

FIGURE 8.5

Lion Gate. Mycenae, Greece

FIGURE 8.6

Lion Lintel. Mycenae, Greece.

bottom like a Minoan column, but the proportions presage the Doric style of early Classical Greek architecture. There are segments of a double platform below, and an architrave with geometric decoration above.

The nearby **Treasury of Atreus** (c. 1250 BCE), a *tholos* tomb, was thought to be the burial place of Agamemnon, although this is disputed. The name Atreus refers to the family of Agamemnon, who in Greek legend endured generations of being cursed by the gods for the actions of Tantalus, the family's founder, who tried to trick the gods into eating human flesh. Agamemnon, whose feud with Achilles is the foundation of the *Iliad*, was the brother-in-law of Helen, the wife of Menelaus, whose abduction or seduction by Paris was the cause of the Trojan War. Angry that Menelaus sacrificed their daughter, Iphigenia, to the gods, Clytemnestra, wife of Menelaus, killed Agamemnon upon his return from Troy. Clytemnestra was aided by her lover Aigisthos,

FIGURE 8.7
Treasury of Atreus. Mycenae, Greece.

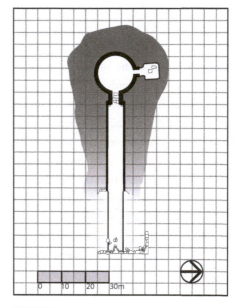

FIGURE 8.8
Treasury of Atreus Plan.

FIGURE 8.9
Mask of Agamemnon (c.1550-1500 BCE). National Archaeological Museum, Athens.

FIGURE 8.10
Tholos or Beehive Masonry. Treasury of Atreus. Mycenae, Greece.

Agamemnon's first cousin. The death of Agamemnon is avenged by Orestes and Electra, son and daughter of Agamemnon and Clytemnestra.

The riches found at the tomb were certainly worthy of a warrior king who was the leader of the Greeks at Troy. The tomb, however, dates from around 1325 BCE, and the destruction of Troy is traditionally placed at 1184 BCE, a date that is more or less supported by the archaeological evidence.

Because of their shape, *tholos* tombs are also called beehive tombs. They have been found at other Mycenean sites, including Tiryns, in the Peloponnese, and Dimini, in Thessaly.

A third Aegean civilization, the Cycladic, was centered in the island group called the Cyclades, and existed from 3200 to 2000 BCE. This culture is almost exclusively known through art and artifacts and is best known for highly stylized female figures, possible earth goddesses, which have a distinctly modern character.

For Further Discussion

In the 1963 film *Jason and the Argonauts*, a film whose special effects are highly praised (and rightly so), the Argonauts capture winged creatures called Harpies by casting nets in a scene filmed at the Temple of Poseidon in Paestum, Italy, a Doric temple built around 600 BCE. The hero Jason, however, was part of the Age of Heroes that lived in the prior millennium. Therefore, showing a classical temple is not correct. What would a temple from the proper time period look like?

FIGURE 8.11

Corbelled Arch. Tiryns Citadel, Greece.

CHAPTER NINE

The Classical World

In the next generation after this, they say, Alexander the son of Priam, having heard of these things, desired to get a wife for himself by violence from Hellas, being fully assured that he would not be compelled to give any satisfaction for this wrong, inasmuch as the Hellenes gave none for theirs. So he carried off Helen, and the Hellenes resolved to send messengers first and to demand her back with satisfaction for the rape; and when they put forth this demand, the others alleged to them the rape of Medea, saying that the Hellenes were now desiring satisfaction to be given to them by others, though they had given none themselves nor had surrendered the person when demand was made.

Up to this point, they say, nothing more happened than the carrying away of women on both sides; but after this the Hellenes were very greatly to blame; for they set the first example of war, making an expedition into Asia before the Barbarians made any into Europe. Now they say that in their judgment, though it is an act of wrong to carry away women by force, it is a folly to set one's heart on taking vengeance for their rape, and the wise course is to pay no regard when they have been carried away; for it is evident that they would never be carried away if they were not themselves willing to go. And the Persians say that they, namely the people of Asia, when their women were carried away by force, had made it a matter of no account, but the Hellenes on account of a woman of Lacedemon gathered together a great armament, and then came to Asia and destroyed the dominion of Priam; and that from this time forward they had always considered the Hellenic race to be their enemy: for Asia and the Barbarian races which dwell there the Persians claim as belonging to them; but Europe and the Hellenic race they consider to be parted off from them.[1]

— from *The History* by Herodotus

According to Hesiod, an early Greek poet, there were successive races of humans: Golden, Silver, Bronze, Heroes, and Iron. The fourth, the age of Heroes, was the age of the famous heroes prominent in art and literature, such as Theseus, Herakles, and Jason. It is also the age of the greatest epics of Greek literature, the *Iliad* and the *Odyssey*. The importance of these two works, which are often called the Homeric epics, and their effect upon the art and literature of the Classical World (ancient Greece and Rome) cannot be overstated.

The Sacrifice of Iphigenea. Imperial Rome IV Style Fresco from Pompeii. Naples Archaeological Museum.

1 Herodotus, Selection from The History of Herodotus, vol. 1, trans. G. C. Macaulay. Copyright in the Public Domain.

The stories of the Trojan War were originally told orally and passed along for several hundred years, until they were written down in the eighth century. At that time, the Greeks reacquired the literacy they had lost during the so-called Dark Age, which lasted from the end of the Bronze Age in the twelfth century until the beginning of the eighth century. The written poems, collectively called the Epic Cycle, were the *Iliad*, the *Odyssey*, and several epics, for which titles are known but the actual poems have been lost. These include the *Ilioupersis*, the story of the attempt of Andromache, wife of Hector, to protect her son; the *Aethiopis*, which describes the death of Achilles; the *Little Iliad*, which describes the sack of Troy; and the *Returns*, which relates the story of how Menelaus and Helen are blown off course and live in Egypt several years before returning to Sparta.

The Trojan War story begins with the legend of Leda and the Swan. Leda is the wife of Tyndareus, the king of Sparta. She has an affair with Zeus, who approached her in the form of a swan. The two eggs from this union produce twins Castor and Pollux and Helen, who will become the most beautiful woman in the world. Clytemnestra is also the sister of Helen.

At the wedding of Peleus and Thetis (who are the parents of Achilles), all of the gods are invited—except for Eris, the goddess of discord, or strife. Eris tosses an apple with the attached words "for the fairest" toward Hera, Athena, and Aphrodite, who all claim the apple. To settle the matter of who gets the apple, they approach Paris, who is tending to his sheep, to decide who is the fairest. Paris is the son of Priam and Hecuba, king and queen of Troy, but he is left exposed when the king and queen hear it prophesized that he is destined to bring destruction upon Troy. The three goddesses try to bribe Paris: Hera with power, Athena with wisdom, Aphrodite with the most beautiful woman in the world. Paris chooses the beautiful woman. That woman is Helen.

Helen is married to Menelaus, the king of Sparta. Paris goes to Sparta, and while a guest of Menelaus, he either abducts or seduces Helen, and takes her back to Troy. This is in violation of the Greek concept of *xenia*, which mandates a fair and just treatment of guests and by guests. Menelaus summons his brother Agamemnon, whose wife is Clytemnestra, to lead an army of Greeks to retrieve Helen. The *Iliad* begins *in media res*, in the middle of the story, and tells of the "wrath of Achilles." The Greek fleet is prevented from leaving the homeland because of unfavorable winds, until Agamemnon, in response to the prophecy of the seer Calchas, sacrifices his own daughter, Iphigenia. A plague later besets the Greeks. This time, Calchas indicates that it is required that Agamemnon return Chryseis, a prized maiden, back to her father, who is a priest of Apollo. Agamemnon takes Achilles' favorite slave girl, Brisies, which angers Achilles. But Achilles refuses to fight. By dishonoring Achilles, Agamemnon has removed Achilles' motivation for fighting.

Achilles lends his armor to his close, friend Patroclus, who is killed by Hector, Paris's brother, the greatest of the Trojan heroes. Achilles kills Hector in battle, and then disrespects the Trojans by dragging the body around with his chariot. Finally, he meets with Priam, serving him a meal. Priam talks about Achilles' own father, and the two men weep. Achilles consents to let the body of Hector, "the tamer of horses," be buried. The *Iliad* ends.

Achilles is killed by Paris. The Greeks use the famous trick of the Trojan Horse to defeat the Trojans.

FIGURE 9.3

Hera and Zeus Metope from Temple E Selinute, Sicily. Palermo Archaeological Museum.

The Greeks sail away, as if they are giving up the battle. They leave the wooden horse. Sinon plays the role of a deserter, and convinces the Trojans to bring the horse inside the city walls. The Trojans bring the horse through the city gate, despite objections by Laocoon, a priest of Apollo. Warnings are also issued by Cassandra, daughter of Priam and Hecuba. As punishment for her refusal of the romantic advances by Apollo, Cassandra has the gift of prophecy—but is fated to be ignored. Laocoon and his sons are killed by serpents. The Greeks then destroy Troy. They commit atrocities, however, such as the assault of Cassandra, who had sought refuge in a temple of Minerva, by the Greek hero Ajax; and the sacrifice of another daughter, Polyxena, to the ghost of Achilles. The traditional date for the fall of Troy is 1184 BCE.

As punishment for their misdeeds at the end of the war, the return of the Greeks to their homeland is filled with difficulties and tragedies. It takes Odysseus 10 years to reach his homeland of Ithaca. Menelaus and Helen spend several years in Egypt before returning home. Agamemnon is killed by Clytemnestra and her lover, Aigisthos. Agamemnon's son, Orestes, avenges this murder by killing his mother and her lover.

The Odyssey begins with Telemachus, Odysseus's son, who was a newborn or an infant when Odysseus left. Telemachus, coming of age, tries to help his mother, Penelope, fight off the suitors, who have taken over Odysseus's property. Odysseus spends several years with Kalypso, after adventures with the Cyclopes Polyphemus, Circe, the Sirens, the Clashing Rocks—all told in flashback. Kalypso promises Odysseus immortality, but Odysseus leaves her. When he finally makes it to Ithaca, Athena disguises him as an old man. Penelope promises the suitors she will marry the man who can shoot an arrow through 12 axes with Odysseus's bow. He wins the contest, and then kills all the suitors. He reveals himself to Penelope, and Athena turns him back to his natural age.

One Trojan escaped the destruction of Troy—Aeneas. He carried his aged father, Anchises, on his back, and fled the burning city. Aeneas then sailed on a long a journey, which, like Odysseus, took him to the underworld. At Carthage (present-day Tunis), he befriended its queen, Dido, but he left her; Dido committed suicide by placing herself on a pyre. He eventually founded Alba Longa and the Roman civilization, fulfilling, no doubt with intent, the prophecy of Homer's *Iliad*. In this way, the *Aeneid* can be seen as Virgil's conscious effort to create a Roman epic in the Greek manner.

Greek culture grew from Iron Age settlements that had existed in the area since at least the sixth millennium BCE. There were three Bronze Age Aegean civilizations: the Cycladic, which existed in the islands called the Cyclades from c. 3000 BCE to 1050 BCE; the Minoan, located on the island of Crete and neighboring islands, lasting from c. 3000 BCE to c. 1400 BCE; and Mycenaean, located on the mainland of Greece, and lasting from c. 2000 BCE to c. 1100 BCE.

Greek history traditionally begins with the first Olympic games in 776 BCE, or 400 years after the collapse of the protohistoric Mycenaean and Minoan civilizations. Those four centuries have been called a "Dark Age" by scholars for two main reasons. First, there is little evidence of significant constructions from that time period, unlike the periods before and after. Second, the Greeks seemed to have lost knowledge of writing, a feat that has not been accomplished before or since by any other culture. Although there were great advances in pottery and in art, there is little evidence of significant works of architecture and literature.

During this period, the city-states that were once controlled by the Homeric Greeks now became controlled by groups of people from the region of Douris, what is now Central Greece, who were called the Dorians. At one time, it was thought there was a Dorian "invasion," though some historians argue that no Dorian culture existed before, and the Dorian people were already present in the Peloponnese, perhaps as a servile class that climbed the economic and social ladder when something happened to the ruling population (such as a victorious, but ultimately disastrous, war fought against a distant adversary).

For all its glory, the Greek "moment" in history was very brief, culminating in the fifth century BCE, the Classical Period. Following the defeat of Persia in the early fifth century BCE, the city-state of Athens gained wealth and prominence, and it was in this period that the greatest Greek works of architecture were built, including the Parthenon. Athens assumed a hegemonic relationship with the other city-states, which were required to pay tribute to a protection organization called the Delian League, which Athens controlled. Acrimony and resentment boiled into the Peloponnesian Wars, ending in 404 with the defeat of Athens by Sparta.

Under Alexander the Great (356–323 BCE), the Macedonians, previously more a peripheral part of Greek culture, conquered the Persians, and eventually ruled over an empire that spread from the Aegean and India to Southern Russia and into Egypt and Ethiopia. Alexander built new cities in the conquered territories, planted them with soldiers and Greek settlers, and thus, expanded the presence of Greek culture. After Alexander died at the age of 32, his kingdom was divided into three main blocks: Macedonia, Syria and Mesopotamia, and Egypt. The Syrian-Mesopotamian kingdom was ruled by the Seleucid dynasty. The Egyptian kingdom was ruled by the Ptolemaic dynasty.

The intimate relationship between the two eminent ancient civilizations of the Mediterranean—Greece and Rome—is unparalleled throughout human history. The coinage of the term *Greco-Roman* is a consequence of the two being closely aligned, although this relationship is not always straightforward. The Romans generally thought of the Greeks as their moral inferiors. Roman men considered Greek men to be too effeminate. Yet many Romans, especially those of the upper class, were *philhellenic*, that is, admiring of all things Greek. While it was true that each culture was ethnocentric, often to a racist extreme—an attitude widely tolerated in the ancient world—Greek culture was considered the more sophisticated of the two. The Greek language was considered the superior language to Latin, and many upper class Romans spoke Greek as a second language. The Greeks, even when conquered, thought of the Romans as inferior, like the Athenians had regarded the Spartans. Yet even some Romans thought this, as well. Horace, the first century BCE Roman poet, observed that "Greece, the captive, made her savage victor captive."

Politically, Greek influence in the ancient world pales when compared to Rome. At its height, the Roman Empire included Northern Africa, the Levant, and most of Europe. Greek civilization was composed of city-states united by culture and language, but not in a formal political structure. The Greek city-states united to defeat the Persians in the early part of the fifth century BCE, and the Athenian hegemony during the Delian Confederacy, for a short period of time, resembled the machinery of an imperial state, but by the end of the century (which concluded with the defeat of Athens by Sparta in the Peloponnesian War), this ersatz empire had disintegrated. Isocrates (436–338 BCE), the great Athenian orator, wrote in *Panegyricus* ("festival oration") that the Hellenes were a people united by similar philosophical and aesthetic viewpoints. Culturally, the situation was different. The Romans adopted many aspects of Greek culture, including mythology, literature, and architecture.

The syncretic relationship of the two mythologies is a major reason why the two are studied jointly more often than singularly. Greek and Roman gods are immortal, but not transcendental; that is, they are of the universe, not remote from it, and they did not create it. They are anthropomorphic, which means that they behave and look like humans, albeit larger, stronger, and more beautiful. The Romans fashioned their gods to be less anthropomorphic than the Greeks.

There are several "generations" of Greek gods. The first generation consists of the primordial gods: Chaos (inactivity), Gaia (Earth), Tartaros (the underworld), and Eros (sexual desire). The mating of these gods produce a second generation: Night, Erebos (darkness), the Ether, Day, Ouranos (the sky), Mountains, and Pontos (the sea). The next generation are the offspring of Gaia and Ouranos, and these are the 12 Titans: Oceanus, Coeus, Crius, Hyperion, Iapetus, Cronus, Thea, Rhea, Themis, Mnemosyne, Phoebe, and Tethys. Some of these gods represent concepts or ideas, such as Mnemosyne (memory), while others represent an aspect of nature. During birth, Cronus castrated his father, Ouranos, who had attempted to push all the children back into the womb of Gaia. The severed genitals were thrown into Pontos, and Aphrodite, the goddess of sexual passion, was born from the foam that appeared, a scene depicted in Sandro Botticelli's masterpiece *The Birth of Venus* (now in the Uffizi Museum in Florence, Italy).

Like his father, Cronus tried to prevent the birth of his children, as well. His wife was his sister, Rhea, and their offspring were the Olympian gods: Demeter (grain and agriculture), Hades (the underworld), Hera (marriage), Hestia (the hearth), Poseidon (sea), and Zeus (the sky). Zeus and the Olympians fought a 10-year war against the Titans. The Olympians were victorious, and Zeus became the most powerful god. Atlas, the son of Iapetus and a daughter of Oceanus named Clymene, was banished to somewhere near the western horizon by the Olympians, because he had sided with the Titans during the war. His task was to hold up the heavens.

The Olympians had their offspring as well, some of whom were the result of unions with humans, mostly a male god and a female human. The most famous of these gods are Apollo, Artemis, Hermes, and Dionysus. Apollo and Artemis is the son and daughter of Zeus and Leto, daughter of the Titans Coeus and Phoebe. Apollo is the god of medicine, music, archery, and prophecy; Artemis is the virgin goddess of wildlife, the hunt, childbirth, and the very young. Hermes is the son of Zeus and Maia, the goddess of Fauna and earth-life who was the daughter of Atlas. Hermes is the god of luck, wealth, roads, and fertility. He is also the messenger god. Dionysus is the son of Zeus and Semele, who was human. Dionysus is the god of wine and poetry. He is linked to the Egyptian god Osiris and to the Roman god Bacchus.

Scenes from the Trojan War and other legendary or mythological tales and images of gods and heroes can be found in *pediment sculpture*, or *tympanum sculpture*, the triangular area that is the uppermost part of a temple; a *frieze*, a continuous horizontal band with decorative sculpture located below the cornice on a temple eleva- tion, or wrapping one or more wall surfaces; in a *mosaic* of tile or painted glass; wall painting; a *fresco*, paintings applied to wet plaster; or a *metope*, the square sculptured areas that alternate with *triglyphs* in the entablature of a Classical temple. Today, the decorative sculpture or mosaic floors are frequently removed from buildings that are exposed to weather and placed in museums, often far removed from the site. Many of the famous sculptural works of the Parthenon are in the British Museum in London. They are called the "Elgin Marbles" after Lord

FIGURE 9.4

Homer. Glypotek Museum Munich.

Elgin, who removed them from the Acropolis in the nineteenth century. The pedimental sculpture of the late-sixth century Temple of Aphaia on the Island of Aegina, which is off the coast of and within the site of Athens and its port, Piraeus, can be found in a museum in Munich, Germany.

The ancient Greeks believed that the center of the world was at Delphi, the sacred sanctuary of Apollo, located north of Athens. The spot is marked by a stone called the *omphalos* (Greek for navel), and located where the *Pythia*, Apollo's priestess, pronounced responses to queries from all over the ancient world. The idea of Delphi as the center of the civilized world at that par- ticular place and time is not farfetched. As the area of the sophistication of human development expanded beyond the river valley civilization of Mesopotamia and Egypt in the second and first millennia, it would be two arms of

Europe that extended into the Mediterranean Sea—the Italian and Greek peninsulas—that would dominate the political and cultural landscape for the next thousand years; and the Mediterranean itself, which had been merely peripheral to those earlier peoples and states, would play a significant role.

The word Mediterranean comes from the Greek *Mesogeios*, which means "between two lands." It is the earth's largest inland sea. Its length, east to west, is about the same as the width of the United States. In an early map of the world drawn by Hecataeus of Miletus, who wrote a book on geography in the sixth century BCE, the centrally located Mediterranean Sea separates the major continents of Europe and Asia-Libya, which, in turn, are surrounded by Oceanus, a perimeter sea or ocean.

The Greeks were the first intellectuals, philosophers, dramatists, and historians. They made achievements in literature, science, medicine, statecraft, law, scholarship, academics, and the arts—painting, sculpture, and architecture. The Romans achieved successes in all these fields and more, but they would never escape from the shadow of the earlier Greek achievements, just as the son of a famous writer or athlete never completely escapes from the shadow of his father. Because the Romans did not have a great cultural tradition, they adopted many elements of the literature, art, architecture, and—significantly—religion of the Greeks.

The Greek temple, the iconic form of Greek architecture, was merely a majestic, more god-worthy version of the ancient Greek house. The word derives from the Latin *templum*, a consecrated open space that is usually quadrangular. The Romans, like the Greeks, considered a *templum* to be a space or a sacred ground, more so than a structure. A building had to be consecrated by a high-ranking priest (Roman *pontiff*) and an augur, a priest assigned to interpret the auspices of the gods. The word "auspice" is derived from the Latin *avis + specere*, signs from birds.

The most significant rite of the Greek religion was the sacrifice. In the Minoan and Mycenaean cultures of the Bronze Age, rituals included human sacrifices, but this practice had disappeared by the time of Classical Greece, and only domesticated animals were used. The purpose of the sacrifice was to give thanks to the god, for

FIGURE 9.5

Temple of Saturn. Roman Forum. The Roman temple form, like many other aspects of Roman culture, is indebted to Greek culture.

past and future intercessions. In the early stages of Greek religion, sacrifices were performed at a modest altar in an open area without any additional structure. The complex temple design of the later Classical period developed slowly, between the tenth century BCE and the sixth century BCE, from diverse, regional housing types into a singular temple "form," with relatively minor variations.

Religious practices evolved to the extent that the personification of a particular god, embodied in a cult image called a *xoanon*, became important. The statue of the seated Zeus in the grand temple of Zeus at Olympia, one of the seven wonders of the ancient world, was of such a scale that if he stood up, his head would have punctured the roof. It was created by Phidias (500–532 BCE), notoriously the most famous of all Greek sculptors.

The rite of the sacrifice began with a procession leading the animal or animals to the sacrificial altar in front of the temple, where a purification rite was performed. The slaughter was carried out by a citizen, not a priest, who served at that post for a specified brief period. After cutting some hair off the animal and throwing it into the flames, the slaughterer would stun the animal, and then cut the animal's throat. The blood would be collected and poured on the altar. The animal was then butchered. The thigh bones were burned with fat and incense. The fumes were offered to the god. The attendant or priest would then pour wine on the fire. Finally, the rest of the meat would be cooked (most likely boiled), and then a communal feast was held. The gods lived on nectar and ambrosia, not meat.

The temple was the house of the god (or gods if it was dedicated to more than one). It served no ecclesial purpose. The *naos* (Latin *cella*) was the innermost chamber, which contained the image of the god. It was typically enclosed on all six sides, with its only available light through opened doors, which were usually bronze. Most temples had a space in front called a *pronaos* and another closed chamber called the *opisthodomos* behind the naos, which served as a treasury of goods offered by individuals or states.

In early temples, there would be a colonnade in front of the pronaos. If this colonnade is set within the *antae*, the flanking walls of the temple, then is called *distyle in antis*; if completely in front, *prostyle*; and if located in the front and rear, *amphiprostyle*. If the colonnade goes all the way around on four sides, this is called a *peripteral*-style temple; a side colonnade is called a *pteron*. *Dipteral* style means there are two rows of columns. The distance between columns of a colonnade is the intercolumniation, which can range from one and a half column widths to four column widths.

Looking at the front of the temple, there are four main parts. The *crepidoma* is the stepped base of the temple. The *stereobate* is the lower platform, and the *stylobate* is the uppermost platform, upon which are placed the columns of the colonnade. The second main part is the *column*, which consists of a base, shaft, and capital. The third part is the *entablature*, the horizontal section above the columns. The entablature is typically divided into three sections: the *architrave*, the lintel spanning the columns; the *frieze*, a decorative central band; and the *cornice*, the uppermost section. The uppermost, or fourth, part is the *pediment*, the triangular area that closes off the gable end of the roof. The flat area within the pediment, typically filled with sculpture, is called the *tympanum*.

FIGURE 9.6
Temple of Aphaia Model. Glypotek Museum Munich.

FIGURE 9.7
Archaic Ionic Capital. Istanbul Archaeological Museum.

FIGURE 9.8
Ionic Capital. Smyrna, Turkey.

An *order* is a system of architectural design that composes of a base, column, and entablature. There are three main orders of classical architecture which are of Greek origin—Doric, Ionic, and Corinthian—and two additional orders developed later by the Romans—Tuscan and Composite. The most obvious differences between the orders are in the columns, which support the portico roof, particularly the capitals. The three Greek orders developed over time from earlier manifestations that were less refined; later constructions gained an increasing level of articulation. The fountainheads of the three orders were from three different regions, although once established, there were no particular boundaries in which they were used. The major extant buildings on the acropolis in Athens, for example, are of two different orders: Doric (Propylea and Parthenon) and Ionic (Temple of Athena Nike, Erechtheion), which are the most predominant styles used in Greek architecture. The same order was typically used throughout an individual structure. The one exception is the Flavian Amphitheater in Rome, commonly known as the Colosseum (70–80), which has Tuscan columns on the ground floor, Ionic on the second, Corinthian on the third, and a composite order on the uppermost level. Of the original three orders, the Romans favored using the Corinthian and Ionic.

The temple was the most important building type in ancient Greece, the one that merited the attention of the best architects, artisans, and sculptors. Unlike the Bronze Age cultures of the Aegean, with a few exceptions, the Greeks paid little attention to tombs, palaces, and houses, preferring instead to make their public buildings grand—temples, gates, and markets. The Romans inherited this fondness for creating public architecture, and expanded on it to a considerable extent. Whereas the Greek baths were modest, Roman baths were triumphs of spatial planning and engineering. While the Greek theater was molded out of the natural landscape, the Roman theater literally doubled the Greek prototype, and was thus called an amphitheater. In the Roman form, it was the most grandiose of all its public buildings, prompting the legend in Rome, for instance, that its fate was intertwined with the fate of the Colosseum.

FIGURE 9.9
See below.

FIGURE 9.10
See below.

FIGURE 9.11
See below.

FIGURE 9.12
The three main Classical Orders: Doric Capital from Temple of Aphaia, Aegina (9.9); Ionic Capital from the Erechtheion, Athens (9.10); and Corinthian capital from the Pantheon, Rome (9.11). Acanthus plant, inspiration for the Corinthian capital (9.12).

The dramatic arts—both tragedy and comedy—were invented by the Greeks, and evolved from an earlier type of production called a *dithyramb*, which was religious in nature. According to Greek tradition, this took place in 534 BCE, when an Athenian named Thespis separated an actor from the chorus and engaged in a dialogue.

Greek tragedies were written for a single performance during the annual Dionysia festival in Athens. These tragedies were performed by three male actors, who wore masks that identified the different characters they played, and a chorus of 12 or 15 males who sang their lines. The chorus is peripheral to the action of the play, providing commentary, typically representing ordinary citizens or slaves. The subject matter for the plays almost exclusively came from Greek myths, although some were based on recent historical events.

A Greek theater consists of the seating area, *cavea*, usually built into a hillside. This includes the *diazoma*, landings between areas of seating; an orchestra (from the Greek *orchestra*, meaning "dancing area"), a circular area where the actors performed; and a *skene* (Latin *scaena*), where the actors changed. The skene was a wooden roofed structure. There were two mechanical devices used in the plays: the *ekkyklema*, which had wheels, and the *mechane*, which was like a crane and was used to move the actors to the roof of the skene, typically when an actor was playing a god.

Examples of Greek theaters are abundant in the Mediterranean. The **Theater of Dionysus** in Athens (originally fifth century BCE; remodeled fourth century BCE; first century AD; third century) is known as the birthplace of Greek tragedy and is the first theater ever constructed in stone. It had a capacity of 17,000 people. Its natural acoustics, along with the acoustics of the **Theater of Epidaurus** (fourth century BCE), which held 14,000 people, are impressive even in their ruined state. Whispers from the orchestra can be clearly heard at the remote seats at the very top of the cavea. The **Ancient Theater at Taormiina** (third century BCE), the **Pergamum Theater** (225–200 BCE), and the theater at Delphi are all sited in spectacular settings. Reminders that the Greek pursuit of perfection in architecture was not limited to its religious structures.

FIGURE 9.13
Theater of Epidaurus, Greece.

FIGURE 9.14
Odeon. Athens, Greece.

Roman theaters differed in several ways. First, the actors performed on the stage, and the orchestra was used for seating for distinguished patrons. The orchestra circle included part of the stage, and thus the scaena is more forward, toward the audience, and is larger and more elaborate than the Greek skene. Theaters were typically built on level ground, and thus have a structural auditorium, not built into a hillside. The first stone theater in Rome was built by the emperor Pompey in 55 BCE; previously, they had been constructed of wood timbers.

The Theater of Marcellus (23–13 BCE) in Rome, the largest theater in ancient Rome, was inhabited by squatters after the fall of the Roman Empire, and today, it houses expensive apartments. It had an estimated capacity of 20,000. The **Antique Theater,** or **Roman Theater** (first century) in Orange, France, still retains its *scaenae frons*, the rear wall of the stage. It had a wooden roof, which no longer exists. The Roman climate is not quite as temperate as Greece, where open-air theaters were practical. The five-story facade of the theater, the part of the *scaenae frons* that faces the exterior, has arched openings on the first level and blind arches on the third level. The *scaenae frons* was restored at the **Roman Theater at Palmyra** (second century) in Syria. Another Roman theater that has survived well is at Leptis Magna in Libya.

For Further Discussion

Explore in more detail one of the many legacies of Greek civilization, such as the epic poem, tragic and comedic

FIGURE 9.15

Theater of Marcellus. Rome, Italy.

drama, religion, sculpture, or architecture. In what ways are the effects of these legacies still visible today?

CHAPTER TEN

Ancient Greece

There is but one entry to the Acropolis. It affords no other, being precipitous throughout and having a strong wall. The g4ateway has a roof of white marble, and down to the present day it is unrivalled for the beauty and size of its stones. Now as to the statues of the horsemen, I cannot tell for certain whether they are the sons of Xenophon or whether they were made merely to beautify the place. On the right of the gateway is a temple of Wingless Victory. From this point the sea is visible, and here it was that, according to legend, Aegeus threw himself down to his death.

For the ship that carried the young people to Crete began her voyage with black sails; but Theseus, who was sailing on an adventure against the bull of Minos, as it is called, had told his father beforehand that he would use white sails if he should sail back victorious over the bull. But the loss of Ariadne made him forget the signal. Then Aegeus, when from this eminence he saw the vessel borne by black sails, thinking that his son was dead, threw himself down to destruction. There is at Athens a sanctuary dedicated to him, and called the hero-shrine of Aegeus.

On the left of the gateway is a building with pictures. Among those not effaced by time I found Diomedes taking the Athena from Troy, and Odysseus in Lemnos taking away the bow of Philoctetes. There in the pictures is Orestes killing Aegisthus, and Pylades killing the sons of Nauplius who had come to bring Aegisthus succor. And there is Polyxena about to be sacrificed near the grave of Achilles. Homer did well in passing by this barbarous act. I think too that he showed poetic insight in making Achilles capture Scyros, differing entirely from those who say that Achilles lived in Scyros with the maidens, as Polygnotus has re presented in his picture. He also painted Odysseus coming upon the women washing clothes with Nausicaa at the river, just like the description in Homer. There are other pictures, including a portrait of Alcibiades, and in the picture are emblems of the victory his horses won at Nemea. There is also Perseus journeying to Seriphos, and carrying to Polydectes the head of Medusa, the legend about whom I am unwilling to relate in my description of Attica.[1]

— from *Description of Greece* by Pausanias

The Greek temple is the most influential building archetype in Western architectural history. Its legacy is constant vindication of the ancient Greeks' obsession with the ideal, even if that quest for perfection came at the expense of innovation. The Greeks did not seek new or different archetypes; they sought to perfect familiar ones.

1 Pausanias, Selection from Description of Greece, trans. W.H.S. Jones and H.A. Ormerod. Copyright in the Public Domain.

A recurring theme in ancient Greek literature is the return of something or someone to its natural state, *nostos*, in Greek. There is a natural state of everything. The world is right when everything is in balance and everything is in proportion. In the Homeric epics, the natural order of things is upset when Helen is abducted from her rightful place, the bed of King Menelaus, and likewise, when Odysseus is prevented from returning to his rightful place, next to his faithful wife Penelope, in the bed he crafted around an olive tree. Thus, it is not the task of architects to compose new systems of order, but rather to put everything in its proper place, reusing and refining established principles. When Isocrates, in *Panegyricus*, boasted of the Athenians' role in the advancement of civilization, he spoke of a "well-ordered life." The order that is manifested in the intricate design of temples and other public works evolved from mere imitation of nature. This concept of order became part of the city, and Isocrates gave the credit "not to the gods but to each other, not one is unconnected with our city."

Greek philosophy began with inquiries about the nature of the universe. Philosophers like Thales of Miletus (c. 625–547 BCE), began to look beyond religion for explanations of natural phenomena. All things are made of water, air, fire, or eventually, "atoms." Protagoras of Abdera (c. 490–420 BCE) is known for the famous first line "Man is the measure of all things." The continuation of this thought is lost, but philosophers see this statement as establishing the idea of individual or cultural perception as the key to experience. This notion was treated with much suspicion by later Greek philosophers, who believed that there exists an ideal that is impersonal. Plato wrote that "the qualities of measure and proportion invariably … constitute beauty and excellence." Aristotle also pursued this concept of an ideal form. Referring specifically to tragedy, but often interpreted as a general aesthetic observation, he wrote that a tragedy must be whole and consists of three parts: a beginning, a middle, and an end. There must be unity of action. The plot—the arrangement of the incidents—is the most important part of a play. Aristotle applies the same basis of judgment to structures as he does to living creatures. They must have an orderly arrangement of parts and a

size that is not accidental, "for beauty lies in the size and arrangement." Both Plato and Aristotle had the benefit of experiencing the great aesthetic achievements of the fifth century BCE in art, architecture, and literature.

For the Greeks, the aesthetics of architecture was theoretically simple: harmony in the relations of the parts led to a harmony of the whole. Humans only had to look at themselves to find the *modus operandi* of Nature's design: the symmetry of the body. Yet the implementation of this harmonic theory was far from simple. Vitruvius, author of *De Architectura*, a detailed compendium on the methodologies of Greek and Roman construction, explained one aspect of harmony, the entasis of columns, as dogged perseverance in the search for perfection. "The eye," he wrote, "is always in search of beauty."

As a rule, Greek temples faced east, to greet the sunrise on the day the foundation was laid. Originally, the exteriors of the temples were solid, with no porches. Columns were added to create open areas on the short sides, at first, and eventually all the way around, like the Parthenon in Athens. What is visible today in the ruins of Greek temples is stone and marble, and (rarely) roof timbers. According to Pausanias, the first temple dedicated to Apollo at Delphi was constructed of laurel boughs, the second of wax and feathers, and the third of bronze. If that sounds a little romantic, it probably is. The archaeological evidence suggests a wooden temple replaced later on with stone.

Historians have divided Greek art into the following periods: **Neolithic** (6000–3000 BCE); **Bronze Age**

FIGURE 10.3

Lion devouring bull from Pediment of Old Temple of Athena. Acropolis Museum, Athens.

FIGURE 10.4

Temple of Athena Polias, or The Parthenon. Athens, Greece.

FIGURE 10.5

Frieze detail from the Parthenon. British Museum, London.

(3000–1000); Cycladic (3000–1000); **Minoan** (2000–1000); **Mycenaean** (1600–1000); **Iron Age** (1050–900); Geometric (900–700) Orientalizing (750–650); Daedelic (700–600); **Archaic** (700–480); **Classical** (480–323); and **Hellenistic** (323 –31). (The bold periods are applicable to Greek architecture as well.) The first temples built in stone were constructed in the Archaic period. Two notable temples from this period are the **Temple of Artemis** (mid-sixth century BCE), Kerkyra (Corfu) and the Old Temple of Athena (c. 525 BCE) in Athens, which was destroyed by the Persians in 480 BCE.

The **Temple of Athena Polias (the Parthenon)** (447–438 BCE) is the masterpiece of Greek architecture, and one of a handful of buildings that are the finest in all of world history. It was designed by Ictinus and Kallikrates and supervised by the sculptor Phidias, who created the statue of Athena inside the temple, itself

another masterpiece. It is a Doric Peristyle temple, 8 columns on the front and rear, and 17 on the sides. It is sited on the highest ground of the Athenian acropolis.

The extant Parthenon is one of several buildings built by Pericles, who was the leader of Athens from 450 to 429 BCE. The Parthenon, located on the Acropolis, was built in the Classical period. There was a Neolithic settlement on the Acropolis from around 2800 BCE. By the Bronze Age, it had been rebuilt as a Mycenaean-type citadel. The Parthenon was the third temple built on the Acropolis dedicated to Athena. The first was built in

FIGURE 10.6

Goddesses Aphrodite and Dione from the East Pediment of the Parthenon. British Museum, London.

FIGURE 10.7

Metope: Centaur and Lapith. Parthenon. British Museum, London.

529 BCE. The second, the Old Parthenon, was built in 490 BCE, but destroyed when the Persians sacked Athens in 479 BCE.

The **Propylaea** (437–432 BCE), a monumental gateway, was designed by Mnesikles, and was designed as a complementary building to the Parthenon, using the same ratio of its plan, 4:9. The diminutive **Temple of Athena Nike** (427–424 BCE), designed by Kallikrates, is perched upon a small protruding area of rock that was used as a bastion in the Mycenaean period. There is an Ionic portico of four columns at each end.

The **Erechtheion** (421–405 BCE), designed by Mnesikles, is remarkable for its south-facing Caryatid Porch, which has six draped female figures used as columns. The temple was built to honor the two gods Athena and Poseidon, who, according to Athenian legend, were participants in a contest to win control of the Acropolis. Poseidon produced an olive tree called the Erechtheis, for which the temple is named, but Athena's olive tree won the contest. The temple is dedicated to the two gods, but the building came to be known as the Erechtheion. The building is unusual in its plan, with its asymmetrical porch appendages, and its section, which is not level, but follows the sloping contours of the site.

The interior of a Greek temple was not a public space, unlike, for example, medieval Christian churches. Rituals

FIGURE 10.9
Temple of Athena Nike. Acropolis, Athens.

took place outside the temple, as did almost all other public activities. The moderate Greek climate certainly affected the planning of buildings and public spaces; it would not have worked in Sweden.

The Greek architect C.A. Doxiadis (1918–1975) studied the ancient Greek public building sites and made several observations. Sight lines, rather than symmetry, dictated the layout of buildings at a particular site, so that each building could be perceived in its entirety as much as possible. Each building form was distinct from others on the site. The organization of the site was comprehensible immediately upon entering the precinct or area.

Percy Gardner, in his book *The Grammar of Greek Art*, described the Parthenon as constructed "on a subjective rather than objective basis" referring to optical "refinements" made by the architects, which also seem to give greater importance to man's "measure of things" than the mathematics of the "things" themselves. These refinements or corrections are as follows. First, the stylobate, the entablature, and pediment were constructed so that

FIGURE 10.8
Porch of the Caryatids. The Erechtheion. Acropolis, Athens.

they curved upward toward the middle, and therefore would appear flatter. On the Parthenon, this measures 6 centimeters (2.4 inches) on the east and west facades, and 11 centimeters (4.3 inches) on the north and south facades. Second, the columns were bowed slightly, an effect called *entasis*, in addition to the normal upward tapering. This corrects the optical illusion created by a series of parallel lines that would tend to make the columns seem thinner at the center. Third, vertical members, such as columns, were inclined inward to correct the illusion that the column is leaning toward the viewer (also 6 centimeters).

The Parthenon and the Classical Age Acropolis are symbols of both democracy and political hegemony. Pericles did not have the power to undertake his expensive building projects alone. In fact, he faced much opposition from those who thought the projects were too costly. It is however, one of the first monumental works of architecture not built by an autocratic ruler. The Athenian people paid for its construction, whether in time or money. At the same time, the tribute paid to Athens by the members of the Delian League created the wealth that allowed such decisions to be made.

The temples of the acropolis in Athens represent only a fraction of ancient Greek temples, and some survive today in relatively good condition. Other notable temples located in Greece and Western Turkey are: The **Temple of Athena**, Assos (fragments in the Istanbul Archaeolgical Museum) (c. 540 BCE); **Temple of Apollo**, Corinth (c. 540 BCE); **Temple of Aphaea**, Aegina (c. 490 BCE);

FIGURE 10.10

Sculpture from the West Pediment of the Temple of Zeus. Olympia, Greece. Apollo (center) intervenes in a fight betweem the centaurs and the Lapiths at the marriage feast of Perithoos.

FIGURE 10.11

Altar (left) and Porch of Temple of Apollo. Delphi, Greece.

FIGURE 10.12

Temple of Poseidon. Sounion, Greece.

FIGURE 10.13

Temple of Hera. Paestum, Italy.

Temple of Zeus, Olympia (468–460 BCE); **Temple of Poseidon**, Sounion (440 BCE); and the **Temple of Apollo**, Delphi (366-326 BCE). Some of the most well-preserved Greek temples can be found in *Magna Graecia,* an area of Greek colonies that included Southern Italy and Sicily. The **Temple of Neptune** (460 BCE), **Temple of Hera** (c. 530 BCE), and **Temple of Ceres** (c. 510 BCE) are all at Paestum, south of Naples. In Sicily, there is the **Temple of Concord** (fifth century BCE) and other temples at the Valley of the Temples in Agrigento, the **Temple at Segesta**, (c. 424–416 BCE); and the **Temples at Selinus** (later half of sixth century BCE).

The Greeks were the first civilization to treat the practice of medicine as a profession, and the first to separate the discipline from mythology. The Hippocratic Oath, the model for the code of behavior for those who practice medicine, traces its roots to the school of Hippocrates (460–357 BCE) on the Dodecanese island of Kos. The **Asklepieion**, or **Sanctuary of Asklepios** (fourth century BCE) on Kos was originally a sanctuary of Asklepius, the son of Apollo and Koronis, who was human. According to Greek myth, a crow told Apollo that Koronis had been unfaithful to him, and so Apollo killed Koronis and turned all crows, which had been white, black. Apollo saved Asklepius, who was then raised by a centaur named Chiron, who taught the boy medicine. When Hippolytus, the son of Theseus and the Amazon Hippolyta, was killed after being thrown from his chariot, Artemis, whom Hippolytus had worshipped, asked Asklepius to save Hippolytus. He did so, but was slain by Zeus with a thunderbolt. In turn, Apollo killed the Cyclopes who had made Zeus's thunderbolt.

Hippocrates turned the Asklepieion into a place of secular healing, seeking and employing biological answers to medical ailments, and encouraging general health of mind and body, including a proper diet. The Asklepieion was built by the disciples of Hippocrates, who continued his practices. The site was a sacred olive grove, and had three terraces. The first terrace was for patient rooms. On the second terrace, there were small temples, rooms for the priests, and a conference area. On the third level, there was a large Doric **Temple of Asklepios** (fourth century BCE). Hippocrates is famous, not only for his writings on medicine, but for his aphorisms as well, including the following famous saying: "Life is short, but the art is long, the opportunity fleeting, the experiment perilous, the judgment difficult." Two phrases incised in limestone at the **Temple of Apollo at Delphi** (366–329 BCE) reveal much about the Greek Classical Age: *mēdén ágan*, which means "nothing in excess," and *gnōthi seautón*, which is translated as "know thyself."' The first is epigrammatic of the aesthetic philosophy of the Greeks; the second of philosophy itself, whose Western foundations are unquestionably Greek, especially the ideas and writings of Socrates (c. 469–399 BCE), Plato (427–347 BCE), and Aristotle (384–322 BCE). Socrates' phrase "the unexamined life is not worth living" is a philosophical anthem for both the ancient and modern worlds.

The sacred precinct at Delphi was originally known as Pytho to Homer, named after the cave of Python, the serpent who was the son of Mother Earth. Eventually it became the cult center of Apollo. The Pythian games, similar to those at Olympia, were held every eight years at first, then every four. The site is located on Mount Parnassos, overlooking the "sea of olives," a plain of olive trees that extends to the Gulf of Corinth in the distance.

The Delphic oracle was very prestigious in the ancient world. Its patrons included ordinary citizens with banal questions about their personal lives, to leaders of the Greek city-states, and even "barbarians" (non-Greeks). A petitioner to the oracle would make a sacrifice of an animal.

The questions were presented on lead tablets to the *Pythia*, a priestess, who sat on a tripod in a small room in the temple called an *adyton*. The tripod was placed over a chasm in the rock, and the Pythia inhaled a *pneuma* (vapor or gas) that emanated from the chasm, which put her in an intoxicated state. Her response, perhaps incoherent, was interpreted by a poet, and then the response was handed over to the petitioner. Often the responses were equivocal; that is, they could have been interpreted in two different ways.

The most famous of these, as cited by Herodotus, involved Croesus, the King of Lydia (present-day Western Turkey). Croesus sent a delegation of Lydians to Delphi with the following question: Croesus, King of the Lydians and other peoples, in the belief that yours is the only true oracle in the world, gives you gifts worthy of your prophetic insight, and asks whether we should wage war against the Persians and whether he should add any military force to his own as an ally.[2]

The response was if Croesus were to wage war against the Persians, he would destroy a great empire. After hearing this news, he sent another delegation to Delphi and asked if he would reign for a long time. This time, the Pythia answered:

> … But whenever a mule becomes king of the Medes,
> Then, tender-footed Lydian, flee by the pebbles
> River Hermus,
> And do not delay, nor feel shame at being a coward.

The empire Croesus destroyed was his own. The "mule," an offspring of mixed blood (a donkey and a horse), was Cyrus of Persia, who was of mixed descent.

The Greek city-states built treasuries at the site to house votive offerings and documents. The **Treasury of the Athenians** (490 BCE) contained spoils from the Athenians' victory in the battle of Marathon against the Persians. It is a Doric distyle in antis, 10 meters by 6 meters. The metopes showed scenes from the lives of Theseus and Herakles.

Near Apollo's sanctuary at Delphi is the Sanctuary of Athena, which included the early fourth century **Tholos Temple**. It consists of a circular cella and a colonnade of 20 slender Doric columns of Pentellic marble. The columns were re-erected, and the cornice and metopes were replicated, so the appearance of the temple is relatively substantial.

---

2   Strassler, Robert B., ed., *The Landmark Herodotus*, New York: Pantheon Books, 2007.

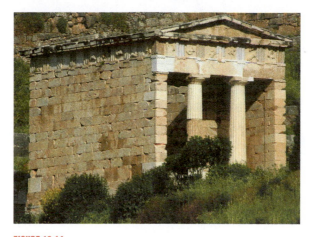

FIGURE 10.14

Treasury of the Athenians. Delphi, Greece.

The quest for perfection, readily apparent in Greek architecture and art, is an essential driving force of the quadrennial festivals held at religious centers, the most famous of which are those that took place at Olympia. They were founded in 776 BCE, which is the traditional—but arbitrary—date historians use as the end of the Dark Age of Greek civilization. The games were peaceful, less violent evocations of the Homeric quest for *kleos*, or glory. There was a Homeric code that was followed. Only Greeks were allowed to perform, and participation in the games was an honor. Competing—and often warring—separate entities found their common bond in the games, which displayed in a triumphant manner what it means to be Greek.

Olympia, like Delphi, owes at least part of its eminence to its splendid natural setting. It is a place that has been occupied since the Neolithic Age (4300–3100 BCE), but even today it is pastoral and idyllic, surrounded by an alluvial plain. In the central area of the site, which is surrounded by facilities for the athletes and priests, is the **Temple of Zeus** (c. 470–456 BCE), a Doric peripteral hexastyle structure designed by Libon of Elis. The temple sits on a man-made embankment, which raised the foundation 3 meters above the natural grade. The pediment sculpture, in the museum on the site, is relatively well preserved.

The east pediment depicts the preparation of the race between Pelops and Oinomaos, the King of Pisa.

According to Greek myth, Pelops wanted to marry Oionomaos' daughter, Hippodameia. Oinomaos stipulated that Pelops could marry Hippodameia if Pelops could defeat him in a chariot race. Oinomaos' charioteer removed the bronze pins from the wheels of his chariot and replaced them with wax. The king crashed during the race and died, and Pelops escaped with the princess.

The west pediment, by the sculptor Alkamenes, depicted the battle between the Lapiths and the Centaurs at the marriage of the Lapith King Perithoos. During the feast, the Centaurs, after drinking too much wine, began to assault women and boys attending the wedding, and even the bride. Metopes from the cella depict the 12 labors of Herakles.

For Further Discussion

Looking at photographs of buildings representing the three Classical orders, Doric, Ionic, and Corinthian, describe them in your own words, starting at the top or bottom and proceeding up or down from there.

CHAPTER ELEVEN

Iron Age Civilizations of the Mediterranean and the Near East

....and there are two divisions of the city (Babylon); for a river whose name is Euphrates parts it in the middle. This flows from the land of the Armenians and is large and deep and swift, and it flows out into the Erythraian sea. The wall then on each side has its bends carried down to the river, and from this point the walls stretch along each bank of the stream in the form of a rampart of baked bricks... This wall then which I have mentioned is as it were a cuirass for the town, and another wall runs round within it, not much weaker for defence than the first but enclosing a smaller space. 183 And in each division of the city was a building in the midst, in the one the king's palace of great extent and strongly fortified round, and in the other the temple of Zeus Belos with bronze gates, and this exists still up to my time and measures two furlongs each way, being of a square shape: and in the midst of the temple is built a solid tower measuring a furlong both in length and in breadth, and on this tower another tower has been erected, and another again upon this, and so on up to the number of eight towers. An ascent to these has been built running outside round about all the towers; and when one reaches about the middle of the ascent one finds a stopping-place and seats to rest upon, on which those who ascend sit down and rest: and on the top of the last tower there is a large cell, 186 and in the cell a large couch is laid, well covered, and by it is placed a golden table: and there is no image there set up nor does any human being spend the night there except only one woman of the natives of the place, whomsoever the god shall choose from all the woman, as say the Chaldeans who are the priests of this god.[1]

— from The History of Herodotus

The Greek historian Herodotus reflects in the opening paragraphs of *Histories* that "human prosperity never remains constant." One of the more famous cities of antiquity, Babylon, has a history that is evidence of the volatility of the ancient world, in particular the persistent changes of fortunes in the Near East. Babylon was a city of relative obscurity until the early part of the second millennium BCE, when it became of the most influential cities of the ancient world under its leader, Hammurabi. His empire fell almost immediately after his death, but roughly a millennium later, in the late seventh century, Nebuchadnezzar (also written Nebuchadrezzar) created an empire that called itself New Babylonia, and built such monuments as the legendary Hanging Gardens of Babylon, one of the ancient wonders of the world, and the Ishtar Gate. The Neo-Babylonians considered themselves descendants of the celebrated Mesopotamian civilizations that preceded them. The rebuilding of Babylon and the short-lived Neo-Babylonian empire was last great ancient civilization to emerge in Mesopotamia.

The first few centuries of the first millennium BCE are generally described as "Dark Ages" throughout the Mediterranean world and lands of the Fertile Crescent to the east after the widespread disruptions of civilizations at the end of the Bronze Age (the end of the second millennium). One cultural group from this era, the Phoenicians, is familiar to readers of both the Old and New Testaments.

---

1 Herodotus, Selection from The History of Herodotus, vol. 1, trans. G. C. Macaulay. Copyright in the Public Domain.

They occupied an area in the Levant in what is now Lebanon and Northern Israel. The name Phoenicia was given to them by the Greeks. Like Greece of the same time period, Phoenicia was composed of city-states, some of which, such as Byblos, Tyre, and Akko, or Acre, were important centers of culture and trade.

Although there are a few extant Phoenician architectural ruins, such as a temple at Byblos from the second millennium BCE, the Phoenicians are best known as craftsmen for other cultures (they were the builders of the Jewish Temple of Solomon in Israel, for instance) and for the city of Carthage, in modern-day Tunisia. Carthage was one of many Phoenician colonies scattered throughout the Mediterranean, including in Spain and Northern Africa. It grew into a formidable presence in the Mediterranean, one that would later muster a challenge, misguided in hindsight, to the expanding Roman dominion. In 146 BCE, Carthage was completely destroyed by the Roman army; the ruins that exist there today are from its reconstruction in the Republican and Imperial Roman periods.

The most dominating and durable of all the Mesopotamian civilizations was Assyria, which occupied a boomerang-shaped area that spanned from Memphis in Northern Egypt, northward to present-day Eastern Turkey, and down to the Persian Gulf. Historians divide this time frame into three periods: Old Assyrian (c. 2000–1363 BCE), Middle Assyrian (c. 1163–1000 BCE), and the Neo-Assyrian (c. 1000–612 BCE). The greatest legacies of Assyrian architecture are the elaborate palaces built by and for its kings, large temple complexes in their cities, each dedicated to a particular god, and fortifications.

Assyria

The ancient capital of Assur, about 300 kilometers north of modern-day Baghdad, Iraq, was occupied from c. 2500 BCE until 612 BCE, when Assyria was conquered by the Medes, from modern-day Iran. Its center was dominated by temples and the royal palace. Temples were built to honor the local god Ashur, the personification and deification of the city; Ishtar, the goddess of sexuality, love, fertility, and of war; Anu, the celestial god; and Adad,

the god of storms. Nimrud (ancient Kalhu) was another capital of Assyria (884–710 BCE). The city was founded by Shalmaneser I toward the end of the Bronze Age. As at Assur, and later capital sites, the ziggurat tradition continued, but now the ziggurat was no longer the most dominant building; palace structures, built by the Assyrian kings, were now predominant.

A doorway in the **Palace of Ashurnasirpal, Nimrud,** (c. 883–859 BCE) is flanked on each side by a *lamassu*, an Assyrian astrological protective deity, depicted in sculptural art as a winged beast with the body of a lion or bull and a human head. The lamassu sculpture is generally integrated into the walls of the gate opening, and thus is not completely three-dimensional. It is the most iconic and most singular feature of Assyrian architectural art.

Two important kings of the Neo-Assyrian empire, Sargon II (r. 722–705 BCE), and his son Sennacherib (r. 705–681 BCE) built palace complexes that are exemplary of Assyrian art and architecture. **The Citadel of Khorsabad** (ancient **Dur-Sharrukin**) (c. 720 BCE), built by Sargon II, consisted of Sargon's palace; the Temple of Nabu, the Mesopotamian god of wisdom and writing; and other structures surrounded by a nearly square city wall. Nineveh is located 100 kilometers north of Assur. Its fortification walls contained at least five gates. The central opening of the *Nergal Gate* (c. 700 BCE) is flanked on each side by a lamassu. Two other gates, the Mashki and Adad Gates, were destroyed by Islamic State militants in 2015. The walls of interiors rooms and courtyard at the **Royal Palace of Sennacherib at Nineveh** (c. 700 BCE) were decorated with bas-relief panels depicting scenes from Sennacherib's military campaigns and hunting expeditions, which are common subjects in Mesopotamian art. In addition, one series of stone slabs show the process of quarrying and transporting the large lamassus to the city, which weighed up to thirty tons. Bas-relief panel sculpture in Assyria predates the Greek practice of friezes, such as the frieze that decorates the naos wall of the Parthenon. The art is descendent from the tradition of bas-relief *stelae*, slabs placed in front of or inside temples, which dates back to the third millennium BCE. Prior to the rise of Assyrian civilization, public art in Mesopotamia was confined to religious subjects.

COPYRIGHTED MATERIAL — DO NOT DUPLICATE, DISTRIBUTE, OR POST

In the Assyrian period, the king, his entourage, and his exploits dominate architectural art.

In 689 BCE, the city of Babylon was attacked by the Assyrians. Sennacherib boasted that he "destroyed, devastated, and burned with fire" the city and its foundations, and later flooded it with canals. By 612, the Assyrian civilization had all but disappeared, its cities destroyed. Nebuchadnezzar, who was crowned king after his father died in 605, rebuilt Babylon City with "walls made from using baked bricks and bitumen." The city was surrounded by an outer perimeter barrier of three successive walls, two of which were made of brick, and an inner barrier made from two brick walls, separated by a 50-meter-wide moat. There were eight gates, the most famous of which is the **Ishtar Gate** (c. 600 BCE), which was removed from its site and rebuilt inside the Pergamon Museum in Berlin. The wall is decorated with glazed bricks whose color is a deep royal blue, and alternating panels of red and white dragons (symbols of the god Marduk, the preeminent Mesopotamian god) and bulls, symbols of Adad, the god of storms and rain. The gate was approached from the north by a processional way called the *Ai-ibur-shabu*, which translates as "may the enemy not cross it." The street was lined with walls also decorated with glazed bricks and panels of lions, symbols of Ishtar, the goddess of love, sexual desire, and war.

Inside this new city, Nebuchadnezzar accumulated an "abundance of royal treasures"—silver, gold, precious gems, and ornamental objects. And in 539, the Babylonians were conquered by the Persians, who, perhaps in deference to its great beauty, did not destroy it. In fact, how it arrived at its ruined state remains a mystery.

Persia

In Herodotus's description of Persia, the story of the first great Persian king, Cyrus the Great, is related in great detail. It is an exceptional birth tale, a common scenario in ancient literature (Oedipus, Moses, etc.), intermingled with verifiable factoids from Persian history. Cyrus was the grandson of Astyages, who had a dream that his daughter's son would overthrow him. He instructs his general, Harpagus, to kill the baby after he

is born. Harpagus gives the child to a herdsman and tells him to kill the baby, and then give him the body. The herdsman's wife, who had just given birth to a stillborn child, convinces her husband to exchange the body of the stillborn baby with the living child. Astyages recognizes the boy ten years later as his grandson, who is play acting as a king. Astyages believes, incorrectly, that the dream is fulfilled by the fact that the boy was playing a king, and allows the boy to live. Astyages punishes Harpagus for disobeying his orders in a brutal manner: he kills Harpagus' son and feeds the flesh to his father. Astyages avenges this act in due time, when he encourages Cyrus to rebel against his grandfather.

The empire that began with Cyrus the Great was known as the Achaemenid Empire (550–330 BC). It was the largest empire of the ancient world, and it loomed large for all Greek-speaking peoples until it was finally defeated by Alexander the Great in the late fourth century BCE. Even after the celebrated defeat of the Persians in 490 and 480 BCE, the Greeks must have assumed another attack was forthcoming. But it never came. Although. the Persians were more organized and outnumbered the Greeks, for some debatable reason, the Persians never again attacked the Greeks until Alexander. During this period, however, Persia (modern-day Iran) built a cultural legacy that is visible today in museums and at sites such as Persepolis, founded by Darius I in 518 BCE.

The **Apadana Hall** (sixth century BCE) is a hypostyle hall with multi-leveled capitals: above the shaft is a

FIGURE 11.2
Lion Devouring Bull from Staircase at Persepolis. Plaster Cast. British Museum, London.

decorated band; then a lotus-like capital similar to those found in Egypt; a rectangular section with double volutes all around; and finally, double projecting bulls or lions. A multi-layered entablature of varying decorative motifs extends beyond the outer bull or lion head.

Etruria

Buried underneath the ruins of Roman civilization—figuratively and literally—in North-Central Italy (present-day Tuscany and part of Umbria), are the archaeological remnants of the Etruscans, who enjoyed some prosperity between the eighth and fourth centuries BCE. They called themselves the Rasenna, but their language has not been completely deciphered. This culture evolved from various autochthonous populations in the region, including the Villanovans, who began to trade with the Greeks in the eighth century. It is this initial contact with the Greeks that established the cultural link with the Aegean and mainland Greek cultures, leading to the adoption by the Villanovans of Greek art, customs, architectural language, and mythology. Etruscan civilization begins around 750 BCE, and consisted of culturally linked city-states, united politically in what is known as the League of 12 Cities.

The emergence of the Etruscan civilization was one of several events in the Mediterranean region that symbolized the end of the period of cultural decline that abruptly began at the end of the Bronze Age. In 814 BCE the Phoenicians founded the city of Carthage in Northern Africa (near modern Tunis). The Olympic Games were established in 776 BCE, signaling an end to the so-called "Dark Age" of ancient Greece. Unlike most other civilizations that existed during this time period, the Etruscans left behind no works of literature, and thus, to reassemble their religious beliefs and social practices, archaeologists and historians have mainly relied on art, artifacts, and architecture.

Like ancient Greece, Etruria was a federation of independent city-states that historians call the Etruscan League. Originally there were 12 city-state members, located in the Tuscany and Umbria regions of North-Central Italy. These communities were built on hilltops, like Greek cities of the Late Neolithic and Bronze ages.

The sites were selected for their available natural resources, as well as their defensibility. Unlike later Greek cities such as Athens in the Classical period, the hilltop was not used exclusively as a sanctuary. Instead, a temple was built on a terrace located in a location that would give it prominence. The Etruscans were very religious and proudly displayed their piety to their neighbors.

Early Etruscan culture clearly had its origins with the autochthonous peoples that occupied the territory prior to the emergence of Etruscan civilization. Their gods were very active in the affairs and lives of humans, who learned the will of the gods through divination—signs and portents found in nature. The most important god was Tinia, who had characteristics similar to the Greek god Zeus and the Norse god Odin. His consort was Uni, a goddess of fertility. Later on, the Etruscans adopted many aspects of Greek religion, including Greek gods and goddesses.

The Etruscans believed that at death, one passed from life into afterlife, an arduous journey to an island of perpetual bliss. The bodies of the dead were either cremated or inhumed. Cinerary urns, used for storing the ashes of human bodies after cremation, and sarcophagi, used for storing the corpse, were works of art, depicting the deceased, often seen reclining, and also depicting scenes from the person's life, or a vision of that person's afterlife. The area where the dead were buried was planned much like a townscape, with streets and "houses" that were carved out of the rock. This is called a *necropolis*, a city built for the dead.

The Banditaccia Necropolis at **Cerverteri** (eighth–third century BCE), ancient Caere, is the largest surviving necropolis of the ancient Mediterranean world of any

FIGURE 11.3
Etruscan Tomb. Cerverteri, Italy.

FIGURE 11.4

Column from Etruscan Tomb. Cerverteri, Italy.

The influence of Greek architecture can be clearly seen in several tombs. The **Tomb of the Capitals** has Aeolian-style columns, a simpler, earlier form of the Ionic order. The shafts of the columns are octagonal. Other tombs have Doric-style columns (c. sixth century BCE) and Tuscan style columns (c. third century BCE).

At the **Monterozzi Necropolis at Tarquinia** (seventh– second century BCE) there are roughly 6,000 underground tombs, many with elaborate fresco paintings that decorate both walls and ceilings. Like at Cerverteri, the negative spaces that have been carved out of the rock emulate the spaces created by houses and temples, including many with sloping gable roofs. Sometimes there is a tympanum created at each end, which like the tympanum of the Greek temple, has a separate, decorated scene, either geometric or representational. Tarquinia is traditionally cited as the oldest city of Etruria. The artwork reflects the various periods of Greek art, from archaic to Hellenistic. The *Tomb of the Leopards* (480–470 BCE) is noteworthy for its architectural form and for its portrayal of a slice of Etruscan aristocratic life. There are two leopards in the tympanum opposite the entrance and a banquet scene on the wall below. Three couples, two mixed and one male, are stretched on a *klinai*, or couch-like bench. Servants, some dressed, some half-dressed, play music and serve libations from various vessels.

There are only a few examples of Etruscan above-ground architecture that have survived above the level of the foundation. The **Etruscan Arch** or **Arch of Augustus**

civilization, with thousands of tombs arranged along the "streets of the dead." The tombs typically have several rooms arranged symmetrically with the entrance through the larger, central room. The houses for the dead were built to resemble the domestic architecture of the Etruscans, with the exception that the structural components of the houses for the living were generally made out of wood, whereas in the tombs these components have been carved out of the tufa stone. Earlier tombs have stone roofs that emulate thatched roofs; later tombs emulate a tile roof. Many of the tombs have built-in furniture, such as chairs and beds. The beds were designed for married couples, as seen in paintings found in tombs. Because of this detail, it has been suggested that women held a comparable, if not equal, place in Etruscan society.

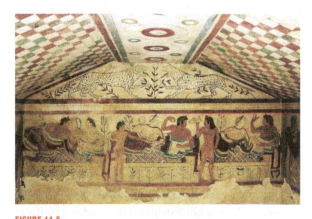

FIGURE 11.5

Tomb of the Leopards. Wall Painting. Tarquinia, Italy.

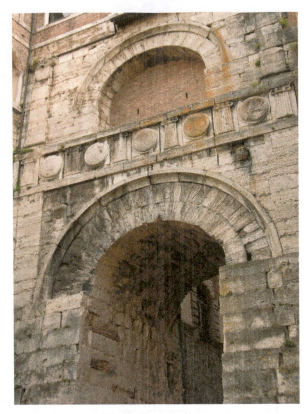

FIGURE 11.6
Etruscan Arch, or Arch of Augustus. Perugia, Italy.

FIGURE 11.7
Etruscan Funerary Urn. National Etruscan Museum of Viterbo.

Ancient Israel

Throughout history, the eastern end of the Mediterranean has been the first step out of Africa for several species of hominids, the crossroads between the East and West, the birthplaces of Judaism and Christianity, the fountainhead of Islamic expansion, the destination of Crusaders, and an epicenter of religious confrontation. In ancient history, all or part of the area was controlled by the Amorites; the Syrians; the "Sea Peoples;" the Phoenicians; the Aramites, the Canaanites, by the tribes of Israel and Judah; the Edomites; the Egyptians; the Hittites; the Persians; the Macedonian Greeks; the Romans; and other tribes and smaller groups who occupied the territory at one time or another.

The history of the Hebrews is recounted in the Hebrew Scriptures, or the Old Testament of the Bible. Abraham is the founding father of the Hebrews. He is called upon by Yahweh to leave his family and settle in the Promised Land, or Canaan, in ancient Palestine. His grandson, Jacob, displaced by famine, moved his family to Egypt. In an event called the Exodus, Moses, a descendant of Abraham, led the Hebrews out of Egypt back to Canaan, of which they eventually gained control. Beyond the Bible, there are few historical records of these events, although biblical archaeology is a well-established field

(second half of third century BCE, restored 40 BCE) in Perugia was originally built as an entrance gateway as part of the city walls. Above the tall arched gateway are elements from the Greek Doric order—alternating metopes with round discs or shields and triglyphs. Another arch, the **Porta all'Arco** or Etruscan Gate (fourth century BCE) in Volterra, has three sculpted heads on its exterior facade.

It is known that the Etruscans adopted the early form of the Greek temple, using the soft tufa stone, sun-dried bricks, and wood, but only the foundations remain of Etruscan public architecture. The Etruscans founded a fourth Order of architecture, called Tuscan, and were skilled engineers, as evidenced by the draining of the wetlands. This became the Roman Forum, a project the Romans called the **Cloaca Maxima**. The legacy of Etruscan culture is ultimately that it served as a platform for the Roman one that followed.

of study. Both Christianity and Islam are linked to Judaism, the religion founded by Abraham. Abraham's son, Ishmael, is considered to be an ancestor of all Arabs. Jesus, the Greek name for Joshua, which means "savior," is also a descendant of Abraham.

The most famous work of architecture in ancient Judea is the **First Temple of Jerusalem** (957 BCE). It housed the Ark of the Covenant, and was a place of assembly for the entire city. The site was the Temple Mount, the legendary site of the Abraham's altar, which he was to use to sacrifice Isaac. The Temple faced the East, and had three rooms of equal width: the *Ulam*, a porch or vestibule; the *Hekhal*, where people assemble for the service; and the *Devir*, the Holy of Holies, the sacred room that housed the Ark. A *yazi'a*, or storehouse, surrounded the building on the south, west, and north sides. This temple was totally destroyed by the Babylonian King Nebuchadnezzar II in 587 BCE, and the Jews were deported to Babylonia. Cyrus II conquered Babylon in 538 BCE, and the Jews returned to Jerusalem. Although no archaeological evidence exists of the building, there is a detailed description in the Torah, or the Christian Old Testament:

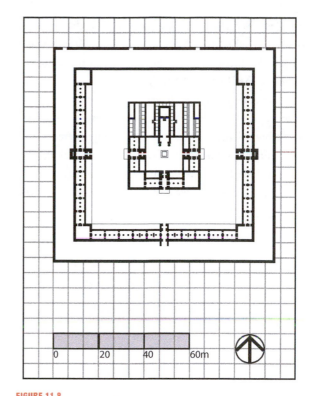

FIGURE 11.8

Temple of Solomon (First Temple) Plan (based upon description in Old Testament).

> And the house which king Solomon built for the LORD, the length thereof was threescore cubits, and the breadth thereof twenty cubits, and the height thereof thirty cubits. And the porch before the temple of the house, twenty cubits was the length thereof, according to the breadth of the house; and ten cubits was the breadth thereof before the house. And for the house he made windows of narrow lights.
>
> And against the wall of the house he built chambers round about, against the walls of the house round about, both of the temple and of the oracle: and he made chambers round about: The nethermost chamber was five cubits broad, and the middle was six cubits broad, and the third was seven cubits broad: for without in the wall of the house he made narrowed rests round about, that the beams should not be fastened in the walls of the house.
>
> And the house, when it was in building, was built of stone made ready before it was brought thither: so that there was neither hammer nor axe nor any tool of iron heard in the house, while it was in building. The door for the middle chamber was in the right side of the house: and they went up with winding stairs into the middle chamber, and out of the middle into the third.
>
> So he built the house, and finished it; and covered the house with beams and boards of cedar. And then he built chambers against all the house, five cubits high: and they rested on the house with timber of cedar.[2]

—1 Kings1:6:7 King James Bible

The **Second Temple of Jerusalem** (515 BCE) was not as elaborate as the first temple. It did not contain the Ark, as that had been lost in 587. Herod reconstructed this Second Temple beginning in 20 BCE, but this temple

---

2 1 Kings 6," King James Bible. Copyright in the Public Domain.

was destroyed in 70 CE. The only portion that survived is what is called the Western Wall (the Wailing Wall), which was incorporated into the wall surrounding the Dome of the Rock in 691 CE.

In medieval Europe, it was believed that the planning of the Temple of Solomon was divinely inspired. Therefore, its dimensions and proportions were studied by architects and builders of Christian churches and cathedrals. The French philosopher and theologian Pierre Abélard (1079–1142) wrote that the proportions of the temple were analogous to the consonances of music. The earthly temple of Solomon is linked to the New Jerusalem, the heavenly city of God.

For Further Discussion

Prepare a timeline of the different cultures mentioned in this text to this point. Where appropriate, place the most important building or buildings discussed from each culture.

CHAPTER TWELVE

Ancient Rome

In a word, the early Romans made but little account of the beauty of Rome, because they were occupied with other, greater and more necessary, matters; whereas the later Romans, and particularly those of to-day and in my time, have not fallen short in this respect either — indeed, they have filled the city with many beautiful structures. In fact, Pompey, the Deified Caesar, Augustus, his sons and friends, and wife and sister, have outdone all others in their zeal for buildings and in the expense incurred. The Campus Martius contains most of these, and thus, in addition to its natural beauty, it has received still further adornment as the result of foresight. Indeed, the size of the Campus is remarkable, since it affords space at the same time and without interference, not only for the chariot-races and every other equestrian exercise, but also for all that multitude of people who exercise themselves by ball-playing, hoop-trundling, and wrestling; and the works of art situated around the Campus Martius, and the ground, which is covered with grass throughout the year, and the crowns of those hills that are above the river and extend as far as its bed, which present to the eye the appearance of a stage-painting — all this, I say, affords a spectacle that one can hardly draw away from. And near this campus is there is another campus, with colonnades round about it in very great numbers, and sacred precincts, and three theatres, and an amphitheatre, pand very costly temples, in close succession to one another, giving you the impression that they are trying, as it were, to declare the rest of the city a mere accessory. For this reason, in the belief that this place was holiest of all, the Romans have erected in it the tombs of their most illustrious men and women. The most noteworthy is what is called the Mausoleum, a great mound near the river on a lofty foundation of white marble, thickly covered with ever-green trees to the very summit. Now on top is a bronze image of Augustus Caesar; beneath the mound are the tombs of himself and his kinsmen and intimates; behind the mound is a large sacred precinct with wonderful promenades; and in the centre of the Campus is the wall (this too of white marble) round his crematorium; the wall is surrounded by a circular iron fence and the space within the wall is planted with black poplars. And again, if, on passing to the old Forum, you saw one forum after another ranged along the old one, and basilicas, and temples, and saw also the Capitolium and the works of art there and those of the Palatium and Livia's Promenade, you would easily become oblivious to everything else outside. Such is Rome.[1]

— from *The Geography* by Strabo

According to Homer's *Iliad*, Poseidon prophesied that Aeneas, the son of Anchises and Aphrodite (Venus) and cousin of Hector, the great Trojan hero, would survive the sack of Troy and found a new city elsewhere. Aeneas was a minor character in the *Iliad*, and not a particularly heroic one at that. Nevertheless, the Roman poet Publius Vergilius Maro (70–19 BCE), known as Virgil, cast Aeneas as the hero of his Homeric-style epic about the birth and growth of the Roman Empire, the *Aeneid*. Although the venerated events depicted in Homer's epics occurred in the twelfth century BCE—the actual beginnings of Roman civilization occurred in the eighth

---

1. Selection from The Geography of Strabo, trans. H.L. Jones. Copyright in the Public Domain..

century BCE—and are, therefore, chronologically incompatible, Virgil's deliberate affiliation of Rome with the gods, kings, and warriors of the heroic age sought to take a hammer, or at least a chisel, to the notion of Greek cultural superiority. The "Pageant of Heroes" scene in Book VI (Aeneas is shown the souls of the future heroes of Rome in the underworld) allowed Virgil to complete the association of the glorified past and the glamorized present.

At the end of the Greeks' long siege of Troy, after the ruse of the Trojan Horse and while Troy is being laid to waste, Aeneas puts his father, Anchises, on his shoulder. Aeneas leads his wife, Creusa, and his son, Ascanius, out of the burning city. Anchises represents the Trojan past; Ascanius represents the Roman future. During the struggle to leave the city, Creusa is killed. She appears to him as a shadow or ghost and discloses to him that he will marry a new bride in his new city.

Aeneas and his fellow Trojans sail for 7 years and take refuge after a storm in Carthage (present-day Tunis). Aeneas becomes the lover of Carthage's widowed queen, Dido. When Aeneas spurns Dido's pleas for him to stay, she commits suicide. Aeneas visits the underworld and sees, among others, his father Anchises, Dido, and the great Roman leaders and heroes of the future. He and the Trojans land finally at the mouth of the Tiber River and fight a war against Turnus and his people, the Rutuli. At the end of the epic, Aeneas, standing over the wounded Turnus, spurns the opportunity to be merciful and kills him with his sword.

The historical tradition is that Ascanius founded Alba Longa, which was situated southeast of Rome. Alba Longa was the first of several villages that were united as the Latin League, or Latium, which were taken over by Rome in the seventh century BCE. The second Roman foundation myth is the story of Romulus and Remus. The traditional date for the founding of Rome by Romulus is 753 BCE.

Rhea Silvia, a daughter of a king of Alba Longa, was raped by the god Mars and gave birth to the twins Romulus and Remus. Rhea Silivia's husband, Numitor, was the rightful king of Alba Longa, but his kingship was usurped by his brother. When the twins were born, they were seen by their uncle as potential threats to him, and thus their lives were endangered. The twins were set adrift in the Tiber River in a basket. Initially they survived because they were suckled by a she-wolf. Then they were found and raised by a shepherd and his wife. When they grew older, they overthrew their uncle and restored Numitor to his throne. Later, after jointly deciding to create a new city, they argued over its location and its name, and Romulus killed Remus. Thus, Aeneas is said to have founded the Roman civilization, and Romulus is said to have founded Rome itself.

The debt of Roman culture to Greek culture is owed to the Etrurians, who traded with the Greeks and adopted aspects of Greek lifestyle. Roman civilization slowly developed between the eighth and third centuries. By the third century, the Roman and Greek cultures were in close proximity with each other at Magna Grecia, which were Greek settlements in Southern Italy and Sicily. Politically, Rome was at first a protector of Magna Grecia, but a defeat of King Pyrrhus in 275 BCE ended Greek independence in Sicily. The ascendancy of Rome as the dominating power of the Mediterranean came when the Romans defeated the Carthaginians in the Second Punic War between 218–201 BCE.

Republican Rome was established around 510–509 BCE. Prior to this time, a regal system of government had been in place. In lieu of a king, there were two consuls and a number of magistrates, who were elected annually by free male citizens. In addition, there was a council of advisers called a Senate, which was chosen by the consuls. The key element in the expansion of Roman territory was the system of inclusion: The conquered people became allies, who were then encouraged, with promised shares of the plunder, to become part of the well-organized military campaigns. In this way, the process was self-perpetuating. The republican era came to an end after a series of civil wars in the first century BCE, an era that included the assassinations of Pompey and Julius Caesar. Octavian, later Augustus, defeated Mark Antony, and established the principate form of government and the Roman Empire. Although a few buildings from the republican era remain, most of the great architectural monuments of ancient Rome that survive today are from imperial Rome.

The identity of Roman culture was established between the late sixth century BCE and the end of the third century BCE. Roman literature traces its roots to Livius Andronicus and Ennius, from the late third century and early second century, respectively. Romans began to acquire a wholehearted interest in Greek sculpture about this time, as well. Architecturally, the early buildings erected by the Etruscans and by the Romans in the Republican Era have almost all disappeared, either because they were damaged by fire, or they were replaced with later buildings on the same site. A good example of this is the **Temple of Jupiter Capitolinus**, which was originally built in 509 BCE but burned in 83 BCE. Its podium is now at the back wall of the Palazzo dei Conservatori on the Capitoline Hill in Rome. Another is the **Temple of Saturn** (497 BCE, reconstructed third century), whose eight portico columns among the are the most conspicuous ruins in the Roman Forum. The nearby **Curia Julia** (44 BCE, reconstructed 305 and 412) was the place of assembly for the Roman Senate.

The effect of ancient Rome's contribution to architecture can be summed up with the simple recognition that 1) in Roman architecture, architectural space was invented; and 2), the Romans created monumental buildings for public use, not just for religious purposes. It is not that Egyptian and Greek temples and public buildings were solid, or that the public did not participate in their functions, this just means that functions took place in courtyards and open spaces—not in spaces enclosed by walls and a roof. The spaces that were created were used to house gods, not people. In addition, it is not that Roman buildings were always, from the beginning, designed with grand interiors—because they were not—they were more Greek. Eventually, Roman architecture, like Roman culture in general, became more Roman without necessarily becoming less Greek. The Greeks introduced philosophy to architecture and, arguably, created the most perfect facade in the entire history of architecture in the Parthenon, but they never created a space as elegant as the interior of the Pantheon.

In time, Roman architecture adopted the persona of the empire. Buildings, such as the Basilica of Constantine and the Baths of Caracalla (both located in Rome),

FIGURE 12.2

Curia Julia (Senate House). Roman Forum.

demonstrate a grandeur not seen since the New Kingdom in Egypt, but in a different way. These were not labors for an autocratic ruler; they were labors for the citizens.

The **Temple of Fortuna Huiusce Diei, or the Temple of Good Fortune on This Day** (c. 100 BCE), one of the **Four Republican Temples** at Largo Argentina in Rome, was built using the Corinthian Order, with tufa foundation, column shafts, and travertine marble bases and

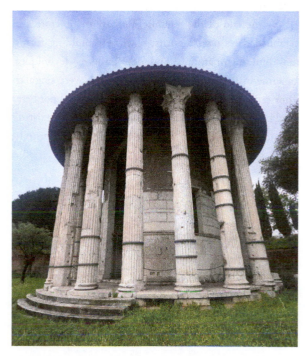

FIGURE 12.3

Temple of Hercules Victor (Round Temple). Rome, Italy.

capitals coated in stucco. Its form is similar to the Tholos Temple at Delphi.

The **Temple of Portunus** (formerly known as the **Temple of Fortuna Virilis**) (c. 80–70 BCE) and the **Round Temple** (commonly the **Temple of Vesta** [c. 100 BCE]) are situated in a small park near the Tiber River in Rome. Portunus was the ancient Roman god of harbors and gates, and when the temple was built, it was located within the harbor area. It is an Ionic tetrastyle temple. The tufa and travertine columns were coated with stucco to give the appearance of a finer marble and to embellish and refine the detail of the molding. The Round Temple was probably dedicated to Hercules, although the attribution is uncertain. The exterior of the temple—columns and cella—were made from Greek Pentelic marble.

The well-preserved **Maison Carrée**, in Nîmes, France (16 BCE), was dedicated to the adopted sons of Augustus, Gaius and Lucius. It is a pseudo-peripteral hexastyle Corinthian temple and rests on a podium that is 3.6 meters high. It owes its magnificent state of preservation to the fact that it was never out of use, first as a Roman temple, then as a church, and finally, as a museum.

By the end of the republic, Roman architecture had established its own identity, with new building forms, new building materials, and new building techniques. In some instances, the Roman inventions were singular: They employed new ideas or methods that had not been used before. In other cases, the Romans adapted existing technology. The Greeks had used an arch, but sparingly,

such as at the entrance to the stadium at Olympia. The Romans adopted it as their own, so much so that they are often given credit for its invention. The Etruscans used a *barrel vault*, which is an arch extended in the perpendicular plane (theoretically *ad infinitum*). While the Etruscans used the vault for minor, utilitarian purposes, such as a culvert, the Romans used it to create large enclosed public spaces. The Etruscans had made small domes, not unlike the tholos structures in Mycenae from the second millennium BCE. Unlike these structures, which are corbeled—meaning that each successive layer of stones is placed slightly more inward from the last—the Romans built true domes, where the structure supports itself. Roads and bridges had long been in use, but the Romans made them art forms. Some are in use to this day.

Suetonius wrote The Lives of the Twelve Caesars, biographies of the Roman emperors from Julius Caesar (c. 100–44 BCE) to Domitian (51–96). He noted that the city of Rome was "not built in a manner suitable to the grandeur of the Empire" when it first came under the control of Octavius Augustus (63 BCE–14), who reigned from the assassination of Julius Caesar, in 27 BCE, until

FIGURE 12.5

Temple of Augustus. Pula, Croatia.

FIGURE 12.4

Maison Carrée. Nîmes, France.

14. As previously noted, Augustus famously boasted that he had found the city built of brick and left it in marble. In addition to upgrading the city's infrastructure, Augustus also established means of dealing with disasters, such as floods and fire. Suetonius is careful to suggest that the elaborate construction program initiated by Augustus was for the public, not for himself:

> May it be my privilege to establish the State in a firm and secure position, and enjoy therefrom the rewards of which I am ambitious, that of being called the author of the best possible government, and of carrying with me when I die the hope that the foundations which I have laid for the State will remain unshaken.[2]

The *Ara Pacis Augustae* or **Altar of Augustan Peace,** in Rome (9 BCE) is remarkable in both its subject matter—an obscure goddess *Pax* (as opposed to a military triumph), and a celebration of the joys of familial and civic leisure—and its architectural art. The altar is surrounded by an enclosure wall, which is decorated with sculpture both inside and out. Processional friezes decorate the upper registers of the north and south exterior walls. The family of Augustus, priests, magistrates, and ordinary citizens are shown in a public parade. For decades, Rome had suffered through almost continuous civil wars. The figures of the frieze are emblematic of the peaceful period, the *Pax Romana* (27 BCE–180), that followed.

Some of the heirs to Augustus's empire, however, did not pass on this torch of magnanimity. Nero (37–78), who among the many people he put to death were his mother, his aunt, his wife, and his father, emperor Claudius, and who infamously set fire to his own city while he dressed up in an actor's garb and "sang the whole of the Sack of Troy." The historian Tacitus is less certain than Suetonius about Nero's culpability for the fire, but acknowledges the rumors of his superciliousness and described the

---

2 Selection from The Lives of the Twelve Caesars by Suetonius, ed. Joseph Gavorse. Copyright © 1931 by Random House LLC.

FIGURE 12.6
Frieze detail from Altar of Peace (Ara Pacis). Rome, Italy.

little effect the efforts had on assuaging the public in the fire's aftermath. Nero's self-empowerment is attested in the archaeological remains of the **Domus Aurea**, or **Nero's Golden House** (64–68), which was more than 200 meters long and had 142 rooms, many with a ceiling higher than 10 meters. Most of it is now buried under ruins and modern roadways.

A substantial labor force allowed the Romans to systematically engage their construction projects, starting with the preparation of construction materials. A standardization of components was invented, which allowed for the stockpiling of materials. The building process became efficient and well organized. Methods were used to increase speed. By using materials like concrete, brick, and small stones in lieu of large stone blocks that had to be cut down to size, the structural process was additive rather than subtractive, which saves both material and time.

The development of concrete as a construction material is one of the great milestones in engineering history. It came about sometime in the third century BCE. It was discovered that when mixed with water, sand, and small stones, a material called *pulvis puteolanus*, volcanic ash from places like Vesuvius, created a plastic, synthetic material that would become extremely hard when *cured*, i.e., when the moisture had substantially evaporated. The most innovative and famous use of concrete was at the Pantheon in Rome.

The **Pantheon** (118–125) is unique among all the temples of antiquity, and *the* masterpiece of Roman architecture. Of all Classical buildings, it is the one building where the evidence of the architectural achievement

FIGURE 12.7

The Pantheon. Rome, Italy.

of each august Mediterranean civilization, Greece and Rome, coexist. The Pantheon consists of a Corinthian classical porch, a short intermediate transitional structure, and a concrete rotunda. The front porch is the quintessential architectural form that symbolizes the Greek pursuit of correctness and beauty; the rotunda is the embodiment of Roman innovation in materials and engineering.

It was erected by Hadrian. The purpose is unknown; the assumption that it was a temple to all the gods is not verified. A quite plausible theory is that the Pantheon was a building where living emperors, self-deified, could be seen in association with the traditional gods. There is record of an imperial edict read out loud in the Pantheon around 370. The idea of the emperor being a "divine ruler" was developed by Caesar Augustus. This was not commonly manifested in Rome, only in the outer provinces.

The building survived beyond antiquity, because it was converted into a church (St. Mary of the Martyrs) in 608. It is often said of the Pantheon that it is an imperfect building, that the two main forms, the drum in the rear and the traditional temple form in front, are somewhat incongruous. This has been given as evidence that it was designed by Hadrian, not by a trained architect, although this, too, is not known.

The extant structure is the third Pantheon temple. The first was built by Marcus Agrippa in 27 to 25 BCE, but was destroyed by fire in 80. Domitian built a second, destroyed by lightning in 110. The inscription "M. AGRIPPA L.F. COS TERTIUM FECIT" reads "Marcus Agrippa, son of Lucius, made this in his third consulship." The inscription beneath reads "PANTHEUM VETUSTATE CORRUPTUM CUM OMNI CULTU RESTITUERUNT," or "with every refinement they restored the Pantheon, worn by age"—*they* being the emperors Severus and Caracalla.

FIGURE 12.8

Occulus and Coffered Ceiling. The Pantheon. Rome, Italy.

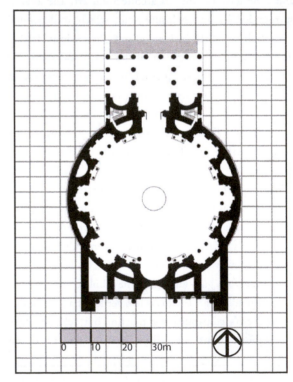

FIGURE 11.9

The Pantheon Plan. Rome, Italy.

As viewed today, the building seems to be low in relation to the surrounding buildings, but originally there were four steps that led up to the porch. The building was at the end of a colonnaded forecourt, so the rotunda would have been less visible than it is today. The presence of a forecourt is further evidence of the importance of the building in antiquity, as a temple precinct, or separated area, was used for those temples of greater stature.

The shafts of the porch columns were made of Egyptian granite; the capitals, entablature, and pediment were made of Pentelic marble. The rotunda originally had a stucco finish over the brick, which is now exposed. The transitional mass is architecturally a second entablature. The diameter of the rotunda is the same as the height. To take the horizontal thrust of the dome, the walls are six meters thick. The dome of the Pantheon was the largest concrete span until 1958. The interior space of the Pantheon marks the first time in architectural history that the design of a building's interior space becomes prominent.

The Romans did not invent the arch and the vault, but they significantly improved the ways and means of building them and exported this technology over their vast sphere of influence. Arches and vaults were used in new building types, and these *were* invented, or dramatically improved or expanded upon, by Roman architects and engineers: the Roman-type theater, the amphitheater, public baths, aqueducts, bridges, private homes, triumphal arches, and basilicas. Roman arches were semicircular in form, and composed of either brick or trapezoidal-shaped stones. An arch transfers the load of its own weight, as well as any load above the arch, to the supports on either side. These supports must be strong enough to withstand a horizontal force. The distance between the supports is called its *span*. The top center stone in an arch is called the *keystone*. The advantage of an arch, as opposed to a lintel, is that it can be constructed of smaller members. A lintel is larger and heavier. A *vault* is an arch that is continuous in the dimension perpendicular to the span of the arch. A barrel vault is one that is formed from a continuous, semicircular arch.

The barrel vaults used in the **Baths of Caracalla** (211–216), in Rome, allowed the architects to create

FIGURE 12.10

The Mosaic of Amphitrite. Baths of Gavias Maximus (Baths of Neptune). Ostia. Italy

wide and tall monumental spaces. The Roman bath was a gathering place for men, although women were accommodated with, a segregated section, \a segregated time period, or a completely separate facility. It was part country club, part athletic club, part social club. One could exercise, swim or bathe, read, hear speakers, or promote business. The capacity of the Bath of Caracalla was around 10,000 people, and included a *natatio* (an Olympian-style pool), a frigidarium and caldarium (cold-water and hot-water baths), and *palaestrae* (exercise rooms). The scale of the building can only be partially perceived looking at the ruins today. It used 20.6 million pieces of brick; over 800,000 full bricks; 210,000 cubic meters of concrete; and 6,000 cubic meters of granite and marble, and it had 252 columns, some of which weighed 50 tons each. The Baths of Caracalla were modeled after the **Baths of Trajan** (104–109), of which little remain. At the **Baths of Gavias Maximu**, or the **Baths of Neptune** (132), in Ostia, Italy, the ancient Roman port, a floor mosaic depicting sea creatures and the god Neptune, a common theme at Roman baths, is well-preserved. The **Roman Baths** at Bath, England, are still operating. Over 250,000 gallons of water are pumped into the site daily. The waterworks are ancient; the bath building was reconstructed in the nineteenth century.

FIGURE 12.11

Interior of the Colosseum. Rome, Italy.

The **Colosseum (Amphitheatrum, or Flavian Amphitheater)** (70–80) was the largest of all the Roman amphitheaters, its two diameters measuring 189 meters by 156 meters. As the name suggests, the Roman amphitheater is, in plan, of a Greek theater mirrored along its long axis. It was begun by Vespasian in 70 and completed by his son, Titus, in 80. The amphitheater was paid for by the spoils of war, probably from the 50,000 kilograms of gold and silver from the Temple at Jerusalem.

Its capacity was about 50,000. On the lowest level sat the senators, then the knights, then plebeians, then the poor, then women, and finally, slaves. The central area where the combatants were engaged was covered with a layer of sand to absorb the blood. It was called the *arena*, named after the Latin word for "sand" or "beach." The *vomitoria* were the exit passages under the seating, constructed with massive arched piers.

Its use differed dramatically from its Greek counterpart, and this difference, perhaps more than any other, is significant of the stark contrast between the personae of the two cultures. In the Greek theater, dramas were presented, where the soul and character of the Greeks came deeply into question. In the Roman amphitheater, a bloodthirst dominated the entertainment. One culture searched for ideals; the other was content with the basest level of human engagement. The Homeric spirit of Greece was evident at the Olympic Games, in which athletic competitions took the place of hand-to-hand combat, and where conflicts between competing political

rivalries were temporarily set aside. Inside the amphitheater, the slaughter—of animals and slaves—was the end, not the means.

Gladiatorial shows were called *munera* (dutiful gifts). Initially, wealthy citizens sponsored the games, and not the state, but later, this changed. Games were held for the New Year's celebration, which took place in December; during funerary rites of an important person; on the anniversaries of deaths; or in celebration of military triumphs.

Animal hunts were featured in the morning, public executions at noon, and gladiatorial contests in the afternoon. In 107, Trajan celebrated a military triumph with 11,000 animals and 10,000 gladiators in a series of games that lasted for 123 days. Gladiators were criminals, prisoners of war, or career professionals (mostly freed slaves), and occasionally women. Fights were staged with elaborate sets. Executions often involved machinery and torture.

The outer facade is 48 meters tall and consists of four stories: The first three with *trabeated* (post-and-lintel) arcading and an uppermost story that is solid, with pilasters and windows located in alternating bays. The first level is Tuscan Order, the next is Ionic, and the top two are simplified Corinthian. The use of the different orders on the facade is a Roman invention. Just above the middle of the upper columns, corbeled stones supported masts, from which hung the **velarium**, a canvas awning that covered the seats.

Another popular entertainment venue for the Roman was the *hippodrome*, a course or arena used for chariot races shaped in an elongated oval, also called a *circus*. Like modern horse races and sporting events, wagering on the races was common. Accomplished drivers became local sports heroes. There were racing teams, the Whites, Reds, Blues, and Greens, which generated rivalries that often escalated beyond the sport itself. The **Circus Maximus** (from the fifth century BCE) could hold up to 150,000 spectators. The **Circus Maxentius** (early fourth century) was built outside the city center. A *stadium* was built for athletic games. The oval shape of the **Stadium of Domitian** (86) is still intact; the seating area became

FIGURE 12.12

Pont du Gard Aqueduct. Vers-Pont-du-Gard, France.

from adjacent mountain streams, 30 miles of which were above ground. Aqueducts, covered troughs with a constant downward slope from the source, were built all over the Roman Empire. The two most spectacular extant ruins of these are at Pont du Gard, near Nîmes in Southern France, and in Segovia, Spain. **Le Pont du Gard Aqueduct** (first century) was originally 50 kilometers long. At the stream called the Gard, the aqueduct is 49 meters high. A spectacular example of the exportation of Roman construction techniques throughout the empire is the **Segovia Aqueduct** (late first century). It was constructed of dry-stone laid granite blocks, with two rows of arched openings, the lower one being substantially taller than the upper one, with a total height reaching almost 28 meters at the tallest point.

apartment buildings, and the open space is now **Piazza Navona,** one of Italy's finest squares.

To supply Rome with enough drinking water and water for its many fountains and baths, Roman engineers built nearly 300 miles of aqueducts to bring freshwater

Triumphal arches were built to commemorate victories or conquests and could be either a single arched

FIGURE 12.13

Segovia Aqueduct. Segovia, Spain.

FIGURE 12.14

Arch of Titus. Roman Forum.

opening or three; one large opening in the center; and two on the side used for pedestrians. Although they were known to have been built since 200 BCE, the earliest to survive is the **Arch of Tiberius** (c. 30 BCE), in Orange, Southern France. Relief sculpture that decorated the arch is well-preserved, with scenes depicting fighting armies, the capture of prisoners, and the trophies of the victorious Romans.

The **Arch of Titus** (81–82), located in the Roman Forum, was built to commemorate the capture of Jerusalem. The columns on either side of the opening are the first examples of a fifth order of antiquity, called the Composite Order. It was completed after Titus' death, and commemorates his deification. In the coffer of the underside of the arch, Titus is shown riding an eagle to heaven. The **Arch of Septimius Severus** (203) was built

to honor the emperor Septimius Severus and his sons, Caracalla and Geta, who "restored the Republic and expanded the dominion of the Roman people." It is a triple arch built on a procession route to the Temple of Jupiter. Originally, the top of the arch held bronze figures of the emperor and his sons riding in a chariot.

The **Mausoleum of Hadrian** (139); was intended to be an artificial mountain in appearance. It followed a traditional design for monumental tombs: a solid cylinder set within a square platform. Because its setting was adjacent to the Tiber River, it was converted into a fortified structure in the third century. Later, it was converted in a papal palace, and renamed **Castel Sant'Angelo** (fourteenth century). It was modeled after the **Mausoleum of Augustus** (first century BCE), also near the Tiber.

FIGURE 12.15
Mausoleum of Hadrian (Castel Sant'Angelo). Rome, Italy.

FIGURE 12.16
Porta Nigra, Trier.

FIGURE 12.17
Temple of Diana. Jerash, Jordan.

Roman towns and cities typically had defensive walls and gates, an urban design element that persisted well after the end of Western the empire. The **Porta Nigra** (186–200), in Trier, Germany, is an example of an elaborate gate, three stories high with a courtyard and barracks.

There is an abundance of sites throughout the extents of the Roman Empire where significant portions of Roman cities are visible today. The most famous of these are **Pompeii** and **Herculaneum**, which were buried in 79 by an eruption of Mt. Vesuvius, discovered in 1599, and uncovered beginning in 1748. Others include **Ostia**, the ancient port of Rome, **Jerash** in Northern Jordan, **Leptis Magna** in Libya, **Caesarea** in Israel, and **Baalbek** in Lebanon. The Romans were not the first planners of cities, but they were the first to establish a systematic approach, and they exported this rational, well-organized methodology throughout the empire.

There were two main axes in each city, the *Cardo Maximus*, the main north–south road, and the *Decumanus Maximum*, the main east–west road. Each city at least has a *forum*, a public outdoor space, which served as a gathering place and market place and where governmental and religious buildings were located. Outside the forum area, smaller streets were arranged in a grid pattern, forming *insulae,* or residential blocks. The wealthy lived in areas where larger houses and villas could be constructed, such as the **Palatine** in Rome. The wealthy would have country villas, as well. **Hadrian's Villa** (second century) near modern Tivoli, not far from Rome, was a complex of 30 buildings covering a square kilometer. One of the most important rooms in Roman villas was the *triclinium*, an elaborate dining room or pavilion.

The majority of the ancient Roman cities did not survive *in toto*, but instead became the foundations of later towns and cities. In some places, a few buildings survived intact, often because they were converted into another use, such as a church. Most buildings were destroyed. The marble that faced many of the public buildings was burned to make lime for stucco and plaster.

A few small temples built during the reign of Augustus in the provincial areas of the empire are noteworthy. At Assisi, in Umbria, Italy, the **Temple of Minerva** (late first century BCE) is a Corinthian building later converted into a church, Santa Maria sopra Minerva, which is its present use. It may have been dedicated to Hercules, not Minerva, who was the wife of Jupiter.

A cult began in the late first century BCE with Julius Caesar, in which Roman emperors were seen to achieve an *apotheosis*, or elevation to divine status. Therefore, there were temples built to honor certain emperors, as the visible evidence of what is called the Imperial culr. The **Temple of Augustus** (c. 2 BCE–14), in Pula, in modern Croatia, has survived in nearly its original state, like the Maison Carrée in France. The inscription of the temple recognized the deification of both Julius Caesar and his adopted son Augustus. The **Temple of Augustus and Livia** (c. 20–10 BCE) in Vienne, France, also well-preserved, was dedicated to Augustus and his wife Livia.

In 16 BCE, Augustus founded a city called Augusta Treverorum, which is modern Trier, the oldest city in Germany. It was named after the local tribes of Celtic people, who were called the Treveri. A three- and four-story gate, the northern gate of its city walls, is called the Porta Nigra (late second century), Black Gate because the sandstone masonry from which it was built, originally light-colored, has turned dark over time.

The segmented façade of the **Library of Celsus** (117–120), in Ephesus, Turkey, is an example of Roman divergence from the static, two-dimensional aspect of

FIGURE 12.18
Library of Celsus. Ephesus, Turkey.

Greek architecture. It is one of the most beautiful edifices in all of the Classical world. Ephesus was founded in the first half of the first millennium BCE and was controlled by the Lydians, Greeks, Persians, Macedonian Greeks, and Romans. Although only a fraction of the ancient city has been excavated, the extant ruins are vast and extensive. The library was built in honor of the governor of the region. It has an elaborate two-story front elevation, but the space beyond is neither deep nor particularly large in area. Nonetheless, it has a capacity to effectively persuade a viewer of the sophistication of Roman planning and architecture, as much as any other Roman ruin.

In *The History of the Decline and Fall of the Roman Empire* (1776–89) Edward Gibbon listed the names of what he called the Five Good Emperors: Nerva (reigned 96–98), Trajan (98–117), Hadrian (117–138), Antoninus Pius (138–161), and Marcus Aurelius (161–180). It is not an accident of history that this period coincides with an era in which many works of public architecture were built. Trajan (53–117) built the two-story, semicircular **Trajan's Markets** (112) and the **Basilica Ulpia** (112). His ashes are buried under a 38-meter-high monument, **Trajan's Column** (113), whose outer surface contains a 200-meter-long helical frieze depicting the story of the Roman victory over the Dacians, who lived west of the Black Sea.

Trajan's successor Hadrian (76–138) built a temple to the deified Trajan near the column. Hadrian directed projects all over the empire, including the Pantheon and his villa at Tivoli, already noted. In Athens, **Hadrian's Library** (132–134) was described by the writer Pausanias as a "building with 100 columns of Phrygian marble." In the ancient world, libraries were places were books and government records were stored, places of learning, and places for lectures. In Athens, this included, appropriately, a school of philosophy. The **Temple of the Deified Hadrian, or Hadianeum** (second century) was turned into a palace in the nineteenth century. **Hadrian's Wall** (122), a fortification wall almost 120 kilometers long in Northern England, was built primarily to register the

extents of the Roman empire, and its impact was more symbolic than practical.

When emperor Diocletian (244–311) came to power, the empire was close to collapsing from outside and from within. More than 20 emperors reigned between 235 and 284. Three emperors were murdered in the year 238 alone. One of the measures he undertook to save the empire was the formation of the *tetrarchy*, a rule by four governors, two emperors and two Caesars. Diocletian retired from his co-emperor role in 305 and moved to Split, in modern Croatia, where he had constructed the **Palace of Diocletian** (285–305). In a single complex structure, the progression of architectural style, from Classical to Medieval, is visible. There are elements of the palace that are *Post-classical*, such as he arched entablature at the **Temple of Jupiter** inside the palace, which is similar to the Temple of Aphrodite (200) at Aphrodisias in Turkey. After the palace was abandoned, squatters moved in, and eventually, the entire complex was a blend of architectural styles.

The **Arch of Constantine** (312), next to the Colosseum, was the last important secular structure built in Rome during the Imperial era. It was built to honor Constantine's victory over Maxentius. Unlike the Arch of Septimus Severus, after which it is modeled, the materials used are all recycled, such as the medallions, which were taken from a building built by Hadrian. Although very visible today, with the Colosseum just behind, it is iconic in that, in spite of its majestic appearance and its homage to one of the most important figures in all of Roman history, upon very close inspection, it lacks the flawless precision of the empire at its zenith.

For Further Discussion

The staging of gladiatorial contests and other such sanguine events in amphitheaters is one aspect of Roman culture that is unique to the Romans, not shared with or borrowed from Greek culture. What other aspects of Roman culture are uniquely Roman?

CHAPTER THIRTEEN

Hellenism

And as they went Hera with friendly thought spread a thick mist through the city, that they might fare to the palace of Aeetes unseen by the countless hosts of the Colchians. But soon when from the plain they came to the city and Aeetes' palace, then again Hera dispersed the mist. And they stood at the entrance, marvelling at the king's courts and the wide gates and columns which rose in ordered lines round the walls; and high up on the palace a coping of stone rested on brazen triglyphs. And silently they crossed the threshold. And close by garden vines covered with green foliage were in full bloom, lifted high in air. And beneath them ran four fountains, ever-flowing, which Hephaestus had delved out. One was gushing with milk, one with wine, while the third flowed with fragrant oil; and the fourth ran with water, which grew warm at the setting of the Pleiads, and in turn at their rising bubbled forth from the hollow rock, cold as crystal. Such then were the wondrous works that the craftsman-god Hephaestus had fashioned in the palace of Cytaean Aeetes. And he wrought for him bulls with feet of bronze, and their mouths were of bronze, and from them they breathed out a terrible flame of fire; moreover he forged a plough of unbending adamant, all in one piece, in payment of thanks to Helios, who had taken the god up in his chariot when faint from the Phlegraean fight. And here an inner-court was built, and round it were many well-fitted doors and chambers here and there, and all along on each side was a richly-wrought gallery. And on both sides loftier buildings stood obliquely. In one, which was the loftiest, lordly Aeetes dwelt with his queen; and in another dwelt Apsyrtus, son of Aeetes, whom a Caucasian nymph, Asterodeia, bare before he made Eidyia his wedded wife, the youngest daughter of Tethys and Oceanus. And the sons of the Colchians called him by the new name of Phaethon, because he outshone all the youths. The other buildings the handmaidens had, and the two daughters of Aeetes, Chalciope and Medea. Medea then [they found] going from chamber to chamber in search of her sister, for Hera detained her within that day; but beforetime she was not wont to haunt the palace, but all day long was busied in Hecate's temple, since she herself was the priestess of the goddess. And when she saw them she cried aloud, and quickly Chalciope caught the sound; and her maids, throwing down at their feet their yarn and their thread, rushed forth all in a throng.[1]

The Argonautica is the only surviving Hellenistic epic poem. It tells the story of the quest of Greek hero Jason and companions (which includes Heracles) to retrieve the golden fleece from the land of Colchis. Along the way, they have several adventures, including encounters with the Harpies, Talos, and the Clashing Rocks.

Aristotle (384–322 BCE), Socrates (469–399 BCE), and Plato (429–347 BCE) are the three most celebrated Greek philosophers. Like Socrates and Plato, Aristotle had an incredible thirst for knowledge, and set out in his life to know as much about the world as possible. "All men," he wrote, "by nature desire to know." His most celebrated contribution to philosophy—one of many—involved the organization of inquiry of all things into what he called causes: the material cause (*of what is it made?*); efficient cause (*what makes it?*); the formal cause (*what gives it its shape?*); and the final cause (*what is its ultimate purpose or reason?*). Aristotle's reputation of having one of the most

---

1 Apollonius Rhodius, Selection from Argonautica, ed. and trans. R.C. Seaton. Copyright in the Public Domain.

prodigious minds of his time gained him not only fame but a modicum of wealth as well, an unusual situation for a philosopher.

In 343 BCE, Aristotle went to Mieza in Macedonia, where he taught Alexander the Great (356–323 BCE), one of the greatest military leaders in history, and Ptolemy (367–283 BCE), one of Alexander's generals who later became King of Egypt. Exactly what Alexander learned or what Aristotle taught is impossible to know, but one conclusion is obvious: the pupil inherited the teacher's passion for knowledge, his sharpness of thought, and his fondness for the Greek approach to life. As he conquered worlds to the East and South, he built new cities and transformed old ones, and in doing so, he expanded the range of influence of Greek culture.

Alexander's lessons with Aristotle were cut short when his father, Philip, was assassinated in 336. At age 21, Alexander took command of his father's army and conquered Persia, the Levant, Egypt, and territories of the Near East as far as the Indus River, stopping only because his army had had enough and refused to go further. He died in 323, which is the traditional date for the beginning of the Hellenistic Age.

Macedonia is situated at the extreme northernmost part of the Greek peninsula. According to Herodotus, it was populated—at least in part—by people who fled Argos, in the Peloponnese, probably during the tumult at the end of the Bronze Age. Although some Greeks discounted the notion that the Macedonians were Greek (which they claimed), Herodotus offered the "proof" in his *Histories*, that Alexander won a dispute once when he sought to compete in a race at the Olympic games, in which barbarians (non-Greeks) were steadfastly forbidden. Alexander was able to prove his "Greek-ness," and tied for first in the race.

Of particular interest to architectural historians is the policy of Alexander to build new cities in the conquered territories, planted with soldiers and Greek settlers. One of Alexander's generals, Seleucus, continued this policy. After the death of Alexander in 323 BCE, Seleucus established an empire of his own, the Seleucid kingdom in the Levant and in Mesopotamia.

The Hellenistic Age is characterized by the infusion of Greek ideas into the conquered territories. Sometimes, this results in a cross-fertilization, often creating a hybrid aesthetic—to some, a corrupted, or "orientalized" Hellenism; to others, a free exchange of ideas. In architecture, this means that forms that were stable for some time now began to experience some transformations.

FIGURE 13.2
Alexander Battles the Persians. Relief from the Alexander Sacrcophagus (4th c. BCE). Istanbul Archaeological Museum

FIGURE 13.3
Temple of Apollo. Didyma, Turkey.

During the Hellenistic Age, the Doric Order declined in usage and popularity, in favor of the Corinthian Order. When the Doric Order was still used, it was often combined with the Ionic. Civic buildings became more common. The development of the roof truss allowed for an increase in the widths of buildings without intermediate supports. All of these changes, and more, were utilized by the Romans. Greek Hellenistic temples are generally more monumental than their predecessors.

The dipteral, decastyle **Temple of Apollo at Didyma** (313 BCE–41) in Ionia (Turkey) was under construction for an unusually long time. According to legend, the shepherd, Branchus, was tending to his flocks when the god Apollo seduced him. Branchus dedicated an altar to Apollo and was given the power of divination; thus, an oracle was established at the site of a sacred spring. The present temple was built to replace an earlier one built in the archaic period in 560 BCE. The Didymeia festival was held every four years and consisted of athletic events, arts, and drama.

The temple measured 45.7 meters by 109.4 meters. It had a *chresmographeion* (the pronaos) at its western end, an elongated naos, and a short vestibule at the eastern end. It was designed by Paeonius from Ephesus, and Daphnis from Miletus. The columns in the corners of the pronaos had representations of bulls' heads and of Apollo and Zeus and Artemis and Leto. Decorated bases from the outer section of the peristalsis are from 37. The crepidoma (base) was 3.5 meters high. The clients purified themselves with water, then offered a goat as a sacrifice. At the pronaos, those who wished to consult with the oracle presented questions.

The chresmographeion was where the answers were written and delivered by the priest. Corinthian columns flanked its entrance. The cella was open to the sky. A giant Medusa head decorated the frieze of the outer architrave.

The dipteral octastyle **Temple of the Olympian Zeus** (174 BCE–131) in Athens was designed by Cossutius, a Roman architect. The temple's Corinthian columns were made of Pentelic marble. It was one of the largest Greek temples. Construction of the edifice began under the Seleucid King Antiochus IV Epiphanes. It was completed by Hadrian, who installed an altar in the temple precinct and, according to Pausanias, many statues of himself.

The Greeks had long admired Egyptian civilization and, in many ways, saw themselves as the heirs of Egyptian culture. When Alexander the Great conquered Egypt, he did not seek to proselytize Greek culture there to the same extent that he did in Asia. He did establish a city named Alexandria, one of many along the path of his over-ten-year military journey to the east.

At the Siwa Oasis in the Libyan desert, Alexander visited an oracle and asked it, "Who is my father?" (Rumors that he was the illegitimate son of an Egyptian father—Nectanebo II, the last native pharaoh—persisted until the Middle Ages). The oracle's answer was "the sun." In Egypt, the pharaoh is divinely linked with the sun god Ra. He was crowned pharaoh and proclaimed a god.

After conquering Egypt, Alexander continued his campaign to the East. On the return journey, after his army refused to continue further, Alexander became ill and died. After his death, his generals divided up what was the largest empire yet in history. Ptolemy became the ruler of Egypt and established the Ptolemaic dynasty of Egypt, which lasted from 323 BCE until the death of Cleopatra in 30 BCE. This Hellenistic influence is usually assimilated into Egyptian history. Hellenistic temples at Kom Ombo, Edfu, Esna, and Dendera are the architectural descendants of Old Kingdom temples, such as at Saqqara, and New Kingdom temples, such as Luxor and Karnak. The layout is virtually unchanged: a linear development, beginning with an outer court, pylons, and inner courts culminating in an enclosed sanctuary. The most conspicuous change in the design is that the decorative treatment of column capitals is often not consistent, sometimes varying from column to column. Colonnades are more prominent; at several sites, they are placed in front of buildings, a practice seemingly influenced by the Greeks.

The complex of structures known as the **Temple of Isis at Philae** (378–341 BCE and 283–47 BCE) was relocated to the nearby island of Agilkia after the construction of Lake Nasser in 1964. Isis, a fertility goddess, was the sister and wife of Osiris and the mother of Horus. She is represented in art with a throne headdress

FIGURE 13.4

Entrance Pylons. Temple of Isis. Philae, Egypt.

FIGURE 13.5

Hathor Columns. Temple of Isis. Philae, Egypt.

or with a sun disk with cow horns on either side. The cult of Isis at one time gained much popularity in Greece and Rome, and persisted in Egypt until the sixth century CE. In later Egyptian history, she is linked with the goddess Hathor, perhaps as the same goddess.

Like Luxor and Karnak, several of the Ptolemaic rulers contributed building projects, up until the last Ptolemaic and early Roman period; e.g., the *Temple of Hathor* was built in the second century BCE, and the Kiosk of Trajan (c. 98–117 CE) became the official entranceway to the site from the river.

The **Temple of Sobek and Horus at Kom Ombo** (c. 205–180 BCE) was built out of sandstone by Ptolemy V.

It was a pilgrimage center of healing, seeking intercession from Horus in his role as the "good doctor." The pilgrims would spend the night within the temple precinct. Sobek, or Suchos, means crocodile. The Greeks associated Sobek with Helios, the god who personifies the sun.

The **Temple of Horus at Edfu** (temple, 237–212 BCE; decoration, 142 BCE; hypostyle hall, 122 BCE; pylon, 57 BCE). The designs of Edfu and Kom Ombo are similar. The temples are surrounded by a perimeter wall that creates a narrow passage all the way around each temple. At each, a hypostyle hall, oriented perpendicular to the main axis, is situated directly behind the front colonnade. Appropriately, the Edfu temple culminates in a single sanctuary; at Kom Ombo, there are two.

The most famous work of Ptolemaic architecture was the **Pharos Lighthouse at Alexandria,** built by Ptolemy

FIGURE 13.6

Hypostyle Hall with Palmette Capitals. Temple of Horus. Edfu, Egypt.

I Soter (r. 323–282 BCE), one of the seven wonders of the ancient world. Its light, from a fire reflected by a large curved bronze mirror, could be seen for 30 miles. It was in operation until 1303, when it was destroyed by an earthquake.

The **Library of Alexander the Great**, also built by Ptolemy I and expanded under Ptolemy II, once contained 700,000 papyrus scrolls. Some were from the library of Aristotle, others were added to by traders to the port of Alexandria, who were required to surrender any books they had onboard their ships. The library had a separate room just for the works of Homer. Unfortunately, the library, and probably most of its contents, did not survive antiquity. In 48 BCE, Julius Caesar's army unintentionally set fire to the building. In the third century CE, it was destroyed further by the attack of the Roman emperor Aurelian. Whatever contents survived this incident were destroyed or dispersed by later religious purging.

In what is today Southern Jordan, a group of people called the Nabataeans, who had originally come from the Arabian Peninsula, established a trade route carrying spices, incense, precious metals, and Chinese silk, among other goods, from Arabia to the Eastern Mediterranean Coast, eventually bound for ports in Greece and Italy. The Nabataeans were nomadic, but they set up camps that were semipermanent. In 321 BCE, they fought off one of Alexander's generals who tried to take control of the region. When the power of the Seleucid kingdom waned, the Nabataean kingdom began to thrive. From c. 168 BCE to 109 CE, a succession of Nabataean kings ruled over this relatively small and remote area.

Nabataean architecture is an amalgam of Occidental and Oriental styles. The most famous building, **El Khazneh**, the so-called **"Treasury" at Petra** (first century BCE), is called Hellenistic, but there is nothing else like it in ancient Greece. The two-story facade is cut into the wall of the *Siq*, a deep gorge. The sandstone is so rich in color and texture that the Greek practice of applying stucco and paint to the architectural facades seems gratuitous, and indeed, there is no evidence that this happened. There are many tombs cut into the rock at Petra. Some are Assyrian style, simple with geometric reliefs; some are Nabataean style, modified from Hellenistic; and some are Roman.

FIGURE 13.7

Approch to El Khazneh, or The Treasury from Siq. Petra, Jordan.

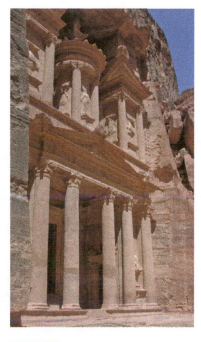

FIGURE 13.8

El Khazneh, or The Treasury. Petra, Jordan.

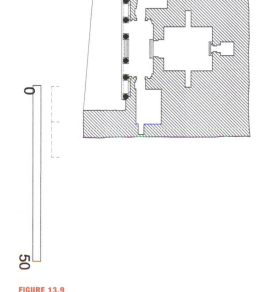

FIGURE 13.9

El Khazneh, or The Treasury Plan. Petra, Jordan.

FIGURE 13.10

Tomb of Zecharias (1st c.BCE). Jerusalem, Israel.

The influence of Hellenism can be seen in the Levant and areas to the east, although in the Near East, now the Middle East, the effect was somewhat diminished by the spread of Islam in the latter half of the first millennium. The so-called **Tomb of Zecharias**, properly the Tomb of Bene Hezir (late second century or early first century BCE) in Jerusalem, Israel, and other so-called Tombs of the Valley located beyond the east city walls, are examples of the range of Greek influence in the later centuries of antiquity.

For Further Discussion

Compare a work of architecture from the Classical Age of Greece with one from the Hellenistic Age. Begin with general influences and approaches, then focus on a certain aspect or detail.

CHAPTER FOURTEEN

Ancient Asia

All the ceremonies of religion scrupulously to be practiced

1. This is the truth:—
The works which the sages (kavi) saw in the sacred sayings
Are manifoldly spread forth in the triad [of the Vedas].
Follow them (ācaratha) constantly, ye lovers of truth (satyakāma)!
This is your path to the world of good deeds.

2. When the flame flickers,
After the oblation fire has been kindled,
Then, between the two portions of melted butter, his oblations.
One should throw—an offering made with faith (śraddhā).

3. If one's Agnihotra sacrifice is not followed by the sacrifice of the new moon and of the full moon, by the four-months sacrifice, by the harvest sacrifice, if it is unattended by guests, or not offered at all, or without the ceremony to all the gods, or not according to rule, it destroys his seven worlds.

4. The Black (kālī), and the Terrible, and the Swift-as-Thought,
The Very-red, and the Very-smoky-colored,
The Scintillating, and the All-formed,1 divine one,
Are the seven so-called flickering tongues [of flame].
Rewards of ceremonial observances

5. If one performs sacrifices when these are shining,
Offering the oblations at the proper time, too,
These (flames) as rays of the sun lead him
To where is resident the one lord (pati) of the gods.

6. Saying to him "Come! Come!" the splendid offerings
Carry the sacrificer with the rays of the sun,
Addressing pleasant speech, praising, and saying:
"This is your meritorious (puṇya) Brahma-world, gained by good works."[1]

— from the **Second Khanda**, *Mundaka Upanishad*, translated by Robert Ernest Hume

---

1   Selection from Second Khanda Mundaka Upanishad, The Thirteen Principal Upanishads, trans. Robert Ernest Hume. Copyright in the Public Domain.

The *Upanishads* are philosophical and religious texts that contain basic precepts and tenets of the religious traditions in South Central Asia that would eventually merge into Hinduism. The earliest texts date from the first half of the first millennium BCE, but the rituals are older, beginning as early as 2600 BCE. One of the basic concepts revealed in the *Upanishads* is *Atman*, the cosmic soul of the universe that is also present in each human. *Brahman*, a manifestation of knowledge and creativity, is also present in each individual. The Upanishads introduced the concept of *samsara*, the cycle of birth, death, and rebirth, which is at the core of Hinduism. This cycle is explained by the concept of *karma*, the inescapable and unchangeable principle of cause and effect.

Hinduism is one of several ancient Asian religions—with Buddhism, Confucianism, Taosim, and Jainism—that have survived until today are among the most populous of all current religions. Buddhism was founded around the fifth century BCE and is based on the teachings of Guatama Buddha, who lived in what is now Eastern India. Confucianism, which is more philosophical than theological, was based on the teachings and sayings of Confucius (551–479 BCE). Taoism, or Daoism, is based upon the *Tao Te Ching*, which is attributed to Laozi (c. fifth–fourth century BCE). Jainism is based upon the teachings of the last *Tirthankara*, or teaching God, Mahavira (sixth century), from modern-day India.

Gandhara Stupa: The Birth of the Buddha. Kushan Dynasty last 2c early 3c. Freer Gallery Washington.

The most spectacular works of ancient Asian religious architecture are Hindu temples, although some were built as Hindu places of worship but later adopted by either Buddhists or Jains. Hinduism descended from two sources, the Harappan or Indus Valley Civilization (c. 3300–1300 BCE) and the Aryan people who migrated from Central Asia around 2000 BCE. In the Vedic Age (c. 1500–500 BCE) *vedas*, hymns written in Sanskrit and dedicated to different gods, were being used by priests. During this period, the most important ritual was a sacrifice, made in an open-air shrine whose design was prescribed in the Vedas and was imitative of a sacred mount with five peaks called Mount Meru. They were simple platforms raised above the ground—uncovered, or covered with an umbrella-like form, or a gazebo-like form, or else protected from the elements by a tree. The square was seen as a sacred form, a symbol of the organization of the universe and of *brahman*. Eventually the *mandala* became the form that used as the basic planar form of Hindu temples. A mandala is a square with an inner circle, with four T-shaped "gates" at the cardinal points. In drawings, images of deities are placed in the center. In mandala-inspired architecture, the center is the location of the *garbhagriha*, a room with a statue of a deity in the center.

In Hindu tradition, the temple is the place where humans are in contact with the gods. The purpose of the temple is to dissolve the boundary between the human and divine worlds. There is an identification with the form of the universe and the form of the temple. Hindu temples are found in India, Cambodia (Khmer), Vietnam, and Indonesia. Hindu temples in India are generally grouped together in two distinct regional styles—northern and southern. In North India, temples a *shikhara*, a tower shaped like an arced pyramid, rises above the garbhagriha. In South India, each layer of the tower, called a *vimana*, is reduced in a regular manner. On two or four sides of the garbhagriha, there are small projections, which serve as vestibules. Scenes from the mythology of the Hindu gods are carved on both the doorways and the towers. The carvings and decoration are integral to the structure, not applied to it; thus, in Hindu architecture, sculpture and architecture become one.

Bhitargaon Temple (fifth century) is one of the earliest of the Hindu temples in India whose complete structure survives. It was made of brick. **Kailasa Temple** (eighth century) at Ellora was carved out of the rock (like Abu Simbel in Egypt). The **Vishvanatha, Temple** and the **Lakshmana Temple at Khajuraho** (tenth–eleventh centuries) epitomize the northern style. The stone figures that decorate the temples at Khajuraho are among the finest works of Indian art. The **Keshava Temple** (thirteenth century) at Somnathpur is a prototypical example of the southern style. It has three identical sanctuaries that resembled inverted cones.

Lao-tzu, a philosopher of the mid-first millennium BCE, wrote that a blurred and indistinct state of calmness and vagueness existed before the creation of heaven and earth. It alone is unchanging, and by its actions the universe itself changes. Its name is unknown, perhaps unknowable, but he called it *Tao*, or *Dao*. *Tao* is not a force or principle of creation—it is a principle of growth. Unlike Western ideas of God, *Tao* is not the master of the universe, affecting every detail. According to Lao-tzu, it loves all things but "does not lord over them."

The earliest vestiges of Taoist traditions can be traced to the Shang, who were a late Bronze Age people who lived in the area called the North China Plain along the Yellow River in Northern China (present-day Hebei, Shanxi, and Henan provinces). As a means of divination (foretelling the future), they used the cracks that resulted from heating an animal bone (typically a shoulder blade) or a plastron, the underside of a turtle. These oracle bones, as they are known, would be inscribed, using a bronze quill, with a question from a Shang king. The response, which was believed to be from the king's ancestors, would be interpreted by an official "diviner" who read the lines that appeared on the surface of the oracle bone. The *I Ching*, or *Book of Changes*, is a divination "manual," based on 64 hexagrams (six-line figures), representing all the possible signs that could appear on the oracle bones when they cracked.

Qi is the breath of life. It circulates within, and thus, animates all living things, creating the complementary forces of *yin*, which is the negative, passive, female, dark, or earthly aspect of all things, and *yang*, those aspects

FIGURE 14.3

Devi Jagadambi Temple. Khajuraho, India.

that are positive, male, heavenly, warm, and light. The concept of qi permeated early Chinese views of philosophy, medicine, art, science, and literature.

K'ung-tzu, or Confucius (551–479 BCE), was a teacher and philosopher, whose book *Lunyu*, or *The Analects*, is one of the most influential works in all of Asian history. He developed a principle of how people could live in harmony with one another by recognizing the Five Great Relationships, which are based on the family but serve as a model for other relationships, using the concepts of hierarchy and reciprocity. Veneration temples to honor Confucius and other important figures of Confucianism have been built since the fifth century BCE. The oldest, largest, and most famous is the **Temple of Confucius** (rebuilt fifteenth century) in Qufu, China.

K'ung-tzu was one of many early Chinese philosophers of the period, which was called the Axial Age, or the Age of the Hundred Schools. One such school, called Legalism, proposed that strong authoritarian leadership is necessary, because humans generally lack the ability to sustain themselves in a communal situation and need guidance. The kings of Qin dynasty adopted this ideology, and through a series of conquests that lasted for several generations of kings, gained control of the region. In 221 BCE, the King of Qin proclaimed himself to be Qin Shihuangdi, which means "First Emperor." He unified the empire by establishing standards for weights and measures, a writing system, and carriages and by

FIGURE 14.4

Terracotta Army. Mausoleum Complex of Emperor QinShiHuangdi. Xi'an, China.

eliminating contrarian thought—he burned books and buried scholars. Qin Shihuani was obsessed with his immortality but ironically died young at the age of 50 in 210 BCE. His reign lasted only 14 years, but he left behind a grandiose memorial of his authoritarian regime: The **Tomb of Emperor QinShihuang** (247–208 BCE), located outside present-day Xi'an.

The site of Emperor Qin's tomb was chosen for its superior *feng shui*, the ancient practice of determining the placement and direction of buildings, as wells as their internal spatial relationships for the optimal circulation of *qi*. Because he believed that life underground after death was a continuation of life on earth, the emperor constructed his tomb as an underground palace covered by a burial mound that was once 115 meters high. According to official records, thousands of officials were killed and thousands of craftsmen were buried alive in order to keep the tomb secret. Over 600 satellite pits and tombs within an area of 56 square kilometers have been found so far. The secrecy plan was successful for a long time. Qin's tomb remained undisturbed until it was discovered accidently by farmers in 1974.

The famous pits of the terra cotta soldiers are, to this date, the most significant of all the discoveries at the site. Four separate pits have been uncovered so far, containing over 8,000 life-size soldiers, horses, and archers. Each warrior has an independently crafted expression. All of the sculptures were originally pigmented. Each soldier carried a weapon. One pit contained infantry soldiers, another cavalryman, and another high-ranking officers. They were aligned in underground corridors, all facing the same direction. These corridors were approximately 5 to 7 meters tall and had brick floors and timber framework walls that supported a timber frame roof, with fiber matting and earth fill above. The corridors are separated by partitions made of rammed earth. There are ramps at the end, so that the soldiers could respond quickly to a battle situation.

Yumenguan Pass, or the **Jade Gate** (c. 120 BCE), near Dunhuang in Western China, is the oldest monumental extant structure in China. It has been substantially eroded by wind but still has an impressive size. Caravans of traders passing through the gate would pay a tariff. In antiquity Yumenguan had an estimated population of 40,000; today, there is no visible evidence of the city except for the gate, which is cube 10 meters

FIGURE 14.5

Han Dynasty Great Wall. Near Dunhuang, China.

FIGURE 14.6

Yumenguan Pass (Jade Gate). Near Dunhuang, China.

high, made from tamped earth. Also near Dunhuang are subterranean Jin Dynasty (265–420) tombs, some of which exhibit a unique architectural style.

Near Yumenguan are the oldest visible remnants of the Han Dynasty (202 BCE–6) portion of the **Great Wall of China** (c. 214 BCE–1644). It is impossible to discuss the Great Wall without first addressing common misconceptions. For one thing, it is not a single wall; it is a series of walls built over time. The portion seen more often near Beijing by tourists and heads of state is only a reconstruction of a wall that was built 500 years ago. The wall cannot be seen from the moon, let alone an astronaut flying in an orbit around the earth. The walls were not effective in keeping the enemy out; they were effective as a political statement. The Western Han Dynasty Wall was built from straw made from grasses and rammed earth, with watchtowers placed between

2 and 5 kilometers apart. The most recent sections of the wall were built during the Ming Dynasty (1388–1644); they were made of stone.

Siddhartha Gautama, known as the Buddha, claimed he had attained *nirvana*, a transcendental state in which suffering, desire, self-awareness, and the effects of karma and samsara no longer exist. This state is also called enlightenment, the freedom from the cycle of rebirth. Guatama was born in Lumbini, in modern-day Nepal, in the sixth or fifth century. He is the founder of Buddhism, which has coexisted with Hinduism in Asia for over 2,500 years as a separate but often similar or complementary religious philosophy. A central principle of Buddhism is the Four Noble Truths: 1) life is unsatisfactory, filled with suffering; 2) the cause of suffering is endless "wanting;" 3) suffering is eased when "wanting" ceases; and 4) cessation can be achieved by an eightfold path.

FIGURE 14.7
Brick Tomb of a General. Near Dunhuang, China.

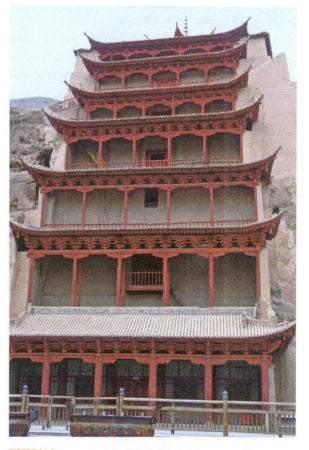

FIGURE 14.8
Mogoa Caves. Near Dunhuang, China.

Near Dunhuang, China, the **Mogao Caves** (fourth century–eleventh century)—also known as the Caves of the Thousand Buddhas—were carved into the mountain and contain a treasure of Buddhist art, including colossi of the Buddha, both standing and reclining, and many paintings. Like the Etruscan tombs at Tarquinia, architectural spaces were carved out of the rock and then decorated. It is believed that a Buddhist monk named Le Zun created the first cave temple. At least 490 more were created during the next 700 years.

The earliest Buddhist shrines were earthen mounds that marked a burial site of a holy person (the equivalent of a monk), either a *bhikkhu* (male) or a *bhikkhuni* (female). Eventually this mound structure would be made of masonry, either brick or stone, thus developing into what is called a *stupa*, a solid domed-structure containing the relics of a Buddhist monastic. A *chedi* is the name for such a structure located in Thailand. The ethnic Sinhalese people of Sri Lanka call it a *dagoba*.

Over time, the design of stupas became more intricately detailed, with each part being symbolic of a particular aspect of Buddhist tradition. Designs may vary from place to place, but in general, stupas sit on a platform called a *medhi,* sometimes called the vase of treasures. An *anda,* or hemispherical mound that symbolizes an earthen mound is next. On top of the mound is the square-shaped *harmika,* which supports a ringed spire representing the *bhumi*, the ten stages of awakening and a *chattra,* a parasol-shaped finial. At the very top is the *nada,* or jewel, which represents the attainment of aspirations. A stupa is enclosed by a *torana,* elaborately carved stone gateways.

The oldest surviving stupa is the **Great Stupa at Sanchi** (originally third century BCE), also the oldest surviving stone structure in India. The **Jetavanaramaya Stupa** (273–301), Anuradhapura, Sri Lanka, is believed to house a sash that belonged to the Buddha. It is constructed of brick, and is the largest stupa in area ever built and one of the tallest. A stupa is the central feature of **Borobudur** (ninth century) in Magelang, Central Java, Indonesia, the world's largest Buddhist temple, called a *candi* in the Indonesian language. It is immediately surrounded by 72 Buddhist statues.

FIGURE 14.9
Wild Goose Pagoda. Xi'an, China.

The pagoda, or *ta*, is the most iconic archetype of Chinese architecture. It developed in China in the first century from the Indian stupa. A multistoried pagoda is a series of single-level stupa-type forms placed atop of one another, typically diminishing in height and breadth as the structure gets taller. They could be constructed of wood, stone, or brick. The interior is hollow, with floors and a stairway. The **Wild Goose Pagoda** in Xi'an, (701–704) has arched doorways on each of its six upper levels on all four sides. Very slim pilasters decorate the walls, with a *tou*, or bearing lintel, above.

Angkor Wat (constructed 1113–1150), like other temple complexes in Southeast Asia, is a model of the Hindu universe. This is a Khmer innovation, although derived from Indian mythology. The moat that circumambulates the entire compound represents the oceans. Inside the moat, there is a series of enclosures, and

FIGURE 14.10

Angkor Wat. Angkor, Cambodia.

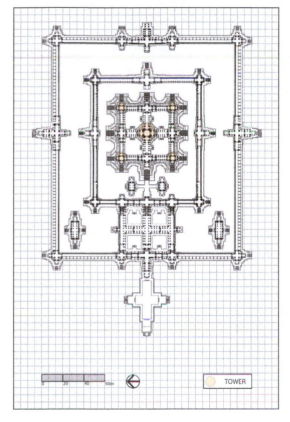

TOWER

FIGURE 14.11

Angkor Wat Plan.

tower, would be—and still are—visible from the entire surrounding countryside for miles on all four sides, not unlike Chartres Cathedral, for example. The floor level of each successive gallery rises as it approaches the center. The obvious, almost banal symbolism—the ascension of stairways that lead to heaven—seems, after hundreds of years, neither too heavy handed nor too simplistic.

Astronomy has been fused with architecture since Stonehenge and the Pyramids, so it is not surprising to see astronomical devices in either Christian or Buddhist-Hindu edifices. At Angkor Wat, the doorways of the ascending *gopura* are aligned in such a manner that a beam of light penetrates the successive openings at precisely the autumnal and vernal equinoxes.

The central sanctuary of Khmer temples consists of a base, a door opening with pilasters and lintel, a tympanum, a pediment, and the reduced stories of the upper part of the tower. The towers of medieval cathedrals rise directly from the doorway, eschewing a base for practical reasons: the pilgrims would bring their animals inside the cathedral. The doorway is flanked by saints and important holy figures. The doorways of Khmer temples are also flanked by religious figures, either freestanding, or in the bas-relief decoration of a pilaster. In both types of edifices, there are richly decorated tympanums above the doorway. Overall, Angkor contains many temple sites distributed through the ancient city of Angkor, the largest city in the world prior to the Industrial Revolution. At **Bayon Temple** (thirteenth century), in Angkor, there are 49 towers carved with colossal faces, probably of its builder, King Jayavarman VII, arranged in an array. **Bantey Srei** (tenth century) is one of the oldest sites and is known for its elaborate sculptural decoration.

The form of the grand Khmer temples at Angkor—the quincunx of towers—help to bestow on Khmer temple architecture attributes that define a masterpiece of Art: unity, singularity, clarity, and monumentality. This form, which was also used at Ta Keo and East Mebon, among others, is one of several temple layouts employed by Khmer builders. A single, dominant tower, located at the center of the inner, or last, enclosure of the temple complex, was used, notably at Baphuon (Angkor), and at **Prasat Phimai** (eleventh–twelfth centuries) and **Prasat**

like the axial progression in the Christian church, the concentric progression of the temple toward the center elevates the status of the worshipper at each stage.

The floor level of the central sanctuary is 75 feet above grade; thus, the towers, especially the main

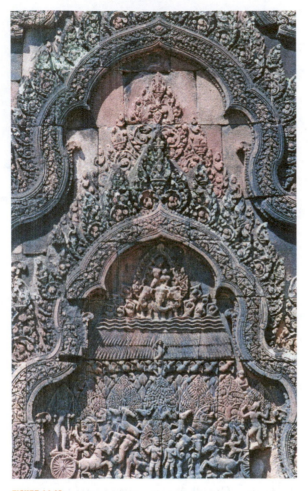

FIGURE 14.12
Bantey Srei. Angkor, Cambodia.

FIGURE 14.14
Phimai Temple Complex. Phimai, Thailand.

For Further Discussion

Compare Eastern and Western cultures from a general perspective. In what ways are they alike? In what ways are they different? Next, compare two works of architecture and explore what cultural factors affected each and made them different from one another.

Phnom Rung (tenth–twelfth centuries), northwest of Angkor in what is now Thailand. An example of a row of three towers is **Prang Sam Yod** (thirteenth century), in Lopburi, also in Thailand.

FIGURE 14.13

Phnom Rung Temple Complex. Phnom Rung, Thailand

CHAPTER FIFTEEN

Ancient American Civilizations

The next morning we reached the broad high road of Iztapalapan, whence we for the first time beheld the numbers of towns and villages built in the lake, and the still greater number of large townships on [Pg 219] the mainland, with the level causeway which ran in a straight line into Mexico. Our astonishment was indeed raised to the highest pitch, and we could not help remarking to each other, that all these buildings resembled the fairy castles we read of in Amadis de Gaul; so high, majestic, and splendid did the temples, towers, and houses of the town, all built of massive stone and lime, rise up out of the midst of the lake. Indeed, many of our men believed what they saw was a mere dream. And the reader must not feel surprised at the manner in which I have expressed myself, for it is impossible to speak coolly of things which we had never seen nor heard of, nor even could have dreamt of, beforehand.

— from *True History of the Conquest of New Spain*, by Bernal Díaz del Castillo (1492–1580), John Ingram Lockhart, transl. (1844)

On Good Friday in 1519, the conquistador Hernando Cortes arrived on the eastern shore of what is now the state of Vera Cruz on the Gulf of Mexico. There, he founded Villa Rica de la Vera Cruz, one of the first European cities in the New World. Later that year, after skirmishing with and defeating the Tlaxcala, Cortes and his soldiers arrived at Iztapalapa. One of these soldiers, Bernal Diaz, wrote an account of this expedition. Already, the cities and villages of the Aztecs had called to mind the fantastic places described in the popular knight-errant tale *Amadis de Gaula*, inspired by medieval Arthurian literature. When Diaz saw Iztapalapa, however, he was astounded. The palace where soldiers were lodged were "spacious and well built, of magnificent stone, cedar wood, and the wood of other sweet-smelling trees, with great rooms and courts … and all covered with awnings of woven cotton."

Later Cortes and his men came to Tenochtitlan, the capital of the Aztec empire, and there, Cortes and Motecuhzoma (Montezuma) met face to face, perhaps the most famous and most symbolic of all such encounters between Europeans and the sovereigns of the previously undiscovered continent. Although somewhat stiff, the meeting was very cordial, however the civility that marked the first meetings did not last, and Cortes and his deputy, Alvarado, eventually took over the city. They then used it as a base for further conquests.

The introduction of two continents with the rest of the world was an event that could only happen once in the lifetime of the earth. From a political and cultural perspective, the result could not have been more catastrophic for the native populations. Some works of pre-Columbian literature and verbal art survive, because they were translated into Spanish, but most were lost. Pre-Columbian art was accumulated into museums and private collections all over the world. The monumental stone architecture of the three most prodigious civilizations of the Americas—the Aztec, Maya, and Inca—together with the images of native North America seen through the eyes of the Europeans in the art, literature, and film depictions of the American West, are the most durable remnants of ancient America.

The Ancient American civilizations descended from migrating populations toward the end of the last ice age,

1 Bernal Díaz del Castillo, Selection from True History of the Conquest of New Spain, trans. John Ingram Lockhart. Copyright in the Public Domain.

around 12,000 years ago. They evolved independently from European, Asian, African, and Pacific Island civilizations. Scholars have long speculated that there may have been some pre-Columbian contact between the Americas and the rest of the world. Recent DNA testing of certain plants has raised at least some questions about some possible interaction. The only recognized evidence of contact before the voyages of Columbus is the archaeological site at L'Anse aux Meadows, in Newfoundland, a Norse settlement from the early eleventh century. History books have long reported that in the year 1001, Leif Eriksson sailed to a place called "Vinland," which is likely to be Newfoundland. Beyond that, it is certainly possible—perhaps even likely—that there could have been an incidental contact: a single sailor or sailors that somehow survived a voyage that, because of a storm or confusion, went too far. Still, there is no evidence that any such contact, if it did happen, had much effect on any of either of the parties involved.

Ancient American culture can be divided into the following regional areas: Native American, Southwestern, Mesoamerican, and South American. Each region was distinct from the other, although there are some shared common characteristics. One such feature is the layout of the Mayan city centers and the layout of Mississippi mounded sites. Both have raised platforms or pyramids surrounded by plaza areas, although there is no evidence that the planning of Mississippi culture sites was influenced by the earlier or contemporary Mayan sites. Ancient American cultures varied in the size of their population, the size of their influence area, when their so-called "Classical" period occurred, and the durations of these periods.

The development of agrarian communities in the Americas came later than in Europe and Asia. Like the early communities of the Near East, Egypt, and Anatolia, increased yields of agricultural products spurred both a population growth and advancement in the level of civilization. In the Americas, this was the result of improvements to the types of maize, bean, and squash crops that were planted. Technologically, American civilizations never reached the same level of sophistication as those in Eurasia. They lacked the domesticated farm

animals used for transportation in other civilizations, and therefore, never used the wheel. Metallurgy was used for personal items like jewelry, but metal tools were never developed. These facts make the architectural and artistic accomplishments of the Mesoamerican cultures all the more remarkable. The lack of beasts for transportation also meant that communication between the various groups of people was more limited than it was in Eurasia.

Some aspects of Mesoamerican civilizations were similar to those developed on other continents. The progression of the development of communities followed a similar pattern—from small tribal villages and larger agrarian towns to cities and city-states. Other similarities were the basic structure of a militarized state, whether for expansive or defensive purposes; the patriarchal autocracy or oligarchy as the form of government; the central, and often domineering, role of religion; the establishment of a writing system; the use of slave labor; division of labor; the distinction of gender roles; the establishment of social classes; trade networks; and the creation of monumental architecture. These similarities suggest that there are common characteristics in the development of any civilization.

The most advanced civilizations in the Americas were located in Mesoamerica and the Andes. Agrarian civilizations appeared in Mesoamerica in the middle of the second millennium BCE. The first large city in the Americas was Monte Alban in the Oaxaca Valley, in present-day Mexico; it had a population of around 20,000 people in 500 BCE. One of the largest pre-European (pre-Columbian) empires in the Americas was the Incan Empire, located in the Andean mountain range in South America (in parts of present-day Peru, Ecuador, Chile, Argentina, and Bolivia). It lasted from the early thirteenth century until the late sixteenth century, when it fell victim, directly and indirectly, to Spanish conquests. Cuzco, in present-day Peru, was the center of the empire and its more important city. Machu Picchu, the estate of the ruler Pachacuti (1438–1472), is its most spectacular architectural site.

In North America, however, civilization never progressed beyond the early stages of an agrarian society, in spite of geographical advantages, and in spite of the fact that ungulates were available for domestication. Native American culture is divided into two eras: the Woodland era, with Indian tribe names such as Cherokee, Sioux, Mohawk, etc., and the Mississippian era. There is archaeological evidence of communities in Eastern North America, beginning in the fourth millennium BCE. The most significant sites were all constructed of earth and wood, as they would be throughout the course of the history of native architecture in North America. The extant archaeological remains are insubstantial and have minimal visual impact; thus, they have been unnoticed or neglected for many years. The use of earthen mounds, either to elevate ceremonial areas or tombs, or as a platform for living facilities, is the dominant aspect of Native American architecture. The earliest example of monumental earth construction was in Louisiana, sometime between 5500 and 3000 BCE. At **Watson Brake** (c. 3900–3300 BCE), near Monroe, Louisiana, there were 11 or more earthen mounds connected by earthen terraces, arranged in a slightly ovate circle 60 meters in diameter and 5 meters tall. Due to its location in the flood plain of the Ouachita River, it is possible that the enclosure mound was constructed for protection from severe, occasional flooding. At **Poverty Point** (1730–1350 BCE), near Floyd, Louisiana, shelters were built in six concentric rows that radiated from an open central plaza area.

Cahokia (1050–1350), located on the flood plain of the Mississippi River near St. Louis, Missouri, is the largest ancient archaeological site in Eastern North America. The site, which occupied about 13 square kilometers, had 120 earthen mounds, which were created by carrying baskets or aprons filled with dirt. The largest is Monks Mound, which was composed of several terraces, located within a main plaza enclosed by a *palisade*, a fence of wooden stakes that surrounded a small village. Monks Mound is about 317 meters by 241 meters by 30 meters tall, or the height of a nine- to ten-story building. It was named after Trappist monks who lived on the mound between 1808 and 1813.

Outside the palisade, there were more than 100 additional mounds. To the west of Monks Mound is what has been called "Woodhenge," due to its resemblance to

FIGURE 15.2

Cahokia Reconstruction. Cahokia Museum. Illinois.

Stonehenge. It is 125 meters in diameter and consists of 48 posts arranged in a circle. Four of the posts are aligned with the four compass points, and there was an additional post placed near the center, which suggests that the arrangement of posts was used for astronomical purposes relating to agriculture.

Cahokia reached a maximum population of an estimated 10,000 to 20,000 people in the thirteenth century, although some estimates go as high as 40,000. At the higher level, Cahokia would have had a larger population than London at the time.

Moundville (1200–1500) in Alabama is the second largest site. It has 20 platform mounds built around a large central plaza area and several smaller plazas. A few houses have been reconstructed at the site.

The Ancestral Pueblo people, formerly called the *Anasazi* (from Navajo, "enemy ancestors"), created the most sophisticated Pre-Columbian architecture north of modern-day Mexico. They built cluster villages using adobe, earth, and stone that appear to be instinctive, but tectonic, appendages to the natural landscape. Few monumental works of architecture show as much respect for their immediate environment; they are at once enterprising and reverential. Ancestral Pueblo Civilization occupied what is now the northern parts of Arizona and New Mexico, Southern Utah, and the southwest corner of Colorado, a region called the "Four Corners" today, named for the geographical point where the four states meet. It is an area rich in protuberant geological features that have evoked an aura of sacredness to those who migrated there roughly 12,000 years ago, and is still as mystifying today.

Ancestral Pueblo civilization has been divided into cultural periods that date from approximately 9,000 years ago—several "Basketmaker" eras that ended around 750 and five "Pueblo" periods that followed. Prior to the construction of pueblos, the populations lived in pithouses, which were built atop flat table-like mountains called *mesas*. During the Basketmaker III (500–750) era, pueblo villages were first created. Between the years 500 and 1350, the Ancestral Pueblo people built the only significant, enduring stone structures in what is now either the United States or Canada prior to the arrival of the Europeans.

During this period, houses were built into natural hollows of cliffs, thus giving rise to the epithet "cliff-dwellers," which is sometimes used to describe the culture. Circular pit structures called *kivas*, similar in design to the older pithouses, were mostly used for communal rituals and gatherings. They originally had wooden roofs, no longer visible at any of the archaeological sites today. A shaft was built to the south which brought in fresh air to the space. Near a firepit in the center was a *sipapu*, a small opening in the earthen floor which is seen to be a symbolic access to the ancestral world that lies below. Benches were built into the side walls. Kivas may also have been used as residences, although to what extent, when, and why are not understood.

At Mesa Verde ("green table") in Colorado, there are over 600 cliff dwellings, among the thousands of archaeological sites now located in a national park. The **Cliff Palace** of **Mesa Verde** (1100–1275) had 220 rooms, 23 kivas, open plazas, and ceremonial towers. Most of the houses shared a common courtyard, probably shared by single clans. Another large house is **Spruce Tree House**, which had 135 rooms.

Pueblo Bonito (c. 750–c. 1150) is the largest of nine Great Houses built at **Chaco Canyon** in Northwestern New Mexico. It had more than 800 rooms and 37 kivas. Because archaeologists have found little evidence of constant occupation, it is seen to be a ceremonial center, a place where the Ancestral Pueblo people assembled for special ceremonies from all over the region. The semicircular plan of the structure resembles a Greek theater. There were smaller kivas for individual clans and two large kivas to accommodate *moieties*, or halves, of the assembly.

The earliest structures at **White House Ruin** at **Canyon de Chelly** (pronounced *dŏ-shay'*) (c. 1100–1300) in Northeastern Arizona were built in a dramatically sited cliff nestled under a massive (240 meters) outcropping of sandstone that curves outward as it rises from

FIGURE 15.3

Cliff Palace. Mesa Verde, Colorado.

FIGURE 15.4

White House Ruin. Canyon de Chelly. Arizona.

FIGURE 15.5

Chaco Canyon. New Mexico.

the canyon floor. **Antelope House** also is sited beneath a cliff, which is 180 meters tall. At **Mummy Cave**, a three-story structure is still *in situ*. Canyon de Chelly and other Ancestral Pueblo sites in the area were abandoned around 1300. The most common explanation offered for this is a dramatic climatic change, perhaps as a result of deforestation.

Mesoamerica refers to the area bounded on the north by present-day Sinaloa, a state in Central Mexico, and on the south by Honduras. Ancient cultures in that region included the Olmec, Zapotec-Mixtec, Teotihuacan, Tenochtitlan, Mayan, and Aztec. Ceremonial centers— large open plazas where the public gathered for religious and community rituals—were the focal point of Mesoamerican communities. Adjacent to the public space were the palaces of the political and religious leaders, the temples, and their ancillary structures. Artwork is generally associated with public buildings, either sculpture or paintings, and as such, is also associated with religion. Mesoamerican cultures had a hierarchal social structure.

The first complex culture in Mesoamerica is the Olmec Civilization, beginning around 1250 BCE, and located in what is the modern-day state of Tabasco. The Olmec created large stone sculptures of four different types: giant bodiless heads (1.6 to 3 meters), depicting chiefs or gods; monolith-style thrones, with sculpted figures on the sides; stelae of different sizes and shapes, some with a hieroglyphic writing, some with figures; and statues of humans or animals. At San Lorenzo in the Valley of Oaxaca, a natural plateau was modified by moving tons of earth to create a platform, which was used for additional smaller platforms that supported public buildings made out of wood and other nondurable materials. In addition, there were other, smaller mounds, which supported residential structures. At the height of their power, the Olmec controlled most of Mesoamerica.

The first large city in the Americas was **Monte Alban** in the Oaxaca Valley, in present-day Mexico; it had a population of around 20,000 people in 500 BCE. Teotihuacan was an independent city-state from the period of 100 BCE to 750 CE with much influence on neighboring cultures, especially during the fourth through the sixth centuries. The site contains several large and small pyramids, arranged about a central axis called the Calzada de los Muertos (Avenue of the Dead). The avenue is not aligned with the true north–south axis, but is rather 17 degrees skewed to the east. The **Pyramid of the Sun** is one of the most important monuments of the pre-Columbian era in all of the Americas. Due to the

FIGURE 15.6

Pyramid of the Sun. Teotihuacan, Mexico.

special orientation and its precise geometry, the pyramid is situated in alignment with a point on the horizon where the sun sets, twice a year on May nineteenth and July twenty-fifth. On these two days, the sun is also directly overhead the pyramid's peak at noon. The pyramid had five tiers made of mud with a stone facing and is 225 meters square and 65 meters tall.

The Mayans (c. 1000 BCE–1250) occupied three main areas: The Pacific Highlands, in present-day Southwestern Guatemala and El Salvador; the central lowlands; and the northern lowlands of present-day Guatemala, Belize, and the Yucatan in Mexico. Their history is divided into several periods: The Pre-Classic; Classic, Early and Late; and Post-Classic. The Pre-Classic period of Mayan civilization consisted of agricultural communities. In the Early Classic Period, the Mayan region was composed of independent states, each of which had its own *kuhul ajaw*, or king. Two states dominated the region: Tikal and Calakmul. The Proto-Classic period is the period when a firm foundation is laid for the artistic accomplishments of the Mayas, including the development of hieroglyphic writing and the Mayan calendar. In the Classic period, populations expanded, and the city-states grew in size and administrative structure. Mayan civilization declined, beginning in the early ninth century; the various causes that have been suggested are overpopulation, declining soil productivity, deforestation, and warfare. The ultimate cause was probably a combination of all of these things.

Mayan culture developed in the tropical rain forests of the lowlands of Central America, and along the Pacific coast and the mountainous area of what is now Southwestern Guatemala. The Maya inherited at least some of their heritage from the Olmec, but also evolved from small communities unaligned with the Olmec. Mayan culture is divided into two general areas: the Guatemalan highlands and lowlands, which include what is present-day Eastern Guatemala, portions of the Mexican states of Chiapas and Tabasco, the Yucatan Peninsula, the entire country of Belize, and Northwestern Honduras.

The most significant developments in art and architecture were made in the lowland area, which is the home of the Mayan pyramids. Although none reached the height of the Egyptian pyramids, some exceeded the area. The Mayan pyramids were terraced, and thus resemble Djoser's pyramid at Saqqara more than they do Khufu's pyramid at Giza. At times, a newer structure was superimposed over an earlier structure. Just as in Egypt, the pyramid form grew from a simple platform, although the original Pre-classic Mayan platform was meant to support a smaller structure on top of it, not to cover a chamber that was buried below it. In this respect, the White Temple of Uruk is more apt as a comparative example. In Classic Mayan pyramids, a tomb chamber was buried into the bedrock below the structure, not within the pyramid, like at Giza.

At the uppermost platform of the pyramid was a small sanctuary or temple building, which owed its form to a wooden hut. It was set on a low plinth, reached by relatively few steps. An ornamental "roof comb" was placed on top of the "roof temple." It should be noted that the entire Mayan pyramid structure is called a "temple," unlike the Egyptian pyramids, where temple and tomb connote two distinct buildings.

A central plaza area was created by excavating the perimeter of a site. At some sites, a separate higher temple platform, called an acropolis, would be constructed. (The word *acropolis* is confusing; actual correlations between the Mayan and Greek usages are minimal.)

At Tikal, the Central Acropolis, is a large palace complex. In ancient Greece, an acropolis was used strictly for religious activities. Tikal, the largest of the Mayan cities, had a central Great Plaza that was a religious, social, economic, and political center, but there were other minor ceremonial plazas that were connected by elevated causeways. The Great Plaza was used for ceremonies honoring the ancestors of the rulers, funerals, rites of ascension, and religious rituals associated with rainmaking and the fertilization of the earth.

In addition to the pyramids, public buildings included palace buildings for the ruling elite, ball courts, and structures for which no function has been attributed. In front of the temples were stelae, upon which were carved glyphs and relief images depicting historic events, and which were political propaganda for the aristocrats who were in control and lived in the palaces, or else they were mythological images. Stele 22 at Tikal, one famous example, shows the ruler preparing to sacrifice a captive.

In Mayan mythology, the rulers who were buried in tombs under the great pyramids were seen as protectors and supporters of the community. The king, or *kuhul ajaw*, controlled the economic, political, and religious aspects of the entire community. He was seen as divine.

Mayan religion evolved over time, with substantial changes coming in the Post-classical period. The gods were either *anthropomorphic* (with human characteristics), *zoomorphic* (with animal characteristics), or associated with natural phenomena, such as the sky, rain, or lightning. The sun, moon, stars, and planets were in a contact cycle of birth and rebirth. *K'in* is the cycle of a single day, when the sun is born at dawn, dies, and descends to the underworld at night.

The Maya believed in the existence of a supernatural entity called the *k'uh*. Unlike the Asian concept of *qi*, the *k'uh* permeated all things in the universe, living and nonliving. Gods and mortals both had a "companion spirit" called the *way*, pronounced like the letter Y.

Human sacrifice was often part of the rites. In the eleventh century, human sacrifice is depicted in artwork in scenes where the heart is torn out of the victim. Some sacrifices involved the additional act of decapitation. The blood that flowed would seep into, and thus nourish, the earth. Rituals also included bloodletting by the religious and political authorities. One who allowed himself to be exposed to pain was considered more devout.

The end of the principal cycles of the calendar were celebrated in the public plazas. The *tzolkin* (divinatory cycle) was 260 *kin* (days). The *haab*, or solar year cycle, was 365 kin. The Long Count, also called the Great Cycle, was 5200 *tun* (360 days in the year).

Mayan architecture was seen as representative of the universe. The Great Plaza (150 BCE–700) at Tikal was the center of activity, where the order of the universe, manifested by both the gods and the *k'uhul ajaw*, is visible to the community. The plaza is bounded by four monumental buildings: the Central Acropolis to the south, Temple II on the west, the North Acropolis to the north, and Temple I to the east. The floor is made of

FIGURE 15.7
Temple I. Tikal, Guatemala.

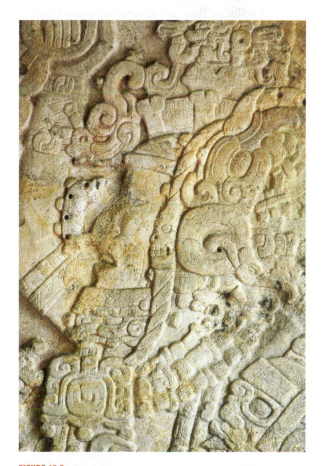

FIGURE 15.8
Stela 31: King Great Jaguar Paw. Tikal.

38 centimeters of plaster, placed in layers at different times between 150 BCE and 700 CE.

Temple I, or the **Temple of the Giant Jaguar** (700) is one of the iconic buildings of Mayan culture. It had nine terraces (the number nine was a sacred number), resting on a foundation of earth and limestone rubble. The *roof comb*, an ornamental sculpture on the uppermost terrace, consisted of two sealed, vaulted chambers, faced with a painted relief of a rotund figure and serpents. The comb is set back from the plaza. The terraces are decorated with moldings that are irregular, in that they are inset and offset, raised and lowered, in relation to the planar surface. As in most Mayan temples, the most prominent feature is the stair, which goes from the plaza to the top of the structure.

The temple has three interior narrow chambers with tall ceilings. They are constructed according to a standard Mayan practice of having the two supporting walls incline toward the center, and filling the space at the top with capstones. The tomb underneath the pyramid was buried there after the temple was completed, but sometime before 900. In the twelfth or thirteenth century, the bones of an additional body were placed in the tomb. In Mayan belief, the bones are essential for the dead, because of the presence of the *k'uh*.

Astronomy played a role in the design of the **Pyramid of Kukulcán**, or **El Castillo** (c. 980) at Chichen Itza. On the days of the spring and fall equinoxes (March 21 and September 23), a shadow-and-light effect creates the appearance of a plumed serpent slowly slithering down the edges of the pyramid, as the sun moves across the sky. This serpent is the god Kukulcán, who is descending to earth to initiate the agricultural season. In addition, there are 365 steps from the bottom to the top of the pyramid, including the upper shrine, which is the number of days in the Mayan calendar. Each of the four sides of the pyramid has 52 stone panels, which is the number of years in the calendar cycle. There is also an observatory, called **El Caracol**, on the site. The name Chichen Itza combines *chichén*, or edge of the well, and *itza*, water sorcerers.

Like many archaeological sites all over the world, the remote location of the Mayan sites led to widespread looting until recently. For example, **The Pyramid of the Masks** (500) at Kohunlich, a temple site in the Rio Bec region of the Yucatan in Mexico, once had eight monumental masks that flanked a grand staircase. Three were looted and only five remain.

Tulum, located in the Yucatan Peninsula in the Caribbean Sea, dates from the Classic Period, but the most of the extant structures at the site date from the Early Post-Classic Period. Notable buildings at the site are El Castillo, a pyramid structure, and the Temple of the Frescoes.

The central ceremonial areas of Mayan sites, which contained temples, large open plazas, palaces for the ruling class, administrative buildings, and ball courts, were raised up from the jungle floor, using earth and rock from the periphery of the site. This was probably done for symbolic as well as practical reasons. The plazas were sloped, draining rainwater to the moat-like areas surrounding the site.

Beginning in the ninth century, the Mayan civilization began to decline. Tikal, which is estimated to have had a population of 20,000 during the Classical period, lost 90 percent of its population. What was once seen by scholars as a collapse is now seen as a deterioration. By the time the Spanish arrived in the sixteenth century,

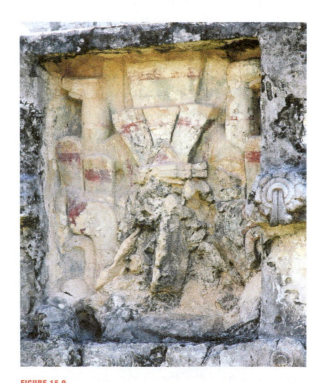

FIGURE 15.9

Descending God. Painted Bas-relief from the Tomb of the Frescoes. Tulum, Mexico.

an empire that had once been fierce and aggressive was conquered with comparative ease. The monuments of the Mayan civilization were overgrown by the tropical forests and were lost to the world until the nineteenth century. Major discoveries of Mayan sites persist into the twenty-first century.

The earliest monument works of architecture in the Americas were built by the Caral, also known as the Care-Supe, or Norte Chico civilization (c. 4000–2000 BCE), who established the first cities in the Americas during the latter half of the fourth millennium BCE— earlier than those in Mesopotamia or Egypt. With the Sumerian civilization in Mesopotamia, the Harappan civilization in the Indus Valley, and the Egyptian civilization along the Nile, it is one of four world-wide river valley civilizations to emerge in the fourth century BCE. Archaeological sites have been found at the confluence of three rivers in Northern Peru: the Fortaleza, the Pativilca, and the Supe.

The **Caral Pyramids** (c. 2600 BCE) were built at approximately the same time as the first Egyptian pyramids. They were constructed of stone that was quarried and carried in bags called *shicra* to the site. The ruins of seven pyramids have been found, ranging in size up to approximately 135 meters by 150 meters.

The Caral was one of several ancient civilizations located in the Andean mountain range, including the Chavin culture (c. 1500 BCE), the Nazca culture (100–800), who created the famous geoglyphs known as the Nazca lines, and the Moche (100–800). The **Cao Viejo**, **Huaca del Sol**, and the **Huaca de la Luna** are pyramids built by the Moche at a site known as the **El Brujo Complex** (200–650). A mummy of a woman was found at the site, dubbed the Lady of Cao, who died around 400 and was buried with jewelry, weapons, sewing needles, headdresses, and cotton.

The Inca Empire was the largest empire in all of the Americas at the time of the European arrival in what the Europeans called the "New World." The domain of the Incas was called *Tawantinsuyu* ("The Four Quarters or Regions"), and was divided into four areas separated by axes whose center was Cusco. From 1438 to 1532, the Incan Empire assimilated an area of diverse geography

FIGURE 15.10
Machu Picchu. Peru.

and independent people into what was to be a single empire of one culture with a common language, a common government, and a common religion. This process was halted by the Spanish conquest.

The greatest architectural legacy of Incan civilization is finely worked stonework, using a *dry masonry* technique, in which large blocks of stone are carefully dressed and placed without mortar. The joints of Incan stone masonry are famously so precise that a knife blade cannot be inserted in them. Stone blocks were pounded into shape using stone tools, and then finished with grinding stones and sand. Incan buildings are simple, rectangular structures, typically one story with few doorways and windows. **Macchu Picchu** ("Old Peak") (c. 1450), near Cusco, Peru, was a citadel or a royal or imperial estate. It is sited on a small flat-top mountain 2,430 meters above sea level. Of the more interesting structures at the site are the Temple of the Sun and the Inti Watana, which was an astronomical clock.

For Further Discussion

Compare an ancient civilization from North or South America with other ancient civilizations from Europe or Asia. Points of comparison should be art, architecture, political structure, technology, language, literature, and social practices. Ignore absolute time periods as bases for comparison, and instead focus on relative levels of development.

PART

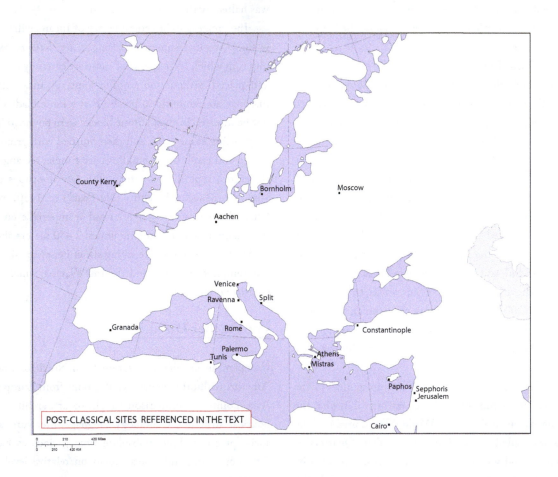

County Kerry

Bornholm

Moscow

Aachen

Venice

Ravenna

Split

Granada

Rome

Constantinople

Palermo

Tunis

Athens

Mistras

Paphos

Sepphoris

Jerusalem

Cairo

POST-CLASSICAL SITES REFERENCED IN THE TEXT

0   210   420 Miles
0   210   420 KM

FOUR

Late Antiquity

Late Antiquity, in general terms, is the period between Roman civilization and the Medieval era. Unlike other great civilizations of the ancient world, which were vanquished quickly in military conflict, the fall of Rome was gradual. It was a tattered carcass of an elephant left alone to decay on barren plain, not an impala devoured by lion, jackal, and vulture. The prime years of Roman civilization were during the first, second, and third centuries. When, in 324, Constantine moved the capital of the empire to Byzantium and renamed it Constantinople, a significant portion of the Roman military muscle moved east with Constantine, thus leaving Rome more vulnerable to invasions from the North. The Byzantine Empire at Constantinople lasted until 1453. Honorius moved the eastern capital to Ravenna in 402, after Theodosius redivided it. In 476, Romulus Augustulus was deposed as the emperor of the Western Roman Empire. He sent his insignia, the official seal of the Western Empire, to Constantinople, an act that, in retrospect, was the last significant event of ancient history.

In AD 400, Rome had 800,000 people, 10 miles of walls, 376 towers, 19 aqueducts, 1,212 fountains, and 926 public baths. The poet, Rutilius Namatianus, wrote that counting the glories of Rome "is like counting the stars in the sky." In 410, the Visigoths plundered the city; the Ostrogoths did the same in 455. In the sixth century, Rome was sacked three times, by both the Byzantines and the Goths. After the fall of Rome, the Forum became a cow pasture, and the Colosseum was used as a quarry for Christian churches. It wasn't until 1462 that Pope Pius II made a declaration forbidding the plundering of ancient buildings, although this was largely ignored.

CHAPTER SIXTEEN

Early Christianity

But, on the same ground, Discord as well as Concord ought to be deified. A hazardous venture the Romans made in provoking so wicked a goddess, and in forgetting that the destruction of Troy had been occasioned by her taking offence. For, being indignant that she was not invited with the other gods [to the nuptials of Peleus and Thetis], she created dissension among the three goddesses by sending in the golden apple, which occasioned strife in heaven, victory to Venus, the rape of Helen, and the destruction of Troy. Wherefore, if she was perhaps offended that the Romans had not thought her worthy of a temple among the other gods in their city, and therefore disturbed the state with such tumults, to how much fiercer passion would she be roused when she saw the temple of her adversary erected on the scene of that massacre, or, in other words, on the scene of her own handiwork! Those wise and learned men are enraged at our laughing at these follies; and yet, being worshippers of good and bad divinities alike, they cannot escape this dilemma about Concord and Discord: either they have neglected the worship of these goddesses, and preferred Fever and War, to whom there are shrines erected of great antiquity, or they have worshipped them, and after all Concord has abandoned them, and Discord has tempestuously hurled them into civil wars.[1]

— *The City of God*, Augustine of Hippo, Book III, Chapter 25

Augustine of Hippo (354–430) was a theologian and philosopher who was perhaps ribbing the pagans in the early fifth century when he wrote the above except from *The City of God*, begging a basic question of polytheism—how do humans appease opposing gods. Augustine lived in an extraordinary time, in which a religion that had endured for hundreds of years was rapidly being abandoned and a new religion, which began as a breakaway cult from a minor religion in a faraway province, was usurping the old and gaining dominance in the greatest empire in all of history. *The City of God* methodically challenged claims by the pagans that it was Christianity that was the cause for the turmoil in the empire, an idea raised again by Edward Gibbon in the eighteenth century, from a different point of view. That view is now seen, ironically for a work of six volumes, as too simplistic.

Not long after the crucifixion of Jesus, a man was stoned to death in Jerusalem for preaching "blasphemous words against Moses and God." He became the first saint of Christianity, and his feast day is celebrated the day after Christmas, the feast of St. Stephen, on December 26. One of those who encouraged the mob to condemn Stephen was Saul, a Pharisee who punished the early disciples of Christ "often," and "compelled them to blaspheme" so that there would be anger incited against them. A few years after the death of Stephen, Saul was on his way to Damascus, and according to his accounts in the *Acts of the Apostles* from the *New Testament*, he was confronted by a bright light that blinded him. He heard a voice speaking in Hebrew, saying, "Saul, Saul, why are you persecuting Me? It is hard for you to kick against the *goads* (sticks for prodding cattle)." He asked the voice to identify Himself.

---

1   St. Augustine of Hippo, Selection from The City of God, trans. Marcus Dods. Copyright in the Public Domain.

"I am Jesus, whom you are persecuting," was the response. At that point, according to the Acts, Jesus instructed Saul to "open the eyes" of others.

Saul's account can either be an unintentional fabrication (he imagined the event but thought it was real), an intentional fabrication, or it can be a truthful account of actual events. No matter what it is, the conversion of Saul to Paul was a crucial event in the history of Christianity, and one that helped to reshape the world. Paul's missions all over the Mediterranean, from the Levant to Turkey, Greece, Malta—and ultimately to Rome—was an integral part of the rapid spread of Christianity. The fact that Roman law allowed citizens unrestricted travel allowed Paul to travel extensively.

At first, many of the believers in Jesus' resurrection, including Peter and James, remained active in the Jewish faith, but eventually, their beliefs led to their expulsion from the Jewish community. In 59, Paul sought protection from the Jews by the Romans, who were historically tolerant of cults as long as they were not seen as threats to the empire. As the Christian movement became stronger, this tolerance decreased. The refusal by Christians to pay homage to the Roman gods nor recognize the deification of the emperor invoked the anger of the emperor Nero, who began to persecute Christians beginning in 67.

A formal structure for Christian beliefs was never established by Jesus himself, who was born Jewish and died Jewish. Groups of believers congregated in private homes called *tituli*, and as populations grew, these became dedicated for congregations. At these tituli, the first Christian art works, both mosaics and paintings, were created. The ritual, or service, includes readings from the Old Testament; a dinner that invoked the Last Supper; the *Eucharist*, in which the bread and wine are consecrated and then consumed; and a sermon by the leaders of the congregation. The Mass, from the Latin *Missa*, which means dismissal, developed from these early congregations of prayer. *Catacombs*, underground rooms and passages used for tombs, were used for burials by Christians, Jews, and pagans alike, but not for formal places of assembly, nor were they secretive places of refuge for significant quantities of Christians, persecuted or otherwise. Like tituli, catacombs in Rome were early sources of Christian art.

Christianity developed footholds in Western Asia and Northern Africa, but the martyrdoms of Peter and Paul in Rome began a chain of events that culminated in Rome becoming the epicenter for the new religion. The persecution of Christians, which had been inconstant since Nero, was revived for one last time under the emperor Diocletian in 303–304, who had divided the empire in two in 293. In 312, Flavius Valerius Aurelius Constantinus, or Constantine I (272–337) became the emperor of the Western Empire. He had been engaged in a civil war with Maxentius. On the eve of the decisive battle with Maxentius at the Milvian Bridge near Rome, he had a dream or vision in which there were the Greek letters *chi rho*, the first two letters in the spelling of the Greek word for Christ, and the message *in hoc signo vinces*, which translates "in this sign you will conquer." Constantine instructed that a *vexillum*, a military standard, be made with the chi rho symbol now commonly referred to as a *christogram*. This new standard with the Christian symbol was named a *labarum*. The next day, Constantine's army routed Maxentius's army, and on the following day, he marched victoriously into Rome. One year later, Constantine signed the Edict of Milan, along with Licinius, the emperor of the Eastern Empire, which formally established religious tolerance within the Roman Empire.

The battle at the Milvian Bridge was memorialized in the inscription of the entablature of the Arch of Constantine (first noted in Chapter Twelve), which was dedicated on the tenth anniversary of Constantine's reign, in 315. A part of the inscription, which would have originally been inlaid with gilded bronze letters, reads: "QUOD INSTINCTU DIVINITATIS MENTIS," or "because of divine inspiration and his own great spirit."

In the early days of Christianity, there was much disagreement among various congregations concerning some of the tenets of the faith. These were resolved at the First Council of Nicaea, a town in Northwestern Anatolia, in 325. There, under Constantine's direction, 300 bishops convened and drafted the Nicene Creed. Although the pagan religion would still be observed by some until the sixth century, the effect of Constantine's conversion was the final push that Christianity needed in its ascendancy to become the world's most popular religion. In 330, Constantine founded the city of Constantinople on the site of the ancient Greek city Byzantium. Fifty years later, Constantinople became the seat of the Eastern Empire.

Several churches in Rome grew from sites which had been tituli, including: **Santa Maria Maggiore** (432), which was a Roman basilica; **San Lorenzo fuori le Mura** (432, 578, 1216), originally two churches whose abutting apses and adjacent walls were removed in 1216 to form one church; and **Sant'Agnese fuori le Mura** (625–38), built on the site of the tomb of Saint Agnes. There were two models for Early Christian churches. The first was the Roman basilica, a building that was used as a law court beginning in the late second century BCE. The name derives from the Greek *stoa basileios*, or royal stoa. The Roman basilica had a nave that was two stories high, and columns all around the perimeter. The aisles were two storeyed, and both communicated with the nave —. a space that was two storiess tall. The *apse* in the Roman basilica, a semicircular projection located at the center of the shorter ends, was incorporated into the Christian adaptation. An altar with a *ciborium*, or *baldacchino*, a canopy structure, was placed above the tomb of the saint or the depository for the saint's relics. If a Christian basilica had an upper floor above the aisle, this was called a *gallery*. Men and women typically occupied separate areas of the nave, but sometimes the women occupied the gallery, in which case it was called a *gynaecea*. The architectural language and methods of construction and construction of Early Christian architecture are essentially Roman. Additionally, the actual materials, in particular, but not limited to, columns and capitals, were taken from Roman buildings, especially as the use of the pagan structures waned.

The establishment of the Christian ritual—the Mass—had a significant effect upon the architectural development of the church. The sacrifices and offerings that were the key elements of the Greek and Roman religions were events that took place outside the religious structure, the temple. The Christian ritual required interior space; therefore, several Roman building types were available: the theater, the public baths, the Pantheon, and the basilica; the basilica is the one that was adopted.

FIGURE 16.2

Basilica Julia. Roman Forum. The basilica form was adopted by Christians for congregational purposes such as the celebration of the Missa.

The ruins of several secular Roman basilicas in the Forum offer a vivid understanding how these buildings were designed. The **Basilica Julia** (12), named after Julius Caesar and located in the Roman Forum, is a well-known example of the Roman basilica prototype. It was a civil court that housed the Court of the Hundred, which dealt with matters of inheritance. It had a wide nave and double aisles. The Basilica Aemelius Paullus (55–34 BCE) was two stories tall and was entirely supported by colonnades. The **Basilica Nova**, or **New Basilica** (306–313) was begun by Maxentius and finished by Constantine, and for years it was known as the *Basilica Constantine*. It has three large coffered vaults still *in situ* and is one of the more recognizable monuments of the Forum.

The first of several churches commissioned by Constantine was **San Giovanni in Laterano, or the Lateran Basilica** (330). Like many churches to follow, its form resembled the secular basilicas: a wide central nave, with narrower side aisles, and an apse at the end. Also like many early churches, the exterior was relatively plain; elaborate decorations were reserved for the interior.

The Basilica Church of St. Peter, or Old St. Peter's, (330) was Constantine's largest building project. It was preceded by a large atrium with gardens and fountains called Paradise. It had double aisles, although a single aisle would become more standard. A mosaic that decorated the arched opening at the western end of the nave (preceding the apse) showed Constantine presenting a

FIGURE 16.3

Fresco of Old St. Peter's Basilica.

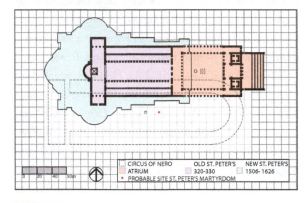

FIGURE 16.4

St. Peter's Basilica Plan.

FIGURE 16.5

Mosaic Floor Map. Church of St. George, Madaba, Jordan. Segment Showing the Old City of Jerusalem (mid 6th c.): note the Church of the Holy Sepulchre (bottom center) and the colonnaded road Cardo Maximus (center).

model of his church to St. Peter. After falling into disrepair, the old basilica was demolished in the sixteenth century and replaced by the current basilica.

In 325 Emperor Constantine sent a letter to Macarius, the bishop of Jerusalem, ordering the construction of a church at the site of the burial place of Christ, the Church of the Holy Sepulcher (326–335). Because the most important tenet of the Christian faith is that Christ was resurrected from his tomb three days after his death, the church is arguably the most important site in all of Christendom. The historical and archaeological support for the authenticity of the site is circumstantial rather than direct, but the body of evidence weighs strongly in its favor. First, in the first half of the first century, the site was an abandoned quarry, and other tombs fashioned from the cavities left by the quarrymen have been found. Second, there was a tradition that liturgical services were held at the site until the year 66. Third, it was located outside the city walls at that period, as was noted in the New Testament. Finally, when the city walls were expanded between 41 and 43, the area was not built over, suggesting that it was a sacred place from the beginnings of Christianity.

The church had four distinct parts: a front atrium, an apsidal basilica, a courtyard, and a small rotunda on the site of the burial place of Jesus. The caliph Hakim destroyed the church in 1009, and only the rear courtyard and rotunda were rebuilt. Since then, the church has been damaged by fire, an earthquake, and years of neglect and inadequate repairs. Today, the site lacks the grandiosity it would naturally be assumed to have, such as the Basilica of St. Peter in Rome, or even the Kaaba in Mecca. The approach is crowded by neighboring buildings. The front façade is a patchwork of repairs and alterations, and thus asymmetrical and plain. It does, however, showcase its beleaguered history, for better or for worse.

Constantine also commissioned the **Church of the Nativity** (339). It was built above the grotto which is revered as the birthplace of Jesus. The church was destroyed during the uprisings in the sixth century against the Byzantine Empire by the Samaritans. The current structure was rebuilt by Justinian, the Byzantine emperor.

At Syagha, in Jordan, a basilica-style church was constructed in the second half of the fourth century at the

FIGURE 16.6

Rope Cross Mosaic. Syagha Monastery Church (late 4th c.). Mount Nebo, Jordan.

site believed the place where Moses was presented the "promised land" and where Moses died (Deuteronomy 34:5). The **Mount Nebo Church** was remodeled in the fifth century and rebuilt in the late sixth century.

The second model for the Early Christian church was a centralized plan, either an octagon or a circle. **Santo Stefano Rotondo** (468) in Rome, which has a circular plan, was modeled after the rotondo of the Church of the Holy Sepulcher, and is the only early circular church that has survived. Two prototypes for a round structure in Rome were the Pantheon, which had a coffered concrete roof, and the so-called **Temple of Minerva Medica** (fourth century), which was actually a *nyphaeum*, a monument dedicated to nymphs. Santo Stefano Rotondo, however has a wood roof, supported by two freestanding Corinthian columns near the center and two smaller columns at the inner circular colonnade.

The destruction of pagan temples began before the end of the fourth century. Although one emperor after Constantine, Julian (reigned 361–363), tried in vain to stem the rise of Christianity and the demise of paganism, by the end of the fourth century the Christian religion had reversed places with paganism. The emperor Theodosius (reigned 378–395) outlawed pagan sacrifices

and ordered the closing of all pagan temples. The use of *spolia*, stone masonry and decorative sculpture taken from ancient buildings, was a common practice in the declining years of the Roman Empire. The **Co-Cathedral of St. Secondiano** (sixth century; reconstructed sixteenth century), in Chisui, Italy is an example of such a practice. It was built on the site of a secular basilica. Capitals, of different designs, were taken from that structure. Subsequent renovations again reused them.

As mentioned in Chapter Twelve, some (though not many) Roman temples were converted into Christian places of worship. The reason so few were adapted is simple: unlike Christian churches, Roman temples were not meant to be places of congregation. The **Tempietto sul Clitunno**, or **Temple of Clitumnus** (converted c. sixth century–eighth century) in Umbria.

Throughout this period, the form of the basilica continued to develop. A *narthex*, an entrance vestibule, was added to the front of the church. A separate *campanile*, or

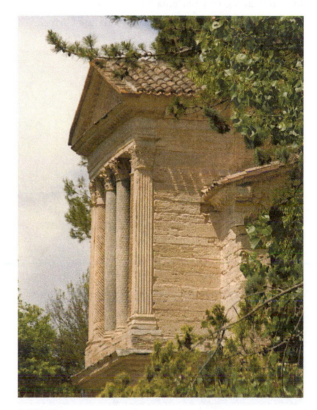

FIGURE 16.7

Tempietto sul Clitunno, or Temple of Clitumnus. Umbria, Italy.

bell tower, became a common feature during the period. Auxiliary rooms for the clergy and baptisteries also were developed.

In the last half of the first millennium, the greatest contribution of art and architecture came during the Carolingian dynasties, especially under Charlemagne, named king of the Franks in 768 and crowned emperor of the reborn Western Roman Empire in 800, by Pope Leo III in Rome. Charlemagne championed a renaissance of the arts, and looked for cultural inspiration from the Eastern Empire even as he competed with the East for influence in Rome.

Not many buildings from this period, often called Pre-Romanesque, have survived, but the best example is the **Palatine Chapel**, or **Aachen Cathedral** (786–805) at Aachen in Germany, which was considerably influenced by what took place in Ravenna earlier in the millennium, specifically San Vitale in Ravenna. Aachen was the location of hot sulfur springs, but was an insignificant town until the arrival of Charlemagne. He built a palace there and ordered the construction of the Palatine Chapel.

FIGURE 16.8

Corinthian Capital with Cross. Basilica of St. John. Ephesus, Turkey.

FIGURE 16.9

Aachen Cathedral. Germany.

When it was completed, it had the largest dome north of the Alps. Charlemagne ruled the Western Empire from Aachen, until his death in 814, and is buried in the cathedral. Otto I, or Otto the Great (936–975) was crowned the German king in 936, and for the next 500 years, most of the German kings were crowned in Aachen.

Carolingian church architecture was characterized by the placement of apses at each end; a design later used extensively in Byzantine architecture. The Carolingian architects preferred a centralized plan, like at San Vitale in Ravenna, whereas Ottonian architects used timber-framed roofs, hallmark features of Early Christian churches such as Sant'Apollinare in Classe in Ravenna. Although historians typically associate the Palatine Chapel, specifically, and Carolingian architecture in general, with Medieval architecture, a more appropriate association is with Late Antiquity. Charlemagne saw his empire as the rightful heir to Rome, and the design of the chapel at Aachen is more closely linked to Roman architecture than it is to the Romanesque.

The nave of Aachen Cathedral, which is the old chapel, is an octagon. Eight massive columns support an open gallery above. The upper story arches are supported by columns that were taken from Roman buildings in Trier, Rome, and Ravenna that were no longer in use.

For Further Discussion

Architects are often given *programs*, which are detailed descriptions of the needs and wishes of their clients. For instance, a corporation building an office building may list the number and size of offices, ancillary spaces such as computer rooms, lunch rooms, and conference rooms. The architect is told, or asks, how many conference rooms, for how many people? He or she may also ask, is privacy an issue for certain employees? If so, for how many? Prepare a brief program for an architect building a church, say in the sixth century, and then prepare a similar one for an architect building a Greek or Roman temple? How would they compare?

CHAPTER SEVENTEEN

The Byzantine Empire

Once out of nature I shall never take
My bodily form from any natural thing,
But such a form as Grecian goldsmiths make
Of hammered gold and gold enamelling
To keep a drowsy Emperor awake;
Or set upon a golden bough to sing
To lords and ladies of Byzantium
Of what is past, or passing, or to come.[1]

— "Sailing to Byzantium," W.B. Yeats (1928)

When William Butler Yeats (1865–1939) wrote the poem "Sailing to Byzantium," the name of the city of Constantinople had not yet been changed to Istanbul; that would take place five years later. Yeats chose to use the ancient name of the city, Byzantium, which was founded in the seventh century. BCE and renamed Constantinople in 330. Yeats's poem is about a spiritual journey, one that takes place in the mind of the narrator of an older man (Yeats was sixty when he wrote it), and Byzantium becomes a metaphor for that journey. He chose it because it was "the center of European civilization and the source of its spiritual philosophy."

Between 330 and 400, Constantinople grew tenfold, from around 35,000 inhabitants to around 350,000. The city became a model for cities of the late Classical and Post-Classical world and became the political and economic center of the Eastern Roman Empire (330–1453). The use of the term *Byzantine Empire* began at the end of the sixteenth century; its citizens would have thought of themselves as members of the Roman Empire until it was overrun by the Ottomans in 1453. They considered themselves protectors of classical traditions in literature and the arts. Nonetheless, as the Romans ultimately sought and discovered their own cultural voice, departing in some respects from Greek influences, the Byzantines forged their own separate culture, adapting and reinventing the Roman ways.

The political boundaries of the empire expanded and contracted almost continuously during its twelve centuries, but as a culture, it remained relatively constant. The most notable exception was the rise and fall of *iconoclasm*, a movement that believes that the use of religious images is heresy. The use of images was an important tool in the spread of Christianity, especially in the conversion of the illiterate, which represented the majority of the population. Iconoclasts rejected the use of images as idolatry, prohibited as one of the Ten Commandments:

> *Thou shalt not make unto thee any graven image, or any likeness of any thing that is in heaven above, or that is in the earth beneath, or that is in the water under the earth.*[2]

1   William Butler Yeats, "Sailing to Byzantium", The Poems of W. B. Yeats: A New Edition. Copyright © 1961 by Macmillan Publishing Company. Reprinted with permission.

2   "Exodus 20:4," King James Bible. Copyright in the Public Domain.

Leo III the Isaurian (reigned 717–741) issued an edict in 726 that ordered the removal of icons from public view. The only image that was acceptable was the cross. In 754, under Constantine V, icons and relics were destroyed by imperial soldiers. Icons were restored by the Seventh Ecumenical Council at Nicaea, but in 815 Leo V (reigned 813–820) revived iconoclasm. Icons were restored again in 843. The iconoclastic periods in the east, although short-lived, further intensified the division between the eastern church, based in Rome, and the western church, based in Constantinople, a division that began ostensibly as a disagreement over minor dogmatic details, but practically as a rivalry for power and influence.

As in Rome, the early Byzantine churches were either in the form of the Roman basilica or they were centralized, either octagonal or circular. In the Middle Byzantine period (843–1204), a plan often used was one in which a *Greek cross* (a cross in which all four arms are of equal length) was set within a square.

The greatest contribution of Byzantine architecture, from a structural viewpoint, is the development of the circular dome perched upon a square base. The circular dome of the Pantheon was related to a circular plan beneath it. The development of the dome over square and octagonal spaces was achieved through a transitional structural element called a *pendentive*, a triangular segment of vaulting, which spans between the arches that support a dome or circular construction above. Another innovation was that bricks were laid in thick mortar beds to create lighter vaults. Domes were sometimes placed in the form of a *quincunx*, a formation of five objects that has one object in each corner, and one in the center, like the five dots on dice or playing cards.

The most important artistic feature of Byzantine architecture was the use of mosaics, the quality of which is unsurpassed by any other period or style in history. Mosaics covered the surfaces of the interiors of domes, walls, apses, and vaults, depicting scenes from the Old and New Testaments, historical figures, the saints and apostles, and the four evangelists. These are accompanied by decorative elements, such as trees, plants, and animals. Background colors are commonly gold, a grass green, or midnight blue. Figures of the Christ, Mary, and the saints are typically shown frontally. Communities that could not afford mosaics used fresco paintings.

Byzantine churches generally have plain exteriors, either of exposed brick masonry, or stucco. The focus of Early Christian, and especially Byzantine, architecture, was the interior space. The relative plain brick exteriors of the Ravenna churches and monuments give little indication of the beauty inside.

St. Helen (c. 250–330), the mother of Constantine, was an influential figure in the sudden upwelling of Christianity during the early fourth century. She is said to have discovered, in Jerusalem, what Christians believe is the cross upon which Jesus was crucified. She is also said to have founded several churches, including the **Panagia Ekatontapyliani**, or the **Church of One Hundred Doors** (326), in Parikia, on the Greek island of Paros. Its beauty is derived from its rusticated stone masonry, not mosaics.

In the later years of the Classical period, the city of Ravenna, a town isolated by the marshes of Northeastern Italy, became a center of cultural prominence. In an attempt to seek refuge from the Barbarian invasions, in 402 the Roman emperor Honorius (reigned 393–423) moved the capital of the Western Empire from Rome to Ravenna, which became known as the "Byzantium of the West." When the Western Roman Empire was overthrown by northern tribes in 476, their leader Odoacer (433–493), became the first king of Italy. From 476 to 576, Ravenna was controlled by the Ostrogoths. The Byzantine emperor Justinian (483–565) believed that the triumph of Christianity was a key to rebuilding Roman supremacy, and in 540 he reconquered Ravenna. He eventually reconquered all of Italy in an attempt to reunite the empire, but in 568 the Lombards took all the land he had taken from the Ostrogoths.

Several monuments from this period are important in the histories of art and architecture. The **Tomba di Galla Placidia** (c. 425–450), was built as a mausoleum for the beautiful and precocious sister of Honorius, who usurped the rule of the Western Empire from her son, Valentinian. Though very small, it is considered the first significant work in the Byzantine style of architecture. The well-preserved mosaics in the interior are of

FIGURE 17.2

Interior of Galla Placidia: Mosaic with Christ and Lambs.

FIGURE 17.3

Exterior of St. Vitale. Ravenna, Italy.

FIGURE 17.4

Interior of St. Vitale. Ravenna, Italy.

predominantly blue tones and are of a workmanship that evokes the classical pursuit of the ideal.

The mosaics of the **Church of San Vitale** (540–548), specifically in the choir and the apse, are, singularly, the masterpiece of Byzantine art. It has an octagonal plan, with a raised concentric dome that is raised like a clerestory to allow light to penetrate into the interior. Like the Tomb of Galla Placidia and the other churches built in Ravenna during this time period, its exterior is simple – exposed brick and unarticulated arched windows, although there is subtle brick detailing. The mosaics in the interior are predominantly green and gold.

The **Basilica di Sant'Apollinare in Nuovo** (493–525) is a basilica-styled church. Mosaics cover the interior wall above the colonnade. On the north side the three Magi and twenty-two virgin martyrs are seen in procession,

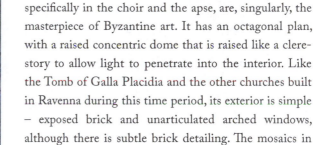

FIGURE 17.5

John the Baptist Baptizing Christ. Dome Mosaics. Arian Baptistery. Ravenna, Italy.

FIGURE 17.6

Interior of Sant'Apollinare in Classe. Near Ravenna, Italy.

The Byzantine Empire 171

FIGURE 17.7

Apse of Sant'Apollinare in Classe. Near Ravenna, Italy. On either side of the central cross are Elijah and Moses; three lambs symbolize the saints St. Peter, St. James and St. John (scene from the Transfiguration of Jesus); below, Saint Apollinaris and twelve lambs, representing the faithful flock.

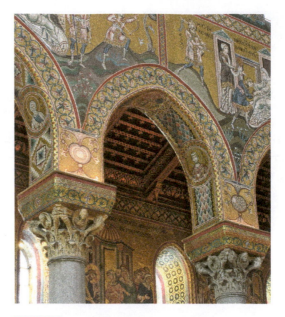

FIGURE 17.8

Interior of Sant'Apollinare Nuovo. Ravenna, Italy.

offering gifts to the Virgin Mary and the infant Jesus. On the south side there is a procession of martyrs. The **Basilica di Sant'Apollinare in Classe** (534–9) is also basilica-style in plan. On the wall above the arched opening at the western, or apse end, are mosaics of the symbols of the four evangelists: St. John, who is represented as an eagle; St. Mark, who is represented as a winged lion, because his Gospel emphasized the royal nature of Jesus; St. Matthew, with an inkwell; and Luke, represented by an ox, an allusion to the sacrifice. Twelve lambs, representing the apostles, climb the "hill" created by the apse. In the apse itself, there is a full-length figure of St. Apollinare, and 12 more lambs in a lush green landscape with trees and birds. In contrast with the later establishment of the religion of Islam and the subsequent standards and laws for the decoration of mosques, Byzantine art is seen as a stimulus for the understanding and contemplation of the Christian faith. It is both symbolic and representational, and it is both decorative and functional.

The **Tomb of Theodoric** (sixth century) is circular in plan, with a flat stone roof made from a single slab. These buildings are the direct descendants of Roman architecture, but as the Romans adapted the Classical language they borrowed from the Greeks, the Byzantine architects—like other Early Christian architects in the

FIGURE 17.9

Interior of Hagia Sophia. Istanbul, Turkey.

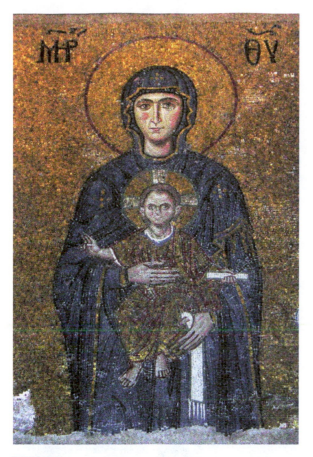

FIGURE 17.10

Mosiac of Virgin Mary and Christ Child. Hagia Sophia. Istanbul, Turkey.

Mediterranean—adapted Roman buildings and made them their own.

The **Hagia Sophia** (532–37) in Istanbul is the masterwork of Byzantine architecture. It was designed by two mathematicians, Anthemius of Tralles and Isidorus of Miletus. Early in the church's history, it was damaged by an earthquake and repaired. It was the center of the Greek Orthodox Church (the eastern St. Peter's), until Constantinople was conquered by Mehmet II in 1453. Mehmet added a minaret (later, three more were added), and converted the Hagia Sophia into a mosque. In 1934 it was turned into a museum. From 537 until the completion of the cathedral in Seville in the sixteenth century, the Hagia Sophia was the largest cathedral building in the world.

The name *Hagia Sophia* means "divine wisdom." It was built by the emperor Justinian (483–565), who ruled the Byzantine Empire at the peak of its prominence. He is said to have exclaimed upon entering the building, "Glory to God who has thought me worthy to finish this work. Solomon, I have outdone you," referring to the Temple of Solomon in Jerusalem. The exterior of the building, which rises gently but emphatically above the skyline, is visible from both the Bosporus and the Sea of Marmara, the bodies of water surrounding the ancient section of Istanbul. The exterior walls are of smooth plaster, currently painted red-orange. The lack of detailing and the overwhelming effect of the massive buttresses (added to protect the building from further damage by earthquakes) are imperfections that diminish the exhilarating effect caused by the scale and positioning of the building during a first impression. The exhilaration returns, however, immediately upon entering the interior. If the Baths of Caracalla had survived antiquity intact, there would be another building of possibly equal stature. As it is, the Hagia Sophia is the first masterpiece in the history of architecture whose main source of beauty—its interior space—survives to the present day.

The building is simple in plan, but complicated in section, and in its structural scheme. A central dome is supported on four massive piers, which in turn support, on the north and south ends, two half domes, and finally two *exedra*e (singular *exedra*), semicircular areas with smaller half domes. The larger half domes serve as buttresses for the horizontal force of the main dome—the natural tendency of the dome to flatten and push outward. In the pendentives are mosaic figures of

FIGURE 17.11

The domes of the Basilica San Marco. Venice, Italy.

FIGURE 17.12

Narthex Mosaic of the Basilica San Marco. Venice, Italy.

FIGURE 17.13

The Translation of St. Mark's Body. Narthex Mosaic, Basilica San Marco. Venice, Italy.

the Archangels Gabriel, Michael, Raphael, and Israfil. Other mosaics were covered by plaster when the church was converted into a mosque, but were restored in the twentieth century.

During the Fourth Crusade in 1204, Constantinople was sacked by the Latins. Some of the Hagia Sophia's relics and works of art were taken to a city that had become the Byzantium of the West, Venice. They would eventually find a home in Venice in **Saint Mark's Basilica**, or **Basilica San Marco** (1063–1073), the second masterpiece of Byzantine architecture. If quality and quantity are combined as a standard of measure, the basilica possesses the greatest collection of mosaics of any location in the world. It is situated at the eastern end of the Piazza San Marco. With the adjacent Piazzetta, which links the basilica to the Doge's Palace and to the lagoon, the basilica is a tour de force illustration of successful urban design. St. Mark's is a combination of Byzantine and Romanesque styles, but like St. Basil's Cathedral (described below), the compartmentalization of its design into any particular style would deny it its distinctive qualities and its particular approach to beauty.

According to Venetian legend, St. Mark, returning from a mission, landed on the site of the future city of Venice when his ship was blown off course by a storm. An angel foretold to him that his body would be returned to the site after his death, and that the site, a loose labyrinth of land and sea, would become a marvelous city. St. Mark continued his voyage, and was buried in Alexandria, the city built by Alexander in the delta of the Nile. In 828 two

Venetian merchants, Buono da Malamocco and Rustico da Torcello, travelled to Alexandria and stole the body of St. Mark. Their achievement, called a "Translation," is depicted in the mosaics of the lateral entrance portals.

The plan of St. Mark's is a Greek cross, created by the addition of two *transepts*, lateral areas of a church that align perpendicularly to the main axis. The narthex is

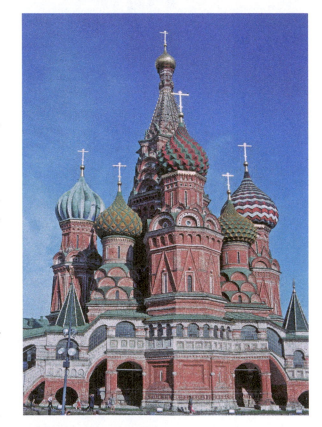

FIGURE 17.14

St. Basil's Cathedral. Moscow, Russia.

U-shaped, extending all the way around to the transepts. The *arcade*—the columns, capitals, arches, and the lower portion of the entablature—is decorated in brightly colored marble. Above the arcade, mosaics cover the walls, the pendentives, and the domes, depicting scenes from the life of Christ, the Old Testament, St. Mark, the Translation of St. Mark's body, and the Apocalypse. The *crossing* dome, where the nave and transept intersect, is called the Dome of the Ascension. Christ is in the center, having ascended into a starry sky, and he is surrounded by the apostles and the Virgin Mary. In the atrium there is a scene depicting the Tower of Babel under construction. The tower is Medieval, not Byzantine, and not Near Eastern, and not too dissimilar from the *campanile* in St. Mark's Square. It was very common for artists to place ancient events that took place in the eastern Mediterranean in a current Western European context, yet part of the mystique of St. Mark's in particular, and Venice in general, is the effortlessness of these transitions. St. Mark's Square, with its long, flanking Renaissance palaces, the Medieval campanile, the facade of the Byzantine basilica, and the adjacent Gothic Doge's Palace—all present their own styles in close proximity. It is the supremacy of craftsmanship that unites them, that makes them seem homogeneous, not style.

The Byzantine style was exported to Russia, but the resulting works of architecture, with their characteristic onion or bulb domes, seem only remotely affiliated with their Western relatives. **Saint Basil's Cathedral**, or more properly, **Cathedral of the Protection of Most Holy Theotokos on the Moat** (1555–1561), is conspicuously located on Red Square in Moscow. Red Square, like Tiananmen Square in Beijing, the Mall in Washington D.C., and St. Peter's Square in Rome, is the public square not only of the city of Moscow, but of an entire nation. It has eight domes, which are of different shapes and sizes and set at different heights. The domes are painted in different colors. The basic elements of Byzantine architecture were blended with traditional Russian vernacular architecture to create a singular design that can be found nowhere else in the world.

The many domes symbolize the 25 thrones of the New Jerusalem, of the Heavenly City, as described in the last book of the New Testament, *Revelation. Revelation*, written in the latter half of the first century, foretells the end of the world—the *apocalypse*—and specifically, the opening of the seven seals, which bring: The four horsemen—conquest, war, famine, and pestilence; the vision of martyrs; the darkening of the sun and moon; and the seventh seal—the seven trumpets of the seven angels and the Final Judgment. In 4:2–5, Jesus Christ, the Lamb of God, describes the Throne as Rome of the Heavenly City, which has a central throne for God the Father. The throne is like an emerald surrounded by a rainbow. Around this central throne are 24 more thrones, upon which the elders sit, wearing white robes and golden crowns.

One of the strengths of Byzantine architecture is its adaptability to local social and economic conditions. Architects and builders in smaller communities, or those of modest means or with limited access to materials, were still able to achieve an elegance of design best described as casual or non-monumental. The **Palace of the Despots** (fourteenth century) and other buildings in the ruined town of Mistra (located in the southern portion of the Peloponnese peninsula in Greece), offer glimpses into simpler Byzantine civic, religious, and residential architecture. Mosaics are replaced with wall paintings and frescoes, and the detailing is less refined; generally, the buildings are less compelling than the masterpieces of Byzantine architecture. Still, the pared-down style maintains many of its aesthetic attributes. A Christ figure, for instance, in the dome of a small church, appears to be of a remote, spiritual world—yet at the same time, accessible to this world.

In the eleventh and twelfth centuries, the Normans, the Scandinavian peoples whose ancestors were the *Norse* or the *Norsemen*, expanded into the Mediterranean, and from the mid-eleventh century until the mid-thirteenth century, they controlled the Southern Italy and the island of Sicily. Later they conquered Malta. Culturally and architecturally, the result was a blend of Norman, Arab, and Byzantine styles. This architecture was also called *Saracenic*.

The **Cappella Palatina** (1132–40) in Palermo, Sicily is a notable example of this blend of styles – Byzantine style mosaics, some of which were create by Greek artists, and Arab style marble geometric decoration. The exterior of **San Cataldo** (1160), also in Palermo, is an amalgam of styles. Its most notable Islamic feature is a row of three small stucco domes, painted red. A bell tower is inspired by contemporary Norman architecture. Its interior shows Byzantine influences. The gold and colored mosaics of the interior of **Monreale Cathedral** (1172–76) have elevated the status of the church to the extent it is mentioned often as one of the finest in all of Italy.

For Further Discussion

The *East–West Schism*, is the division between the Roman Catholic and the Eastern Orthodox churches took place in 1054 and has perpetuated ever since. Research three significant rituals that take place in one and not the other, and explore how these differences would affect the architectural design of the churches.

CHAPTER EIGHTEEN

Islam

Passing from the court of the Alberca, under a Moorish arch way, we entered the renowned Court of Lions. No part of the edifice gives a more complete idea of its original beauty than this, for none has suffered so little from the ravages of time. In the centre stands the fountain famous in song and story. The alabaster basins still shed their diamond drops; the twelve lions which support them, and give the court its name, still cast forth crystal streams as in the days of Boabdil. The lions, however, are unworthy of their fame, being of miserable sculpture; the work, probably, of some Christian captive. The court is laid out in flower-beds, instead of its ancient and appropriate pavement of tiles and marble; the alteration, an instance of bad taste, was made by the French when in possession of Granada. Round the four sides of the court are light Arabian arcades of open filigree work supported by slender pillars of white marble, which it is supposed were originally gilded. The architecture, like that in most parts of the interior of the palace, is characterized by elegance, rather than grandeur; bespeaking a delicate and graceful taste, and a disposition to indolent enjoyment. When one looks upon the fairy traces of the peristyles, and the apparently fragile fret work of the walls, it is difficult to believe that so much has survived the wear and tear of centuries, the shocks of earth quakes, the violence of war, and the quiet, though no less baneful, pilferings of the tasteful traveller; it is almost sufficient to excuse the popular tradition that the whole is tected by a magic charm.[1]

— from *Tales of the Alhambra* (1832) by Washington Irving (1783–1859).

In Washington Irving's collections of essays and stories, *Tales of the Alhambra*, descriptions of the Alhambra, such as the one above, are mixed with the retelling of stories and legends about the palace and the city of Granada, from both the Islamic and Spanish periods of occupation. The palace at Granada is the most famous example of Islamic architecture in Western Europe. The Muslim controlled much of Spain from the eight century to the end of the fifteenth century and left behind both the influence of Islamic architecture in subsequent Iberian architecture, as well as some entire Islamic structures that were left unscathed after their expulsion.

The relationship between Europe and the Near or Middle East has been fraught with political and religious conflict since the initial expansion of Islam during the Umayyad conquests in the eighth century, and thus the *Reconquista*, the recapturing of the Iberian Peninsula for Christianity, an eyewitness to surrender of the Alhambra noted that the Spanish royals, Ferdinand and Isabella, met Muhammad XII, the last Muslim ruler of Granada as the latter was leaving the palace with his entourage. By previous agreement, as part of the accord which ended the conflict, the sultan offered to kiss the hands of the king and queen, and the offer was declined.

Arabian, and by extension, Islamic culture has, in spite of religious and political tensions, has piqued the interest of Westerners for centuries. The stories that Scheherazade tells King Shahryar in *The Arabian Nights' Entertainment*, or *The Thousand and One Nights* are like watercolor vignettes of the Oriental world, from Turkey to India,

---

1   Washington Irving, Selection from Tales of the Alhambra. Copyright in the Public Domain..

stories that were once passed on orally from generation to generation. They are stories within a story. Shahryar, whose kingdom is located somewhere in Southern or Central Asia, discovers that his queen has been unfaithful to him. He kills her and her lovers, and in a vengeance against all womankind, selects and marries a virgin from his kingdom, sleeps with her one night, and then orders her execution the following morning. He has done this for a thousand nights until Scheherazade, his vizier's virgin daughter, convinces the king to listen to a story before he sends her, too, off to her death. He consents, but she does not finish the story in one night. The story is so fascinating that the king allows her to finish it the following night. She does, and then starts another story. This goes on for one thousand and one nights, until the king's heart is finally softened.

Islam comes from the Arabic words *islam*, meaning "submission" and *aslama*, meaning "to submit." It was founded by Mohammed (also Muhammad, (c. 570–632), who was born in Mecca (Arabic, *Mak-kah*), an oasis town in Western Saudi Arabia. In Mecca, Mohammed received the revelations from God through the angel Gabriel. This later became the basis of the *Koran* (also *Quran*), which contains the dogma of the Islamic faith. His teachings were at first rejected by the Meccans, and in 622 he was forced to leave. This is when he made his journey, later called the *Hegira*, or *Hejira*, to Medina. He and his followers returned to Mecca and fought with them, until Mecca surrendered to Mohammed's forces in 630. By the time of his death two years later in 632, Islam had spread throughout much of Arabia. In the early days of Islam, there was a bitter division of the faith into two separate groups concerning recognition of the first three caliphs after Mohammed. (A *caliph* was the title of the religious and political leader of all of Islam, until it was abolished in 1924.) The friction between the two groups—the *Sunni* and the *Shia*—persists even today.

The Koran contains 114 chapters called *suras*, and is written in verse, which the Muslim faithful learn from memory. The Koran is believed to be the word of Allah, (from the Arabic, *al ilah*, the God). The five principles of the Islamic faith, called the "Five Pillars," are: *hadj*, (also *haj*, or *haji*), a pilgrimage to Mecca that each Muslim

FIGURE 18.2

Geometric and Calligraphic Mosiac Decorated Mihrab (1354–55) from Isfahan, Iran. Metropolitan Museum of Art, New York.

make at least once in a lifetime; the *salat*, daily prayers five times a day; the *sawm*, fasting from sunrise to sunset during Ramadan, the ninth month of the Muslim year; *shahada*, an affirmation of Allah as the one and only God; and *zakat*, giving to the poor.

The *mosque*, or *musjid* (*Arabic*, place of prostration), is a place for communal prayers. It is the religious, social, and political center of Islamic life. Five times a day, at dawn (*fajr*), midday (*dhuhr*), afternoon (*asr*), sunset (*maghrib*), and nightfall (*isha'a*), and also on Friday evenings, the muzzein, the servant of the mosque, announces the *adhan*, the call to prayer, traditionally from a tower called the *minaret*. Men and women pray in their own areas, separated by a decorative screen called a *magsura*. The imam, the leader of the prayers at that particular mosque, intones for the prescribed recitations called the *rakah* from the *minbar*, or pulpit. The faithful face the *mihrab*, a niche that indicates the *qibla*, the direction of Mecca, specifically the Kaaba, which is a monument that marks the location of an ancient shrine built by Abraham. (The practices described above are for the Sunni branch of Islam. Those of the Shia branch are slightly different, such as the prayers being three times a day, not five.)

A wall separates the mosque area from the rest of the town or village, and a gate, called an *iwan*, or *liwan*, leads into the *sahn*, a courtyard area, which may be used for prayer. In Iran, this arch is called a *pishtaq*. The *iwan* developed gradually from what was, in the early days of Islam, a modest opening in the outer wall. Perhaps influenced by religious centers built for royal families, or perhaps in the spirit of competition, it was embellished over time.

Historically, the main materials used for decorative elements of the mosque are stone, brick, stucco, and terra cotta, depending upon the availability of natural resources. Stucco is common in Iran, as it was in ancient Persia. Stone was used where it is available, such as in Anatolia (modern Turkey). In the desert areas of Western Asia, brick was the most common structural material, again, as it was in antiquity. Terra cotta was used almost exclusively in Iran.

Unlike Christianity, the religious figure is, with rare exception, never used in the decoration of a mosque; Muslim law prohibits it. Decorative elements are typically geometric, architectural, vegetal, or inscriptive (mostly in Arabic, and typically a passage from the Koran). An *arabesque* is a pattern or decoration in which geometric components are intertwined with one another. A common architectural decorative element is the *muqarnas*, a section of a vault that resembles a stalactite or honeycomb. Although it may have been derived from a structural use, the muqarnas is typically used to give the surface a three-dimensional effect. In general, the decorations are used strictly for aesthetic purposes, and the clear intention is to prevent the ornamentation from distracting those who would be submitting their attention to God.

There are four main building types that are common in Islamic architecture: the mosque, the tomb, the palace, and the fort. Typically, Islamic architecture was adapted from local styles—in Egypt, Persia, Byzantium, or Visigothis (Spain). Characteristic architectural features are the horseshoe arch, the ogive, or pointed arch, the dome, the minaret, portals, courtyards, and geometric decoration.

The original place of prayer for Mohammed was a simple house that he built in Medina made from mud brick walls, and a flat roof of palm trunks and branches. His congregation at that point faced Jerusalem. In 624 Mecca became the focal point for Islamic prayer.

Islamic architecture is prevalent in Northern Africa, the Arabian Peninsula, and Southern Asia. In other areas, like Spain, its presence is significant, and in other areas there may be isolated examples. Although Arabic influence can be seen in all Islamic architecture, the style is adaptive to local materials, methods, and customs.

The **Haram esh-Sharif**, commonly known as the **Dome of the Rock** (688–691) in Jerusalem, was the first noteworthy Islamic structure. It has a mathematical design, both in its plan and section, which accounts for much of its aesthetic appeal. Although it is similar in plan to San Vitale in Ravenna, and the Mausoleum at the Palace of Diocletian in Split, the proportions of those buildings do not impress as much, and the clarity of the design, which can be seen from miles around, is greater. The building is Jerusalem's iconic work of architecture. Al-Mukadassi, a writer from Palestine from the tenth century, wrote of the building,

> *… in all of Islam I have not seen the equal; neither have I heard tell of anything built in pagan times that could rival (its) grace.*

The Dome of the Rock was built on the site of the most famous work of architecture of ancient Judea, the **Temple of Jerusalem** (957 BCE). The original temple housed the now-lost Ark of the Covenant. The site was the Temple Mount, the legendary site of Abraham's altar, which he was to use to sacrifice his son, Isaac. That temple was totally destroyed by the Babylonian king

Nebuchadnezzar II in 587 BCE, when the Jews were deported to Babylonia. Cyrus II conquered Babylon in 538 BCE, and allowed the Jews returned to Jerusalem. A second Temple of Jerusalem was completed in 515 BCE, enlarged by Herod in 20 BCE, then destroyed by the Romans in 70 CE. The only portion that survived is what is called the Western Wall, or the Wailing Wall, which was incorporated into the wall that encloses the Dome of the Rock. With the Church of the Holy Sepulcher nearby, the old center of Jerusalem is often referred to as one of the few places where the three dominant religions of Western civilization—Islam, Judaism, and Christianity—come together.

After the destruction of the second temple, the site remained barren until a mosque was built from spolia in 670. For Muslims, the building commemorates the place of Mohammed's Night Journey, which has two parts, the *Isra*, during which Muhammed traveled on a steed named Buraq to the "farthest mosque," and the *Mi'raj*, during which he traveled to heaven and spoke with God. Muslims believe that God related to Muhammed the instructions on how to pray.

The eponymous rock is located behind a wooden screen that dates from 1198. It is believed that Mohammed prayed at the rock, which lifted itself in the prophet's honor. The *mihrab* is the oldest surviving one in all of Islam. Mosaics that evoke a garden or an earthly or heavenly paradise, decorate the interior.

A second purpose of the building in addition to the commemoration of the Night Journey is clear from an Arabic inscription that decorates the octagonal exterior wall. It reads, in part: "The Messiah, Jesus, son of Mary, is only an apostle of God…God is only one God. Far be it from his glory that he should have a son." The prospective audience for this affirmation of "pure" monotheism, which dismisses the Christian concept of the Trinity, can be easily discerned.

The two small domes of the **Great Mosque** (eighth century–eighteenth century) in Tunis, Tunisia, were built in 864. They do not cover the assembly space, but rather a vestibule. The prayer hall has a flat roof. The minaret is square in plan, and is decorated with screen-like geometric stonework. The **Mosque of Ibn Tulun** (876–879) in Cairo

FIGURE 18.3
The Great Mosque. Tunis, Tunisia.

was designed by a Syrian architect, who wrote a letter while he was in prison to try and convince the builder, Ahmad, into hiring him; he succeeded. The entire structure is made from brick covered with stucco, into which is carved its decoration. It had been the desire of the caliph not to rob churches of their columns, which was a common practice, so the capitals are original. The Corinthian capital of acanthus leaves was restyled with vine leaves.

The **Sulemaniye Mosque** (c. 1560) in Istanbul, Turkey, was commissioned by Suleiman the Magnificent (1520–1566) after military successes in Iraq and the Balkans. The architect was Mimar Sinan (1491–1588), who constructed nearly 200 buildings in Constantinople. Sinan began as a mason, and worked his way up to be chief architect. Sinan combined elements, such as portals, with the structural logic of the Byzantine domes into a

FIGURE 18.4

Exterior of the Blue Mosque. Istanbul, Turkey.

FIGURE 18.5

Interior of the Blue Mosque. Istanbul, Turkey.

seamless unity. The **Blue Mosque** (1609–1616), also in Istanbul, was built by Sultan Ahmet I when he was 19 years old. The architect was Mehmet Aga.

Another important prototype of Islamic architecture is the madrasah (from the Turkish madrese). A madrasah is an Islamic theological seminary and university, which focuses on the Koran, but has a curriculum that includes law, mathematics, literature, astronomy, and other disciplines. The Ulugbek Madrasah (1417–1420) at Samarkand, Uzbekistan, is one of the great architectural masterpieces of Central Asia. It is named after the Timurid ruler, Ulugh Beg ("Great Ruler"), who was a mathematician and astronomer.

Moorish architecture refers to the buildings built by the Moors, the Islamic people who occupied Northern and Northwestern Africa, the Iberian Peninsula, Sicily, and Malta during the Medieval period. The **Alcazaba of the Alhambra** (1013–1090, 1230–1272), later **El Alhambra** (1334–1391), in Granada, Spain, was originally a hilltop fortress, or *alcazar* (Spanish, from the Arabic *al-kasr*, meaning "the castle") that became a lavish palace during the Nazirid dynasty (1236–1492), the last Muslim emirs in Spain, who were expelled on January 2, 1492. The word Alhambra comes from the Arabic *al-hamra*, which means "the red."

If architectural history was only concerned with the outward appearance of buildings, then the Alhambra would not be given much consideration. The exterior, with its plain stucco walls and tile roofs, gives only subtle hints

FIGURE 18.6

Ulugbek Madrasah. Samarkan, Uzbekistan.

FIGURE 18.7

Stalactite Ceiling of the Hall of the Abencerrajes. Alhambra Palace. Granada, Spain.

Court of the Lions. Alhambra Palace. Grenada, Spain.

of the elaborate decoration inside. The ornamentation of its interior, however, is as sumptuous as any residential interior space has ever achieved. The materials are mostly wood and plaster, both of which are normally considered too impermanent for the extensive detailing that has been applied. The richness of the architectural language, such as the stalactite arches and ceilings, gives the modestly sized spaces an ethereal quality, without compromising human scale. The most magnificent rooms—the Court of the Lions, the Court of the Myrtles, the Hall of the Ambassadors, the Hall of the Kings, and the Hall of the

FIGURE 18.10
Taj Mahal. Agra, India.

FIGURE 18.9
San Cataldo. Palermo, Sicily.

FIGURE 18.11
Detail at Main Entrance. Taj Mahal. Agra, India.

Two Sisters—have an individual identity, but do not compromise the uniformity of the overall design.

The Normans, who conquered England in 1066, conquered Sicily in 1061. From the late eleventh century until the mid-thirteenth century, an unusual mixture of cultures resulted in the development of Arab-Norman, or Sicilian-Norman architecture. The church of **San Cataldo** (1154) in Palermo, Sicily, with its distinctive three red domes, is an example of a harmonious blend of the two styles. Amalfi Cathedral (ninth century–thirteenth century), in the Campania area of mainland Italy, was predominantly built in the Sicilian-Norman style.

The **Taj Mahal** (1631–1643) is the mausoleum of Mumtaz Mahal, the favorite wife of the Mughal emperor Shah Jahan. During the period of the Mughal Dynasty (1526–1857), there was a peak in the quality and quantity of cultural achievements. Shah Jahan reigned from 1627 to 1658.

The Taj was designed to evoke the Islamic vision of the garden of paradise. It is surrounded by a wall that encloses an entrance court and gateway, gardens, the lotus pool, and finally, the mausoleum, flanked by a small mosque and hall, which are placed upon a platform 95 meters square and 6.7 meters high. At the corners of the platform rise four minarets that are 40 meters tall. Latticed marble screens filter daylight into the interior spaces. The light is soft, yet rich in color. This attitude and approach to daylighting in buildings is one of the trademark characteristics of Islamic architecture. It has been theorized that the Crusaders returning from the Levant and Egypt arrived with new ideas about architecture. These ideas were both literal—the ogive arch for instance—and conceptual.

PART

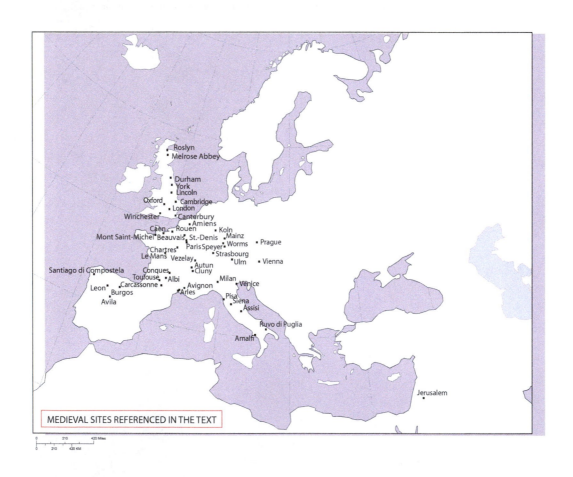

Roslyn
Melrose Abbey
Durham
York
Lincoln
Oxford
Cambridge
London
Winchester
Canterbury
Amiens
Caen
Rouen
Koln
Mont Saint-Michel
Beauvais
St.-Denis
Mainz
Prague
Paris
Speyer
Worms
Chartres
Strasbourg
Le Mans
Vezelay
Ulm
Vienna
Autun
Santiago di Compostela
Conques
Cluny
Toulouse
Albi
Milan
Venice
Leon
Carcassonne
Avignon
Burgos
Arles
Pisa
Siena
Avila
Assisi
Ruvo di Puglia
Amalfi
Jerusalem

MEDIEVAL SITES REFERENCED IN THE TEXT

0   210   420 Miles
0   210   420 KM

FIVE

The Middle Ages

The Medieval Period in European history is generally descriptive of that period between the end of antiquity and the beginning of the Renaissance. The Dark Age was an era of upheaval, resulting from the power vacuum that followed the decline of the Roman Empire. In the early years of the Middle Ages, the Vikings constantly raided the European continent. Thus, it was an era marked by civic and social instability. "Everywhere brute, improvident force reigned," is how Viollet-le-Duc described the era. The collapse of Rome, and its ability to organize all aspects of civic life, affected the stability of towns and cities all over the former empire. The economic growth, and the accumulation of wealth that had flourished in the imperial system, retreated as well. Trade, which depended both upon the safety of travel and the upkeep of Roman roads, bridges, and ports, declined. Disease and civil strife resulted in population decline. Large building projects—trademarks of the Roman world—were extremely rare in the Dark Ages.

By the first years of the second millennium, a revitalization of towns and cities had begun. Agricultural production increased, which contributed to an increase in population. The development of water mills and windmills helped spur the development of the textile industry. The maintenance and construction of roads and bridges were both aided by a new sense of civic duty. Medieval art and literature, heavily influenced by a widespread devotion to the Christian faith, forged an identity that broke away from Classical influences. Cults of the saints and the Virgin Mary fueled the construction of stone churches and cathedrals.

CHAPTER NINETEEN

Castles and Fortified Towns

To Hrothgar was given such glory of war,
such honor of combat, that all his kin
obeyed him gladly till great grew his band
of youthful comrades. It came in his mind
to bid his henchmen a hall uprear,
a master mead-house, mightier far
than ever was seen by the sons of earth,
and within it, then, to old and young
he would all allot that the Lord had sent him,
save only the land and the lives of his men.
Wide, I heard, was the work commanded,
for many a tribe this mid-earth round,
to fashion the folkstead. It fell, as he ordered,
in rapid achievement that ready it stood there,
of halls the noblest: Heorot he named it
whose message had might in many a land.
Not reckless of promise, the rings he dealt,
treasure at banquet: there towered the hall,
high, gabled wide, the hot surge waiting
of furious flame. Nor far was that day
when father and son-in-law stood in feud
for warfare and hatred that woke again.
With envy and anger an evil spirit
endured the dole in his dark abode,
that he heard each day the din of revel
high in the hall: there harps rang out,
clear song of the singer. He sang who knew {1d}
tales of the early time of man,

how the Almighty made the earth,
fairest fields enfolded by water,
set, triumphant, sun and moon
for a light to lighten the land-dwellers,
and braided bright the breast of earth
with limbs and leaves, made life for all
of mortal beings that breathe and move.
So lived the clansmen in cheer and revel
a winsome life, till one began
to fashion evils, that field of hell.
Grendel this monster grim was called,
march-riever mighty, in moorland living,
in fen and fastness; fief of the giants
the hapless wight a while had kept
since the Creator his exile doomed.
On kin of Cain was the killing avenged
by sovran God for slaughtered Abel.
Ill fared his feud, and far was he driven,
for the slaughter's sake, from sight of men.
Of Cain awoke all that woful breed,
Etins and elves and evil-spirits,
as well as the giants that warred with God
weary while: but their wage was paid them![1]

— from Beowulf *(anonymously written), trans-*
lated by Francis Gummere.

---

1   Selection from Beowulf, trans. Francis B. Gummere.
Copyright in the Public Domain.

The bloodline of J.R.R. Tolkien's twentieth-century heroic narratives *The Hobbit* and *The Lord of the Rings* can be traced all the way back to the end of the first millennium. Before writing the Middle Earth novels, Tolkien was a formidable medieval scholar. In 1936 he published a paper entitled "*Beowulf:* The Monsters and the Critics," which re-characterized *Beowulf*, not as a folk tale, but as an accomplished work, one that belonged in a pantheon of masterpieces of world literature. What *Beowulf* had to overcome was not insignificant—the traditional view of the Early Middle Ages as a cultural black hole.

Beowulf was written in Old English, and dates to sometime in the late first millennium. In the epic poem, Beowulf, who is from a kingdom in present-day Southern Sweden, travels to Denmark and kills a monster called Grendel, who had been terrorizing the inhabitants of a kingdom reigned by King Hrothgar. The monster would enter the king's mead-hall in the middle of the night, after those inside were in a deep sleep induced by food and drink. Grendel abducted, and then butchered, as many as 30 men in a single night. Beowulf kills Grendel, then returns to his homeland as a hero. He becomes king. Beowulf rules for 50 years, until a dragon begins to attack his own citizens. He slays the dragon, but later dies of his wounds.

Although there are several references to the Old Testament in *Beowulf*, it is not a religious text. It is a work of epic literature, comparable to both the *Iliad* and the *Odyssey* and the *Aeneid*. After killing Grendel, Beowulf arrives at the mead-hall holding the head of the slain monster by the hair and dragging it across the floor (it is obviously too heavy to lift, even for him) to display it to the king. He tells his audience that he could not have succeeded in killing Grendel without the help of God. The gods of the Homeric texts were seen to directly intercede and interfere in the actions of the heroes. In *Beowulf*, the intercession is more vague, but still effective.

Some early scenes in *Beowulf* take place in a mead-hall, a prototypical structure of Northern Europe and Scandinavia used for social and civic purposes. It is also known as a *longhouse*. The archaeological remains of royal mead halls, such as the one described at the beginning of Beowulf, have been discovered in Denmark and Sweden, and other locations in Scandinavia dating from the mid-sixth century. Because they were constructed of wood, there are only evidentiary remains of these buildings still in existence, although there are reconstructions at archaeological sites and outdoor museums. Longhouses ranged from 50 to 80 meters long. Their ancient equivalent, in both form and function, was the Greek *bouleuterion*.

With the fall of the Roman Empire, together with the dearth of urban centers north of the lands that had constituted the empire, evidence of monumental architecture in the latter two-thirds of the first millennium is largely absent today, compared to the Classical era that preceded it. This fact certainly has helped to perpetuate the description, first conceived by the Italian writer Francesco Petrarca (Petrarch) (1304–1374), that the Middle Ages were Dark Ages. Petrarch's term of disrespect was originally a criticism of literature, not culture in general, but today the term apples to all the arts. The decline of arts such as drama, philosophy and painting sculpture affected mostly the upper classes. The decline of architecture and civic monuments affected everyone, and affected towns and cities—how they looked and how they functioned. The creative well was not completely dry. As Christianity expanded into the north, churches were built, but many were small, others were lost to destruction by fire or by man, and others still were demolished at a later date so that a larger, more contemporary—Romanesque or Gothic—one could take its place.

The order that had characterized the Roman Empire was gone. The systematic approach throughout the empire, which had provided roads and other infrastructure, a monetary structure that had facilitated trade, legal machinery, and a bureaucracy for the collection of taxes and the distribution of government services—in essence all of the essentials of civic life—had vanished as well. Some of the monumental structures from the empire survived, but most did not. They fell into ruin, and thus were constant reminders of a glory that no longer was. To add insult to injury, the stone and marble that once made the towns and cities seem majestic, was removed from structures and burned to make lime, for use as stucco for more common structures, and as fertilizer for farmers' fields.

The word *medieval* is derived from the Latin words *medium* and *aevum* ("middle" and "age.") Francesco Petrarch (1304–1374) first used the expression in the fourteenth century as a derogatory label of the period between two eras he considered to be more enlightened—ancient Rome and the Renaissance. The approximate date of the Medieval Age in art and architecture is from the late tenth century to the late fifteenth century. *Late Antiquity*, discussed Part Four, has traditionally been labeled the Early Middle Ages. In this chronology the Middle Ages span from the end of the Roman Empire, beginning in either the fourth or fifth century, until the beginning of the Renaissance during the 1400's. In addition to the secular architecture from this period described in this chapter, there are two styles of art and architecture that dominate this period: *Romanesque*, which is subdivided into Pre-Romanesque and Romanesque (some historians use *Early* and *Late Romanesque*), and *Gothic*, which is subdivided into Early, Middle, and Late, or *Flamboyant*. Regional adaptations are prevalent in both styles. Although the terms *Romanesque* and *Gothic* are most often used to describe religious architecture, the language that was predominantly created for these non-secular works was used for secular building types as well, such as palaces and public buildings.

The rise of medieval architecture was predicated upon the winding down of the Viking invasions, which had been relentless; a moderation of the climate, which increased agricultural production, and thus allowed some stability and prosperity to occur; and an increase in the influence of the Church upon communities. The church dominated the physical appearance of towns and cities as well as their socioeconomic structures. This model would endure without being substantially altered until the urban sprawl of the twentieth century diluted cityscapes and townscapes in Europe and the rest of the world.

The most dominant characteristic of medieval secular architecture is its defensive posture. Most towns had walls that encircled them. Individual landowners, who were often at odds with the ruling authority of the region, also created an architecture that was designed for protection, the *castle*, which comes from the Latin word *castellum*, or fortified place. The owners of castles, and of more importance, the lands around them, were the *nobility*, a hereditary class of both power and wealth. The nobles of the Middle Ages were a warrior class; they constantly fought among themselves, mostly for greater power and greater wealth. The individual warriors who fought for the nobility were called *knights*, who had extensive training and expensive equipment—armor, weapons, horses, and an entourage that serviced these tools of fighting. A third class of people, the peasants, was by far the most populous. Some were free, other were serfs or slaves, but no matter their situation they were not immune to the violence that plagued their masters and lords. A fourth class, of skilled workers and merchants, would gain traction during the period, and would gain in status, wealth, and numbers.

The European Middle Age was a period of piety and religious commitment. The devotion of people of all classes was, for the most part, unquestioning. It was singular—*the Church* meant the Roman Catholic Church, and obedience to church dogma was to that which preceded from the Catholic hierarchy, and ultimately the pope. Yet it was also a period in which the populus—the believers—also played an important role. Pilgrimages to the holy sites, the sites of the martyrdom of saints, the Holy Land where Jesus lived and died, and places of known intercessions, or miracles became extremely popular. Individuals made the journey to seek intercessions on their own behalf, or to seek forgiveness from God for sins. Along the well-traveled paths of these journeys, monasteries, churches and cathedrals prospered, allowing abbot, bishops, and priests the opportunity to improve their structures, in both size and in beauty. Pilgrims visited the churches to see the relics of the saints. A relic could be a part of the body that was preserved, a skull, or hair, for instance. It could be a tunic or some other item of personal property. The relics were seen by some pilgrims to have powers to heal or otherwise intervene, a notion that was not dispelled by the church until 1563. Most important churches had a *reliquary*, a shrine in which the relics were stored. Some were designed so as to visible to the pilgrims.

The *Crusades*, military expeditions to the Levant to reclaim control of the Holy Lands, were both pilgrimages and holy wars. The First Crusade (1095–99), which has been called the "People's Crusade" was referred to as a pilgrimage until 100 years after it took place. Despite some initial failures, the First Crusade was successful in retaking Jerusalem for Christianity. Jerusalem was retaken by the Muslim leader Saladin in 1187. Saladin allowed the second **Church of the Holy Sepulcher** (1048) to remain open to Christians. It had been rebuilt after it had suffered damage at several times in the first millennium, including the final destruction in 1009 by the Muslims. The effects of the Crusades upon architectural history are two-fold. First, was the construction of Crusader castles all along the paths in Europe from the homelands of crusaders to the Mediterranean and the Levant. Second, was the introduction of architectural motifs from the Levant to the Europeans, such as the ogive arch, to be discussed in Chapter Twenty-One.

Some of the crusaders military Christian orders and self-proclaimed "soldiers of Christ." An *order* is a society, or fraternity, of monks, priests, or nuns devoted to a stated regulations and standards. The **Convent of Christ Castle** (1160) in Tomar Portugal is a crusader castle built by the Knights Templar, or the Poor Fellow-Soldiers of Christ and of the Temple of Solomon. The Temple of Solomon was the Templar name for the occupied Dome of the Rock, which became the Templar headquarters in Jerusalem during the Christian occupation of the city between 1099 and 1187. A second formidable military order was the Knights Hospitaller, or the Order of Saint John, which was established before the crusade began. The **Palace of the Grand Master of the Knights of Rhodes** (fourteenth century), Rhodes, Greece is a castle built on the site of a Byzantine citadel. It is a fortified castle with sporadic Gothic detailing on the exterior, such as the at the main gate, and throughout the interior.

The **Krak des Chevaliers** (twelfth century) in present-day Syria is the most distinguished of the crusader castles, castles built during the military expeditions made by the Europeans to reclaim the Holy Land from Islamic control from the eleventh through the thirteenth centuries. It could house up to four thousand soldiers.

The earliest castle prototype in England and Western Europe was the Iron Age *hillfort*, a settlement or place of refuge built upon a hill or hillock, often with several layers of earthen fortification walls or stockades. **Maiden Castle** (c. 600 BCE), in Dorset, England, had two and three layers of earthwork walls. It was kidney shaped, and had entrances at the shorter ends. Maiden Castle was called impregnable, which does not surprise. Concentrically walled towns and concentrically walled castles had a significantly higher rates of successful defense than ones with single walls.

As late as the eleventh and twelfth centuries castles were still being built out of earth and wood, not stone. A natural mound was flattened in the center, with its sides steepened to create a perimeter ditch. This reshaped mound was called a *motte*. The center flat area contained a timber house or a single tower called a *keep*, that could be used as a place of refuge or for defense. A *bailey* was a separate area enclosed by a *palisade*, a wooden fence, or a *curtain wall*, made of stone, that was connected to the motte by a bridge.

FIGURE 19.2
Tower of London. England.

FIGURE 19.3
Windsor Castle. England.

Of the more than 1500 surviving masonry castles in England, the two most famous are **Windsor Castle** (1170) and the **Tower of London** (c. 1086–1097). The oldest part of the Tower of London is the **White Tower**, built by William the Conqueror (r. 1066–1087). Among the many storied events in the history of the Tower of London, the most famous is the execution by beheading of Anne Boleyn, the second wife of Henry VIII. After more than three years of marriage, in which she had failed to produce a male heir to the king, she was tried and convicted for incest and adultery. In 1533 her marriage to Henry, and the subsequent excommunication of both Henry and Thomas Cranmer, the Boleyn family priest who had been appointed archbishop of Canterbury, triggered the separation of the Church of England from Roman Catholicism.

Castles often had their own private chapel, either built within the exterior castle walls, or as a separate structure on the estate. The royal palaces at Windsor and London were of exceptional design. **St. John's Chapel** (1077–97) at the Tower of London's White Tower is Romanesque in style. St. George's Chapel at Windsor was built later in the Gothic style.

The castle is a visible embodiment of social hierarchy. Most castles were built on the tallest and most strategic promontory of the area in which they were built, and is symbolic of the domineering relationship the castle and its occupants possessed over the towns people who lived below. The Czech writer Franz Kafka explored this nuance of "Old World" Europe in a surreal manner in his 1926 novel *Das Schloss*, or *The Castle*. The occupants of the castle are seen as aloof, alienated from the people who live in the village.

The situation of **Caerphilly Castle** (1268–1290) in Wales is unusual, in that instead of being perched high on a hilltop, it is located within a bowl, surrounded by low hills. Its major defensive elements are a man-made lake that completely surrounds the castle, and double ring walls. It was built for an earl, Gilbert "the Red" de Clare, not a king.

Burg Eltz, or **Eltz Castle** (ninth century–1540), situated high above the Moselle River in Germany, is one of only a few castles in Europe that have survived

FIGURE 19.4

Caerphilly Castle, Wales.

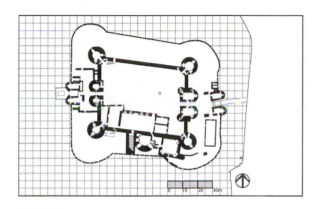

FIGURE 19.5

Caerphilly Castle Plan.

without significant destruction. The whitewashed walls of **Hohensalzburg Castle** (1077) in Salzburg, Austria are visible from throughout the city below. The octagon-shaped **Castel del Monte** (c. 1240), in the Apulia region of Italy, was built on the top of a promontory, and thus is visible from miles around. A ceremonial gateway entrance has the form of a triumphal arch, although the language is Gothic. The design of the castle was influenced by crusader castles its builder, Friedrich II, had seen in the Levant.

FIGURE 19.6

Castel Del Monte. Apulia, Italy.

The design of fortified towns had many aspects in common with castles, the main difference being that castles were built for a single king or lord and his family. The *battlement*, a parapet wall broken by slots, is the most conspicuous feature of the walls and towers of fortified towns and castles. The slots are called *crenels*, or *embrasures*, beveled openings in a parapet. A *merlon* is the alternating solid portion of the battlement. A *turret* is a small tower, sometimes corbeled, extending above a parapet. If a wall has turrets or battlements, or both, it is said to be *crenelated*, or *castellated*. If the uppermost parapet projects outward, it is called a *machicolation*, and the projection characteristically achieved through corbelled arches.

Town walls from the Medieval era can be seen today in all of Europe. Some of the most notable cities with extant walls are: Dubrovnik, Croatia; York, England; Lucca, San Gimignani, and Montereggione, Italy; Avignon, Aigues Mortes, and Saint Malo, France; **Rothenburg-ob-der-Tauber, Cochem, and Nordlingen, Germany; and Tallinn, Estonia.** The meticulously-constructed walls of **Avila,** in North-Central Spain, were built between 1088 and 1091. There are 88 cylindrical towers called *cubos*. When spaced closer together, they form the nine gates

The practice of building defensive walls that encompass a city is as old as the city itself, being first used at Jericho around 10,000 years ago. The walls of larger cities would be rebuilt outward from the central core when needed as populations grew and the city expanded. The estimated population of ancient Rome, on the other hand, had a population that peaked at around 1 million people. At the beginning of the fifteenth century, the population had decreased to around 20,000 people. A project to shorten the walls in the sixteenth century was abandoned, however, after only a few sections were built.

Some medieval towns had the appearance of a single, monumental work of architecture from a distance. This was achieved by the uniformity of its building materials—indigenous or natural stone walls, or white stucco, or a common roof material, such as clay tile. The defensive walls that surrounded a town could also help to create the effect of a singular construction. Some have survived without significant change until today.

Carcassonne (twelfth–thirteenth centuries) is a fortified town in Southern France. Due in part to its aggressive restoration by the renowned French architect Viollet-le-Duc in the nineteenth century, it has maintained its medieval character. Its most visible features are its two ring walls and 53 towers, most of which have roofs that originally looked like Chinese hats, but were restored by Viollet-leDuc to their present taller, conical shape. Inside the walls, two buildings are prominent, the church and the *chateau*. There are two main gates. Each gate is protected by a *barbican*, a fortified tower or outpost that projects beyond the natural line of the defensive wall, and thus exposes an attacking army on its flank. Additional round towers are spaced approximately 40–50 meters apart.

The siege of a medieval town could be attempted in four ways: using an overwhelming number of attackers

FIGURE 19.7

Carcassonne, France.

FIGURE 19.8

Le Mont St. Michel, France

FIGURE 19.9

Nykirke. Borholm, Denmark.

to minimize the effect of the defensive advantages of the fortifications; using siege engines to batter the walls; undermining the walls by digging under them; or simply surrounding the town and cutting off its link to resources needed for survival. In 1240 Carcassonne was attacked by the viscount of Beziers. Siege engines proved ineffective against the thick stone walls, so the attackers reverted to mining the gate near the church. The defenders used a technique called countermining, and successfully turned back the assault.

Le Mont St. Michel (tenth– fifteenth centuries) in Northern France comprises a monastery and village built on an outcropping of rock rising above the sandy plain called the *greve* at the Bay of Mont St. Michel. The site has two natural defense mechanisms: first, there are pockets of quicksand that make the greve hazardous on foot; second, the high tide, which comes in rapidly, surrounds the entire rock outcropping, turning it into an island. Shallow water boats that approach at high tide are stranded at low tide. Above the houses of the village is the monastery, with architecture of both the Romanesque and Gothic styles.

On the island of Bornholm, which is situated in the Baltic east of mainland Denmark and south of Sweden, are some examples of religious architecture that is secular in its character. An emphasis upon security and protection is clearly visible in some distinctive church architecture built more than a century after Viking raids had ended elsewhere. Because of its isolated position, the island was vulnerable to raids from both the Northern European mainland and from Sweden. During the twelfth century, residents of the island built four round churches that have a unique appearance among Christian church buildings. They were places of worship, but were also places of shelter in the case of an external raid. **Nykirke** (1150), in the village of Nyker, is the smallest of these churches. Its thick white-washed stone walls have small openings, effective for defensive purposes, but also helpful as combatants against winter storms. The other three churches on the island are Østerlars Church, Nylars Church, and Olsker Church.

For Further Discussion

Il Palio is an annual horse race that takes place twice each summer in the Piazza del Campo in Siena, Italy, a fan-shaped Medieval square. Research events in other cities which are Medieval traditions or are associated with Medieval architecture or public space. What is the relationship of these events with Medieval architecture?

CHAPTER
TWENTY

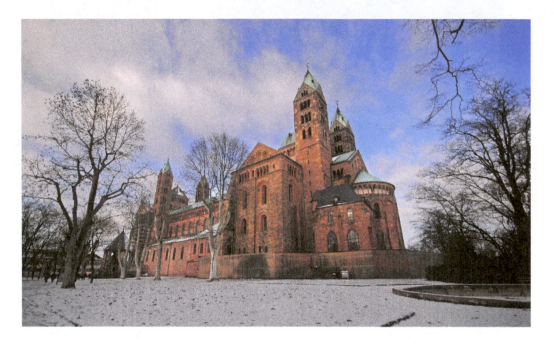

Romanesque

Elements of Roman architecture were reused and adapted to new functions. The groin vault was an innovation of Late Romanesque architecture, and became a prominent feature of Gothic architecture. A vaulted ceiling is one that is formed with a continuous arch. *Groins* are the curved edges of intersecting vaults. A *groin vault* is the vault formed by the intersection of two perpendicular vaults.

In Roman vaulting, the *voussoir*, the wedge-shaped stones that form the vault, act together as a curved planar surface. In *rib vaulting*, which superseded the Roman vault at the beginning of the twelfth century, structural stone "ribs" frame the edges of the vault, and lighter stones are used to infill the space between. If the section of the vault is divided into four parts, it is called a *quadripartite* vault. If it is divided into six parts, then it is called a *sexpartite* vault.

Blind arcades, decorative arches that resembled arched openings or arcades and attached to a blank wall, were another feature used frequently in France, Italy, and Germany. The main entrance of the west facade was embellished with either figurative or geometric decoration.

Territorial adaptations of the Romanesque style responded to recent architectural trends of the region. In France, the side aisle of the church was continued around the choir or chancel, the area in the front of the church reserved for the clergy. This is called an *ambulatory*. In England, the zigzag motif was used at the *arris*, the sharp edge of a curved surface. In Spain, an occasional Moorish element infiltrated the design. Various colored marbles in Italy were used as veneers on facades, many laid with exuberant, geometric patterns. A large round window, either a *rose window* or *wheel window*, appeared on the facades.

A *rose window* is simply a round window with stone (*tracery*) or metal dividers (*cames*), creating the pattern of a rose. In a *wheel window*, the radial lines are emphasized. Romanesque Italian architects were not complacent; the style varies, sometimes significantly, from city to city.

Two ancillary structures came into use during the Romanesque period in Italy: the *baptistery* was a separate building reserved for the sacrament of baptism, which was traditionally performed at Easter, the Pentecost, and the Epiphany; and the *bell-tower*, the Italian *campanile*.

In the decades that preceded the end of the first millennium, several dynasties gained prominence in western Europe and had sufficient longevity to experience a minor flourish in the arts and architecture. These are the Merovingian dynasty (fifth century–eight century), the Carolingian Empire (800–924), and the Ottonian dynasty (919–1024). Caroligian architecture, discussed in Chapter Sixteen, was essentially Roman in character. Merovingian and Ottonian architecture, while owing much to Roman structural and engineering methods, were more independent. All three are labeled *Pre-Romanesque* by architectural historians.

The **Abbey of Pomposa** (c. 800–c. 1100) near Ferrara, Italy is a transitional church with elements of Early Christian, Byzantine, and Romanesque styles. The interior resembles the naves of the Ravenna Byzantine churches, with the exception that mosaics, which decorate the apse and site wall above the colonnade, are now frescoes. The Abbey was founded in the Carolingian era.

The Romanesque style emerged gradually, not spontaneously, during the first half of the eleventh century from experimental design features in individual churches in what today is France, Western Germany, and Northern

Spain near the Pyrenees. At the time, this region consisted of *duchies* (territories of a duke or duchess) or *comté* ("free" regions). These included Bretagne, Normandie, Lotharingia in the north, Aquitaine in the west, and Bourgogne and Champagne in the east, and Toulouse, Aragon, and Cataluna in the south, as well as smaller regions. One of the earliest of the new features of the Romanesque style that appeared was the three-story nave, consisting of a colonnade at the lowest level, a *triforium* gallery, a series of three smaller arches situated above the arched opening of the lowest level, and an upper story, the level of clerestory windows. This layout is visible at the church of **Saint-´Etienne** (1050), Vignory. France.

In the north, an important development was that of a clearly articulated *westwerk*, or west front, the western entrance façade of the church consisting of a central rectangular tower corresponding to the interior nave flanked by bell towers. **Sankt Pantaleon** (late tenth century), in Cologne, Germany, had a single broad arch at the entrance. The **Abbaye-aux-Hommes,** or **St. Etienne** (1066–1086) in Caen, was begun by William the Conqueror (c. 1027–1087), the first Norman king of England, and was influenced by Speyer Cathedral. Its western facade, with its square towers and octagonal pinnacles, was a model for Gothic architects for the next several centuries. There are nine towers, topped with spires of varying heights, dispersed around the perimeter. Four of the towers are located at the east end, two close set at the beginning of the apse, and two that flank the apse, separated by flying buttresses.

In the south, the unmistakable influence of extant Roman ruins, which were more visible than in the north, can be seen in several churches. The façade of Abbey Church of Saint-Gilles (twelfth century– fifteenth century), St. Gilles-du-Gard, France, evokes the triumphal arch at Orange, with a central ceremonial arch flanked by two smaller arches. At Orange, the arches are, obviously, true openings. At Saint-Gilles, they become three portals, a ceremonial entrance, and two side entrances to accommodate the crowds exiting the Mass at the end of the service. The basilica form is seen behind this entrance porch. All of the arches are accentuated by both architraves, a banded molding around the outer surface

FIGURE 20.2

West Front. Abbey-aux-Hommes, or St. Etienne. Caen, France.

of the arch, and archivolts, concentric bands of molding at the arch's recesses.

The façade of **St. Trophime** (twelfth century–fifteenth century), Arles, France, evokes a single-arched triumphal arch, such as at nearby Glaunum. The west porch, built in the late twelfth century, is classically inspired, but clearly demonstrates the Romanesque quality of *joie de vivre,* especially in its sculpture. The porch is symbolic and decorative, not quite functional, as it only protrudes from the façade a short distance. The main portal arch springs from three columns on either side, which, uncommonly, have a sculpted base. The Old Testament figure Daniel is seen between two lions in one. Samson fights a lion in another. In another Samson is seduced by Delilah. The columns capitals of the cloister, also built at the end of

FIGURE 20.3

Entrance Porch of Saint Trophime. Arles, France.

the twelfth century, have various themes. from simple foliage to Christ's entry into Jerusalem. The *tympanum*, the semi-circular stonework above the wooden entry doors, shows Christ in his Majesty with symbols of the four evangelists.

The **Cathedral of St-Lazare, Autun** (1120–1178) is characteristic of the development of the Romanesque style in Southern France. The tympanum above the main entrance door is an example of an angular style created by the sculptor Gislebertus in 1135. The subject is *The Last Judgment*, a theme commonly used in such locations in both the Romanesque and Gothic periods.

There are several late Romanesque churches in France that are considered to be transitional to the succeeding Gothic period. The **Abbey Church at Vézelay**, also known as **Sainte-Madeleine** (1089–1206), is an

FIGURE 20.4

Cloister Column Capital. Saint Trophime. Arles, France.

FIGURE 20.5

Abbey Church of Cluny. France.

FIGURE 20.6

Main Portal. Cathedral of St. James. Santiago de Compostela, Spain.

FIGURE 20.7

Church of St. Madeliene, Vezelay Abbey. France.

early instance of a vaulted crossing, which occurs when perpendicular vaults intersect with one another. The nave features ribbed vaults with alternating dark and light stone. Romanesque churches do not always bring in sufficient light into their naves; that would be a special feature of Gothic churches. However, the nave at **Vézelay** is lighter than most churches of the period, thanks to high clerestory windows.

The **Abbey Church, Cluny** (1086–1131) was the largest Christian church in the world until the construction of St. Peter's in Rome. The church was badly destroyed during the nationalization of Church property in the aftermath of the French Revolution.

The abbey churches at Vézelay and Cluny are among those that gained status and wealth following the inception of the *Camino de Santiago*, the pilgrimage to Santiago de Compostela in northwest Spain. In his book *On the Deaths of the Fathers*, Isidore of Seville wrote that the body of St. James, one of the 12 apostles, was buried at Santiago de Compostela. Around 75 years later in 813, the relics of the body of the apostle Saint James were discovered by Theodemir of Iria Flavia. There is archaeological evidence of buildings from the Roman city of Asseconia buried under the present church at Santiago de Compostela, which was built up at the intersection of two Roman roads, so the story is plausible, if not verifiable. The discovery of the relics had a profound effect in the Middle Ages. Beginning in the latter half of the tenth century, pilgrims began to visit the site, using a walking stick and wearing a hat that was decorated with a scallop shell, the saint's symbol. During the peak of the pilgrimages, around 500,000 people made the journey. Churches all along the various pilgrim routes in Spain and in France became important stops for the pilgrims, and were remodeled and expanded. The **Cathedral of Santiago de Compostela** (1060–1211) was almost 100 meters long. Like at other pilgrimage churches, the aisles continued into the chevet, the eastern end of the church, so that monastic devotions, called the Liturgy of the Hours, which took place up to eight times a day, could take place and not be disturbed by pilgrims visiting the relics.

The Romanesque style in Germany is also known as the Rhenish style, meaning of the Rhine, near which

FIGURE 20.8
Mainserdom. Mainz, Germany.

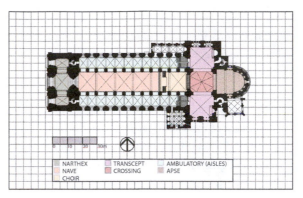

FIGURE 20.9
Plan of a Medieval Cathedral.

FIGURE 20.10
Wormser Dom. Worms, Germany.

most of the churches are located. **Speyer Cathedral** (1080–1106), was the earliest church that was built with stone vaulting for its nave and its aisles, the first to articulate the wall faces of the nave, and one of the earliest to have twin towers at the entrance (western) facade. Its design is pivotal in the establishment of the Romanesque style. There is a wider, but lower, octagonal tower at the eastern and western ends, and a unique external gallery on the upper level between the two ends. There are octagonal apses at each end of **Worms Cathedral** (1181), but the eastern end is more complex and more fully developed than its western end. **Mainz Cathedral** (eleventh), also known as the **Mainzerdom** was complete in the Romanesque style, but is no longer pure in style, due to later alterations in the Gothic and Baroque periods, and thus is an example of a work of architecture that both a witness to and participant in the history of architecture. The west end of **Maria Laach Abbey** (1093–1156) features a porch and atrium, called the *paradisium*, a garden area that was common in Early Christian churches. There are 12 Romanesque churches in the center of the city of **Köln** (Cologne) Germany,

and though they all suffered major damage during World War II, most have been restored, such as **St. Gereon** (1075–1227), **St. Kunibert** (1215–1247), and **St. Aposteln**, or **Church of the Apostles** (1035–1220).

There are four regional styles of Romanesque architecture in Italy: the Lombard Style, in north and Central Italy; the Pisan style, in the Tuscany area; the Florentine Style, in and around Florence; and the Sicilian-Norman

Style, in Sicily and Southern Italy. There were distinctive innovations in each region. The basic form of the Italian Romanesque church was the basilica, with some modifications. The Lombard style featured a front facade that was heavily sculpted, with a lion porch and a vaulted interior. The most noticeable feature of the Pisan style is the placement of rows of upper-level arcades on the front elevation. The Florentine style is characterized by the use of white and green marble on the exterior. The Sicilian-Norman style is Lombardian with Islamic influences.

Although its fame, for centuries, has been magnified due to the seemingly precarious tilt of its *campanile*, or bell tower, the cathedral complex at Pisa merits considerable attention for the delicate detailing of its buildings and the *campo* upon which they are placed. The grouping of the Cathedral, the Baptistery, the Tower, and the Monumental Cemetery located on the **Piazza dei Miracoli**, or the Square of Miracles, form one of the most harmonious complexes of architecture in the world. Unlike the rest of Europe, where the bell tower was typically attached to the cathedral, at Pisa they are separate, and so is the baptistery. Although the cathedral and the baptistery share the same axis, the arrangement of the buildings provides has a dynamic effect. As one strolls through the campo, which is simply a green carpet of grass, the way the buildings influence each other and relate to one another constantly changes.

Pisa Cathedral (1063–1272) was built according to a basilica plan, which is clearly expressed in its three-dimensional form. The westerly façade is composed of five arcades. The lowest is the tallest and widest, with the central span slightly wider than the others to accommodate double entry doors. The upper arcades are of a similar height, with the exception of the one at the pediment. The walls are striped with red and white marble veneer.

The titling of **Pisa Campanile** (1173–1372) began almost immediately, after the completion of only the second of eight floors, and is attributable to two factors. All structures bear upon a *substrate*, the surface of the earth directly below the constructed elements of a building. The natural soil, that which was *in situ* before any disturbance to the site, may consist of any or several of a variety of soils that vary in their stability when subjected to the weight of a structure. If the soil is not considered stable enough, it can be removed and stronger soil be brought it to replace it, or else piles can be used to transfer the load further down until it reaches a solid bearing. In the case of the Pisa bell tower, the subsoil was clay, and was not uniform. When subjected to loads, the soils compressed to one side causing the leaning. The second structural issue was the shallowness of the foundation. Some recent remedial work has stabilized the structure, although it still leans about 4 degrees, or 3.9 meters, somewhat less than at its maximum tilt of 5.5 degrees.

The architectural design of the tower was far more successful than its engineering. The first floor and the top floor are blind arcades, with the top floor set back.

FIGURE 20.11
Cathedral. Ruvo di Puglia, Italy.

FIGURE 20.12
Piazza dei Miracoli. Pisa, Italy.

The blind arcade of the first floor, being solid, creates a visual sense of stability (albeit a false one). The middle six floors are colonnades—circular loggias that help to create a harmonic relationship with the cathedral. The Leaning Tower of Pisa is not the only campanile, or tower in general, to lean in Italy, it is just leans more severely than the others. The tower and the rest of the buildings would be a UNESCO heritage site even if the tower was perfectly straight.

The bells of *campanile* were rung before religious services and for the seven canonical hours of prayer: *Matins*, or First Hour at 6am; Third Hour, or Trece at 9am; Noon Prayer, or *Sext*; Ninth Hour at 3pm; Vespers, or Evensong at 6pm; Compline at 9pm; and Midnight Prayer. They would also ring for special events, such as for baptisms, weddings, and funerals. Baptisms were once important events in Italy, ones that were as ceremonial as weddings or funerals. It is a tradition that continues, to a lesser extent, even today (as depicted in the climactic scene from the film *The Godfather* from 1972). The **Baptistery** (1153–1265) was begun in the Romanesque style (the first two floors) and completed in the Gothic style (upper level and gable screening). The **Cremona Baptistery** (1167) and the **Parma Baptistery** (1196–1270) are other examples of Romanesque freestanding baptisteries.

The **Basilica of St. Francis of Assisi** (1228–53) has two levels, the *Basilica superiore* or Upper Church and the *Basilica inferiore*, the Lower Church, originally a crypt before a new crypt was added in the nineteenth century. The Lower Church in the Romanesque style and the Upper Church in both the Romanesque and Gothic styles. The church is dedicated to St. Francis, the founder of the Franciscan order. Among the many important frescoes in both churches are the ones in the Upper Church that are a series of 28 frescoes that depict the life of St. Francis. Francis was the son of a wealthy Assisi merchant who renounced the patrimony of his father and lived a life void of possessions.

San Zeno Maggiore, Verona (twelfth–fourteenth centuries) is characteristic of the Lombard style and of Italian Romanesque in general, owing to its elegant simplicity. A freestanding porch is supported by lion columns. Above the porch is an early example of a rose

Basilica San Francesco (St. Francis) Assisi, Italy.

window in Italy. The projecting porch is narrower and slightly taller than the one at St. Trophime, in Arles.

In the British Isles, there are two styles of Early Medieval period: Anglo-Saxon (fifth century–1066), which is Pre-Romanesque, and the Norman (eleventh century–twelfth century), the Romanesque style of England, Scotland, Ireland and Wales. Two examples of Anglo-Saxon churches that have survived without much alteration are the **Chapel of St. Peter-on-the-Wall** (late seventh century), located in Bradwell-next-the-Sea, Essex, and **St. Laurence's Church** (early eleventh century) in Bradford on Avon, Wiltshire, which has some Romanesque influences.

A characteristic of the English-Norman or English Romanesque style of architecture is the use of geometric ornament that decorates the architrave or archivolt of arched openings. Often at least part of a church was transitioned into the Gothic style in mid-construction, or else remodeled or replaced later on, such as at **Durham Cathedral** (eleventh–thirteenth century). **Winchester Cathedral** (1079–sixteenth century), one of the first Norman church projects, is another example of a religious structure that is a composite of both medieval styles. In spite of some obvious, quite visible differences

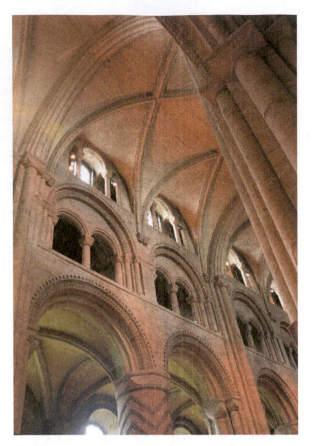

FIGURE 20.14

Nave of Durham Cathedral. England.

between the two, the more dominant Gothic parts of the church blend relatively easily with earlier Norman style. This may be attributed to some facets of each that are shared. Both styles aspired to verticality. Both allowed the richness of the masonry and the structure to inform the aesthetic, on both the exterior and the interior. Both were organized into sections (bays). In other words, the styles are different but compatible, which cannot be said for the relationship between Classical and Gothic, for example.

For Further Discussion

The Medieval period is the earliest in the music history in which a significant body of works are known. It was an important period in the history of music, one in which fundamental principles such as using musical notation that signifies both the pitch and timing of the sounds of voices and instruments. What was the character of the music from this age? Did it have anything in common with the art and architecture? How would Medieval architecture have affected the music?

CHAPTER TWENTY-ONE

Gothic

There was a housewife come from Bath, or near
Who—sad to say—was deaf in either ear.
At making cloth she had so great a bent
She bettered those of Ypres and even of Ghent.
In all the parish there was no goodwife
Should offering make before her, on my life;
And if one did, indeed, so wroth was she
It put her out of all her charity.
Her kerchiefs were of finest weave and ground;
I dare swear that they weighed a full ten pound
Which, of a Sunday, she wore on her head.
Her hose were of the choicest scarlet red,
Close gartered, and her shoes were soft and new.
Bold was her face, and fair, and red of hue.
She'd been respectable throughout her life,
With five churched husbands bringing joy and strife,
Not counting other company in youth;
But thereof there's no need to speak, in truth.
Three times she'd journeyed to Jerusalem;
And many a foreign stream she'd had to stem;
At Rome she'd been, and she'd been in Boulogne,
In Spain at Santiago, and at Cologne...[1]

Geoffrey Chaucer (c. 1343–1400). was already an accomplished poet and writer when he assembled a collection of stories and used a pilgrimage to Canterbury as the framework for Canterbury Tales (c. 1386–1400). Harry Baily, the proprietor of the Tabard Inn in London, proposes to a group of 30 pilgrims that they entertain each other by each telling four stories, two on the journey to Canterbury and two on the return journey. They are going to Canterbury to pay homage to seek spiritual assistance from the popular saint Thomas Becket, who is buried there.

On December 29, 1170, four knights answering Henry II's call for some men to help rid himself of a "turbulent priest," entered Canterbury Cathedral armed with their swords. One of them called out, "Where is Thomas Becket, traitor to the king and to the realm?" Thomas Becket, the archbishop of Canterbury, answered them, saying, "Lo! Here am I, no traitor to the king, but a priest. I am ready

---

1 Geoffrey Chaucer, "The Wife of Bath," Canterbury Tales. Copyright in the Public Domain.

to suffer in His Name who redeemed me by His Blood." The knights demanded that Becket rescind some recent excommunications, which had tested the balance of power between the king and his former chancellor, whom he appointed archbishop. When Becket refused, the carnage began. The first blow inflicted knocked off Becket's crown. The second was also a blow to the head, but Becket stood firm. Another blow dropped Becket to his knees, and while he was prostrate he prayed, "For the name of Jesus and the protection of the Church I am ready to embrace death." He received one final, devastating blow to the head, and one of the knight's assistants cried out in triumph, "Let us away, knights, this fellow will rise no more." The account above was told by Edward Grim, an acolyte of the archbishop, who witnessed the assassination first hand. The story of the rise and fall of the deep friendship of Becket and Henry II is a classic tale. Jean Anouilh's play *Becket, or the Honor of God* was the basis of a 1964 film, *Becket*, with Richard Burton in the title role and Peter O'Toole as Henry II. Among their many richly worded encounters is an exchange in which O'Toole says to Burton: "So what in most people is morality, in you it's just an exercise in … what's the word?"

Becket's answer is "Aesthetics."

Pope Alexander III canonized Thomas Becket in 1173. Soon thereafter, Canterbury was a popular destination for pilgrims. Between the eleventh through the fourteenth centuries, pilgrimages were very popular for both the rich and the poor alike. Because the journey was long, arduous, and sometimes dangerous, people traveled in groups. The stated purpose for pilgrimages was to visit the relics or burial places of saints, but the lure of travel and adventure was also part of their appeal. The most popular destinations were St. Peter's Cathedral in Rome, the birthplace of the Church, St. Denis, near Paris, and Santiago de Compostela, in Northwestern Spain. Because of this surge of activity, the construction of churches and cathedrals in France and Northern Spain—both of new structures and the remodeling of older ones—swelled considerably.

Near the end of his life, Geoffrey Chaucer (c. 1343–1400), an accomplished poet and writer, assembled a collection of stories, and used a pilgrimage to Canterbury as a framework. Chaucer called the assemblage *The Canterbury Tales*, now considered one of the epic works of English literature. Harry Bailey, the proprietor of the Tabard Inn in London, proposes to a group of 30 pilgrims that they entertain each other by each telling four stories, two on the journey to Canterbury, and two on the return journey. He promises them he will reward a free dinner to the pilgrim who tells the best story. The stories that are told, as well as the descriptions of mannerisms of those telling the stories, are both entertaining and instructive of medieval life.

One such pilgrimage church that found prosperity was at Saint-Denis, a village north of Paris, which held an annual fair to celebrate relics of the Passion that had been given to the church by the emperor Charles the Bald. St. Denis was the first bishop of Paris. He was tortured and beheaded in about the year 250, during the period of persecution of Christians under the reign of the Roman emperor Decius. It was said that after he was beheaded, he walked ten kilometers, head in hand. An abbey and church were built at the site in 475 and expanded during the Carolinginan period, but it was remodeled extensively in the twelfth century. These renovations would have a

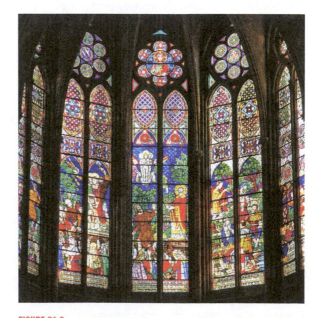

FIGURE 21.2

Stained Glass Windows in Choir. Basilica of St.-Denis. France.

profound effect upon architectural history for the next few hundred years.

On March 12, 1122, a monk named Suger (1081–1151) was installed as the abbot for the royal abbey of St. Denis. Suger's rise to prominence began when he was a student at Saint-Denis and befriended the future king Louis VI. It is difficult now not to underestimate the position and importance of Saint-Denis as one of the most important churches of medieval Europe, being the burial place of French kings, and as the birthplace of Gothic architecture. History is often affected by circumstances, and in this particular situation, it was the vision of a single person, thrust into a position of authority by a fortuitous association at an early age, which changed the course of architectural history. Suger, for his part, seemed ready for the challenge, as can be gathered from this passage from his writings:

> … I see myself dwelling, as it were, in some strange region of the universe which neither exists entirely in the slime of the earth, nor entirely in the purity of Heaven; and that, by the grace of God, I can be transported from this inferior to that higher world in an anagogical manner.

Suger guided the construction of a new narthex and a new choir of the **Basilica of Saint-Denis** (1130–1140). Both of these elements were innovations that advanced this new style, architecturally and structurally, beyond the limits of the Romanesque style of building. What was achieved was a delicacy of design previously unseen in masonry architecture in Western culture. The walls and columns became lighter and more slender, yet the height of the spaces had increased. A significant contributing factor in this structural development is also the most visible architectural transformation–the *ogival*, or pointed arch, which transfers loads supported by the arch more vertically than semicircular arches, which transfer more of the load horizontally.

The west front was inspired by Saint-Étienne in Caen. The *narthex*, or antechamber, was a medieval adaptation of Christian churches to accommodate large groups of pilgrims that would enter the church at a particular time.

Passage through the western doorways affirms several beliefs for pilgrims: that Christ was resurrected, that he was born to Mary, the Mother of God, and that he will welcome those who have believed in Him and followed his moral teachings at the Last Judgment. The western front is a remnant of the Roman *castrum*, or castle gate. Once the pilgrim, or believer, passes into the church, he or she is protected from the enemy (Satan), just as the Roman gate protected against a physical enemy. The central door is aligned with the altar at the eastern end, and was used for ceremonies. The normal entrance to the church was through the two side doors. In this aspect, it is not dissimilar functionally to a three-opening Roman triumphal arch.

The *nave* is the central open main assembly area of the church used by laypersons, and often their beasts. The *transepts* are the lateral arms of the church that face north and south, often having portals that are of similar design to the main west portal, but are less grandiose. The *aisles* of the church on either side of the nave, which previously ended at the transept, were extended at Saint-Denis to create an ambulatory that passed completely around the eastern end of the church. The *choir*, the eastern end of a Gothic church from the transept forward and in the shape of a segmented curve, is the most significant variation from the past. The separation of the individual chapels that radiate around the perimeter of the choir have opened up by the use of a structural technique called buttressing. From a practical standpoint, the ambulatory allowed laypersons to get closer to the most sacred part of the church, which was reserved for the clergy, yet contained the relics and much of the finer artworks.

Suger's accomplishments at Saint-Denis are remarkable, in that his ideas were in stark contrast to the influential Cistercian movement, which proposed a return to the more austere approaches to ornamentation and design common in early Christianity. The abbot and theologian, Bernard of Clairvaux (1090–1153), argued that art had become a spiritual distraction, and diluted the sense of seclusion of monasticism.

The term *Gothic* is derived from the French word *gothique* or from the Latin *Gothi*, referring to the infamous Goths of Central and Northern Europe who invaded the Roman empire. *Gothic* was first used by Vasari in the sixteenth century. The English Renaissance architect Sir Christopher Wren used the word Gothic as a term of reproach. It is called the *style ogival* in France.

A Gothic church is easily identified by its iconic visual elements: the pointed arch, ribbed vaulting, stained glass, pinnacles, flying buttresses, and the verticality and visible energy of its form. It is the first style in architectural history to give great importance to the entrance of light into the interior space of a building. Daylight was introduced into the building, not merely through windows, but through the walls themselves, which became transparent, a transformation that prefigured modern architecture. This was as much a spiritual innovation as it was an architectural one. In his book *The Gothic Cathedral*, Otto Von Simpson observed that medieval builders regarded light as "the most noble of the natural phenomena, the least material, the closest approximation to pure form." This notion is derived from Plato.

In Gothic architecture, form and function became ideologically intertwined. All of the components of a Gothic building were not only plainly visible, but they were—or at least seemed—necessary for the existence of the whole structure. There is little that is hidden. The ribbed vaulting system alone is a subject of considerable interest. The stone vaulting of the ceiling, or the "roof proper," is in the shape of a pointed arch. The outer roof, or "roof mask," is a gable made out of timber beams.

In his *Dictionnaire raisonné de l'architecture française du XIe au XVIe siècle* (1854–1868), Viollet-le-Duc (1814–1879) presented a clear distinction between Gothic and Classical architecture: scale. Greek and Roman temples used proportion to determine the dimensions of the components of a building. In a small temple for a minor god, for example, a molding or design would have been smaller than a similarly used molding or design in a temple built for Zeus. In Gothic architecture, columns may get taller or shorter, but the "balustrades, supports, socles, platforms, galleries, friezes, bas-reliefs, and the like" will be of similar scale. This is because there is the unifying element of *human scale* in the Gothic. No matter how grandiose it may appear, it is nevertheless "constructed according to the measure of man."

The human scale Viollet-le-Duc refers to is in juxtaposition to, and perhaps in competition with, the grand ascendancy of the interior space, made possible by the enormous ribbed arches and columns that evoke the Hypostyle Hall of the Temple of Amun at Luxor more than they do the columns of the Parthenon or Pantheon. Even still, there is a proper order, as Victor Hugo admired in *The Hunchback of Notre Dame* (1832):

Everything has its place in that self-created, logical, well-proportioned art. By measuring the toe, we estimate the giant.

Gothic architecture evolved in France from the Romanesque, and then spread throughout the rest of Europe. There are three sub periods of Gothic style, per M. de Caumont: the *Primaire*, or *Gothique a Lancettes* of the twelfth century; the *Secondaire*, or *Rayonnant* of the thirteenth century; and the *Tertiaire*, or *Flamboyant* of the fourteenth to sixteenth centuries. The Gothic period of architectural history is the only period in the history of European architecture dating to the beginning of the Classical Age until the nineteenth century that was not influenced by Classical ideals—a span of roughly 2300 years.

The philosopher Thomas Aquinas (1225–1274) wrote in his eminent work *Summa Theologiae* that there are three requirements for beauty: *integritas sive perfectio, proportio sive consonantia, claritas* (integrity or perfection, proportion or consonance, and clarity. When Aquinas was a student in Cologne he studied Aristotle, but this work is not just a reiteration of ancient Greek philosophy. For Aquinas, beauty is also a personal or human experience. Beauty is transcendental: a ray of light penetrating through clouds in a sky possesses the quality of beauty as much as it possesses luminosity. However, it is our experience of the object that completes the relationship—the interaction between ourselves and the object. The qualities of integrity and consonance are validated by our perception of them. This is the importance of clarity, ever present in the medieval art and architecture.

Like the Greek architects of the Parthenon, who manipulated the object to preserve the perception of beauty to the beholder, Aquinas recognized the roles the senses and intellect play in our appreciations of what is good and what is beautiful:

Beauty and goodness in a thing are identical fundamentally; for they are based upon the same thing, namely, the form; and consequently goodness is praised as beauty. … Hence beauty consists in due proportion; for the senses delight in things duly proportioned, as in what is after their own kind—because even sense is a sort of reason, just as is every cognitive faculty.[2]

Unlike Classical architecture, Gothic architecture is emotionally vibrant. In his essay *The Nature of Gothic*, John Ruskin (1819–1900), the most influential critic of art and architecture in the nineteenth century, wrote that the Gothic style is both the most moral and the most "humanized" of all architectural styles. His six "characteristic or moral elements" of the Gothic are: savageness, changefulness, naturalism, grotesqueness, rigidity, and redundancy. These apply to the buildings themselves; to their builders or architects, these characteristics are: savageness or rudeness, love of change, love of nature, disturbed imagination, obstinacy, and generosity. Of the latter group, Ruskin is obliged to explain further, since one would not normally concede that being called "rude," or "obstinate," or "disturbed" is a good thing for an architect, even if it were true. Ruskin intended "no reproach" in his use of the word "savageness," and he stated that "wildness of character" and "roughness of work" are honorable characteristics. He implies that the Northern climates, to which he attributes the origin of the style, give men more "hard habits" than ones with more sunshine.

The artists working on the Gothic cathedrals were given somewhat more freedom than their predecessors of the Romanesque era, and substantially more than the Classical periods. This freedom led to a variety of images and forms. Ruskin claims that Gothic is the *only* rational architecture, because it is adaptable to the particular needs of the client and program. This same freedom allowed the Gothic sculptors to use their love of nature to create realistic, but personal, images. The artists also had

a "tendency to delight in the fantastic and the ludicrous, as well as (the) sublime." Although this love of the grotesque would later be criticized in the Renaissance, few visitors to Notre Dame Cathedral are not fascinated by these flights of fantasy, whether in the gargoyles or in the statuary of the portals. The *rigidity* that Ruskin alludes to is not a personality trait, but rather an attribute of the movement of lines that define the form of a Gothic work. They are more like lighting, and sinuous like a snake. Finally, the *redundance* (redundancy) that Ruskin alludes to is of generous ornamentation. He asserted that a building without ornamentation is haughty, because it implies that it is perfect without it. Humility, he contended, is the "accumulation of ornament." He may or may not have been trying to be prophetic with his observation on the eve of the modern movement.

At times, Ruskin seems to be both passionate and distant in his admiration for Gothic architecture, much like how a man entrapped in upper-class airs would regard with much interest a pretty woman of a lower class—not unlike the archdeacon's fascination with Esmerelda in *The Hunchback of Notre Dame*.

William Durandus (1237–1296), who was an expert in canon law, wrote a treatise about the meaning of the various components of Gothic architecture called *The Symbolism of Churches and Church Ornaments* (1286). The glass windows are the Holy Scriptures (the Old Testament and New Testament). They keep out the wind and the rain, which are harmful, allowing the light of the sun, or God, to enter the church. The door of the church is Christ. The piers, the means of support, are bishops and doctors. The pavement is the "poor of Christ," those who "humble themselves in all things." The beams are princes and preachers, because they "join together the church."

Of the structural system of Gothic architecture, Viollet-le-Duc wrote, "It is impossible to remove a single one of its 'organs' without killing the entire organism." The entire building is separated into *bays*, structural segments that span from column to column and extend from the floor to the roof. The elements of these bays differ only in character, not in function, from their Romanesque predecessors. In general, the rounded arches and vaults of the Romanesque are replaced with

---

2   St. Thomas Aquinas, Selection from Summa Theologica, trans. Fathers of the English Dominican Province. Copyright in the Public Domain.

pointed arches and vaults of the Gothic. The *ogive*, or pointed arch, had its origins in ancient Assyria. After the Muslim conquest of Persia, it became a common feature of Islamic architecture. When the Normans recaptured Sicily for Christianity, they found the pointed arch in use there.

The *flying buttress* is a new element of Gothic architecture. A buttress is simply a projecting pier intended as a counterforce against the horizontal thrust of the main vaults. A flying buttress uses a *rampant arch*, in which one support is taller than the other. The vertical piers of the buttresses often were extended to form *pinnacles*, which came to a point.

The great Gothic cathedrals in the medieval cities of Europe were more than just religious centers. They were civic centers as well, a point well illustrated in Hugo's novel. There is much symbolism in the image of the church towering above the commercial and residential buildings, thus dominating medieval towns and villages, and the symbolism rings of truth. The Church, as the social philosopher Lewis Mumford (1895–1990) noted in *The City in History* (1961), "dominated every aspect

of medieval life." Medieval literature, however, is an assembly of reverence and irreverence, of both exceptional piety and disdain for human excessiveness, in such works as *The Divine Comedy* by Dante Alighieri (1265–1321), *The Canterbury Tales*, *The Decameron* by Giovanni Boccaccio (1313–1375), and in the writings of Francesco Petrarca, Petrarch (1304–1374). The compelling coupling of diligence and decadence, of reason and indulgence, is also found in the art of medieval architecture.

The purpose of medieval art, from its origins in the early days of Christianity, was to instruct visitors to the church about the historical life of Jesus, especially the critical circumstances of his birth, death, and resurrection; to bring to life the narratives of the Old and New Testaments; to honor the saints and martyrs of the church; and to reveal the moral precepts from the teachings of Jesus. There were no public schools in medieval towns and cities, so education was reserved for the elite. Because the majority of the laic population was illiterate, didactic artwork was an important instrument in delivering the message of Christianity to the masses. When theologians, such as Bernard of Clairvaux, objected that

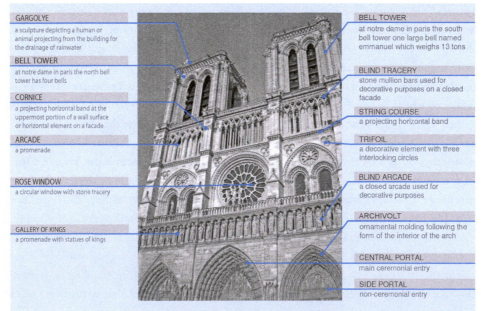

ELEMENTS OF WEST FRONT OF A GOTHIC CATHEDRAL (Notre Dame, Paris)

FIGURE 21.3

medieval art had become distracting, Suger and others countered by citing art's dual purpose: to express both the basic ideas and tenets of Christian teachings for the *illiterate*, and the more complicated aspects to the ecclesiastical *literati*.

With the possible exception of the Hindu temples of Southern and Southeastern Asia, no other period in history achieves a more perfect fusion of art and architecture. In Gothic architecture, art is perceived to be integral with the structure, and not applied. The artistic program begins with the *westfront*, the western and most important facade of the church, and continues throughout; no architectural component, no surface is immune from decoration. *Tympana* (singular, *tympanum*), the flat surfaces above the doors in arched portals, and *lintels*, single stones spanning the flanking columns of doorways, were important, because they were both easily and commonly seen by churchgoers and pilgrims. Common scenes portrayed were the Last Judgment, the Ascension, and the Second Coming. Jamb sculptures decorated the segmented recess of the doorway. At Saint-Denis and at Chartres Cathedral, jamb statues were introduced, depicting prominent laic or religious figures, seen as protecting the entrance to the church. The jamb statues at Chartres, images of Old Testament kings such as David and Solomon, have an exaggerated verticality that emphasizes their significance as "pillars" of the faith.

Gothic cathedrals are renowned for their windows made of *stained glass*, which consists of individual *tesserae* (singular, *tessera*) of colored glass, connected by lead strips and set into an opening. The pattern of the lead is often a geometric design that is independent of the subject matter of the window. The color in the glass is achieved by adding metal oxides to heated, molten glass. Detailing is painted onto the glass, and then the glass is reheated, so that the painted surface bonds to the glass. A *lancet* window is a thin, vertical window with a round (Romanesque) or pointed (Gothic) top. It can be used as a singular element or in groupings of two or three, and occasionally as a series of windows, such as at **Sainte-Chapelle** (1239–1245), the former royal chapel in Paris. A *rose window* is a circular window with flowerlike *tracery*, the pattern of stonework within a window. The

stained glass at the cathedrals in Chartres and Lyon is considered exemplary; however, there are fine specimens of stained glass all over Western Europe.

The capitals of columns can either be descendant from one of the Classical Corinthian order, or be independent from Classicism, with a decorative motif of animal or human figures, foliage, or geometry. Individual ornamental devices include the *gargoyle*, a grotesque human or animal figure that is used as a scupper from the drainage of water; a foil, intersecting three (*trefoil*) or four (*quatrefoil*) circles; a *pinnacle*, a small-scale pointed tower; or *crockets*, stone flowers or leaves that project from a spire or pinnacle.

The nave of **Sens Cathedral** (1140–1534), begun just after the alterations at Saint-Denis, was wider, and therefore taller. At the time, the prestige of Sens surpassed Paris. The cathedral possessed important relics—a piece

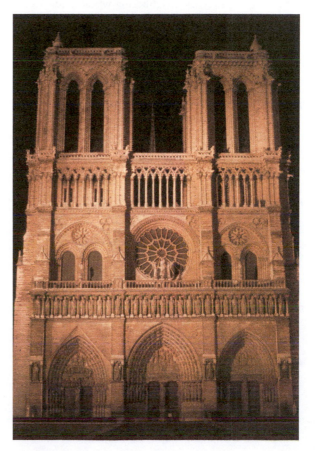

FIGURE 21.4

Notre Dame Cathedral. Paris, France.

of the True Cross, and the vestments of Thomas Becket. However, during the thirteenth century in North-Central France, a competition arose to build the tallest cathedral, a situation not unlike one that would arise in the early twentieth century to build the world's tallest skyscraper.

For a short period of time, Notre Dame was the tallest. Just as the Parthenon is the idealized form of the Greek temple, Notre Dame Cathedral (1163–1250) in Paris is the idealized form of Gothic architecture. Like the Parthenon, it displays a precise symmetry; it is located on a site that maximizes its visibility; and its city rose to a prominent stature, thus facilitating the lavishness of its construction program.

The idea that medieval art is a language, and that the cathedral is the instrument through which that language takes form, is epitomized at **Chartres Cathedral** (1194–1260), which dominates the town and can be seen towering over the neighboring wheat fields from a significant distance. Christian dogma is presented here in stone and in glass, more than in any other medieval cathedral. In addition to the religious iconography, astrology and the calendar also are there, with many representations of astrology. In medieval thought, there were three stages to God's designs for the universe: the creation, the period represented by the astrological signs Aries through Cancer; the rise of self-awareness of humanity, from Leo to Scorpio; and the reunification with God, from Sagittarius to Pisces.

The construction of the church faced many setbacks, the most severe being three separate fires, in 1020, 1134, and 1194. In spite of these—and in spite of the fact that its two towers were built centuries apart—there is unity of design that is often admired. The north tower was struck by lightning in 1506 and rebuilt in a different style than the south tower, which was completed in 1165.

The most important relic of Chartres Cathedral was the tunic Mary wore at the Nativity, which was thought to have been destroyed in the 1194 fire. When it was later found that it had been stored in the crypt and thus spared

FIGURE 21.5
West Front. Chartres Cathedral. France.

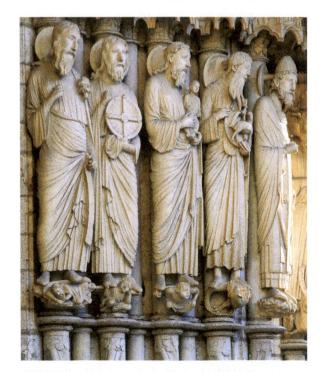

FIGURE 21.6
Portal Statues. Chartres Cathedral. France.

from the fire, the impetus to rebuild the cathedral after the fire was given a great boost. After this, Chartres became the most important center for the cult of the Virgin Mary, which was extremely popular in the Middle Ages. Symbolically, the Church is the Bride of Christ. Mary is the virgin Mother of God, but she was also seen as the Bride of Christ. The physical church thus has a close association with Mary. Chartres Cathedral was built in honor of the Assumption. Others, such as the cathedral in Paris, are simply named *Notre Dame*, "our Lady."

Malcolm Miller, a scholar who conducted tours at the cathedral for years, once remarked that one reads Chartres "like a book," in which the "architecture is the binding, its text is in the glass and sculpture." One of the most celebrated works of stained glass (not just at Chartres) is the *Notre-Dame de la Belle-Verrière*, sometimes referred to as the "Blue Virgin Window." Mary is shown seated upon her celestial throne, wearing a crown and a blue tunic. Her face is surrounded by a blue halo, and above her is a dove that represents the Holy Ghost, and from whom the halo receives its luminescence.

The *Portail Royal* of the western façade contains some of the finest works of Medieval sculpture. It consisted of the now traditional (since the Romanesque period) central ceremonial door and two side doors. Flanking each door are elongated figures—the famous jamb statues—representing the royalty of France and leaders from the Old Testament, such as David and Solomon. Although the figures are almost completely three-dimensional, they belong, spatially, to the pilaster shafts that support the concentric archivolts that form the portals. Stepping back from the portals, it becomes clear that the sculpture and architecture are integrated as one entity. No individual subject, great or small, seems amiss from the whole. In this way, Chartres Cathedral, and Gothic architecture in general, rivals Classical architecture, even as it dismisses much of the language as too static, not audacious enough.

The first miracle of Gothic architecture—unprecedented height and unprecedented illumination of the interior with daylight—was made possible by the use of flying buttresses, the iconic structural innovation of the entire Medieval period. At Chartres these buttresses are sculpted and airy. The columnar shaft of the buttress

splits into two and supports the nave wall at the top and bottom of the clerestory windows. The area between is a series of lancet-like arches. The second miracle of Gothic architecture is its lightness. Romanesque architecture was heavier, more massive, and less daring.

The height of the nave of **Amiens Cathedral** (1220–1270) is 42 meters, and thus the second tallest ever planned, and tallest one completed. The deeply recessed sculptured portals of the west front are richly detailed. The west front is not quite symmetrical; the north tower is slightly taller. These towers and the rose window were built in the fourteenth century, during the later High Gothic period, in France known as the *Rayonnant* (c. 1240–1350).

FIGURE 21.7
Crossing and Choir. Amiens Cathedral. France.

FIGURE 21.8
Rouen Cathedral Tower. Rouen, France.

FIGURE 21.9
Vaulted Ceiling of Choir. Beauvais Cathedral. France.

FIGURE 21.10
Chevet Butresses. Beauvais Cathedral. France.

The impressionist artist Claude Monet (1840–1926) painted thirty-plus views of **Rouen Cathedral** (1202–1230, alt. through nineteenth century) from an apartment he had rented across the street. Each painting showed the cathedral in a different light—morning, full sunlight, etc.—which demonstrates the perceptive skills of the artist, the richness of the sandstone, and the seemingly endless capacity of Gothic architecture to stimulate the senses. The nave of **Le Mans Cathedral** (1217–1254) is Romanesque, but the Gothic choir, with a tall double ambulatory, was built in the thirteenth century, and the transepts were built a century later. The Gothic fascination with verticality reached its upper limits at **Beauvais Cathedral**, or the **Cathedral of Saint-Pierre** (1247–1568), whose nave is 48 meters tall. In 1284 some vaults and buttresses collapsed. An open masonry spire 157 meters tall, built above the crossing transept, collapsed in 1563. Today, it is still imposing, in spite of the fact that it's only completed parts of the church are the choir and the transepts. The nave is the original Romanesque structure.

The **Albi Cathedral** or the **Cathedral of Sainte-Cécile** (1282–1330) in Southwestern France has a singular design not found elsewhere. It walls are rounded, and made of smooth red brick. It has an austere military aspect, which is an acknowledgment of its situation as the domain of the most ruthless of all the inquisitors in medieval church history, Bishop Bernard de Castanet. His violent suppression of heresy and the subsequent fear of reprisal necessitated its style. Other notable examples of French Gothic religious architecture are **Laon Cathedral** (1160–1225), **Soissons Cathedral** (1180–1225), **Lyon Cathedral** (1180–1480), and **Reims Cathedral** (1211–1290).

English Gothic architecture differs from the French in several ways. The English churches tend to be longer and narrower than the French. Transepts are longer, and therefore project out further from the nave. Side chapels are more prevalent in the French and are rarer in the English churches. The *chevet*, or the rounded east end of the French choir, is typically rectangular in England. English aisles are always singular. English churches are more likely to have a single western tower, as opposed to two. The bay width is narrower in English cathedrals. Flying buttresses are less common in England. The rose window on the western facade, a prominent feature of French design, is not used in the English fronts, but relegated to the transepts. Medieval periods in England are divided into Anglo-Saxon (550–1050); Norman (1050–1150); Transitional (1150–1200); Early English Gothic (1190–1280); Middle Gothic, or Decorative (c. 1280–c. 1380); and Perpendicular Gothic (1380–1550).

At **Canterbury Cathedral** (1070–1503) it is possible to see much of the history of medieval architecture in England all in one structure, one that has a reputation for its historical significance and architectural prominence. The murder of Becket took place in the northwest transept. The nearby doorway to the cloister, from which the knights entered, is still in the same location. The transformation of the cathedral from an earlier structure

FIGURE 21.11

Stained Glass Window Group: Christ Descending from the Cross. Lyon Cathedral. France.

into the "French," or Gothic, style was done between the years 1070 and 1077 after a fire in 1067, but many alterations and additions followed thereafter. The earlier structure, built after 1011, replaced one from the sixth century. It was destroyed by the Danes, who abducted the archbishop Alphege, who after he refused to allow

FIGURE 21.12

Crossing of Canterbury Cathedral. England.

ransom to be paid for his release, was pelted to death by oxbones, which were discarded after a feast.

As is often the case, the *crypt*, the underground area of the church used as a chapel or for burials, was not substantially altered during the rebuilding process and still maintains its Norman character. The cathedral has two pairs of transepts, an embellishment which would be imitated elsewhere in the British Isles. The second, easterly, pair of transepts served the clergy and allowed easy access for pilgrims to the shrine of Becket in the Trinity Chapel. The ceiling of the crossing of the Eastern transepts is characteristic of the English style of *splayed* vaulting, in which the ribs of the vault are spread out like the fingers of an open hand.

Westminster Abbey (1042–1745) is the most historic church in London, and, by extension, all of England. It has been the setting for coronations of kings, royal weddings, and funerals and memorials for some of the most famous names in English history. The abbey served as the dramatic setting for the crowning of all English kings since William the Conqueror in 1066, the weddings of Henry I and Queen Elizabeth II and many in between, and many royal funerals, as well as the funeral of Diana, the Princess of Wales in 1997. Figures from the humanities have been buried there as well, including Isaac Newton, Charles Darwin, Henry Purcell, and Geoffrey Chaucer. An area called the Poet's Corner was established near the Chaucer's grave and contains memorials to many English writers and poets. The abbey was begun in the Norman style, and rebuilt in the Gothic style by Henry III (1207–1272) in honor of Edward the Confessor, the last Anglo-Saxon king of England who was canonized as a saint in 1161.

Another one of the earliest churches to adopt the Gothic style in England was **Durham Cathedral** (1093–1490). It is located high on a bluff above the River Wear, its towers barely peeking above the trees in spring and summer. It has the reputation of being one of the finest cathedrals of any style in any country, in spite of some "over-restorations" and alterations of the eighteenth century. Prior to that, the architecture is an example of a mellifluous mixture of Norman and Gothic. Pairs of towers, two octagonal towers at the corners of the north

transept, and two towers at the west end, have Norman bases and Gothic upper sections. The round Norman pillars in the nave are very stout: a circumference of seven meters. The vaulting over the nave is the only surviving example of Norman nave vaulting in all of England.

Lincoln Cathedral (1073–1311) was the first to be built in a style that could be called purely English, influencing the construction others in England, such as **Ely Cathedral** (1080–fourteenth century), **Beverly Cathedral** (twelfth century–fifteenth century). When its 160-meter-tall tower was completed, became the tallest building in the world, surpassing the Great Pyramid at Giza, which held that distinction for roughly four millennia. Later the spire on top of the tower fell during a strong gale, and was not replaced.

The west front of **Wells Cathedral** (1175–1239) is 45 meters wide and 30 meters tall, and thus a 1:1.5 proportion. For comparison, York Minster has a width of 32 meters wide and 60 meters high, or a 1:.5 proportion. In spite of its squatness, a sense of verticality is achieved through the use of six projecting buttresses, two at each of the flanking towers, and one on either side of the main portal. The history of **York Minster** (current: 1080–1472) tells of the many forces, both man-made and natural, that can imperil even such a robust structure as a cathedral. The first building on the site, from the mid-seventh century, fell

FIGURE 21.13
Wells Cathedral.

FIGURE 21.14

Interior of York Minster. England.

FIGURE 21.15

Interior of Winchester Cathedral. England.

into disrepair, the next was destroyed by fire, the next was damaged by William the Conqueror, the next destroyed by the Danes, the next damaged by fire, and parts of this last building gave way to innovations in style.

Due to its very brief period of construction, **Salisbury Cathedral** (1220–1266) was built to a single design style from start to finish. Like many English cathedrals it is set inside a *close*, an area owned by the bishop and used for ancillary purposes. At Salisbury the close contains a green area that surrounds the cathedral, thus allowing the full majesty of the building to be appreciated in full. English cathedrals have a greater divergence in the design of their western fronts. One expecting to see a mild variation of York would be disappointed in Salisbury's main elevation. One that welcomes variety would not.

The later Gothic Period in England saw the development of the *fan vaulting*, or *fan-tracery vaulting*, fan-like

FIGURE 21.16

Chapter House. Wesminster Abbey. London, England.

vaults that spring from a column and diverge outward. The technique was first developed at **Gloucester Cathedral** (1089–1499). It quickly gained popularity and was used

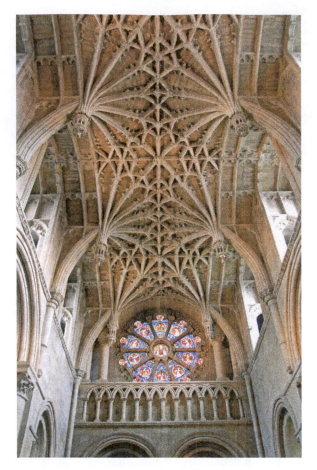

FIGURE 21.17

Interior of Roslyn Chapel. Near Edinburgh, Scotland.

in parts of many other cathedrals in England, including **Bath Abbey**; **Christ Church**, Oxford; the crossing of **Canterbury Cathedral**; the Lady's Chapel and Chapter House at **Westminster Abbey**, London; **Peterborough Cathedral**, the remodeled nave of **Winchester Cathedral**, **Roslyn Chapel** in Scotland, and the **Wells Cathedral** Crossing.

The masterwork of Late English Gothic architecture is **King's College Chapel at Cambridge** (1446–1515), which inspired three sonnets by the poet William Wordsworth (1770–1850). In the poem "Inside of King's College Chapel, Cambridge," he refers to a "branching roof," which is the fan vaulting:

> *So deemed the man who fashioned for the sense*
> *These lofty pillars, spread that branching roof*

Self-poised, and scooped into ten thousand cells,
Where light and shade repose, where music dwells
Lingering—and wandering on as loth to die;
Like thoughts whose very sweetness yieldeth proof
That they were born for immortality.[3]

In Spain, several towns situated along the pilgrims' road to Santiago built great cathedrals, usually with the assistance of French architects. There are several distinguishing features of the Spanish Gothic style. The choir, reserved for the clergy, called the *coro* in Spain, is west of the transept, and thus part of the nave. The sanctuary area is often enclosed. A *cimborio*, a tall square space at the crossing of the nave and the transepts, lit by clerestory windows, is a common feature borrowed from Rouen and Canterbury. **Burgos Cathedral** (1221–1457) has twin towers on its western front that resemble those at Cologne. **Leon Cathedral** (1255–1303) also is French in character. **Seville Cathedral** (1402–1520) is the second largest medieval cathedral in Europe.

The Gothic style arrived late in Italy, and like the Romanesque invasion of a few centuries before, it was not imported *en masse*, but with substantial modifications. While the style never achieved the popularity it gained in France, England, Germany, and Spain, there are many outstanding interpretations of the Gothic style, especially in Northern Italy. The most notable difference between the French and Italian Gothic styles is that the Italian Gothic is less elegantly tall and slender. The second significant distinction is the use of marble and tile on the facades, rather than limestone or sandstone. A third difference, no less significant, is that that the sculpture is less integrated with the structure.

The facade of **Orvieto Cathedral** (1290–1580) is a combination of brightly colored mosaics, marbles, and finely detailed bas-relief sculpture. Its unique qualities and character help diminish a legitimate criticism of the work as a whole: the facade is a false front. Its walls extend outward beyond the actual exterior walls in a manner similar to the false fronts of buildings in western frontier towns or those in a Hollywood movie set. The

3   Wordsworth, William. "Inside the King's College Chapel, Cambridge". Public Domain.

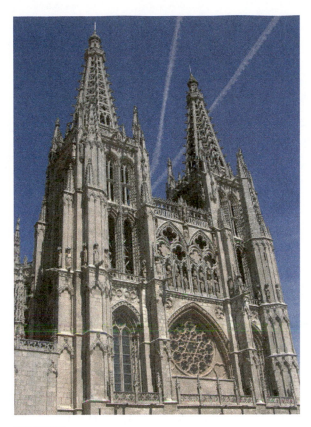

FIGURE 21.18
Burgos Cathedral. Spain.

FIGURE 21.19
Orvieto Cathedral.

small town of Orvieto, 100 kilometers north of Rome, sits on an elongated outcropping of rock that overlooks the vineyards and farmlands below. The cathedral faces a narrow, linear *piazza* (square), which emphasizes the importance of the western facade and diminishes the importance of the rest. The approach is rational and practical, but architecturally less pure, a fact that those who admire its singular beauty are willing to accept. The inspiration of the cathedral at Orvieto was **Siena Cathedral** (1226–1380), which also has a *frontispiece*, a separate or distinctive facade, and striped marble columns and walls elsewhere.

The walls of the Florentine style of Italian Gothic are flatter than elsewhere, and decorated with geometric panels of different colors of marble. **Santa Maria del Fiore** or **Il Duomo** (1296–1462) in Florence continued the tradition, established in the Romanesque period at sites such as Pisa, of having a separate campanile and separate baptistery. The **Campanile** (1334–1359) was

designed by Giotto (c. 1266–1337), one of the founders of modern painting. Additional churches at Florence are **Santa Maria Novella** (1278–1350) and **Santa Croce** (1294–1442). The basic configuration of **Milan Cathedral** (1385–1485) was designed by a French architect, and is one of the "pure" Gothic buildings in Italy.

Strasbourg Cathedral (1230–1365) is an example of a church where the Romanesque and Gothic styles are blended. Strasbourg is located west of the Rhine, but was under German influence until the seventeenth century. The west front and the nave are Gothic; the transepts and choir are Romanesque. It has one spire on its north tower, 142 meters high. The west front is dominated by a 13-meter diameter rose window. Sandstone quarried from the Vosges mountains in France gives the entire building a reddish hue. The Pillar of Angels in the south transept is a three-dimensional representation of the Last Judgment. **Köln (Cologne) Cathedral** (1248–1880) is the most important Gothic cathedral in Germany, and the largest Gothic church in all of Europe. The height of the nave is almost that of Beauvais. Its tall twin towers of the west front are closely spaced together, creating an impressive appearance from the Rhine. Although the construction was extremely protracted, most of the work completed in accordance with the original designs.

Until the completion of La Sagrada Familia in Barcelona (c. 2026), the tallest church in the world is **Ulm Minster** (1377–1492), whose spire is 164 meters tall. It was redesigned to surpass the height of Cologne

FIGURE 21.20

Koln Cathedral. Germany.

Cathedral, which had been the tallest building in the world from 1880 until 1884, the year the Washington Monument was completed. Like many churches in Germany, it converted from Roman Catholicism to Lutheran in 1531.

The Gothic style lost its fuel and its energy beginning in the fourteenth century. The difficulty of sustaining the focus, attention, and financial support of the community—even without the additional burden of political turmoil—is easy to understand. Although it was common for a monarch to have a small church or chapel within the confines of the royal residence, the cathedral of Prague, **St. Vitus Cathedral** (1344–1929) is located within **Prague Castle** (nineteenth century–eighteenth century). Completed after six centuries of work in the twentieth century, **it** is an example of the difficulties of maintaining a continuity of design through long periods of construction.

In the centuries that followed the dissolution of the Roman Empire, various aspects of civic and rural life that had once been serviced by the bureaucracy were left unattended. For example, the system of road building that was a hallmark achievement of the empire, was no longer in place. Maintenance of the existing roads was left to local governments, which were mostly ineffective or nonexistent. In the realm of social services, it was the monasteries that filled the vacuum. They provided hospitals for the sick, asylums for the mentally impaired, alms for the poor, and the education of the young. They educated farmers. They employed workers who could build and decorate churches and cathedrals. They also prayed for souls. They were given land and gifts by those who believed that by their giving, they were following the words of Christ:

Jesus said unto him, If thou wilt be perfect, go and sell that thou hast, and give to the poor, and thou shalt have treasure in heaven: and come and follow me.[4]

The wealth amassed by the monasteries in England was the source of envy and scorn by some, who saw in monastic power the inhibition of individual and religious freedom. Some of the monks had violated their vows. The removal of the papacy from Rome to Avignon (1309-1377) for security reasons, followed thereafter by Great Schism of the Catholic Church, inspired distrust from the English who saw in the Catholic Church an alliance with their enemy, France. When Henry VIII, who was devout in his religion, sought an annulment from Catherine of Aragon so he could marry his mistress Anne Boleyn, he was refused. He countered his excommunication by the pope after his marriage to Boleyn was made public and created the Church of England, of which he became the *de facto* pope, a position the king or queen of England holds today. After Boleyn, whom he later beheaded for adultery and incest, he married four other wives.

The effect of the creation of the Church of England upon the monasteries of England was swift and violent. Some abbots and monks were executed. Buildings, books, works of art, and the instruments of religious service were sold. The new secular landlords, by all accounts, were more oppressive. The properties were taken from the abbeys and sold or given to social or familial

---

4   King James Bible. Matthew 19:21.

relations. There were over 800 abbeys seized by the king in the so-called "Dissolution of the Abbeys." The ruins of many can be seen all over the British Isles today. Even in their disintegrated states, the abbey ruins are informative and formidable, and maybe even easier to admire and understand both the complexity and the simplicity of Gothic architecture.

Jedburgh Abbey (twelfth century), in Southern Scotland, rose in status from a small *priory*, a small monastery run by a *prior*, who was subservient to an abbot. Its nave was narrow and very tall. The zigzag moldings that decorate the portals at its west front and at the entrance to the cloister are indications of the artistic potential of the Norman style. Scottish churches were influenced by the French, except in such details like the archway moldings. The reputation of the abbots and monks at the abbey, like the architecture, was distinguished. However, under the Scottish king James V (1512–1542), the practice of granting *sinecures*, gifted unmerited titles, became common. At Jedburgh this practice destabilized the moral fabric of monastic life. Other ruined abbeys of note in Great Britain are Melrose Abbey, Scotland, and Tintern Abbey in Wales, whose bucolic setting stimulated the self-reflection of William Wordsworth's poem "Lines Composed a Few Miles Above Tintern Abbey,

FIGURE 21.21

Melrose Abbey Ruins. Scotland.

on Revisiting the Banks of the Wye During a Tour, July 13, 1798."

The Gothic period in architecture in many ways prefigured the modern era. It is the first period in Western architectural history to declare independence from classical thought. It was the first to try to "push the envelope" (to use a modern expression) of structural exploration and invention. The building of Gothic cathedrals required communal energy, a unity of purpose, civic identity, and unwavering piety and devotion, but above all it required imagination— inspired by nature, by God, and by the achievements of others.

CHAPTER TWENTY-TWO

Secular Culture and Architecture in the Late Middle Ages

And the good Master said: "Even now, my Son,
The city draweth near whose name is Dis,
With the grave citizens, with the great throng."

And I: "Its mosques already, Master, clearly
Within there in the valley I discern
Vermilion, as if issuing from the fire

They were." And he to me: "The fire eternal
That kindles them within makes them look red,
As thou beholdest in this nether Hell."

Then we arrived within the moats profound,
That circumvallate that disconsolate city;
The walls appeared to me to be of iron.

Not without making first a circuit wide,
We came unto a place where loud the pilot
Cried out to us, "Debark, here is the entrance."[1]

— from *The Inferno* (1320). Dante Alighieri.

In the nine circles of Dante's hell, which are arranged into concentric circular levels, each one placed deeper into the earth from the one above, there is described only one city, Dis, which incorporates the last four circles. The upper most circle, the first one visited by Dante, is limbo, and is the eternal domain of the unbaptized, including the virtuous pagans like Virgil, his guide for the journey. The other eight circles are reserved for those whose greatest sins were, in order: lust, gluttony, greed, anger, heresy, violence, fraud, and treachery. It is no accident that the city of Dis, with its iron walls, gates, moats, and bridges, appears as an infernal carnation of a medieval town. Dante himself participated in an intercity war, one that pitted his native Florence against Arezzo in 1289, part of the ongoing conflict between the Guelfs, who supported the Pope, and the Ghibellines, who supported the Holy Roman Emperor.

Four years later, in 1293, the Ordinances of Justice was enacted which established the Republic of Florence, an event which marked a significant change in Europe. By the end of the Middle Ages, there were both monarchies and republics throughout the continent. These political changes, and corresponding social changes, had multiple

---

FIGURE 22.2

Ideal City (c. 1480-90). Oil on Table. Attributed to Luciana Laurana. Galleria Nazionale di Marche. Urbino, Italy.

effects upon both architecture and planning. The feudal system of the medieval world had a rural emphasis, with much of the population indebted to the few. This was changed by the redevelopment of trade, which had diminished after the fall of Roman. A monetary system was needed for trade, and bankers and lawyers were needed for both. More merchants were needed to service the greater populations living in cities. Towns grew bigger; some grew into cities. Rivalries between towns and states would persist, but the architectural effect of these changes was that there were less fortified castles being built and more in-city *palais* and *palazzo*, as well as more civic buildings and structures.

A *palace, palais (Fr.)*, or *palazzo (It.)*, is simply a large residence having a stately presence. It may also be a civic building. In Florence, the **Palazzo Vecchio** (1298–1314) dominates the Piazza della Signoria, which, because the open space of *Il Duomo*, the cathedral of Florence, is encumbered by the Baptistery, is the largest public space in the city. It was designed by Arnolfo di Cambio (c. 1240–c. 1300). A large tower, 94 meters high, is atypically in that it neither centered nor at one end. Arnolfo di Cambio had to incorporate an existing tower into the design of the building. Tall towers had been a part of old Florence, which was divided into neighborhood factions. The nobility built towers so that they would be protected against prosecution, and thus the towers were symbols of the absence of universal law. In the new republic, the

towers were required to be lowered. The tower at the Palazzo Vecchio was reused for surveillance of the hills that surround Florence. Both the tower and the parapet of the main building are fortified.

The adjacent open structure, the **Loggia dei Lanzi** (1376–1382), now contains statues from antiquity, although loggias were built as public assembly or ceremonial spaces. In England, another type of open structure was the *market cross*, a building placed in a public space that designated the space was allowed to have a market or fair on a regular basis. Larger markets were another type of open-sided structure.

Between the eleventh and the fourteenth centuries, the city of **Venice** was one of the dominant powers of the Mediterranean. Its rise to prominence was partly due to

FIGURE 22.3

Palazzo Doge. Venice, Italy.

a favorable location for trade, and partly because of the ambition and industry of its citizens. Architecturally, the city is an amalgam of the Byzantine, Gothic, Renaissance, and Baroque styles that share a common characteristic of "noble ornamentation," to borrow a phrase from John Ruskin's *The Stones of Venice*. The *urban fabric*—the patterns and relationships of buildings, streets, open areas, waterways, and infrastructure—of Venice is unique among all the cities of the world.

Venice is built on small islands in a large lagoon, protected from the Adriatic Sea by the Lido, a long barrier island. The main public space is the uniquely designed Piazza San Marco, the square in front of the Basilica, and the adjacent Piazzetta, which connects Piazza San Marco with the lagoon. In addition, there are many small public spaces that form the nuclei of neighborhoods. Each of these smaller public squares had their own well or fountain for freshwater, its own market, and often a statue or clock tower, or some similar feature. A church facing the square would identify not only the square, but the whole neighborhood, or parish. This neighborhood square is called a *campo* (plural: *campi*), or sometimes *campiello* (plural: *campielli*), if it is smaller. The division of the city into clearly defined neighborhoods is a fundamental feature of medieval urban planning, and one that affected the design of cities for centuries to come.

Like Piazza San Marco and La Piazzetta, the *campi*, and *campielli* in Venice are sometimes trapezoidal, having two parallel sides. This is less apparent in the neighborhood squares, however, because the buildings do not have a continuous design, which is the case at Piazza San Marco. Other squares are irregular, or L-shaped. There are two means of communication in Venice, composed of its famous waterways—the *canali*, and pedestrian walkways and open areas. *Fondamenta* are large walkways along canals that create a public area between a building and the water. Many structures, however, are built to the face of the canal, creating narrow passage for gondolas and small boats.

After the cathedral and its public space, the second most important element of a medieval city or town was the town hall, known as the *hôtel de ville* in France, the *Rathaus* in Germany, and the *palazzo del comune* in

Italy. In Venice, the **Doge's Palace**, or **Palazzo Ducale** (1309–1424), served a dual purpose: It was the political center of Venice, as well as the residence of the doges, who were the rulers and chief magistrates of Venice between c. 700 and 1797. Its position, between the sea and the Basilica of St. Mark's, is both physical and symbolic. On Ascension Thursdays, the Doge, dressed in gold, and sailing in a gilded vessel called Bucentaur, sailed into the lagoon and tossed a ring overboard, thus renewing the wedding vows between Venice and the sea, uttering the words "We wed thee, Sea, in token of our perpetual rule."

The palace is divided into three horizontal areas plus the roof, which is visible only from the lagoon. There are arcades on the first two levels, the one on the second level having twice the amount of columns as the first. The walls of the uppermost level are clad in white and pink marble, which creates a diagonal pattern. This is the tallest section, attributable to the Venetian tradition of having the most important rooms, and thus the rooms with the tallest ceilings, on the upper floor.

Ruskin called the Ducal Palace 'the principal effort of her imagination," with 'her' being the city of Venice. At the three exposed corners of the building, there are sculptural groups representing the Judgment of Solomon, Adam and Eve, and Noah's Drunkenness. Adam and Eve occupy the corner facing the Piazzetta, standing beneath a fig tree that grows like a vine from foliage of the corner capital. It is a fragment of architectural sculpture that embodies most, if not all of Ruskin's "moral elements" of the Gothic. Savageness, changefulness, naturalism is easy to detect, and *redundance* even more so. The Old Testament figures have little function, and the building would have achieved its majesty without them. For Ruskin, however, art in architecture is an "uncalculated wealth."

The tower of the **Palazzo Pubblico** (1289–1309) in Siena, is similar in design to the one in Florence, rising dramatically from the roof of the building in a similar way and having a similar machicolation at top, but it was built after the palazzo was built, and is a separate structure connected by a continuation of the blind arcade at the second floor. The Palazzo is located on the shell-shaped *Piazza del Campo*, or *il Campo*. The building a central courtyard, a common design for palazzos that

FIGURE 22.4

Palazzo dei Priori. Perugia, Italy.

allows rooms that are not located on the main façade to receive light and ventilation. These spaces contained large assembly rooms and chambers used for the administration of civic and commercial affairs. *Palazzo pubblichi*, or *communali* were, with the *cattedrali*, the vibrant centers of daily life in Italian cities (as were similar buildings in other European cities). In Perugia, the **Palazzo dei Priori** (1293—1443) and the cathedral flank a large piazza, called Piazza IV Novembre today. In the center is the Fontana Maggiore (1277–78) by Nicola Pisano and Giovanni Pisano.

FIGURE 22.5

Allegory of Good and Bad Government (1339). Ambrogio Lorenzetti Palazzo Publico. Siena, Italy.

On the ground floor and second floor, the walls are decorated with large frescoes that that have both secular and non-secular themes. A fresco in the *Sala Della Pace O Dei Nove* (Room of Peace or of the Nine) (1338–40), by Ambrogio Lorenzetti (died c. 1348), entitled *Allegory of Bad and Good Government*, proclaims a message that a good government enables and empowers this relationship of the town to its people. Lorenzetti portrays both subjects – the town of Siena and its people – with equal importance. Siena became a republic in 1115, and despite problems with factional conflicts, it lasted for four centuries.

Palazzo Publico, like the Palazzo Vecchio in Florence, was, in itself, was both the symbolic and material center of daily life. The **Cappella di Piazza** (1352–76), literally 'chapel of the square', is a loggia at the base of the tower used for ceremonies.

The **Castel Sant'Angelo** (originally 134–139; conversion fourteenth century) occupies a prominent position on the Tiber River in Rome near the Vatican. It was originally built as a mausoleum for the emperor Hadrian. It was converted into a papal fortress because conditions in Rome had deteriorated in the Middle Ages. In the opera *Tosca*, by Giacomo Puccini (1858–1924), Tosca, the heroine, commits suicide at the castle by climbing over the machicolated parapet and leaping to her death.

Two events in the fourteenth century, one known at the Babylonian Captivity of the Papacy, which began in 1309, the other the Great Schism, which began in 1378, created the greatest crisis in the history of the Roman Catholic Church. The crisis began in earnest with the assertion by Pope Boniface VIII in a papal bull that the papacy controlled not only the spiritual realm of the faithful but the temporal realm as well, a position that had been at odds with the Holy Roman Empire for some time. The deteriorated environment of Rome as well as the intricacies of European politics led to the abandonment of Rome by the French Pope Clement V and the relocation of the papal court to Avignon, in Southern France. In 1378 Gregory XI moved the court back to Rome, but after he died, a dispute over his successor resulted in there being two popes, each claiming the other to be illegitimate "antipopes." This schism was short-lived, ending in 1417, but significant damage was done to the credibility of papal authority.

The **Palais des Papes**, or the **Palace of the Popes** (1316–64) in Avignon, France was the residence of six popes during this period. In spite of its label, the palace is in essence a fortified castle in appearance, whose scale is quite massive. Though mostly homogenous in style, the structure has a mixture of window and opening styles, both semicircular and ogive. The most conspicuous feature of the main façade that faces an elongated square is a series of pointed arcaded pilasters, of varying widths, that form a narrow parapet on the first floor overlooking the square.

The **Hôtel-Dieu de Beaune (1452)** in Beaune, France was built after the Hundred Years' War, one of the deadliest and most devastating conflicts in Europe

FIGURE 22.6

Palace of the Popes. Avignon, France.

FIGURE 22.7

Hôtel-dieu (1443). Medieval Hospital in Beaune, France.

prior to the twentieth century, has both Medieval and Renaissance characteristics and elements. It was built in an era where basic services for the poor, including medical treatment and maternity assistance, were administered by the Church, with economic assistance from benevolent members of the aristocracy.

Since antiquity, the defensive walls of towns and cities have had architectural detailing decorative functional or non-functional elements. The Lion Gate at Mycenae, and the glazed tile walls and gates of Babylon are two examples. Toward the end of the Medieval period, the gates of city walls became works of architecture in themselves. For example, the **Powder Tower** (1475) in Prague has an inscription that reads "to pay honor and tribute to the inhabitants of the town." In a ceremony, the king, Valdislav II, laid the foundation stone for the tower, but it was paid for by the people. The inscription is a subtle indicator of the rise of an idea in Late Middle Ages that came to be known as *Humanism*, a movement that placed greater emphasis upon the cognitive ability of human beings, independent of political and religious influence. Although cathedrals were the works of the people-the masons, laborers, and skilled workers-they ultimately belonged to the Church. Castles and palaces belong to the royalty and aristocracy. A gate, town hall, or clock towers, was the domain of the citizenry, whether they paid for it, as in the case of the Powder Tower, or not.

The **Charles Bridge** (1357) connected the town with castle, located across the Vltava River on an overlooking hill. It has towers at each end, the Old Town Bridge Tower and the Lesser Quarter Bridge Tower. Its famous statues of saints, thirty in all, that line both side of the bridge, were added in the Baroque period.

The design of medieval fortifications changed dramatically in latter years of the Middle Ages and during the Renaissance period that followed thereafter. The *star fort*, a fortification composed of acute-angled bastions, resembling a star, gained prominence in the fifteenth century and persisted until the nineteenth century. A *bastion* is the projecting part of a fortification. The development of weapons using gunpowder, which began in the fourteenth century, significantly changed siege warfare, and required a major reconsideration of fortified towns and forts. The

FIGURE 22.8

Forte Michelangelo. Civitavecchi, Italy.

eminent Italian Renaissance architect Michelangelo experimented with **Forte Michelangelo** (1508–1537) in Civitavecchia, the port of Rome in 1528, Papal armies threatened to attack Florence after the Medicis had been deposed. Michelangelo designed bastion walls that were a series of acute angles that proved very successful – the Florentines defended their town. Michelangelo's walls were irregular and purely functional, although the idea of the avoiding right angles to improve the capability to attack an invading force from multiple vantage points, became a standard in fortification design. A star shape, which could take many forms, was a natural succession to the idea to architects of the Renaissance (Chapter Twenty-four) to create idealized geometric forms.

Star forts were built in the New World as well. The first was the **Castillo San Felipe del Morro** (1539) in San Juan, Puerto Rico. The first in what is now the continental United States was the **Castillo de San Marcos** (1672) in St. Augustine, Florida. The unfinished **Fort Jefferson** (1847), in the Dry Tortugas, the western end of the Florida Keys, is the largest masonry structure, by area in plan, in the Americas.

In *The City in History*, Lewis Mumford wrote that the "habits and forms of medieval life were still active at least three centuries after its 'close'." From an architectural perspective, the issues that created the iconic tectonic images of the Medieval era still existed, but they were no longer as dominant as they once were. Mercantile capitalism and the expansion of trade were two factors that helped to change towns and cities, both practically and physically. The nobility still existed, but the intangible and physical characteristics of urban life were no longer as comprehensively affected by lords, princes, and kings. Architecture in the next era, the Renaissance, would still be affected by political intrigue, but, with the exception of those structures intended to fortresses, architecture would generally lose its pugnacious tone. Niccoló Machiavelli's early sixteenth century political treatise *The Prince* (c. 1513) mentions the Guido Ubaldo, Duke of Urbino, who chose to "razed to the foundations all the fortresses in that province.," with the reasoning that without the fortifications, Urbino would be less attractive to a potential usurper:

> *And this question can be reasoned thus: the prince who has more to fear from the people than from foreigners ought to build fortresses, but he who has more to fear from foreigners than from the people ought to leave them alone.*[2]

---

2   Nicolo Machiavelli, Selection from Chapter XX, The Prince. Copyright in the Public Domain.

PART

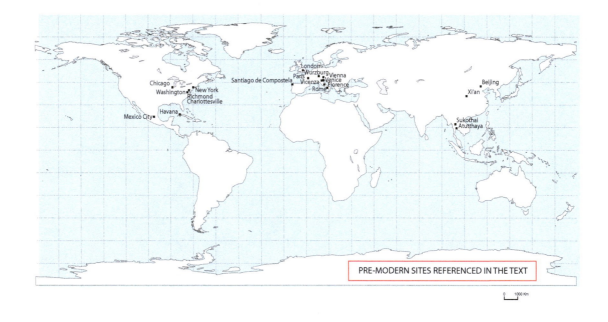

PRE-MODERN SITES REFERENCED IN THE TEXT

0   1000 Km

SIX

Pre-Modern

The most significant transformation of the Pre-Modern era, one that ultimately affected all aspects of civilization, was the simple fact that world grew smaller. The continents moved closer to another and cities and populations that lived on those continents moved closer to one another as well. All this was done metaphorically, of course. What really happened were two events: the invention of the printing press (c. 1455), which triggered the subsequent expansion of collective knowledge, and the expansion of the European sphere of influence, including a new awareness of two continents which had never before been part of its consciousness. In Europe, this period begins with the Renaissance, which is known as a fecund period for art, architecture, literature, science, commerce, and industry. During the fourteenth century, Europe suffered through a great plague, which decreased the population of towns and cities. In the aftermath, the feudal system that had characterized the Middle Ages, began to gradually dissolve. However, the changes that took place in the Pre-Modern era were not limited to Europe; they were visible in Asia and the Near East as well.

CHAPTER TWENTY-THREE

The Far East

In Xanadu did Kubla Khan
A stately pleasure-dome decree:
Where Alph, the sacred river, ran
Through caverns measureless to man
Down to a sunless sea.

So twice five miles of fertile ground
With walls and towers were girdled round:
And there were gardens bright with sinuous rills,
Where blossomed many an incense-bearing tree;
And here were forests ancient as the hills,
Enfolding sunny spots of greenery.

But oh! that deep romantic chasm which slanted
Down the green hill athwart a cedarn cover!
A savage place! as holy and enchanted
As e'er beneath a waning moon was haunted
By woman wailing for her demon-lover!
And from this chasm, with ceaseless turmoil seething,
As if this earth in fast thick pants were breathing,
A mighty fountain momently was forced:
Amid whose swift half-intermitted burst
Huge fragments vaulted like rebounding hail,
Or chaffy grain beneath the thresher's flail:
And 'mid these dancing rocks at once and ever
It flung up momently the sacred river.
Five miles meandering with a mazy motion
Through wood and dale the sacred river ran,
Then reached the caverns measureless to man,
And sank in tumult to a lifeless ocean:

And 'mid this tumult Kubla heard from far
Ancestral voices prophesying war!

The shadow of the dome of pleasure
Floated midway on the waves;
Where was heard the mingled measure
From the fountain and the caves.
It was a miracle of rare device,
A sunny pleasure-dome with caves of ice!
A damsel with a dulcimer
In a vision once I saw:
It was an Abyssinian maid,
And on her dulcimer she played,
Singing of Mount Abora.
Could I revive within me
Her symphony and song,
To such a deep delight 'twould win me
That with music loud and long
I would build that dome in air,
That sunny dome! those caves of ice!
And all who heard should see them there,
And all should cry, Beware! Beware!
His flashing eyes, his floating hair!
Weave a circle round him thrice,
And close your eyes with holy dread,
For he on honey-dew hath fed
And drunk the milk of Paradise.[1]

—from *"Kubla Khan,"* by Samuel Taylor Coleridge (1772–1834)

---

1   Samuel Taylor Coleridge, "Kubla Khan," Christabel, Kubla Khan, and the Pains of Sleep. Copyright in the Public Domain.

In the twelfth century, the romance became a popular source of entertainment in Europe. At first written in verse, then later in prose, romance literature created stories of love, adventure, and mysticism that were, in part, based upon the classics, either from antiquity or the Early Middle Ages. Writers, such as Chrétien de Troyes, became famous. One such writer, Rustichello da Pisa, met a Venetian named Marco Polo (c. 1254–c. 1324) while they were both imprisoned in Genoa. Polo told Rustichello of a trip to and from Cathay (Northern China) and his 20-year stay as one of the *semu ren*, (foreign-born officials, or literally "people with blue eyes") in the court of the Khublai Khan. Around 1300 a book entitled *Livres des merveilles du monde*, or *Books of the Marvels of the World*, was published in Old French. Later, that book became known as *The Travels of Marco Polo*.

Polo's journey, still fascinating and intriguing, was not particularly remarkable, in the sense that it was unique or new. Christopher Columbus had a copy of a subsequent publication of *The Travels* in which he had made marginal notes, and this was certainly inspirational—his voyage in 1492 was a journey to the *East*. Polo's book prompted an invigorated interest in the Orient by Europeans. Yet the most telling aspect of the story is the reaction of the Europeans to Polo's stories: disbelief. The book was nicknamed *Il Milione*, in one part referring to Polo's use of the name *Emilione*, and in the other mocking the book for its telling of "millions" of lies. This reaction is a reminder of the cultural divide that existed between the East and West, in spite of trade and travel, through such means as the Silk Road, had endured for centuries. This divide still exists, though to a rapidly decreasing extent, even today. It is natural for Westerners to see vastly different cultures through "Western eyes," but it is far more rewarding to view these cultures from within their own context.

In 1266, when Marco Polo and his brother visited the palace of Kublai Khan, called **Shangdu**, or **Xanadu** (c. 1271; destroyed 1369), they were well received. Khan gave the Polo brothers a gold tablet 30 centimeters by 7 centimeters which commanded the Khan's subjects to grant hospitality upon the travelers, including horses, guides, food lodging. Kublai Khan has remained a legend in western eyes ever since Polo wrote his travelogue. Khan's palace was described by Polo as follows:

Departing from the city last mentioned, and proceeding three days journey in a north-easterly direction, you arrive at a city called Shandu, built by the grand khan Kublai, now reigning. In this he caused a palace to be erected, of marble and other handsome stones, admirable as well for the elegance of its design as for the skill displayed in its execution. The halls and chambers are all gilt, and very handsome. It presents one front towards the interior of the city, and the other towards the wall; and from each extremity of the building runs another wall to such an extent as to enclose sixteen miles in circuit of the adjoining plain, to which there is no access but through the palace.[2]

Until the twentieth century, Chinese architecture never completely abandoned its indigenous roots of prehistory and early history. The basic systems of structure and decoration, its two most essential aspects—the two most important qualities of any architecture—remained constant for nearly two thousand years. Chinese architecture is described as *organic*—in harmony with its environment—which can be attributed to its invocation of the Taoist philosophical concept of *qi*, its adherence to and compliance with the fundamental forces of nature, and the use of wood as the most predominant material.

The Chinese timber-frame building consists of three main elements: a platform or base made of rammed earth or stone; a post-and-beam skeleton made of wood timbers; and a pitched roof with large, overhanging eaves. Because walls and window openings are independent elements, they can be adapted for various climate conditions, which in China range from subtropical, to highland, to semi-arid, and arid. In Western architecture, this concept came into vogue in the twentieth century. The large overhangs and porches have two important functions. They protect the exterior walls and fenestrations from experiencing a direct heat load from the sun, and thus allow for cooler air to pass through the openings. They also protect the timber frame and other

---

2   Marco Polo and Rustichello da Pisa, Selection from The Travels of Marco Polo the Venetian, ed. Ernest Rhys. Copyright in the Public Domain.

FIGURE 23.2

Dougong. Imperial Palace. Beijing, China.

FIGURE 23.3

Great Wall of China. Mutianyu, China.

wood components of the building from rainwater damage. Wood architecture is vulnerable to rotting, due to excessive moisture, and also to fire. Thus, the quantity of historical Chinese structures is limited when compared to Western architecture.

One of the most important and most characteristic elements of Chinese architecture is the *tou-kung* (also *dougong*), or bracket set, which is placed on top of a column. It replaces the capital of Western architecture, but is much more complicated than a capital. Its basic function is to reduce the span of lintels or beams, thus allowing for an increase in the spacing between columns, and to reduce the cantilever—the unsupported extension of a structural member—for the overhang. The *lu-tou* is the main square block that rests on the column. Brackets, or arms, called *hua-kung*, support smaller square blocks called *tou*, which then support the structural members of the roof. Traditionally, like other components of Chinese timber framing, this is accomplished without nails. The tou-kung supports an eave purlin called the *liao-yen-fang* that is offset from the lintel spanning between the columns. From this purlin extend the *yen-ch'uan*, or eave rafters, and perhaps *fei-ch'uan*, or flying eave rafters.

Like the ancient Greeks, the Chinese used an entasis in shaping a *chu*, or column. The column diameter gradually decreased in the top one-third of the height, although the proportions of columns are not governed by any fast rule. The columns are gradually decreased in height toward the center of the building. Both of these optical corrections are done for giving the structure a greater sense of stability.

The proportions of buildings are determined by a practice of using a module for measurement called a *ts'ai*. The ts'ai is divided into 15 equal parts called *fen*. The width is established as a 2:3 ratio, or ten. From this basic proportion, the sizes of structural members, the slope and curve of the roof, and all other measurements in the building are established according to a system of eight different grades. In multistory buildings, or buildings with more than one horizontal plane, an intermediate module of 6 fen is then used, called a *ch'i*. One complete module of one ts'ai and one ch'i is called a *tsu-ts'ai*.

There are generally two sets of columns in a structure, one at the exterior, and one set in the interior, which are taller to accommodate the slope of the roof. The curved roof of a Chinese building is created by the method called *chu-che*. The ridge, the uppermost part of a sloping roof, is raised up, and the "normal" plane of the rafters is depressed. The entire process is called the *che-wu*, or bending the roof. Roofs are either tiled or thatched, depending upon the importance of the building or the wealth of the builder.

The wooden members of the building are painted with a scaled complexity that also reflects the status of the building. The primary colors of red, green, and blue are combined with black, white, and yellow to create the typical palette of colors used. Warm and cool colors are contrasted with one another.

FIGURE 23.4

Ceiling of Temple of Heaven. Bejing, China

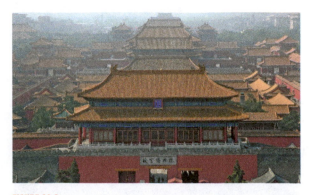

FIGURE 23.6

Gate of Heavenly Purity. Imperial (Gugong) Palace. Beijing, China.

Qinian Dian, or the **Hall of Prayer for Good Harvests**, commonly called the **Temple of Heaven** (1420) in Beijing, is the Parthenon of Chinese Architecture, a paradigm of Chinese architectural balance and symbolism. It is circular in plan, which is the symbolic shape for heaven. The predominant color of the building is red, which is a symbol of royalty. The roof tiles are blue, the symbolic color of heaven.

Once a year, at the winter solstice, the emperor would make a ceremonial trip from his palace to Tian Tan. He would pass through a triple gate at the entrance to the site. The two flanking portals were used by the emperor and by other officials, and the center portal was reserved for the gods. After stopping at the Altar of Heaven to make a sacrifice, the emperor would then process to the Hall of Prayer and pray for a good harvest.

The present structure was built in 1890, to replace the previous one that burned down in 1889. The four interior columns, which are 20 meters tall, are called the Dragon

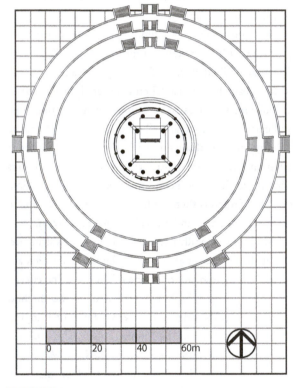

FIGURE 23.5

Temple of Heaven Plan.

The Ming Dynasty (1368–1644) is considered the greatest cultural era in Chinese history. Politically, it was a time of relative stability, strength, and power. Not coincidentally, the arts and literature peaked in both quality and quantity. Many of the iconic works of Chinese architecture were constructed during this period.

FIGURE 23.7

Hall of Supreme Harmony. Imperial Palace. Beiking,China.

Well Pillars. They were constructed from wood shipped from Oregon, as there were no trees available in China that were big enough. These center pillars represent the four seasons of the year. On the site where *Ta-tu*, the palace of the Khublai Khan, was sacked and ruined, a new imperial complex was built in the fifteenth century. **Gugong**, or **the Palace Museum**, commonly called **the Forbidden City** (1406–1421), was the royal palace of 24 emperors during the Ming and Qing dynasties, from 1421 to 1911, when Puyi, the last emperor of China abdicated. The name "Forbidden City" comes from the ancient Chinese name for the innermost part of the star of the universe, which was called the Purple Forbidden Enclosure, or what Western astronomers call Polaris. Inside the enclosure was the Purple Palace, the residing place of the heavenly emperor. The earthly emperor, seen as the Son of Heaven, lives in the earthly Purple Palace.

The Forbidden City is surrounded on all four sides by a moat. The palace area, which contains 720,000 square meters, is protected by a moat on all four sides and four corner towers. It is divided into front and rear, corresponding to *yang* and *yin*, respectively, in traditional *yin-yang* theory. There are four gates: the *Wu Men*, or Meridian Gate, in the south faces the present-day Tiananmen Square. The Outer Court symbolizes the yang, the front, or official part of the complex, for business and ceremony. Five bridges, representing the five elements of Confucianism—*ren* (humanity), *yi* (righteousness), *li* (ritual), *zhi* (knowledge), and *xin* (integrity)—cross the Inner Golden River Water, which is used for drainage and fire protection. The *Taihe Dian*, or Hall of Supreme Harmony, is where the most important imperial events took place. It is the largest wooden hall structure in China. It sits on a three-tiered marble base. The *Baohe Dian*, the Hall of Preserving Harmony (1615), one of several buildings that have been rebuilt after fires, was where the emperor changed clothes before attending a ceremony, but was later converted into a reception hall in the Qing Dynasty. The Inner Court is accessed through the *Qianqing Men*, or wo Gate of Heavenly Purity. The last emperor of China was evicted in 1924 and the site is now officially a museum.

FIGURE 23.8

Five Pagoda Temple. Beijing, China.

The **Wuta Si Temple** (1473), commonly known as the **Five-Pagoda Temple**, and formerly known as the Zhenjue Temple, is a Buddhist temple in Beijing that is heavily influenced by the quincunx tower arrangements of temples, such as Angkor Wat. It has two distinct parts, a five-story square base, and the five pagodas that rise from the top level.

Japan

The oldest religion in Japan is the Shinto, which means "the way of the kami." *Kami* are gods or sprits, who are worshipped in shrines called *jinja*, a *torii* is a gate that is placed at the entrance to a shrine, which, is a simple configuration of two posts joined by two cross beams. Passing through the tori, one passes from the worldly to the spiritual world. There are two rooms that make up the shrine itself: the *haiden*, the place of worship, and the *honden*, which is the inner sanctum only accessible to priests where an object such as a stone or jewelry is placed. The *kami* visits this object, called a *shintai*.

Traditional Japanese styles of architecture were influenced by the traditional architecture of China. Shrines and temples were typically made from wood, using a technology to the Chinese. Horyuji Temple (693) is the world's oldest extant, in situ wooden structure. Himeji Castle (1333–1618) in Himeji, Hyōgo Prefecture is the largest castle in Japan, consisting of 83 buildings, of both wood and stone.

Southeast Asia

The predominant religion in Thailand after the fall of Khmer civilization in the thirteenth century has been Theravada Buddhism. The religious architecture of this period is linked with the important kingdoms that came to power in what was called Siam by the Western civilization: Sukhothai (mid thirteenth century–fifteenth century), Ayutthaya (mid fourteenth century–late eighteenth century), Lanna (mid thirteenth century–nineteenth century), and Rattankosin (from late eighteenth century). *Chedi*, bell-shaped relic shrines originally developed in Sri Lanka, were common in the Sukhothai period. *Prangs*, tectonically sculpted towers, and chedi were common in the Ayutthaya period. Gilded chedi and *wihans*, assembly halls, were often partially gilded in the Lanna period. There are Lanna temples at the Northern city of Chang Mai. Temples and other buildings became more ornate during the Rattanakosin period, whose style is sometimes called Bangkok style. **Wat Pho** (c. 1780) in Bangkok is an example of this latest period of traditional Thai architecture.

The old city of Sukhothai, now abandoned, was first developed in the thirteenth century. Several religious structures have survived and now are part of a UNESCO

FIGURE 23.9

Wat Chang Lom. Si Satchanalai, Thailand.

FIGURE 23.10

Chedi at Wat Phra Si Sanphet. Ayutthaya, Thailand.

FIGURE 23.11

Sitting Buddha. Sukkothai, Thailand.

World Heritage site set in a park-like setting, including **Wat Mahathat** (1240–1346). Another Sukhothai site is located at Si Satchanalai. The Sri-Lankan form of **Wat Chang Lom** (thirteenth century) consists of four concentric square platforms; on the top platform is a bell-shaped chedi. On the lowest platform are forty elephant statues-thirty-six looking outward and aligned with each side, and four standing obliquely at the corners. The elephant was the symbolic guardian of the temple and of the Buddha, as opposed to the Hindu god Ganesh that has an elephant head. A staircase for pilgrims leads to the second level.

Unlike the Khmer monuments, which were mostly made of stone, monuments in the Ayatthuya period were often made of bricks, then finished with stucco. The old city of Ayatthuya was founded in the middle of the fourteenth century. **Wat Phra Ram** (c. 1448–88) has a corncob shaped prang. A series of chedis aligned in a row accentuate the linear arrangement of **Wat Phra Si Sanphet** (early sixteenth century)

The first unified civilization of Burma, or Myanmar, was the Pagan Kingdom (ninth–thirteenth century). At the ancient city of Bagan, there are thousands of structures set in a park. The *zedi*, (chedi) and *pahto* (temple) are the two most common types of monuments at the Bagan Archaeological Park.

Tibet

The large monastery known as **Potala Palace** (1645–95) in Lhasa, Tibet is the center of Tibetan Buddhism. It was a built of wood and stone on a small hill that rises above a plain surrounded by the Himalayas in Central Asia. There are two standout features of the palace-its predominant red and white colors and its height, 200 meters at the highest point from its mid-summit.

A central aspect of Tibetan Buddhism is that humans constantly experience a transcendence from one state into another. The transitional states in between are called *Bardos*. When a person dies, he or she enters a transitional state called a *bardowa*, which lasts for seven seven-day periods. The *Tibetan Book of the Dead*, like the ancient Egyptian *Book of the Dead*, is a guide for people immediately after dying, to help one recognize a state of pure awareness and ultimately be freed from the cycle of rebirth.

FIGURE 23.12

Potala Palace. Lhasa, Tibet.

The Modern Era

In the last one hundred to one hundred fifty years, architecture in the Far East has largely abandoned its traditional heritage. Some of these changes took place due to British and French colonial influences. More recently, it has been the result of the globalization architectural style. In the years after the founding of the People's Republic of China in 1949, a concerted effort was made to build new public buildings in a "modern" style of architecture. The so-called "Ten Great Constructions" in Beijing were completed for the tenth anniversary for the founding of the republic. The new buildings blended traditional Chinese architecture with Western architecture. The **Great Hall of the People** (1959) on Tiananmen Square, near the Forbidden City, is used for State dinners and an assembly building for the Chinese parliament.

In the late twentieth century, and continuing into the twenty first century, coincidental with a rapidly expanding economy, Chinese architecture became completely immersed in global ideas, methods, and technology. The venerated traditional monuments of the past became museums; buildings of lesser-value became subjects of debates concerning the merits of historic preservation.

CHAPTER TWENTY-FOUR

The European Renaissance

To this sollitarie place thus desiredlye comming, with vnspeakeable delight, at pleasure I behelde the straunge manner of the arte, the hugenesse of the frame, and the woonderfull excellencie of the woorkmanship. Maruelling and considering the compasse and largenesse of this broken and decayed obiect, made of the pure glistering marble of Paros. The squared stones ioyned togither without anye cement, and the pointed quadrangulate corner stones streightlye fitted and smoothlye pullished, the edges whereof were of an exquisite vermellion coulour, as is possible to bee deuised: and so iust set, as betwixt the ioynts, euen the enemie to the woorke (if euer there were anye) could not deuise to hide the point of the smallest spanish needle vsed of the best workewomen. And there in this so noble a piece of worke, I found a proportioned substance to euery shape and likenesse that can be thought vpon and called to remembrance …

Then comming to the myddle fronture of the great and excellent woorke, I sawe one sole large and marueylous porche worthy of great estimation, proportioned according to the huge quantitie of the rest of the whole work, which was placed betwixt and continued in building from the one and the other of the mountaines hare lipped, and aboue arched, whose space betwixt as I doe coniecture was in measure sixe furlongs, and twelue paces. The top of which mountaines were perpendicularly equall eyther of them touching the azur'd skey …

Vpon this massie frame and mightie woorkmanship, which I take to be in heigth from the roofe or top to the foote, fiue parts of a furlong, was placed a high and woonderfull Pyramides, after the fashion of a square poynted Diamond, and such incredible workemanship that could neuer be deuised and erected, without inestimable charge, great helpe, and long time…

Euery side or quarter of this foure squared frame, wherevpon the foote of the Pyramides did stand, did extend themselues in length six furlongs, which in compasse about euery side æquilatered of like bredth, dooth multiplie to 24 furlongs. … And of the same stone of Paros as were the steps: which cube and square stone was the Basis and foote set vnder the Obilisk, which I haue in hand to describe.[1]

— from Hypnerotomachia: The Strife of Love in a Dreame by Francesco Colonna

On its surface, the *Hypnerotomachia Poliphili* ("Poliphili's Dream of the Strife of Love") (1499) is an epic that prefigures the common modern literary formula *boy-meets-girl, boy-loses-girl, boy-reunites-with-girl*. It is a romance and also an allegory, both popular literary forms in the Middle Ages and beyond. At the same time, it is a phantasmagoric narrative of one man's long erotic dream. It is a philosophical discourse on aesthetics. Finally, it is a paean to architectural beauty.

The purpose expressed by its probable author, Francesco Colonna, on the very first page is to show that "all human things are but a dream," and "many other things (are)

---

1 Selection from Hypnerotomachia Poliphili ("Poliphili's Dream of the Strife of Love"), trans. Francesco Colonna and Robert Dallington. Copyright in the Public Domain.

Joseph Sold By His Brothers. Bronze Panel from North Baptistery Doors. Santa Maria del Fiore. Florence, Italy.

worthy of knowledge and memory." The book's hero is named Poliphili (Greek, "lover of many things"), and the heroine's name is Polia (Greek, "many things"). Among the countless visions in the narrative are: seven male and seven female dancers who have dual faces, a smiling face in front and a weeping face in the rear; Cupid shooting an arrow into a starry sky and causing a golden rain; a bronze winged horse on a pedestal, but moving at a rapid speed, which foiled the efforts of young children struggling to mount it. There are monuments with inscriptions, which, like the text itself, are in Arabic, Hebrew, Latin, Greek, and a fusion of Latin and Italian. There are imagined temples meticulously constructed with words, and described in great detail. Because of its fascination with and sophisticated treatment of architecture, it was once thought that the architect and writer Leon Battista Alberti was the author of the book, although there are mathematical inconsistencies and discrepancies in the text that dismiss that notion convincingly.

Throughout the narrative, there is the sense that Poliphili's quest for *all things* (Polia) is pervasive. It is a dream that the dreamer never wants to end, unless that quest is successful and all things have been loved. The carnal lust of Poliphili's dream is a metaphor for the author's lust for beauty and knowledge, and thus *Hypnerotomachia Poliphili* is also a subtle portrait of the fruitful and prolific mind, specifically the arts and architects who helped to fashion the visual elements of the cultural revolution known as the Renaissance.

Brunelleschi's Model for Lantern. Santa Maria del Fiore. Florence, Italy. Museo di Duomo.

Il Duomo, or Santa Maria del Fiore. Florence, Italy.

In the early part of the fifteenth century, Filippo Brunelleschi (1377–1446), the Florentine goldsmith, spent more than a dozen years in Rome—not the Rome of Hadrian, or even Constantine—but a city that had shriveled up in size, had retreated in area that approximated its Republican era limits, and living conditions had become problematical. Contemporary drawings showed cows wandered freely through the Forum. Still, the ruins of the Roman Empire still maintained an inescapable inspirational presence, and Brunelleschi spent many hours digging among them and making notations in Arabic and in a secret cryptic code. He studied the traditional classical orders, which the Romans had borrowed from the Greeks. He also studied the Roman method of vaulting and the use of concrete, such as at the Pantheon. These years studying the ancient arts would prepare him for his architectural career, which would culminate in the iconic architectural masterpiece of the Renaissance, the dome of the **Cathedral of Santa Maria del Fiore**, commonly referred to as **il Duomo** (1296–1462), in Florence. Europe. Leon Battista Alberti (1404–1472), perhaps seeing the dome from a hill south of the Arno,

mused that the dome of the cathedral could have held all of Tuscany in its shadow.

Santa Maria del Fiore was originally designed in a transitional Italian Romanesque-Gothic style by Arnolfo di Cambio, (1232–1301). In 1418 the Wool Merchants guild, which was in control of the building program of the cathedral known as the Opera del Duomo, announced that a reward would be paid to "whoever desires to make any model or design" for the cathedral dome. The building by that time had been under construction for roughly 120 years. Brunelleschi was a goldsmith, who had recently lost a competition to Lorenzo Ghiberti, to create bronze doors for the adjacent baptistery. The competition for the dome came down to Brunelleschi and Ghiberti, and they were instructed by the Opera del Duomo to work together. It was Brunelleschi's idea for the dome that was constructed, and eventually he took full control of the project. The dome has an octagon plan, with ribs meeting at a compression ring at the top. Compared to the dome of the Pantheon, the sides are very steep. Unlike the Pantheon, which is made from concrete, the structure of the dome is made from stone and bricks. A series of nine concentric rings, each one smaller than the next, create bracing for the nine main ribs, which form the dome. A lantern was built on top of the compression ring, which allows light in, like the opening in the Pantheon, but closed to the elements.

Brunelleschi's other works in Florence are the **Ospedale degli Innocenti** (Foundlings' Hospital) (1421–1445), the **Chiesa di San Lorenzo** (Church of Saint Lawrence) (1421–1460), and the **Capella Pazzi** (Pazzi Chapel) at

FIGURE 24.5

The Pazzi Chapel. Basilica di San Croce. Florence, Italy.

FIGURE 24.6

Ospedale degli Innocenti, Piazza Sanctissima Annunziata, Florence Italy

the **Chiesa di Santa Croce** (Church of the Holy Cross) (1294–1442).

Brunelleschi was not the first artist to make the Rome journey, and he was not the last. Leon Battista Alberti (1404–1472) wrote in his book *De Re Aedificatoria* (1485) that a building is a "form of body," which echoed similar thoughts by Vitruvius a millennium and a half earlier. Alberti designed a new façade for thirteenth century Gothic basilica of **Santa Maria Novella** (1279–mid fifteenth century) that was a only a frontispiece that did not have a corresponding relationship with the structure behind it. Alberti was interested in pushing architectural design forward from the Middle Ages and therefore the principles and guidelines of proportions outweighed any obligation to register the new with the old. He introduced a pair of volutes to ease the otherwise abrupt transition between the wider lower form of the elevation that included the aisles, with the taller elevation of the nave. This element would be used again by Renaissance and Baroque architects. He reintroduced to the façade a pediment, which had disappeared in the Gothic era. **San Sebastiano** (1459) in Mantua was designed in the shape of a Greek cross, not the traditional Latin cross. It was the first Italian church of the Renaissance to explore a form that the Renaissance architects thought was more mathematically pure. Brunelleschi and Alberti were both influential in the reunification of architecture and Classicism. For the next several hundred years, the ancient orders were reintroduced into the facades of all important buildings, at first in Italy, then all over.

The Renaissance may have been a rebirth of classical ideals, but there was something else going on as well. Alberti agreed with the ancients that Nature guides the hands of the artist, but he also proposed that the artist's mind is equally a factor. In architectural history, the Renaissance is the age of the individual. In history, up to the Medieval Ages, architects were not always identified with buildings, although a few, such as Iktinos, the architect of the Parthenon and the Temple of Apollo Epikourios at Bassae, gained notoriety that endured well beyond their lifespan. During the Renaissance, the architects became more visible, but more importantly, the buildings they designed acquired the traits that could be identified with them.

The symbols of the Renaissance, according to Mumford, were the "straight street, the unbroken horizontal roof line, the round arch, and the repetition of uniform elements, cornice, lintel, window, and column on the façade." Italy was a ripe environment for the birth of Renaissance architecture. The soaring styles of Gothic architecture, ever present in France, England, Spain and Germany, never gained much momentum south of Milan.

Movements and trends, whether in art or politics, are often reactionary to prior movements and trends. We only have to look at recent political history to see the ebb and flow of conservative and liberal ascendancy. It should not be surprising, then, that some of the impetus of Renaissance thought was a contradictory response to the Middle Ages. When Alberti suggested in *De architectura* that the whole should "not be lost in the attention of the individual parts," it was an undisguised criticism of the dispersion of systematic order in Gothic architecture. Antonio di Piero Averlino, known as Il Filarete, an architect who worked on the old St. Peter's Church in Rome, in a treatise on architecture written between 1461 and 1463, attacked the most iconic Gothic device of all, the pointed arch:

> *If the Romans had doubted it [the strength of the round arch] at all, they would have made two arches one above the other, but they would never have used any of these pointed ones [arches]. Since they did not use them, we should not use them.*

Renaissance architects used rhythm as a basis of composition. Sometimes an element is merely repeated, but often an element is contrasted with another element to form a pattern, and then the pattern is repeated. If an ancient building had a pleasing rhythmic organization, it was said to have *eurythmos*, according to Vitruvius. Like in poetry or music, an element can be stressed to create variation, and also like in poetry and music, these stressed elements create a metric rhythm. On a facade, the patterns may be the shape of the fenestration element (window or door),

FIGURE 24.7

Il Tempietto. San Pietro in Montorio. Rome, Italy.

the size, or its articulation, its decorative elements that frame the opening. For a porch or colonnade, the pattern is created by the columns and the *intercolumniation*, the space between the columns.

The *Quattrocento* and the *Cinquecento* (the fifteenth and sixteenth centuries) were the most fecund art periods in Italian history, and together, they are one of the most important periods ever in the history of art. Each prototype "Renaissance Man," beginning with Brunelleschi, would come to be great heroes, especially after the publication of Vasari's biographies. *Lives of the Artists* begins with Brunelleschi and the *Duomo*. The ancient builders, Vasari wrote, "never dared to compete with the heavens" as Brunelleschi's dome does.

Donato Bramante (1444–1514), who was born in Urbino, began his career in Rome in 1500. He originally studied to be a painter, but he was inspired after a visit to Milan Cathedral to devote his attentions to architecture. His first commission in Rome, however, was to paint a fresco over a doorway at the Basilica de San Giovanni in Laterano (St. John Lateran), the oldest church in the city. By the end of the decade, Bramante would become known as Rome's greatest architect. He is given credit for the invention of the rhythmic bay. His most famous structure is a small round temple called the Tempietto (c. 1502) in the courtyard of San Pietro in Montorio. It was built on the supposed site of St. Peter's crucifixion, but this turned out to be an error. Although it is inspired by ancient buildings, most notably the Temple of Vesta near the Tiber, Bramante's hand is well apparent, a condition that Vasari lauded:

> It seems to me that we should be as grateful to Bramante as we are to the ancients; for, if the Greeks invented what the Romans copied, Bramante not merely imitated—he also embellished.[2]

A portrait of Bramante (as Archimedes, the Greek mathematician and philosopher) can be seen in *The Reconciliation of Philosophy and Astrology with Theology*, commonly called *The School of Athens* painted by Raphael Sanzio (1483–1520). Raphael was also from Urbino, and was a distant relative of Bramante. He came to Rome at the request of Bramante, because Bramante had secured the commission from Pope Julius II to decorate some rooms in the Vatican. Raphael's greatest contributions are his paintings and frescoes, but his integration of art into architecture, especially visible in the *School of Athens*, is significant.

Leonardo da Vinci (1452–1519), the archetypal Renaissance Man, left behind many interesting architectural drawings, but there are no buildings that are attributed to him. Among those sketches are ones for an idealized church design. It has been suggested these sketches may have been known at the time he was preparing his first designs for St. Peter's in Rome (see below), however there is no historical evidence of this. Another church that symbolizes the Renaissance quest for the ideal form is Santa Maria della Consolazione (1508–1607) in Todi, Italy. Cola di Matteuccio da Caprarola (unknown–after

2   Vasari.

FIGURE 24.8

Santa Maria della Consolazione. Todi, Italy.

1519) is recorded as being the architect from at least 1510. In 1574, however, a monsignor wrote that Bramante was the architect. In 1490 Leonardo did submit a model for a competition to design the central tower at Milan Cathedral, but it was rejected. It is one of the great mysteries of the Renaissance that Leonardo,

FIGURE 24.9

Basilica of St. Peter. Rome, Italy

whose collective genius in the many disciplines of the arts and sciences was unsurpassed, and who had a clear interest in architecture, never had the chance to practice the trade for a real project.

Of all the great heroes of the Renaissance, no individual had greater skills in all three of the visible arts—painting, sculpture, and architecture—than Michelangelo Buonarroti (1475–1564). The ceiling of the Sistine chapel in the Vatican and the Florentine David are unequivocal masterpieces. His architectural work, although less transcendent, would have nonetheless gained for him a similar reputation on its own merit. The secret to his success was unwavering faith and devotion to his work; his motivation is revealed in his own words:

> *True art is made noble and religious by the mind producing it. For those who feel it, nothing makes the soul so religious and pure as the endeavor to create something perfect, for God is perfection, and whoever strives after perfection is striving for something divine.*

The construction of Basilica di San Pietro in Vaticano (known to the world as Saint Peter's Cathedral (1506–1614) was guided by the greatest artists and architects of the Renaissance and Baroque periods, although Michelangelo's contributions, specifically the nave and the dome, are considered the ones that contribute the most to its prestigious reputation as one of the masterpieces of religious architecture in all of history. It replaced an original basilica that was completed in 326. Around 1450 it showed signs of collapse. Pope Nicholas V commissioned Bernardo Rossellino, Leon Battista Alberti, and Giuliano di San Gallo to rebuild it. Bramante worked on the new Saint Peter's Cathedral, from 1506 until his death in 1514. Under his guidance, much of the old church was torn down, and he designed the new church in the form of a Greek cross. Because he destroyed so much of the old church, Bramante gained a nickname, Maestro Ruinante. He envisioned a dome that would rival the Pantheon in scope. Raphael briefly took over for Bramante as the architect of St. Peter's. He changed

FIGURE 24.10

Palazzo Farnese. Rome, Italy.

Bramante's plan, but it was later changed again. For much of the middle part of the sixteenth century, little work was done on the church, for various reasons, including the sack of Rome during the Reformation in 1527. Michelangelo assumed the role as the architect for St. Peter's in 1546; he abandoned the Pantheon model for one based upon Brunelleschi's Duomo, with a facade like the Pantheon. The drum was completed by the time of his death in 1564. After his death, Giacondo della Porta, with his assistant Carlo Fontana, finished the dome, and added two smaller domes. Carlo Moderna completed the facade, and the church was consecrated in 1626. Bernini took over in 1629. He designed the interior, and created the grand circular plaza in front in 1656–1657, thus completing a process that began more than two hundred years before.

Although it may appear at first that this composite design process created a unified whole, there are some noteworthy problematic issues worth discussing. Bramante's form for the church, the Greek cross (which Michelangelo revived), was scuttled once again in 1608. A Greek cross has four equal sections radiating from a central point. A Latin cross has three equal sections and one elongated section. This elongated section is the nave of a church, where the people congregate. For large numbers of people, the Latin cross is far more practical. The dome disappears as one approaches the facade. Le Corbusier, the twentieth-century French architect, thought that Michelangelo's design was ruined. "The eye would have taken it in as one thing," he lamented. "Mankind lost one of the highest works of human intelligence."

When Michelangelo died, the two architects who received the commission to carry on the construction process were Pirro Ligorio and Giacomo da Vignola who were instructed by the pope to follow Michelangelo's designs. Ligorio was fired because he did not follow this directive. Giacomo della Porta, Vignola's successor, continued work on the dome, but modified the dome by increasing its steepness, and therefore, its height. If you look at the city of Rome today from a high vantage point, and see the numerous Renaissance and Baroque churches, you will see many domes that emulate the one at St. Peter's—not Michelangelo's dome, but the modified one by Giacomo della Porta.

The most esteemed work of secular Renaissance architecture in Rome is the **Farnese Palace** (1514–1589) in Rome, begun the direction of Antonio da Sangallo, but completed, after Sangallo's death in 1546, by Michelangelo, who reconfigured the upper story and changed the facade above the main entrance. For the upper story, Michelangelo created a full-scale mock up in wood, 14 feet long. The building is admired for the clarity of its design.

The palazzo prototype owes its origin to the typical house of ancient Greece and Rome: rooms arranged around a central courtyard, (which can be seen at sites like Herculaneum and Pompeii). This arrangement allowed for cross-ventilation of the rooms, an important consideration in Mediterranean climates. Renaissance *palazzi* were three-story adaptations to this same concept.

FIGURE 24.11

Piazza del Campidoglio. Rome, Italy.

FIGURE 24.12

Palazzo della Ragione. Vicenza, Italy.

The elegance of the facade of the Palazzo Farnese was created by the judicious use of its classical components—strong but restrained; by its self-determining compliance with classical ideals; its unerring proportions; and its subtle blending of repetition and contradiction. If you eliminate the decorative stonework that surrounds the windows and accentuates the floors and roof, what is left is a regular pattern of windows. There are three horizontal zones articulated on the facade, corresponding to the three floors. The bottom floor was for the servants and for ancillary functions, and has the lowest floor-to-ceiling height. The second story was where the members of the family lived, and the ceiling height is therefore taller. Behind the facade of the upper level is the most important space in the palace—the public rooms. Here, the ceiling height is the greatest. From the bottom, each cornice defining the floor levels becomes more substantial, culminating in the roof cornice, which extends five feet outward from the building. The effect created by Michelangelo is bold, yet fitting.

Each of the three zones has distinct fenestration articulation. The bottom floor is the plainest. The second floor, by San Gallo, employs a repeated *a:b* pattern of rectangular and semicircular pediments above the windows. Michelangelo added the coat of arms and changed the center window into a door, with a balcony above the main entrance. On the third floor, a semicircular window protrudes into the space where the pediment

would normally have been. The effect is the lifting of the opening, and thus, the hierarchy is achieved, because the windows seem larger than they actually are, without sacrificing on the overall effect of consistency. Even the embellishment of the second floor fenestration at the center, and the additions of the coat of arms above and the balcony below, do not disturb the order that was created by the elements of the facade. The strong horizontal planes that articulate the internal functions are not compromised; the rhythm of the fenestration is not even interrupted. The horizontal repetition is resolved in the luxuriant cornice at the roof. The vertical repetition is resolved with the hierarchical adjustments at each level, and by the subtle but dramatic accentuation at the center. It is not surprising at all that Vasari called the palace the "finest in all of Europe."

If achievement in the other visible arts—painting and sculpture—is not a factor, then Andrea Palladio (1508–1580) is the leading architect of the Renaissance. Immediately upon the publication of his treatise *I Quattro libri dell'architettura* (*The Four Books of Architecture*) in 1570, he became one of the most influential architects in history. Like other Renaissance architects, he was inspired by Vitruvius. For Palladio, the three aims of architecture had not changed in a millennium and a half: they are convenience, durability, and beauty. What makes a building beautiful? Palladio repeated the classical mantra: a complete form, whose parts correspond with each other and the whole, agree with each other, and are necessary to complete the whole.

Palladio's best-known works are his villas, in and around Vicenza; the **Palazzo della Ragione**, or the Basilica (1549) in Vicenza, an addition and alteration to a medieval hall; churches in Venice, and the Teatro Olimpico (1580–1584), a theater inspired by Roman models, also in Vicenza. A *villa* is simply an agricultural estate; the *casa di villa* is the house of the master of the estate.

The **Villa Almerico, or Villa Rotonda, or La Rotunda** (1567–), near Vicenza, Italy, is one of the masterpieces of Renaissance architecture. It has a plan that is purely symmetrical. A circular rotunda rests upon a square building below, with porticos that project outward on all four sides. That said, the creation of a perfect plan

FIGURE 24.13

Villa Capra, or La Rotunda. Near Vicenza, Italy

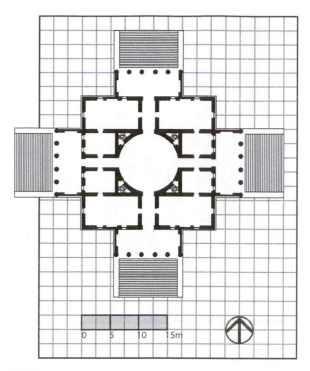

FIGURE 24.14

Villa Capra Plan

does not guarantee that the three-dimensional structure that arises above will also be perfect. Palladio borrowed the basic form from the Pantheon in Rome: a classical porch, an intermediary rectangular area (in the case of La Rotunda a cube), and finally a dome. This relationship is repeated on all four sides. When the German writer Goethe visited the site in 1786, he noted that each side "would be satisfactory as the front view of a temple." It was the site that guided Palladio's design: a small hill with a river on one side but views on all four sides, "one of the most pleasing and delightful one could find.,"

Villa Barbaro (1557–58), near Maser, Italy, has a central two-story section with a broken pediment and four columns, flanked on either side by a long arcades which disguise a two-story space beyond, and finally bookended by pavilions, which are solid basilica-shaped frontispiece pavilions with large sundials above arcaded openings below. Daniele Barbaro, Palladio's client, had great praise

FIGURE 24.15

Villa Barbaro. Maser, Italy.

FIGURE 24.16

San Giorgo Maggiore. Venice, Italy.

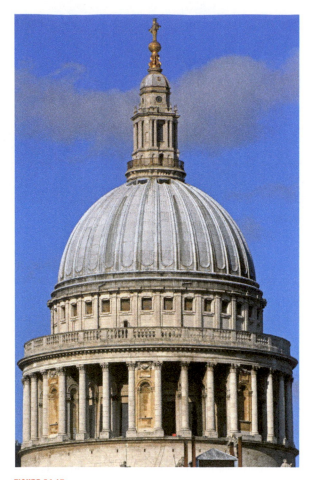

FIGURE 24.17

St. Paul's Cathedral. London, England.

for his architect, whom he thought "best understood the true meaning of architecture." The nearby Tempietto Barbaro (1570), is essentially the Pantheon in plan, with small projecting wings on three sides, and two bell towers flanking the front temple-like hexastyle porch. They are more nimble than the ones that Gian Lorenzo Bernini added to the Pantheon that were removed in 1883.

Palladio designed two prominent churches in Venice; **Il Redentore** (Church of the Redeemer) (1577–1592), on the Isola della Guidecca, and **San Giorgio Maggiore** (St. George Major) (1566–1610), located on the minute Isola di San Giorgio across from the Piazzetta and the Ducal Palace. Of all the landmarks in Venice, including the Basilica San Marco, Palladio's two churches inform the image of the city the most. Seen from the Piazzetta and across the Canale della Guidecca, they are visible reminders of what makes Venice unique among all the cities of the world, a city that seems like it floats upon the water. The façade of Il Rendentore is composed of pediments and roofs at various levels and of different sizes, in addition to a dome and two bell towers that have reminiscent of Islamic minarets. The multitude of forms is unified by the use of a white marble which has a quieting effect.

The main pediment on the façade, as well as a smaller one that frames the main entrance below, are examples of how Renaissance architects sometimes used Classical language in ways that are purely or nearly purely decorative.

The four columns that support the larger pediment and the two columns that support the smaller one do not really do anything. Both pediments project from the main wall surface, but only slightly. The projection seems necessary for the columns, not vice-versa.

The English architect Inigo Jones (1573–1652) also made the pilgrimage to Rome to see the ancient buildings; but in addition, he visited and studied Renaissance works in Northern Italy as well, including those of Palladio. His famous buildings are the **Banquet Hall at Whitehall Palace** (1619–1622) and **Covent Garden** (1631–1635) in London, and the **Queen's House** (1616–1635) in Greenwich.

For the first 30 years of his life, Christopher Wren (1632–1723) was an astronomer and mathematician, who dabbled in architectural engineering. After the

Great Fire of London (1666), though, a rebuilding committee appointed him Surveyor General of London, in charge of the entire reconstruction effort, which included **St. Paul's Cathedral** (1675–1710) and 45 churches spread throughout the city. The effect of this was an unprecedented occurrence in architectural history: a city had been made or remade according to the guiding principles of a single architect. Wren's city would become the city of Dickens and Queen Victoria. In fact, not until the latter half of the twentieth century would Wren's domes and towers diminish in visibility. While the Italian architects looked mainly to Rome for their inspiration, Wren expanded his precedents. "The Orders are not only Roman and Greek," he wrote "but Phoenician, Hebrew, and Assyrian."

The Renaissance Style in England is sub-classified into Elizabethan, Jacobean, Stuart, and Georgian. The latter, having the dates 1702–1830, was highly influential on American architecture. Elsewhere, but particularly in Italy, Spain, and Germany, The Renaissance is divided into three periods: *Early, Middle* and *High Renaissance. Mannerism* is a style that was part of the High Renaissance. It is a name that is applied to certain buildings or time periods of Renaissance architects. In art works, the composition of the subjects in a canvas may not be completely balanced or resolved. In architecture, a composition or form may result from subtle manipulations.

Palazzo Massimo alle Colonne (1532–36) in Rome is an example of a Renaissance building that has been

FIGURE 24.18

Chateau Chenonceau. France.

also called Mannerist. It was designed by Baldassarre Peruzzi (1481–1537), one of many talented architects who worked in Rome at that time period. It was built on top of the foundations for the Odeon of Domitian (c. 90), which dictated its curved façade, An odeon was a semi-circular shaped theater, although the arc of the palazzo is not a complete semicircle. The exterior of **Saint John's Co-Cathedral** (1572–77) in Valletta, Malta by Girolamo Cassar (c. 1520–c. 1592) exemplifies another aspect of Mannerist architecture. The components and Classical language of the façade–pediment, lunette, a di-style porch, bell towers, niches, etc. are disconnected, both physically and stylistically.

CHAPTER TWENTY-FIVE

Baroque

The hasty multitude
Admiring enter'd, and the work some praise
And some the Architect: his hand was known
In Heav'n by many a Towred structure high,
Where Scepter'd Angels held thir residence,
And sat as Princes, whom the supreme King
Exalted to such power, and gave to rule,
Each in his Herarchie, the Orders bright.
Nor was his name unheard or unador'd
In ancient Greece; and in AUSONIAN land
Men call'd him MULCIBER; and how he fell
From Heav'n, they fabl'd, thrown by angry JOVE
Sheer o're the Chrystal Battlements: from Morn
To Noon he fell, from Noon to dewy Eve,
A Summers day; and with the setting Sun
Dropt from the Zenith like a falling Star,
On LEMNOS th' AEGAEAN Ile: thus they relate,
Erring; for he with this rebellious rout
Fell long before; nor aught avail'd him now
To have built in Heav'n high Towrs; nor did he scape
By all his Engins, but was headlong sent
With his industrious crew to build in hell.
Mean while the winged Haralds by command
Of Sovran power, with awful Ceremony

And Trumpets sound throughout the Host proclaim
A solemn Councel forthwith to be held
At PANDAEMONIUM, the high Capital
Of Satan and his Peers: thir summons call'd
From every and Band squared Regiment
By place or choice the worthiest; they anon
With hundreds and with thousands trooping came
Attended: all access was throng'd, the Gates
And Porches wide, but chief the spacious Hall
(Though like a cover'd field, where Champions bold
Wont ride in arm'd, and at the Soldans chair
Defi'd the best of Panim chivalry
To mortal combat or carreer with Lance)
Thick swarm'd, both on the ground and in the air,
Brusht with the hiss of russling wings. As Bees
In spring time, when the Sun with Taurus rides,
Poure forth thir populous youth about the Hive
In clusters; they among fresh dews and flowers
Flie to and fro, or on the smoothed Plank,
The suburb of thir Straw-built Cittadel,
New rub'd with Baume, expatiate and confer
Thir State affairs.[1]

—from *Paradise Lost*, Book I, by John Milton.

Like Dante's Dis, Pandaemonium, Milton's city in hell, has much in common with cities of the living and of heaven as well. In fact, Satan's architect Mulciber also worked in heaven before his fall from grace. *Paradise Lost* is a retelling, in epic form and in flowing, rhythmic language, of the story of Adam and Eve from Genesis in the Old Testament. Every detail of the story is lush and rich, as is Satan, or Lucifer, himself, who in spite of being a villain whose depravity could never be exceeded, is seen as being quite powerful and perhaps of greater interest than the other major characters in the poem-Adam, Even, and God. This richness, applied universally and without

---

1 John Milton, Selection from Paradise Lost. Copyright in the Public Domain.

timidity, is not surprising in an age where all the arts have a similar hyper-energetic spirit, an age where excessive is a word that is rarely applied.

In his book *The Art of Counterpoint*, which is Part III of *Le Istitutioni Harmoniche*, first published in 1558, Gioseffo Zarlino defines counterpoint as a "concordance or agreement" that is created from "diverse parts." The arrangement of tones or voices must be separated by intervals that are "commensurable" or "harmonious." Zarlino had previously argued in *Le Istitutioni Harmoniche* that proper harmony (*harmonia propria*) results from a mixture of tones that "strikes the hearing smoothly," arising from consonance and dissonance, and "induces the mind to various passions."

Like others before and after, Zarlino related music and numbers, and defined a *numero sonoro*, a sonorous number, as a number related to musical tones that is artificially reproduced in a sounding body, such as the hollow body of a violin or guitar. This association was first seen by Greek philosopher Pythagoras (c. 580–c. 500 BCE). In Chapter IV of Book V of *Ten Books of Architecture*, which is devoted to harmonics, Vitruvius

FIGURE 25.2
Façade of Il Gesu. Rome, Italy

FIGURE 25.3
Nave of Il Gesu. Rome, Italy.

argued that fourths and fifths and their corresponding octave extrapolations are intervals that are natural. The idea of proportion having an objective foundation is one that endured throughout antiquity, continued in the Middle Ages (Zarlino cites Boethius, as well), and flourished in the Renaissance.

During the seventeenth and early eighteenth centuries, the period of musical history named *Baroque* was in full fashion. Composers, such as Johann Sebastian Bach (1685–1750), Antonio Vivaldi (1678–1741), Alessandro Scarlatti (1660–1725), George Frideric Handel (1685–1759), Henry Purcell (1659–1695), and Arcangelo Corelli (1653–1713), using expanded methods of musical notation, built upon the harmonic foundations established in the Renaissance, and created music that was quicker, more complex, and more elaborate than anything previously composed. The number of instruments used at one time increased as well.

Le quattro stagioni (*The Four Seasons*), from *Il cimento dell'armonia e dell'inventione* (*The Dispute Between Harmony and Invention*) by Antonio Vivaldi, is one of the period's masterpieces. Each of the four concertos evokes a different mood corresponding to the four seasons of the year, beginning with Concerto No. 1, Spring. Four sonnets, written by Vivaldi, paint a picture of what the composer had in mind; they are not essential in appreciating or understanding the work. The range of emotions displayed in the piece has few parallels in musical history.

If, as the German poet and scholar Johann Wolfgang von Goethe (1749–1832) once proposed, architecture is "frozen music," then Baroque architecture has much in common with *The Four Seasons*. It is often brash, and simultaneously reverential. It is serious *and* playful. Spaces can exhilarate, as well as subdue, the occupant. Finally, Baroque architecture is conventional, as well as personal. Architects, as individuals who found identity in the Renaissance, explore this new-found freedom of expression.

At the same time that Renaissance architecture began to occupy the attention of architects in the rest of Europe, architecture in Italy was already evolving into the next phases, first to High Renaissance, then to Mannerism, and then to the Baroque. Like at St. Peter's in Rome, projects that exercised the minds of a succession of builders and architects often became fluid in the design process. Churches that began in the Renaissance, or even the Gothic period, were modified, or they added a Baroque element, such as a chapel.

The word *baroque* may have been derived from *baroko*, a complex syllogism, or from the Portuguese *barroco*, an irregular pearl, or the Arabic *buraq*, an uneven pavement surface, such as of pebbles or stones, or from all of these. The use of the term "Baroque" began in the late eighteenth century, more than a century and a half after its inception. The word *baroque* was initially a pejorative term, generally describing an excess or absurd object or idea conceived from a variation of a more revered source of inspiration. Francesco Milizia (1725–1798), in his *Dizionario delle belle arti del disegno* (1797), wrote that "Baroque is the ultimate of the bizarre: it is the ridiculous carried to extremes." Among critics, there were more detractors than supporters of the movement until the early twentieth century. For some, it will always be a symbol of excessive wealth—whether of the Church (evidence of which exists today in the abundance of gilded churches), or the State (whose excesses are readily apparent at palaces like Versailles). One could argue, though, that only a small fraction of monumental architecture in history has *not* been excessive.

Sant'ivo alla Sapienza: Courtyard

Sabt'ivo all a Sapienza: Plan

Santa Maria della Salute, Venice

The Baroque period in art and architecture is labeled by some historians as a separate period, and by others as the culmination of the Renaissance. The Renaissance is the embodiment of the Age of Reason, and a focus upon rational thinking, and the Baroque continues that philosophy, but also is an appeal to the emotional aspect of human behavior. Baroque architecture shares with its counterparts in music and art the common characteristics of emotion, flamboyance, movement, indulgent ornamentation, fluidity, and sensuality. Baroque buildings are experiments in spatial illusion, the contrasting of light and color, and the contrasting of forms.

The interiors of Baroque buildings are said to have spatial unity. For example, ever since the adaptation of the Roman basilica up to the Renaissance, there had always been a perceptible segmentation of spaces in Christian churches. The side aisles had a different scale and geometry than the nave and the narthex. Beginning with the Jesuit church **Chiesa del Gesù**, or **Il Gesù** (1568–1584) in Rome by Iacopo Barocci Vignola (1507–1573), this division of spaces became less prominent. Freestanding columns that before were clear expressions of structure, were now integrated into a more solid wall that defined the central assembly space. The continuous aisles of the basilica plan evolved into separate, distinct side chapels in the Baroque. Furthermore, when you walk into the Gesù, you can see all the way to the altar at the opposite end of the church. The façade of the church, by Giacomo della Porta,

The most striking feature of il Gesù, however, is its almost seamless integration of art and architecture, although the interior decoration was not completed until a century or more later. The nave ceiling fresco, *The Triumph of the Name of Jesus*, by Giovanni Battista Gaulli (1639–1709), is an early example of *quadratura*, an illusionistic painting device that creates depth of field through painted natural scenes and painted rather than real architecture, and *sotto in su*, which uses perspective techniques meant to be seen from below the painted surface. A barrel-vaulted ceiling painted with gold coffers, suddenly opens up to the sky. Stucco figures in front of the barrel vault complete the three-dimensional effect, and an imagery of the faithful's journey from devotion and worship to paradise in heaven.

Il Gesù is the mother church of the Jesuit order, begun not long after its founding in 1540. It was founded by Ignatius Loyola was a soldier who was wounded by a cannonball in a battle at Pamplona in Spain. Thereafter he became a "soldier for Christ." The order he founded was known for its discipline and deep devotion to God, and the key role it played in spreading Christianity to the New World and other areas of European exploration and colonization. They were spirited proponents of the Counter-Reformation, the response by the Roman Catholic Church to the Reformation which sought to uphold the traditional values of the faith, and, at the same time, implementing come reforms to correct some of many charges that came about during the period.

Martin Luther's campaign for reform began when he published the single-page *Ninety-five Theses* 1517, which mainly critical of the practice by the church of the selling of indulgences, the reduction of temporal or spiritual punishment through acts of mercy or through donations. While performing an act of penance or enduring a punishment as recompense for sins had always been part of the Christian traditional faith, the practice had deteriorated into *quid pro quo* relationships between the faithful, especially the rich, and the clergy and church hierarchy. When Luther refused to rescind his statements at the Diet of Worms, he was excommunicated. The resulting birth of alternative churches, or *Protestantism*, affected the way Christian churches were designed. Some differences were relatively minor, such as the altar, the focus of Roman Catholic Church interiors. In lieu of the Mass, the Roman Catholic rite that gave importance to the altar, in protestant churches there was a greater focus placed upon the sermon, preached from the pulpit. However, the greatest difference, architecturally, is in one of the basic tenets of the Protestant faith, which diminishes the role the church plays in the salvation of souls. The Council of Trent (1545–63), reaffirmed the role the church plays in the faith, including the seven sacraments-baptism, the Eucharist, confirmation, confession, priesthood, marriage, and the anointing of the sick- which were eliminated or reduced in Protestant faiths.

Some churches and cathedrals were arrogated by Protestant political leaders, while others were taken over when the populations of certain areas changed religions. In the years that followed the Reformation, Protestants did not build monumental or richly decorated places of worship. On the other hand, Baroque architecture Europe, especially in Italy, is a product of the Counter-Reformation.

Vignola, from Bologna, is considered to be the founder of the Baroque movement in architecture. He wrote an influential treatise on architecture called *The Five Orders of Architecture* (1562). Two other architects who also worked almost exclusively in Rome were Gianlorenzo Bernini (1598–1680), the most accomplished artist of the period, and Francesco Boromini (1599–1667), the most innovative architect. Together, they transformed the city of Rome to a similar extent that Christopher Wren transformed London. Of all the periods of its long history, it is the Baroque architecture in the center of Rome that is the most visible today, seen in the ubiquitous fronts of churches that are often mere interruptions of or insertions into the residential fabric.

The rivalry between Boromini and Bernini is one of the great personal narratives in the history of architecture. If you visit Piazza Navona in Rome today, your guide or guidebook will point to Bernini's great sculptural work in the middle of the plaza, the *Fontana dei Fiumi*, or the Fountain of the Rivers (1651). Four godlike figures personify four of the world's rivers: the Danube, the Ganges, the Nile, and the Plate, representing the continents of Europe, Asia, Africa, and the Americas. The figure of the Plate, which faces Boromini's church **Sant'Agnese in Agone** (1652-1672) has his left arm raised above his head, "covering his eyes so that he may not see the facade of Sant'Agnese." Actually, the planning of Boromini's church did not begin until one year after the fountain was completed, so the anecdote is inaccurate. Nonetheless, it makes for a good story, and the rivalry was genuine.

An element of the design of Sant'Agnese, or St. Agnes, is one that is an iconic feature of Baroque architecture-two towers that bookend the main façade, flanking a dome in the middle. At Sant'Agnese, Boromini designed a concave surface between the two towers, thus making the full height of the dome visible. The *drum*, the segmented or curved cylindrically-shaped base of the

FIGURE 25.4

Baldachin. Basilica of St. Peter. Rome, Italy

dome, was lengthened, something that would become a second iconic feature of the Baroque style.

Francesco Boromino was born in a town near the border of Italy and Switzerland in 1599. At the age of 16, he went to Rome, which for centuries had been a veritable architectural classroom. He apprenticed as an *intagliatore*, or decorative sculptor, for Carlo Moderno, the *architetto della fabbrica di San Pietro*, the architect of the work of Saint Peter's, until Moderno's death in 1629. Boromini no doubt thought he would have been given the title of architect for the cathedral, but it was given to Gianlorenzo Bernini instead, who had less experience with matters of building and engineering. But Bernini was well liked, and was already an accomplished sculptor, of *Apollo and Daphne* and *David*, two masterpieces that are both now in the Borghese gallery in Rome. Despite the slight, Boromini agreed to work for Bernini. They worked together at St. Peter's for nine years, from 1624 to 1633. During this time, Bernini, with significant assistance by Moderno and Boromini, created the *Baldacchino*, the first Baroque architectural masterpiece.

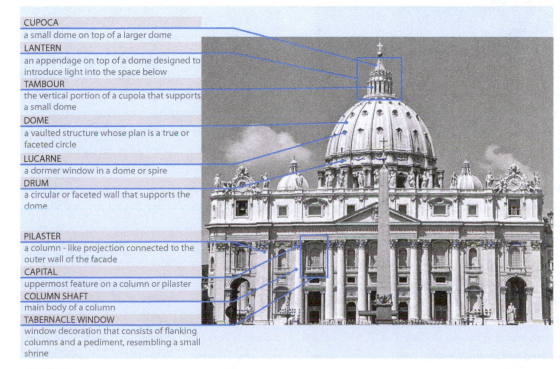

CUPOCA
a small dome on top of a larger dome

LANTERN
an appendage on top of a dome designed to introduce light into the space below

TAMBOUR
the vertical portion of a cupola that supports a small dome

DOME
a vaulted structure whose plan is a true or faceted circle

LUCARNE
a dormer window in a dome or spire

DRUM
a circular or faceted wall that supports the dome

PILASTER
a column - like projection connected to the outer wall of the facade

CAPITAL
uppermost feature on a column or pilaster

COLUMN SHAFT
main body of a column

TABERNACLE WINDOW
window decoration that consists of flanking columns and a pediment, resembling a small shrine

FIGURE 25.5

FIGURE 25.6
Façade of San Carlo alle Quattro Fontane. Rome, Italy

FIGURE 25.7
Interior of San Carlo alle Quattro Fontane. Rome, Italy

The Baldacchino (1633) is a cast bronze canopy structure over the altar, directly underneath Michelangelo's dome. The bronze used in the casting was removed from the ceiling of the portico of the Pantheon, under the reign of Pope Urban VIII—prompting the lampoon, *Quod non fecerunt barbari fecerunt Barberini*, or "what the barbarians could not do, Barberini did." (Barberini was the family name of Urban VIII.) A bronze canopy rests on four twisted columns (a reference to Solomon's Temple in Jerusalem, where Jesus was said to preach), which then are supported by four short marble bases; all of this placed upon the tomb of St. Peter, the symbolic foundation

of the Catholic Church. It was actually Moderno who began the project, who conceived the idea of combining a ciborium, an altar structure consisting of four columns supporting a dome, and a baldachin, a different, less formal type of canopy. Bernini took over the project before Moderno's death, and revised his design. Bernini was willing to take chances, a trait that can secure great fame and success for an architect, or else become a *bête noir*. For Bernini, like many others before and since, the one did not come without the other.

The collaboration between the two artists worked well for a while, but a bad business deal—one involving kickbacks paid to Bernini—soured the relationship between them. Bernini's reputation suffered many assaults, many of which were of his own doing (including a sexual scandal, when he was punished for arranging for the disfigurement of his lover, after he discovered she had been unfaithful to him).

The reason that Bernini was able to overcome misfortunes and scandals was due in part to his affable personality, his brashness, and his political acumen. Boromini, on the other hand, had a volatile personality, was not as comfortable in his relationship with patrons and clients, and was somewhat reclusive. He committed suicide in 1667 by impaling himself on a sword.

Of the two, Boromini is considered the better architect. Two small churches in Rome, **San Carlo alle Quattro Fontane**, (1638–1641 and 1665–1667) and **Sant'Ivo alla Sapienza**,(1642–1650), are tour de force masterpieces of architectural history. Because of their small scale, the potentially cloying impact of Baroque overindulgences is mitigated. Conversely, each sculptural detail becomes more appreciated, because it does not become lost in a profusion of other attention-grabbing objects.

A sculptor begins with a rectangular block of marble. Using chisels, points, compasses, rasps, scrapers, and abrasives, the sculptor gradually fashions an object or figure. Boromini was a sculptor of space; that is, he began with a plane geometric solid and removed material from the inside (this is actually impossible) to create a space. In modern jargon, this is called designing from the inside out.

The space created by the walls of San Carlo alle Quattro Fontane is no larger than one of the grand pillars supporting the dome of Saint Peter's Cathedral. The geometry of the floor plan begins with two symbolic geometric forms—the circle and the triangle. The circle in Christianity represents eternity, for a circle has neither beginning nor end. The equal-sided triangle represents the Holy Trinity: God the Father, God the Son, and God the Holy Spirit. Boromini placed two equilateral triangles, so that they had one common side. Then he drew two circles at the centers of each of the two triangles, to form an ellipse. The shape of the ellipse, literally set in the white marble and gray stone floor and echoed above in a dome that seems to rise much higher than it actually does—an optical illusion produced by the carved octagon, hexagon, and cross shapes that get smaller as they reach the center cupola. The cupola is the only source of light in the church; there are no windows. The walls are white, and so the generous light that comes into the space seems miraculous.

Boromini obtained his next commission, the university church of Sant'Ivo, in part because Bernini had

FIGURE 25.8

Sant'Ivo Alla Sapienza. Rome, Italy.

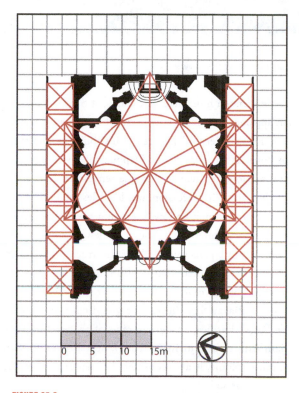

FIGURE 25.9

Sant'Ivo Alla Sapienza Plan

FIGURE 25.10
Santa Maria della Salute. Venice, Italy.

FIGURE 25.11
Interior View of Dome. Salzburg Cathedral. Austria.

recommended him. Like San Carlo, at Sant'Ivo there is an apparent reticence to overstate the decorative play. It is ironic that Bernini's genius was his ability to tell a story in stone, like his Apollo and Daphne, filled with emotion and tension, so much so that one senses that live actors, the best in their profession, would be less real. He was a competent painter, and even wrote a play. Bernini's architectural reputation, although somewhat undermined in his day by a perceived weakness in structural expertise, in time has eclipsed that of Boromini, thanks to the visibility of his most famous project, the seventeenth-century **Piazza San Pietro,** the grand court in front of St. Peter's Basilica, a magnum opus of civic architecture. **Sant'Andrea al Quirinale** (1678), near Boromini's San Carlo in Rome, is also considered a masterpiece of the Baroque period.

Twice in his career, Bernini was hired to design an addition of twin towers to a venerable building, first to the Pantheon, and then to St. Peter's Basilica. The towers added to the Pantheon, begun in 1629, were called Bernini's "ass ears" and were much criticized, although they were not removed until 1883. The problem at St. Peter's was an even greater embarrassment to Bernini, as cracks appeared during construction, work was halted—and finally the project was abandoned. As far as we know, he was never called upon to alter the Colosseum, but if he had done so, he would have completed a trifecta of sorts, of having violated the purity of three of the most revered buildings, in a city where architectural pride runs deep.

Santa Maria della Salute (1632–82), is a conspicuous Baroque church located at the end of the Grand Canal in Venice. It was designed by Baldassare Longhena (1598–1682). The grouping of domes of various sizes creates a picturesque scene commonly chosen as a subject by both artists and photographers.

The city of Rome was blessed with an abundance of talent in the seventeenth century, and there was plenty of work to spread around to these fortunate artists and architects. Pietro da Cortona (1596–1669), an accomplished painter, designed a semicircular portico (porch)

FIGURE 25.12

Nave of St. Paulinus. Trier, Germany.

for the facade of **Santa Maria della Pace** (1656–1657). The two twin churches in the Piazza del Popolo, **Santa Maria di Montesanto** and **Santa Maria dei Miracoli** by Carlo Rainaldi (1611–1691), were placed between three roads that merged together at the square. In the previous century, Sixtus V had established Piazza del Popolo as one of the main landmarks that were linked by straight roadways terminating in public large squares, each with an obelisk in its center. Other architects of the period include Carlo Dotti (1670–1759), who designed the *Madonna di San Luca* (1723–1757); Alessandro Specchi (1668–1729), and Francesco de Sanctis (1693–1740), the architects of the famous *Scala di Spagna* (Spanish Steps) (1721–1725); Nicola Salvi (1697–1751), who created the *Fontana di Trevi* (Fountain of Trevi) (1732–1762); Alessandro Galilei (1691–1737), who designed the main facade of **San Giovanni in Laterno**; and Ferdinando Fuga (1699–1780), who designed the main facade of

Santa Maria Maggiore. Guarino Guarini (1624–1683) and others exported the Baroque style from Rome to the rest of Italy. Guarini's chapel, designed to house the Shroud of Turin, continued the exploration of complex geometries as a means of manipulating interior space.

Although its origins were in Italy, the Baroque architectural style was adopted by architects all over Europe. The secular use of Baroque architecture expanded greatly north of the Alps, in buildings such as the **Palace of Versailles** (1623) near Paris, the **Schönbrunn Palace** (sixteenth–seventeenth century) in Vienna. The Rococo style, also known as Late Baroque, was more fanciful and capricious than the Baroque, and was popular in France, Germany, and elsewhere in the seventh century and eighteenth century, **Salzburg Catehdral** (1614–1628) was one of several projects by the Italian architect Vicenzo Scamozzi, although the design of Salzburg was modified by Santino Solari.

The importance of Spanish and Portugese Baroque architecture lies not only with the churches, cathedrals and secular buildings located throughout the Iberian peninsula, but for the exportation of the style to the Americas during the sixteenth, seventeenth, and eighteenth centuries. As towns grew, most churches built in the early colonial years were replaced by large cathedrals, in the style that had been in vogue in the "old country," normally High Renaissance or Baroque. **Mexico City Cathedral** (1563–1667) has a wide plan with three aisles, which creates a separation of the flanking bell towers from the central portal, adding two side portals like the Romanesque style. The decoration of the front facade is a mixture of Baroque and Classical detailing. The **Virgin of the Immaculate Conception Cathedral**, popularly the **Cathedral of San Cristóbal** (1748–1758) in Havana, Cuba, is a characteristic Colonial Baroque church. Its common name properly refers to St. Christopher, but also honors Christopher Columbus, whose body was entombed at the cathedral until it was moved to Seville in Spain, after Cuba gained its independence in 1902. The cathedral's main facade faces south-southeast, and features a stately Baroque frontispiece, flanked by two asymmetrical bell towers.

FIGURE 25.13

Cathedral of St. James. Santiago de Compostela, Spain.

FIGURE 25.14

Cathedral of Sam Cristobal. Havana, Cuba.

For Further Discussion

Listen to a recording of some Baroque music. Write down impressions of the music as it plays, words that describe its character, its emotions, or its flavor. Select a work of Baroque architecture, and using the list you created for the musical selection, relate as many as you can to the architectural work.

CHAPTER TWENTY-SIX

Historicism

Thou still unravish'd bride of quietness,
Thou foster-child of Silence and slow Time,
Sylvan historian, who canst thus express
A flowery tale more sweetly than our rhyme:
What leaf-fringed legend haunts about thy shape
Of deities or mortals, or of both,
In Tempe or the dales of Arcady?
What men or gods are these? What maidens loth?
What mad pursuit? What struggle to escape?
What pipes and timbrels? What wild ecstasy?

Heard melodies are sweet, but those unheard
Are sweeter; therefore, ye soft pipes, play on;
Not to the sensual ear, but, more endear'd,
Pipe to the spirit ditties of no tone:
Fair youth, beneath the trees, thou canst not leave
Thy song, nor ever can those trees be bare;
Bold Lover, never, never canst thou kiss,
Though winning near the goal—yet, do not grieve;
She cannot fade, though thou hast not thy bliss,
For ever wilt thou love, and she be fair!

Ah, happy, happy boughs! that cannot shed
Your leaves, nor ever bid the Spring adieu;
And, happy melodist, unwearièd,
For ever piping songs for ever new;
More happy love! more happy, happy love!
For ever warm and still to be enjoy'd,
For ever panting, and for ever young;

All breathing human passion far above,
That leaves a heart high-sorrowful and cloy'd,
A burning forehead, and a parching tongue

Who are these coming to the sacrifice?
To what green altar, O mysterious priest,
Lead'st thou that heifer lowing at the skies,
And all her silken flanks with garlands drest?
What little town by river or sea-shore,
Or mountain-built with peaceful citadel,
Is emptied of its folk, this pious morn?
And, little town, thy streets for evermore
Will silent be; and not a soul, to tell
Why thou art desolate, can e'er return.

O Attic shape! fair attitude! with brede
Of marble men and maidens overwrought,
With forest branches and the trodden weed;
Thou, silent form! dost tease us out of thought
As doth eternity: Cold Pastoral!
When old age shall this generation waste,
Thou shalt remain, in midst of other woe
Than ours, a friend to man, to whom thou say'st,
'Beauty is truth, truth beauty,— that is all
Ye know on earth, and all ye need to know.[1]

---

1   John Keats, "Ode on a Grecian Urn," The Oxford Book of English Verse: 1250–1900, ed. Arthur Quiller-Couch. Copyright in the Public Domain.

—from *"Ode on a Grecian Urn"* by John Keats

One of the enduring legacies of British colonialism, which spanned from the early fifteenth century until the late twentieth century was its effects upon scholarship in arts and ancient architecture. One needs to spend just a few minutes the British Museum or the Victoria and Albert Museum in London to appreciate the impact that it had. Until the late twentieth century, travel to the major and minor sites of the ancient world was limited to the privileged or to scholars.

Neoclassical architecture is often referred to as a period of Classical revival between c. 1720 and c. 1820, one of several periods of Historicism that included *Neo-Gothic*, *Neo-Romanesque*, and *Neo-Renaissance*. The term *Greek Revival* is sometimes used to describe this period, especially in England. Unlike the transition between the Romanesque and Gothic periods, or the Gothic and the Renaissance periods, the physical distinctions between Renaissance and Neoclassical are not always apparent, and the chronological divisions are not straightforward. The general term *Classical architecture*—architecture strongly influenced by Greek and Roman precedents—is used to describe all such architecture from the Renaissance to the present day

Paul Frankl, in *Die Entwicklungsphasen der neueren Baukunst*, "refused to call the entire period the Renaissance," as Sir Bannister Fletcher did, partly due to the fact that he considered the Renaissance and the Baroque periods to be "polar opposites." He called all architecture between 1420 and 1900 "post-medieval," divided into four periods, commonly referred to as Renaissance, Baroque, Rococo, and Neoclassicism, although Frankl purposely attempted to avoid those terms. Instead, he organized his study of the periods based upon a building's four "basic elements": space, corporeality (massing or form), light, and purpose.

There are several examples of Classical buildings in Paris that are conspicuous due to their location. The **Madeleine**, or the church of **St. Mary Magdalene**, (1806–1842) in Paris, designed by Pierre-Alexandre Vignon (1763–1828), is a Roman temple with

FIGURE 26.2
The Propylea. Munich, Germany.

Corinthian columns, set on a high platform approached by steps extended almost the full width of the front. In lieu of a scene from Classical mythology, the tympanum sculpture represents the Last Judgment, with Christ in the center at the tallest portion of the pediment. The tympanum of the facade of the **Chambre des Députés** (*Palais Bourbon*) (1847), a similar temple-like building, also with Corinthian columns, depicts a personification of France holding its constitution, flanked by Liberty and Order, Commerce, Agriculture, and Peace. The **Pantheon** (1757–1790) by Jacques Germain Soufflot (1713–1780), has two dominating features: a Neoclassical portico with Corinthian columns, and a Renaissance dome that is raised up on a pedestal, a situation necessitated by the shape (a Greek cross), and the length of the wings. The discontinuity of these elements, reinforced by the plainness of the windowless walls between the two, is unsatisfying, considering its prominent location and esteemed namesake.

The **Propylaea** (1862) in Munich was designed as a ceremonial city gate, and used the Propylaea at the Acropolis for its inspiration. It uses the Doric order on the exterior and the Ionic order on the interior. Ironically, it was designed to commemorate Otto of Greece, the Bavarian born king of Greece (1832–1862), who

FIGURE 26.3
Church of St. Martin in the Fields. London, England

FIGURE 26.4
Library. University of Virginia. Charlottesville, Virginia.

a copy of the Arch of Septimius Severus in the Roman Forum. The *Arc de Triomphe de l'Étoile* is reminiscent of—but not a copy of—the Arch of Constantine near the Colosseum.

The *Beaux-Arts* style was a style that developed from the École des Beaux-Arts in Paris in the late eighteenth century. The **Opera House** (1861–1874) in Paris by Charles Garnier is the quintessential Beaux-Arts structure. It was built over a lake, and became the fictional retreat of the phantom in Paul Leroux's *Phantom of the Opera*. It has a false ceiling that was painted by Marc Chagall in 1964.

In London there are several notable Classical churches: **St. Marylebone** (1813–1818) by Thomas Hardwick (1752–1829); **St. Pancras** (1819–1822) by H.W. Inwood and William Inwood, father and son; and **St. Martin-in-the-Fields** (1722–1726) by James Gibbs (1683–1774). John Nash (1752–1835) has the greatest

FIGURE 26.5
Library Interior. University of Virginia. Charlottesville, Virginia.

abdicated his position after a coup not long after the building was completed.

The **Arc du Carrousel** (1806), by Charles Percier (1764–1838) and Pierre F.L. Fontaine (1762–1853), is

FIGURE 26.6

The Capitol Building. Washington, DC.

FIGURE 26.7

Neuschwanstein Castle. Near Fussen, Germany.

reputation among English Classical architects, for his architectural works and contributions to city planning.

Thomas Jefferson, the third president of the United States, was a Renaissance Man in every sense of the word. In addition to being a statesman and politician, he was the founder of a university (the University of Virginia), an inventor, scientist, and architect. **Monticello** (1770–1775 and 1796–1808), his residence near Charlottesville, Virginia, is filled with many of his inventions and devices, ranging from a handwriting duplicator, to weather vanes and clocks. Jefferson modeled Monticello after a Palladian villa. He taught himself what he needed to know about architecture and building by reading Palladio's *Four Books of Architecture*. There was no school of architecture in Virginia, but it is questionable whether Jefferson would have had the time to attend a university even if there were. There are some aspects of the design of the residence that branch away from the influence of

Palladio in particular, and of Classicism in general. Of all the Renaissance artists, Jefferson is most like Leonardo da Vinci, who was never an architect. They were both addicted to curiosity. Jefferson's design of the student housing on the lawn of the University of Virginia demonstrates this. It is a series of pavilions, separated from one another by small rooms that are like monk cells in a monastery. The different orders of classical architecture are alternated in each pavilion. At one end, on a hill, is the **University of Virginia Library** (1817–1826), which is inspired by the Pantheon. Jefferson also designed the **State Capitol Building** (1789–1798) in Richmond, Virginia, which is modeled after the Maison Carrée in Nîmes.

The symbolic values of Renaissance and Classical architecture—endurance, integrity, and strength—were well suited for government buildings, banks, and institutions that sought to project those qualities through

FIGURE 26.8

St. Louis Cathedral. New Orleans, Louisiana.

their architecture. The **United States Capitol Building** (1792–1867), designed by the amateur architect Dr. William Thornton (1761–1828), was also inspired by Palladio, through Sir Christopher Wren. The building was rebuilt after it was damaged during the War of 1812, by B.H. Latrobe (1764–1820), who also restored the **White House (**1792–1829). The **Lincoln Memorial** (1911–1912) by Henry Bacon (1866–1924) and the **United States Supreme Court Building** (1932–1935) by Cass Gilbert (1859–1934), the architect of the Woolworth Building in New York, owe their appearance directly to the Greek temple.

Although neoclassical architecture may be the most familiar historical style, there are many other important examples of Historicism. **Neuschwanstein Castle** (1869–86) near Füssen in the Bavarian region of Germany is an example of Romanticism in architecture, a medieval or Romanesque Revival castle whose language and function was long obsolete when it was built. It was

built by the king Ludwig II of Bavaria, and inspired by operas of medieval German romances, such as *Lohengrin* (1850) by Richard Wagner (1813–83), who was patronized by the king.

Trinity Church (1872–77) in Boston is another example of Romanesque Revival architecture. It was designed by the American architect Henry Hobson Richardson (1838–86), whose eponymous style Richardsonian Romanesque is characterized by rusticated masonry, turrets, and a heaviness or massiveness of structure often associated with the Romanesque style. **St. Louis Cathedral** (1789–1850) in New Orleans is an example of Renaissance Revival architecture, and is the oldest cathedral in the United States.

There were five separate movements within the general *Neo-Gothic* or *Gothic Revival* architecture style-period that began in the mid nineteenth century. First, there was the emergence of "Anglo-Catholicism" within the Church of England that sought to recognize the Catholic roots of Anglicanism. The many finely-detailed Neo-Gothic local Anglican churches in England, and Episcopalian churches in America, and Anglican churches globally are a result of this philosophy. The second movement was the construction of universities and schools in the Gothic style, deferential to the oldest universities in England, Oxford and Cambridge, and the famous Gothic building at those institutions dating back to the thirteenth century. A third movement, in the late nineteenth century, for secular architecture, was simply the fatigue of classicism and a corresponding rethinking of the merits of Gothic style, influenced by writers such as John Ruskin. A fourth movement looked to the soaring nature of the style as a perfect fit for tall urban buildings. The fifth movement was a residential style, called Victorian Gothic, named for the Queen of England.

The Neo-Gothic style was chosen for the **Palace of Westminster** (1840–70), located on the Thames River in London. It is the assembly building of the two houses of Parliament for the United Kingdom. One of the reasons for choosing the style was that it was the opposite of the Classical style, which the Americans had used to build their new government center in Washington. The adjacent bell tower, **Elizabeth Tower** (1859) houses the

FIGURE 26.9

Reliance Building. Chicago, Illinois.

FIGURE 26.10

Flatiron Building. New York City, NY.

Big Ben clock, a visual and aural icon of the city. The **Hungarian Parliament Building** (1885–96), well-sited on the Danube in Budapest, is Neo-Gothic as well, except for a Neo-Renaissance dome.

The skyscraper is a uniquely American contribution to the history of architecture. From the late nineteenth century until 2004, the title holder of "tallest building in the world" changed many times, but was always an American building, and always located in Chicago or New York. In the twenty-first century, this significantly changed. In the spring of 2011, only one American building, the Willis Building (formerly the Sears Tower), ranked among the top ten tallest buildings in the world.

Although tall masonry buildings had existed in the Medieval Age, most of them residential towers, the origins of the skyscraper began in the late nineteenth century, as a consequence of several innovations in the building industry. In 1852 Elisha Otis announced his invention of an elevator with a safety mechanism that would prevent a catastrophe in case of a breakdown. It was first installed in a building in 1857. The elevator set the stage for increasing the number of floors in a building, beyond the four or five that were considered to be the practical limit. The use of iron to create a steel frame, thus reducing the weight and massing of a tall structure, was accomplished in the **Home Insurance Building** (1884–1931) in Chicago, by William LeBaron Jenney. It was the first skyscraper in architectural history. Structural steel was first used in

FIGURE 26.11

Woolworth Building. New York City, NY

the **Wainwright Building** (1891) in St. Louis by Louis Sullivan (1856–1924).

Other early tall buildings were also in Chicago. The 16-story **Monadnock Building** (1891), by Burnham and Root, was the last tall structure in Chicago using load-bearing masonry. The frame of the 15-story **Reliance Building** (1894), also by Burnham and Root, is faced with terra cotta.

The **Flatiron Building** (1902) in New York City, by Daniel Burnham (D.H. Burnham & Co.), occupies a special site, where Fifth Avenue and Broadway come together and form an acute triangle. It was the tallest building in the world when it was completed. Like the Reliance Building, it has a steel frame skeleton, with terra cotta facing. The decorative style is French Renaissance.

H.G. Wells, the science fiction writer, after seeing the building in the late afternoon sunlight, thought the building looked like a "prow ... ploughing through the traffic of Broadway and Fifth Avenue."

On April 24, 1913, Frank W. Woolworth hosted a dinner party on the 27th floor of his newly completed skyscraper in lower Manhattan, a building variously described by the New York press as the "crowning glory of the builder's art," the "marvel of the age," and "the greatest mountain of steel and stone ever erected by man." The guest of honor was the architect of the building, Cass Gilbert, who in the process of the design, had prodded his client into adding 102 two feet to the height of the building. This was done so that the new structure bearing Woolworth's name (and Gilbert's and Woolworth's images carved in lobby beams) would be the tallest skyscraper in the world, a position it maintained for 13 years, until the Chrysler Building was completed.

The building's design was inspired, at Woolworth's suggestion, by the Victoria Tower of the Parliament Building in London. The pomp and grandeur of this celebration, basked in critical and popular glory for the building's creators, suggest that the premodern reverence for aesthetic ideals, first conceived in the age of Greek and Roman domination of Western culture, and reconfirmed in the Renaissance, was still influential, in spite of the recent trembling of a sociocultural revolution in western Europe, and signs of a uniquely American architecture arising in the Midwest.

Nine years later, the *Chicago Tribune* announced a design competition to create the "world's most beautiful building," an irresistible challenge that attracted entries by at least 260 architects. Although the winning solution was historically derivative, the competition was, in many ways, a watershed, allowing the idea of modernism to establish a foundation within the mainstream of public and private opinion, at least regarding important architecture. The winning entry, by Howells and Hood, borrows from the late Gothic Rouen Cathedral for its base and the terminus of the tower. Because the heaven-piercing spirit of the Gothic meshed perfectly with the fascination with the skyscraper, just like in the Woolworth Building, a new American archetype—albeit borrowed from the Old

Tribune Tower. Chicago, Illinois.

Grundtvig's Church. Copenhagen, Denmark.

World—was born. Although some critics rued that the opportunity to advance a more homegrown ideology (the Chicago School) had been ignored, the success of the winning entry can hardly be disputed. Some of the "modern" entries were unremarkable or lame, such as the one submitted by Walter Gropius and Adolf Meyer, whose works would receive considerable attention in Weimar, Germany, several months later. Adolf Loos, whose works presaged the modern movement in the twentieth century, submitted an intentionally camp Doric column.

Attempts to blend historical styles with modern architecture have generally not been well received, with some notable exceptions. One of the more unique works of the twentieth century is the early Expressionist work **Grundtvig's Church** (1913–26) in Copenhagen, Denmark by P.V. Jensen-Klint (1853–1930). The basic design begins with a Danish vernacular church building, which is then made Gothic in scale and language, and finally the language of both is transfigured with a modern simplification of form.

The language of Classical architecture was revived in the Postmodernism movement, which gained popularity in the 1980's. Some Postmodern works are more properly labeled *Postmodern Classicism*, the use of Classical decoration and traditional motifs in modern contexts, often by playful means. Classical language, once dogmatic, became an instrument of personal expression. Unlike Neoclassical buildings, which were typically monochromatic, Postmodern works of architecture were washed

FIGURE 26.14

Sony Tower, or 550 Madison Avenue Building. New York City, NY.

FIGURE 26.15

Piazza d'Italia. New Orleans, Louisiana.

in bright colors, which, ironically, how ancient Classical buildings appeared before their colors faded over time.

The Vanna Venturi House (1962–64), designed by Robert Venturi for his mother, is considered the vanguard of the movement, even though it predates most of the iconic works by a couple of decades. **Piazza d'Italia** (1978) in New Orleans, designed by Charles Moore, was one of the first Postmodern works to gain widespread attention. Moore employed all five orders of antiquity: Doric, Ionic, Corinthian, Composite, and Tuscan to create an Italian style public space, with arcades and a large fountain.

The **Portland Building** (1980), in Portland, Oregon, by Michael Graves, and the **Chicago Board of Trade Extension** (1982) by Helmut Jahn were the first large-scale Postmodern works to integrate form, color, and Classical motifs. At **Antigone** (1978–2000), in Montpellier, France by Ricardo Bofill, classical elements are used in a monumental scale. Other Postmodern architects included Mario Botta, Rob and Leon Krier, Aldo Rossi, Thomas Gordon Smith, and Stanley Tigerman.

The **Sony Building (**nee **AT&T Building)** (1984) by Philip Johnson and John Burgee, is one of the iconic monuments of Postmodernism. Its most famous feature is the broken pediment at the top of the 36-story building, somewhat called a "Chippendale" top, in reference to the highboy furniture that it recalled. Its second significant homage to historicism is its 65-foot arcaded entranceway, which evokes both the porch of the Pantheon and an Egyptian Hypostyle Hall.

For Further Discussion

Search for some local examples of historical architecture and determine the styles or stylistic elements used. Determine, if possible, any local or regional influences upon that generic style.

PART

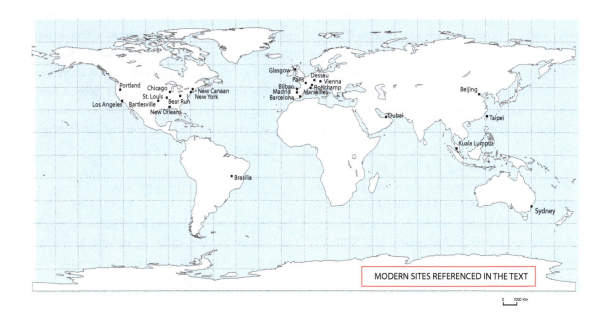

MODERN SITES REFERENCED IN THE TEXT

0   1000 Km

SEVEN

The Modern Era

The seeds of the modern era were planted during the French Revolution (1789). but they were also sown by the gradual erosion of the wealth and power, of both the Church and the aristocracy, and the transfer of wealth that had been born with land ownership in the days of feudalism to industrialists, bankers, and financial tycoons, who, along with state, regional, and local governmental institutions, became the ones that hired architects, builders, and craftsmen. Regions that had been previously separated into smaller factions became unified into single nations. Revolutions wrested power away from monarchies. The dissolution of the Ottoman Empire created independent states in Northern Africa, the Eastern Mediterranean, the Near East, the Balkans, Greece, and Turkey. Italy was united in the late nineteenth century, after a revolution led by Giuseppe Garibaldi. In Russia and in China, reactionary events against oppressive and wealth-hoarding rulers led to the rise of communism, and ultimately a philosophical divide between the East and the West.

In 1928, at a dinner in Washington, Herbert Hoover gathered a brain trust to create a comprehensive report about American society entitled *Recent Social Trends*, which intended to be useful in making policy decisions in his administration. It unveiled social and economic forces that hurried the country "from the days of the frontier into a whirl of modernisms." This sense of rapid change would invade every aspect of design, affecting planes, trains, automobiles, ships, buildings, furniture, furnishings, and much more. Even as the recession of 1929 worsened into the Great Depression, the public's fascination with modernity gained great popularity.

CHAPTER TWENTY-SEVEN

Proto-Modernism

*The next morning, as soon as the sun was up, they started on their way,
and soon saw a beautiful green glow in the sky just before them.
"That must be the Emerald City," said Dorothy.
As they walked on, the green glow became brighter and brighter, and it
seemed that at last they were nearing the end of their travels. Yet it
was afternoon before they came to the great wall that surrounded the
City. It was high and thick and of a bright green color.
In front of them, and at the end of the road of yellow brick, was a big
gate, all studded with emeralds that glittered so in the sun that even
the painted eyes of the Scarecrow were dazzled by their brilliancy.
There was a bell beside the gate, and Dorothy pushed the button and
heard a silvery tinkle sound within. Then the big gate swung slowly
open, and they all passed through and found themselves in a high arched
room, the walls of which glistened with countless emeralds.
Before them stood a little man about the same size as the Munchkins.
He was clothed all in green, from his head to his feet, and even his
skin was of a greenish tint. At his side was a large green box.
When he saw Dorothy and her companions the man asked, "What do you wish in the Emerald City?"
"We came here to see the Great Oz," said Dorothy.[1]*

— from *The Wonderful Wizard of Oz* by L. Frank Baum

In the years that preceded the dawn of a new century-the twentieth since the birth of Christ-there were plenty of reasons for artists and writers-those who pay attention to the general shape of things-to be optimistic about the future, and be confident it would be filled with new thoughts and ideas, and new perspectives on all facets of civilization. The nineteenth century had seen an explosion of inventions that changed how people lived and worked, beginning with the electric battery in 1800, and followed by electromagnetic induction, the reaper, the elevator, the typewriter, the refrigerator, the light bulb, structural steel, the camera, the telegraph, the electric trolley, trains, the automobile and electricity. In spite of these changes and innovation cities generally had not changed much in appearance. Many works of new architecture still relied heavily upon a language that was two millennia and a half old, and Renaissance, Baroque and Neo-Classical buildings from previous centuries were still plentiful. In the late nineteenth century there still existed remnants of the Middle Ages as well. It is not surprising, then, when

---

1   I. Frank Baum, Selection from The Wonderful Wizard of Oz. Copyright in the Public Domain.

Dorothy dreams of the Emerald City in the land of Oz, its basic structure, a palace surrounded by a wall whose entrance was through a protected gate, is a form that is a thousand years old. However, Baum adds color to the wall, clearly indicating that Oz is not only not Kansas, but not traditional Western civilization as well. In the 1939 film *The Wizard of Oz*, Oz is given an art deco flavor, popular at that time. Baum's Oz is a city on the cusp-not quite old, not quite new.

The French Impressionist composer Claude Debussy (1862–1918) was one of the first composers of Classical music to experiment with nontraditional tone collections. Like many of his works, the intrigue of *Prelude to the Afternoon of A Faun* (1892) is not its rhythm or harmony, but the overall effect how the tones of piece come together, in segments, and as a whole.

Early Modern Architecture, or *Protomodernism*, is a transitional period characterized by use of some classical elements and ideas, but expressing an expanding degree of creative freedom. Art and architectural styles from this period include: Utopianism and Socialism, Arts and Crafts, Art Nouveau, Beaux-Arts, Belle Epoque, Fin de Siecle, Romantic, and Art Deco. In the late eighteenth century, nineteenth century, and early twentieth century, architects such as Louis Sullivan (1856–1924), Frank Lloyd Wright (1867–1959), and Eliel Saarinen (1873–1950) were champions of modern ideas in architecture, but at the same time recognized the contribution of the decorative arts to the overall beauty of architecture.

New Lanark (1786) is a mill village located in a lush river valley in Southern Scotland. It was planned and built by Robert Owen (1771–1858), whose Utopian vision was to create a community where people lived and worked that would be crime-free and poverty-free. The mills, which were one of the largest in the world at the beginning of the nineteenth century, were operational until 1968. Another example of a utopian community is the **Garden City** (project) by Ebenezer Howard (1850–1928), a series of communities interspersed with *green belts*, open areas of land consisting of parks and other natural areas where buildings are restricted to only those serving those uses.

The *Arts and Crafts* movement began in the last nineteenth century and lasted for about 30 years. It was a response to the Industrial Age, and the loss of individual craftsmanship in the rapidly expanding milieu of machine reproduction. Its most outspoken proponent was William Morris (1834–1896), who wrote in an essay entitled "The Prospects of Architecture in Civilization" (1881) that "Simplicity of life, even the barest, is not misery, but the very foundation of refinement." In America, like sentiments were expressed by writers such as Henry David Thoreau (1817–1862) and Ralph Waldo Emerson (1803–1882).

The *Art Nouveau* style began in the 1890s and lasted for several decades. As in the works of Gaudí, it is

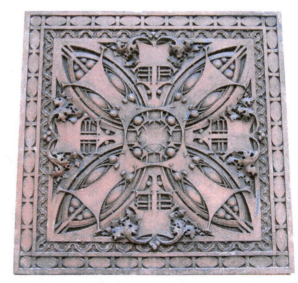

FIGURE 27.3
Terra Cotta Panel Felsenthal Store by Louis Sullivan (1905). Chicago, Illinois. Art Institute of Chicago.

FIGURE 27.2
New Lanark, Scotland.

FIGURE 27.4

Jugendtil Style Generic Mythological Figures from Helsinki Central Train Station. Eliel Saarinen. Helsinki, Finland.

FIGURE 27.5

Metro Station (c. 1912). Hector Guimard. Paris, France.

the Netherlands; the *Stile Liberty* in Italy; and the Tiffany style in the United States, after the jewelry, furnishings, and lamps created by Louis C. Tiffany. The Secession Building (1897–98) in Vienna was built as an exhibition center for Secessionist artists such as Gustav Klimt (1862–1918). Above its main entrance is an inscription which reads *Der Zeit ihre Kunst. Der Kunst ihre Freiheit*, or "To every age its art, to every art its freedom." On the roof above is a gold globe of entwined laurel branches. It was designed by Josef Maria Olbrich (1867–1908). Otto

generally a highly personal and experimental style, with the aforementioned organic or free forms. It is highly decorative, both in religious and secular works. **Rue Paul-Émile Janson No. 6** (1892) and the **Hôtel Tassel** (1892), both in Brussels, Belgium, by Victor Horta (1861–1947), are the earliest Art Nouveau works of architecture. The overall form of the building is simple, but architectural elements, such as doors and staircases, are highly stylized with stained glass and wrought iron, respectively.

The Art Nouveau style was known by different names in different European countries: *Jugendstil* ("youth style") in Germany; *Arte joven* ("youth art") in Spain; *Szessionstil* ("secession style") in Austria; *Nieuwe Kunst* ("new art") in

FIGURE 27.6

Secessionist Building. Vienna, Austria.

Proto-Modernism 287

Wagner (1841–1918) was the leading Austrian architect of the period. His works include the **Majolica House** (1898) and the Post Office Savings Bank (1904–12), both in Vienna.

Two noted French Art Nouveau architects were Hector Guimard (1867–1942) and August Perret (1874–1954). Guimard designed the famous entrances to the **Paris Metro Stations** (1900–1920s). Of over 200 stations that were built, there are 83 stations still in existence with the original design. August Perret used concrete to frame vertical columns of large areas of fixed glass and windows, some projecting forward, at the **Rue Franklin Apartments** (1903–1904), prefiguring similar designs by architects of the modern era.

Antoni Gaudí (1852–1926) was only 31 years old, and had been practicing as an architet for only five years when he took control of **Templo de la Sagrada Familia** (1882–), located in the Eixample suburb of Barcelona, Spain. The project was the conception of a bookseller, Josep Maria Boccabella, who collected the money needed to buy the land under some tiles in his bookstore. His

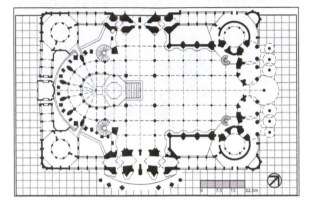

FIGURE 27.7

La Sagrada Familia Plan.

FIGURE 27.8

Nave of La Sagrada Familia. Barcelona, Spain

FIGURE 27.9

Fruit Pinnacle. La Sagrada Familia. Barcelona, Spain.

vision was to create an "expiatory temple," one financed entirely by donors. Gaudí took over the project after the original architect, who had designed a neo-Gothic building, had resigned, and slowly reinterpreted the vegetal and figural forms of the Gothic language. Guadí's highly personal and organic decoration of the temple is often classified as *art nouveau*, while his architecture is linked with a movement called *structural rationalism*. He proposed that construction methods and materials be used in accordance with the laws of nature, and not artificially imposed principles, such as symmetry and apparent form.

The plan of La Sagrada Familia is a Latin cross measuring 94m by 60m. A module of 7.5 meters square is established within this perimeter. Several technical innovations were used in designing the structure of the church. Gaudi created a *catenary* or *funicular arch*—an arch whose curve is formed by a cord fastened at each end and subjected only to gravitational forces—turned upside down. This allowed the building to achieve its great height without the need for buttressing, as was done in Gothic cathedrals. The columns were inspired by trees; at mid-height, a single "trunk" branches out. They are titled toward the directions of the forces, and as such, are less heavy in appearance than traditional columns. When the cathedral is completed, it will be, at 170 meters high, the tallest ever built, surpassing Cologne Cathedral, and more than twice as tall as Notre Dame in Paris.

The appearance of the temple is dominated by its 18 towers—12 bell towers that are dedicated to the apostles, and six *cimborios*, towers with openings that illuminate the interior. Four of the cimborios are dedicated to the evangelists, one to the Virgin Mary, and the tallest one to Jesus. The pinnacles of the towers are of all different designs, tiled in bright colors. Between 1936 and 1954, the project was, for all practical purposes, abandoned. Its popularity has increased substantially in recent years.

Gaudí's unique style evolved while working on the temple and other projects. Early works, such as the **Palau Güell** (1888) in Barcelona, the **Casa de Botines** (1892–1894) in Leon, and a palace for the bishop in Astorga, show both a dedication to the Gothic style and a penchant for the eccentricity that became more apparent as he matured. **Park Güell** (1900), a park and garden

FIGURE 27.10
Casa Mila. Barcelona, Spain.

overlooking Barcelona, is Gaudí's first project where his own personal language overpowered the historical language. **La Pedrera**, or **Casa Mila** (1906), an apartment building, has a unique undulating facade that wraps around the corner at the intersection of two Barcelona boulevards. It illustrates clearly two aspects of Gaudí's work. First, the organic forms he uses are adaptive, and not invented. The context of the building—the surrounding architecture and infrastructure—is disrupted, but not destroyed. Second, Gaudí's personal intervention in the construction process of his buildings was a mandatory element. Drawings, diagrams, and models were merely the first step in the design process. The free-flowing nature of the walls and balconies is described as being *plastic*, three-dimensional forms in art and architecture not limited by traditional geometric shapes. The nearby **Casa Battló** (1907) continued the exploratory nature of Gaudí's approach to design.

Although he achieved a modicum of success in his lifetime, the reputation of the Scottish architect Charles Rennie Mackintosh (1868–1928) gained a significant portion of its stature after his death. He was both a creative and inventive architect and a talented artist, and thus a twentieth century Renaissance man. He suffered some disappointments in his career and did not leave

FIGURE 27.11
Entrance. Glasgow School of Art. Scotland.

FIGURE 27.12
Willow Tea Room. Glasgow, Scotland.

behind a substantial omnibus of built projects when he died. Nonetheless, his contribution to architectural history is securely placed. Although his building designs retained many of the patterns of traditional architecture, he demonstrated the ability—and the need – to finally break free from the Classical language of architecture. He thought it absurd "to see modern churches, theaters, banks, museums, exchanges, municipal buildings, art galleries, etc. made in the imitation of Greek temples."[2]

In 1900, Mackintosh married Margaret Macdonald (1864–1933), a talented painter and decorative artist and they collaborated together on many projects. Mackintosh's **Glasgow School of Art** (1897–1909) embraced one aspect of modernism—the rejection of historical style—but clung to another, the use of ornament. The north wall of the school has large panels of glass, which allow for the infiltration of north light, the optimum light for artists. Decoration of the facade is largely achieved through items that are functional in use, but stylized in design. The building is not symmetrical. The proportion and size of the fenestrations are not classical. There are no historical references. Mackintosh succeeds in breaking free from historical tradition, but the building is not purely a functional response. In this way, it prefigures the expressionist modern architecture of the twentieth century. Mackintosh's popularity, like

2   Mackintosh, Charles Rennie, from "Architecture," in *Charles Rennie Mackintosh: The Architectural Papers*, edited by Pamela Robertson, MIT Press, Cambridge, 1990

that of Gaudi, has increased in the past half-century. The **Willow Tearooms** (1903), also in Glasgow, still thrive.

Cubism was mainly a movement of artists such as Pablo Picasso (1881–1973) and George Braque (1882–1963), in which objects of a subject or subjects, such as a man with a guitar, were abstracted into familiar forms and then re-amassed in a new composition. A minor architectural movement of the same name existed in Bohemia, now a region in the Czech Republic. The **House of the Black Madonna** (1912) in Prague by Josef Gočár abstracts the Baroque Bohemian architecture.

The *Art Deco* style, also called *Style Moderne*, was a movement that affected art and architecture beginning in the 1920's. It first gained international notoriety with the *Exposition Internationale des Arts Décoratifs et Industriels Modernes*, held in Paris in 1925. Art Deco artists and

FIGURE 27.13
House of the Black Madonna Building. Prague, Czech Republic.

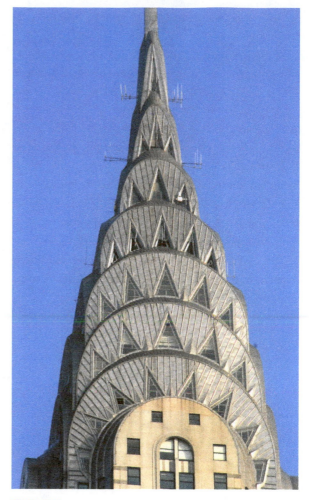

FIGURE 27.14
Chrysler Building.New York City, NY.

architects shared a common aesthetic with industrial designers such as Norman Bel Geddes (1893–1958), a theatrical and industrial designer who designed airliners, floating and revolving restaurants, ocean liners, and aerodynamic cars and motor coaches, or buses, a "house of tomorrow," and even a "Skyscraper" cocktail serving set. Futuristic-looking streamlined designs, which sought to increase speed by reducing resistance to air or water, were an integral part of culture, manifested in trains, planes, automobiles, and cruise ships, and mimicked in housewares, furniture, jewelry and appliances.

In 1927, Carl Breer, the chief engineer of the Chrysler Motor Corporation, observed what he thought was a flock of geese in the sky, which turned out to be a V-formation of airplanes. Not long thereafter, he proposed his design of the Chrysler Airflow, which had streamlined corners, and other aerodynamic features. At about the same time, his boss, Walter Chrysler, was engaged in a vastly different project, but one that shared similar aesthetic visions.

The plans for the **Chrysler Building** (1930) by William Van Alen originally called for it to be 925 feet tall. The nearby Bank of Manhattan building was being built to a height of 927 feet. The race was on to build the world's tallest building, and it seemed as if Chrysler was going to lose. Chrysler, however, had instructed Van Alen to keep a 123-foot tower hidden until the last possible moment. The building then measured 1,048 feet, and

it was now taller than the Eiffel Tower in Paris, which had been the world's tallest structure of any kind to that point. The tower was covered with stainless steel, creating the distinctive pinnacle-shaped crown, for which the building is famous.

The tower and the lobby are two masterpieces of the *Art Deco* style, also called *Style Moderne*. Each of the four sides of the tower has five arches made from stainless steel, which diminish in height and width toward a final icicle pointed upward toward the sky. Triangle-shaped windows are set into the arches, radiating from the top portion of an eight-story rounded-top massing that is inset from stories below it. The effect is like a series of stainless steel sunsets, one on top of another, emitting a constant energy and radiation, regardless of the condition of the sky.

The reign of the Chrysler Building as the world's tallest building did not last long. The **Empire State Building** (1931) by William Lamb of Shreve, Lamb & Harmon, was the first building to have more than 100 stories. Also an Art Deco building, it was the tallest building in the world until the World Trade Center supplanted it in 1972. Its reputation for years as the tallest building in the world has always overshadowed its architectural merits. Nonetheless, its place in history is well established, in no small part due to its star presence in movies like *King Kong, An Affair to Remember* and *Sleepless in Seattle*.

The **Art Deco District**, properly the **Miami Beach Architecture District**, in Miami Beach, Florida. Miami Beach was in the middle of a "building boom" which triggered the construction of many buildings of the same style. The boom suddenly ended in the late 1920's when two significant hurricanes devastated south Florida. The area remained relatively quiet until a "rediscovery" took place in the 1980's which transformed the architecture into an element of pop culture.

For Further Discussion

The Proto-Modern period in architecture is the last in which art was almost always integrated into serious works of architecture. Find some examples of buildings since that period that continued the tradition.

CHAPTER TWENTY-EIGHT

Modernism

By day the skyscraper looms in the smoke and sun and has a soul.

Prairie and valley, streets of the city, pour people into it and they mingle among its twenty floors and are poured out again back to the streets, prairies and valleys.

It is the men and women, boys and girls so poured in and out all day that give the building a soul of dreams and thoughts and memories.

(Dumped in the sea or fixed in a desert, who would care for the building or speak its name or ask a policeman the way to it?)

Elevators slide on their cables and tubes catch letters and parcels and iron pipes carry gas and water in and sewage out.

Wires climb with secrets, carry light and carry words, and tell terrors and profits and loves—curses of men grappling plans of business and questions of women in plots of love.

Hour by hour the caissons reach down to the rock of the earth and hold the building to a turning planet.

Hour by hour the girders play as ribs and reach out and hold together the stone walls and floors.

Hour by hour the hand of the mason and the stuff of the mortar clinch the pieces and parts to the shape an architect voted.

Hour by hour the sun and the rain, the air and the rust, and the press of time running into centuries, play on the building inside and out and use it.

Men who sunk the pilings and mixed the mortar are laid in graves where the wind whistles a wild song without words

And so are men who strung the wires and fixed the pipes and tubes and those who saw it rise floor by floor.

Souls of them all are here, even the hod carrier begging at back doors hundreds of miles away and the brick-layer who went to state's prison for shooting another man while drunk.

(One man fell from a girder and broke his neck at the end of a straight plunge—he is here—his soul has gone into the stones of the building.)

On the office doors from tier to tier—hundreds of names and each name standing for a face written across with a dead child, a passionate lover, a driving ambition for a million dollar business or a lobster's ease of life.

Behind the signs on the doors they work and the walls tell nothing from room to room. Ten-dollar-a-week stenographers take letters from corporation officers, lawyers, efficiency engineers, and tons of letters go bundled from the building to all ends of the earth.

Smiles and tears of each office girl go into the soul of the building just the same as the master-men who rule the building.

Hands of clocks turn to noon hours and each floor empties its men and women who go away and eat and come back to work.

Toward the end of the afternoon all work slackens and all jobs go slower as the people feel day closing on them. One by one the floors are emptied ... The uniformed elevator men are gone. Pails clang ... Scrubbers work, talking in foreign tongues. Broom and water and mop clean from the floors human dust and spit, and machine grime of the day.

Spelled in electric fire on the roof are words telling miles of houses and people where to buy a thing for money. The sign speaks till midnight.

Darkness on the hallways. Voices echo. Silence holds ... Watchmen walk slow from floor to floor and try the doors. Revolvers bulge from their hip pockets ... Steel safes stand in corners. Money is stacked in them.

A young watchman leans at a window and sees the lights of barges butting their way across a harbor, nets of red and white lanterns in a railroad yard, and a span of glooms splashed with lines of white and blurs of crosses and clusters over the sleeping city.

By night the skyscraper looms in the smoke and the stars and has a soul.[1]

— from "Skyscraper" by Carl Sandburg

In a famous scene from the 1949 film classic *The Fountainhead*, based upon the 1943 novel by Ayn Rand, Gary Cooper, playing Howard Roark (owing much to the individualist spirit of Frank Lloyd Wright), silently stews and simmers while his clients add cardboard Neoclassical decoration to the model of a building he has designed for them in a sleek and modern style. Finally, he says to them, "If you want my work, you must take it as it is or not at all." Although Rand pointed to Wright as a source of inspiration for the hero-protagonist of her novel, in the film, the architectural drawings and sketches are more generically (and ironically less individualistically) modern. What is clear in the film is that the *pastiche* elements the other architects add so easily to the facades are superfluous. The genius of the design—economy and efficiency—is unchanged by their addition. Roark's building had its own inherent beauty; the cardboard add-ons were unnecessary.

Howard Roark, the rugged but elegant individualist, is a hero to architects, because he strikes a blow (literally, actually) against what they perceived to be an oppression which they had suffered for centuries—the archaic prescriptive language of Classicism. At the end of the movie, after the manipulative, dogmatic critic has been defeated, the sympathetic but apprehensive patron has succumbed to self-destruction, and the cynicism of the alter-ego heroine has been subdued, the hero and heroine ride a

construction elevator up a sleek skyscraper that seems a mile high, as if to say, "the impediments to modernism now gone, the sky is the limit." This image of the noble architect, laden with lofty ideals and principles, embattling his practical-minded, often conservative client is emblematic of the period. It is a scene that was played out many times over throughout the twentieth century with the rise of modernism, by far the most industrious era in the history of building. The message of the modern architects: the beauty is the form of the structure itself; any decoration is gratuitous.

The modern approach to form has manifested itself in various stylistic approaches, which can be classified under two general categories. There are various labels for each one, and each broad style has several specific styles associated with it. The first category is referred to as the *modernist* style, or *pure modernism*, or perhaps *minimalist*. The next chapter will explore the second broad category, expressionistic. The term *modern* is often used to describe works of architecture in either broad category, but there are significant, fundamental differences that distinguish one from the other.

The most famous painting in Western civilization, the *Mona Lisa* by Leonardo da Vinci, measures only 53 centimeters by 77 centimeters (21 inches by 30 inches). By comparison, *Liberty Leading the People*, by Eugène Delacroix, measures 325 centimeters by 260 centimeters (128 inches by 102 inches). The *Mona Lisa*, *or La Gioconda*, is a portrait of a woman who is neither queen

[1] Carl Sandburg, "Skyscraper." Copyright in the Public Domain.

nor princess; she is the wife of a silk merchant. *Liberty Leading the People* depicts a watershed moment in French history: the July 1830 uprising against Charles X. The central figure of *Liberty* is Marianne, a national emblem. What makes the success of the *Mona Lisa* remarkable is that it is an exception. Most great works of art until the nineteenth century depicted grandiloquent subjects from history, religion, mythology, or sovereignty. In the late nineteenth century, with works of art such as Édouard Manet's *Le Dejeuner sur l'Herbe* (*Luncheon on the Grass*—1863), the use of ordinary subjects by artists became more frequent, anticipating the twentieth century, when common subjects were nearly a mandate. The greatest works of literature, with few exceptions, also focused on an epic hero or event, such as *Gilgamesh*, the Homeric epics, *Beowulf*, and *Paradise Lost*. In the modern era, *Ulysses*, by James Joyce, is consistently named as the most important novel of the English language (by the Modern Library, for example). It is the story of a single day in the life of an ordinary man. In contrast, *Citizen Kane*, consistently the top-rated film of the American Film Institute's rankings of English-language films, is the story of a celebrated man whose life's grandeur becomes his undoing, and who ultimately laments having been denied a more unexceptional youth.

The important works of architecture throughout most of history were also larger than life. With few exceptions, they were large-scale public works, whether secular or religious. Similar to developments in art and literature, the substance of architecture changed considerably in the modern era. Residential structures, excluding palaces for the ruling elite, were studied for their contribution to our understanding of the lifestyles of civilizations, but were rarely singled out for their aesthetic contributions. , In the twentieth century, monumentality became less significant in judging a work's cultural significance. The single greatest work of American architecture, according to a survey of architects by the American Institute of Architects, is Frank Lloyd Wright's Falling Water, a single-family residence built over a stream in the woods of Pennsylvania.

Until the modern era, townscapes of villages, towns, and cities were dominated by religious buildings. In the modern era, both the Church (the domineering institution) and the church (the physical embodiment of any organized religious institution), lost their pre-eminence in their placement and their importance in the community. There was a dissipation of faith into sundry and diverse directions, and a corresponding dispersal of religious structures. At the same time, the scale and amount of secular buildings substantially increased. From the aspect of urban planning, a church could still dominate a neighborhood, but no longer a community, let alone a larger urban area.

The basic structure of towns and cities changed little from the beginning of the Middle Ages, until the eighteenth century, when the agrarian model of civilizations—in which the majority of people worked as farmers or peasants—was transformed by the Industrial Revolution. To accommodate a rapidly increasing population, combined with a rapid influx of people moving into cities, the city itself was transformed, with structures that were either new or had completely revamped functions: factories; office buildings; densely populated residential structures; buildings for an expanding governmental complex; cultural buildings; and the necessary infrastructure to accommodate concentrated populations.

In 1917 the French architect Tony Garnier (1869–1948) published *Une Cité Industrielle: Étude pour la construction des villes* (*An industrial city: A study in the construction of towns*), a model city made completely out of reinforced concrete. It was inspired by a novel entitled *Travail*, published in 1900 by Emile Zola (1840–1902).

From an architectural perspective, the initial response to the Industrial Revolution was adaptation; ultimately, this changed to innovation. In the twentieth century, all facets of architecture—the appearance of structures, the spatial quality of structures, the engineering and mechanics of buildings, the process of design and construction—were analyzed from a fresh perspective. Many architects looked at traditional means and methods, and came to the conclusion that they were no longer relevant.

The new design theories were often so much unlike the old, that the two could rarely subsist side by side without causing friction, thus polarizing public opinion into two distinct camps—traditionalists and modernists. The dramatic, ubiquitous juxtaposition of premodern and modern—of old and new—in cities and towns all over the world is at the crux of the discussion about modern architecture. Where the disciplined patterns and symbols of the ancient world meet the emancipated and uninhibited patterns and symbols of the modern world, there is tension, one that is unlikely to ever be resolved. Neither one is necessarily wrong; they are just different. Bernard Bosanquet, in *A History of Aesthetic*, anticipated this conflict in 1892, long before the modern movement had gained much steam. He wrote that the *bête noire* of modern art is its constant "contradiction" with history.

The origins of modern thought began in the eighteenth century with Immanuel Kant (1724–1804), who was an important contributor to the study of aesthetics. He expressed the notion that the matter of taste is subjective, thereby denying the object its right to please. The objects themselves have identity, in a particular space and time, and our reaction to them is forever momentary. It is the perspective of the viewer that addresses its character. This "judgment" is divided into logical and aesthetic, or "contemplative," sections. It follows then, according to Kant, that the dicta of Vitruvius and the dicta of the revivers of the Classical form, which had guided the hands of architects for most of architectural history since antiquity, were no longer relevant.

Some would argue that the "modern" basis for the interpretation of beauty was not really new. It was, ironically, 23 centuries old. Bosanquet, paraphrasing Plato and Aristotle, provided a platform for modern theory, proposing that beauty is "purely formal, consisting in certain very abstract conditions which are satisfied, for example, in elementary geometrical figures as truly as in the creations of fine art." The connotation of the word *modern* is subject to continuous transformation and renewal. It can mean "up to date," and could apply equally to technology and ideas. *Modern* can also mean "of or relating to the present or recent times." The use of the word *modern* to describe art, architecture, or music, could be used in this sense. An Elvis Presley or a Beatles song on the radio was once considered to be modern music, but is now just a "golden oldie." However, the term Modern Architecture, like Modern Art, has become fixed in time, referring to a specific cultural period.

FIGURE 28.2

Goldmanand Salatsch Building. Vienna, Austria.

At the close of the nineteenth century and the beginning of the twentieth century, there were two significant values in question: the use of Classical forms, order, and decorative elements, and the purpose and usefulness of ornament. The former was challenged first, then followed by the latter. One of the earliest challenges against Historicism came from the German philosopher Friedrich Nietzsche, who wrote in 1872 that the "inartistic and half-artistic … do not want greatness to rise; their method is to say, 'See, the great thing is already here!'"

In the twentieth century, innovation became the most important factor in the success of cultural works. As a result, works of art, music, and architecture were more self-conscious than in any other period in history. The Avant-garde (French: "before the guard) movement in the arts, whose works are highly experimental, and profess to be at the forefront of artistic movements or trends, often purposely sacrificing content for the sake of ideas, as in these examples.

In 1908 Adolf Loos (1870–1933) published a provocative essay called "Ornament and Crime," in which he stated that the "lack of ornament is a sign of intellectual power." He chided his fellow architects for applying corbels and "garlands of fruit" made out of cement to ersatz palaces of clients. His design for the **Goldman & Salatsch Building** (1910), now called the **Looshaus**, is one of the earliest completely modern buildings of any significance. Its minimalist design caused a minor scandal in Vienna.

The term *Modern architecture* is more general than other styles, in that there are many diverse substyles within the broader context of *modernism. Early Modern architecture*, or *Protomodernism*, is a transitional period between the Classical period and the modern, characterized by the use of some Classical elements and ideas, but expressing a high degree of creative freedom. Substyles of this period include *Arts and Crafts*, a reactionary movement against the Industrial Age that emphasized natural materials and designs; *Beaux-Arts*, a highly decorative style born in the École des Beaux-Arts in Paris; *De Stijl*, a Dutch movement that focused on simple, rectangular forms; *Fin de Siècle*, a style of the late nineteenth century and early twentieth century, known for its opulence; and *Art Deco*, a highly decorative style influenced by nontraditional sources (Egypt, rather than Greek or Roman, for example).

High Modern Architecture is characterized by the absence of classical motifs and forms, the exploration of abstract forms, and the minimal, or lack of, use of applied ornamentation. Substyles are *Bauhaus*, *Expressionist*, and *Modernist*. Late Modern Architecture is characterized by absolute simplification of form, an emphasis on function, the exposition of structure, and the exposition of construction materials. Its two prominent styles are the *International Style* and *Brutalism.*

The fundamental philosophy of modern architecture is that the art of architecture is *tectonic*, relating to the structure. It is implicit and inseparable from the building's form, and is not applied. The application or association of art with a building is superfluous. For some, this means that such an inclusion of art is detrimental to the purity of the design. For others, art can be a welcome, if nonessential, element.

In 1907 the *Werkbund* was founded by Hermann Muthesius in Germany, to promote cooperation between artists and craftsmen and trade and industry. In 1910 Walter Gropius (1883–1969), a *Werkbund* leader, published, with Peter Behrens, *Memorandum on the Industrial Prefabrication of Houses on a Unified Artistic Basis*, which advocated a move toward the synthesis of technology and art. In 1919 Gropius combined the Weimar Arts and Crafts School with the Weimar Art Academy and created the *Bauhaus*, whose teachers included Johannes Itten, Lyonel Feininger and Gerhard Marcks. In the next four years the school added Adolf Meyer, Georg Muche, Paul Klee, Oskar Schlemmer, Wassily Kandinsky, and Laszlo Moholy-Nagy, all of whom either were, or became, accomplished artists of the period. The founding principal was stated in *The Theory and Organization of the Bauhaus* (1923):

Human achievement depends on the proper coordination of all the creative faculties. It is not enough to school one or another of them separately: they must all be thoroughly trained at the same time.

The curriculum at the Bauhaus included hands-on instruction in the materials, such as stone, wood, metal, clay, glass, furniture, and textiles; as well as empirical studies of form, color, geometry, space, and nature; and technical instruction in construction and representation. "Bauhaus evenings" brought those accomplished in art, architecture, and other fields, such as music and science.

Le Corbusier, né Charles-Édouard Jeanneret (1887–1965), was, in many respects, the most influential architect of the twentieth century. In 1923 he published *Vers une Architecture*, which was translated to *Toward a New Architecture* when it was published in English in New York. Echoing the phraseology of Loos 15 years earlier, Le Corbusier pronounced that style is "a lie." He proposed that the aim of architecture is to "achieve a state of platonic grandeur, mathematical order, speculation, and the perception of harmony which lies in emotional relationships." It is the one art that has the capability of doing so.

He famously expressed the idea that a house is "a machine for living," which paved the way for a complete rethinking of not only what a house should look like—its aesthetics—but its function as well. His **Villa Savoye** (1928–1931), near Poissy, France, explored several ideas previously not expressed or seen in residential architecture: the house was lifted up on *pilotis*, or stilt columns and piles, so that the main living level was on the second floor; it had no traditional exterior or interior supporting walls, thus the plan was "free"; the wall was cantilevered

FIGURE 28.3
Unite D'Habitacion.Marseilles, France.

FIGURE 28.4
Roof Detail. Unite D'Habitacion.Marseilles, France.

FIGURE 28.5
Balcony Detail. Unite D'Habitacion.Marseilles, France.

beyond the columns, freeing the facade from columns, thus giving complete freedom to the fenestration, which became a horizontal band of glass; and the roof was used as a garden. These innovations would later be used in the *ribbon glass* style of office building design that still is used in some buildings today.

The **Unité d'Habitation** (1946–1952) a large "community" apartment building in Marseilles, France, employed the pilotis concept on the ground floor, and expanded the idea of a roof garden into a large public square built on the roof, which included a swimming pool, gymnasium, a nursery, and an area for lounge chairs. On the middle floor of the building were community facilities and a small shopping area. Although many of these items have become common, they were considered pioneering at that time. Other innovations included

FIGURE 28.6
Interior of Barcelona Pavillion. Barcelona, Spain

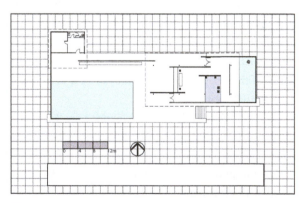

FIGURE 28.7
Barcelona Pavillion Plan

the use of *brise-soleil* (French, "sun break"), sun-shading devices. The balconies were already recessed from the exterior wall line. The concrete side walls of the balconies were stained in different colors, creating an irregular pattern. A ventilation intake on the roof was designed to look like a piece of sculpture. Le Corbusier was one of the first architects to use exposed concrete walls, called *béton brut*. On the ground floor, Le Corbusier's Modular Man is incised into the concrete.

The **Barcelona Pavillion** (1929–1930; rebuilt 1986) was designed for the 1929 International Exposition in Barcelona by Ludwig Mies van der Rohe (1886–1969). A series of innovations in the building were the reason why the unusual step of rebuilding a building that had served its intended purpose and had been demolished. The roof seems like it is floating; instead of columns, it supported by vertical planes (walls). The distinction between indoor and outdoor space is blurred; the glass walls extend from floor to roof; the floor and ceiling surfaces seem continuous through the exterior wall. The veins of the marble are meticulously matched on the most prominent interior wall. There is no need for a work of art tube hung on the wall; the architectural material becomes the art.

In 1932 Phillip Johnson (1906–2005) and Henry-Russell Hitchcock (1903–1987) published *The International Style: Architecture Since 1922*, which accompanied an exhibition or show at the Museum of Modern Art in New York called "Modern Architecture—International Exhibition. The three main characteristics of what they called the "International style" were: a prohibition of applied ornament; an emphasis of volume instead of mass; and an organization based upon "regularity," rather than symmetry. The International style was a universal style, as opposed to the diverse revival styles of the nineteenth century. Earlier manifestations of the modern style were "fragmentary and contradictory." According to Johnson and Hitchcock, the International style was as significant as any other style of the past. From a structural perspective, the International style was innovative and expressive, like the Gothic style. From a design perspective, it was like Classical. Functionally, it was better than either one. "There is now a single body of discipline," they exclaimed, "fixed enough to

FIGURE 28.8

Phillip Johnson House, "The Glass House". New Canaan, Connecticut.

FIGURE 28.9

Farnsworth House. Plano, Illinois.

permit individual interpretation and to encourage general growth."

Johnson's **Glass House** (1949), in New Canaan, Connecticut, like Mies van der Rohe's **Farnsworth House** (1952) in Plano, Illinois (from which it drew inspiration), became famous as an icon of modernity. It was one of several buildings Johnson built on his estate during his lifetime. Functionally, it was better suited as a pavilion for entertaining than a single-family residence, and that is what it became. The use of large panels of glass as exterior walls is one feature of what became known as *Mid-Century Modern* architecture.

In 1955 Johnson published "The Seven Crutches of Modern Architecture," a transcription of a talk he delivered to students at the Harvard Graduate School of

Design the previous year. The crutches—history, pretty drawings, utility, comfort, cheapness, serving the client, and structure—constitute a language of design tools. A few decades earlier, Le Corbusier had called style a lie, and now Johnson, the one architect in the twentieth century who was, at once, an integral part of the modern movement—and yet sufficiently detached from the movement to be an objective critic—had admitted that stylistic rules and restrictions, which the modernists had considered the bête noire of the historical styles, had not disappeared with modernism, they had merely changed.

In the talk, Johnson declared "I do not strive for originality," and disdained the "perpetual revolution" of architectural design. Twenty-five years later he unveiled his design for the **Sony Building**, nee **AT&T Building** (1984) in New York City that was no longer modern, and became one of the iconic buildings of early Postmodernism. Johnson's intellectual journey, which lasted nearly a century, is a personification of the entire profession of architecture in the same period.

In 1977 Charles A. Jencks (b. 1939) summarily declared in his book, *The Language of Post-Modern Architecture*, that Modern architecture "had expired finally and completely" in 1972. The event he cited was the demolition of Pruitt-Igoe, an urban renewal housing project consisting of 33 buildings with 11 stories each that had been completed only 16 years earlier. The complex had been designed by the architect Minoru Yamasaki (1912–1986), who also designed the World Trade Center (1970–2001).

Howard Roark, the fictional architect of *The Fountainhead*, also designed a housing project that was demolished, but his was destroyed while it was still under construction—and he was the one who destroyed it. Roark had agreed to be the "ghost-designer" for Peter Keating, his alter-persona, in part because he wanted to pursue the "potentialities of our modern world." When the builders altered his design, discarding its aesthetic nature but retaining the ingenuity of its solution, he dynamited the entire complex. In Roark's (and Rand's) viewpoint, he was merely retrieving intellectual property, for which he was not paid. By his own admission and his own stated philosophy (Rand's Objectivism), he did not

care for the people who lived in the slums. His interest was in the solution, not the problem.

The second-place submission in the Tribune Tower competition of 1922, by Eliel Saarinen, is perhaps one of the most influential, unsuccessful, unbuilt designs in the history of architecture, and it would have been the winning entry had it not been submitted one month late. Saarinen, born in Finland in 1873, had achieved great success in his native country with groundbreaking works like the Helsinki Railway Terminus. He created a design that was uniquely non-derivative, creating a new language for the skyscraper (a building type still in its infancy), one that relies almost wholly on massing instead of detailing. Raymond Hood would use the ideas proposed in this design for the grandiose project now known as **Rockefeller Center** (1930–1933) in 1931, a complex of buildings now universally beloved by both the casual admirer and the disciplined critic, and which the architect Robert Stern later admired was a great example

FIGURE 28.10

"Wisdom", Painted Low-relief Sculpture over Main Entrance to Rockefeller Center. (1933) . Lee Lawrie. New York City, NY.

"of what urban design can achieve within the grid pattern of development." John D. Rockefeller enjoined his designers only to make the building "as beautiful as possible consistent with maximum income"—in other words, "do more with less." The project was originally conceived by Otto Kahn, an investment banker and a board member of the Metropolitan Opera. He thought that an office project would help finance a new home for the Opera, and at a dinner party at the Metropolitan Club in 1928, Kahn approached Rockefeller, the son of the founder of Standard Oil. Rockefeller was intrigued and took on the project, but in 1929, at the start of the Depression, the Metropolitan Opera withdrew from the project. Rockefeller was thus faced with the daunting task of effecting the 12-acre development on his own. Certainly, only a handful of entrepreneurs in America would have been able to pull the strings on the largest privately funded architectural project in world history.

The *Exposition Internationale des Arts Décoratifs et Industriels Modernes* in Paris in 1925 opened a door for sleeker, less static design, and Picasso and other cubist painters had established a cabal of avant-garde partisans. Rockefeller's wife, Abby, was a founder of the Museum of Modern Art, and a collector of contemporary art. It did not hurt the Hood team that Hood's design for the *Daily News* building in 1930 had been a clear rejection of Gothic idioms.

Rockefeller Center would thus become the first monumental testing of the waters of modernism. The early reaction was substantially negative. Raymond Hood and his partners did not enjoy the heroic stature awarded Cass Gilbert two decades earlier. Ironically, in Chicago, Hood's design was criticized, because it did not embrace modern ideology, and in New York it was criticized—because it did. The *Herald Tribune* thought the exterior was "revoltingly dull and dreary." The *New York Times* called it a composition of "architectural aberrations." Yet the modern movement gained a momentum, which lasted for the next several decades.

The Great Depression, which began in 1929 and lasted throughout much of the 1930s, is most often remembered for the severe hardships caught in black-and-white photographic images from the era, such as the Stock Market Crash of October 29, 1929, and the panic that followed; the bread lines, or the Dust Bowl of 1933, which caused tens of thousands of farmers to abandon their property and migrate to other portions of the country, the subject of John Steinbeck's novel *The Grapes of Wrath* (1939); and of the classic film adaptation by John Ford in 1940. In the arts, however, this period is of great imagination and forward thinking, as if the constant pressing-on of modernity was not going to be deterred by economic realities.

Rockefeller Center was an example of the streamlined style popularized in the 1930's, which was sometimes accompanied by Art Deco decoration and detailing, though not always. The **Johnson Wax Administration Research Tower** (1944–1950), by Frank Lloyd Wright (see Chapter 29), was not influenced by the Art Deco movement. However, the streamlined effect is clearly visible in the tower, which has a single structural and circulation core, and was inspired by the structure of a tree.

The **United Nations Secretariat** (1950) was New York's first all-glass skyscraper. It is a thin slab, 38 stories tall, with blue-green glass curtain walls on its longer facades, and marble at the shorter ends.

FIGURE 28.11

Johnson Wax Research Tower. Racine, Wisconsin. (Frank Lloyd Wright)

FIGURE 28.12
United Nations Building. New York City, NY.

FIGURE 28.13
Lever House. New York City, NY.

An international team of architects from all over the world, with Le Corbusier and Oscar Niemeyer, a modernist architect from Brazil, having the most influence. The building plays a starring role in the 1959 Alfred Hitchcock masterpiece *North by Northwest*, including the title credits, inspired by the pattern of mullion on the building's glass facades, a brief sequence near the building's entrance with Cary Grant that was surreptitiously filmed by the director, because filming was forbidden at the site, and a murder scene that takes place in the building's lobby, recreated in Hollywood.

The **Lever House** (1952), designed by Gordon Bunshaft, a partner in the large commercial firm Skidmore, Owings & Merrill, was one of the most influential building projects in the years that followed the hiatus of construction activity during and immediately after World War II. It was one of the first buildings to use a pure curtain wall, which is an exterior wall system that is supported by the building's structure, but is non–load-bearing, and typically attached to the face of the building skeleton. The composition of the building consists of two narrow rectilinear slabs that are perpendicular to one another. The vertical element is a 24-story office building, with the stainless steel and green glass curtain wall. The horizontal element at the base of the building is a single story raised above the ground plane, to create an open plaza below the building.

Bunshaft's client for the project was Charles Luckman (1909–1999), who at the age of 30 was on the cover of *Time* magazine, which called him the "Boy Wonder of American Business." Luckman had studied architecture at the University of Chicago, but because jobs were scarce in architecture during Great Depression, he went into sales, and became president of Pepsodent Toothpaste at the age of 30, and after that, Lever Brothers. Soon after working with Skidmore, Owings & Merrill on the Lever House, and before it was completed, he returned to his roots and practiced architecture.

Lever Brothers manufactured soap and detergent, so it was important that their building, in a very prominent location on Park Avenue, always look clean and fresh. The soot and dirt that collects on buildings is a problem for masonry surfaces. Glass, on the other hand, is easily cleaned.

While the Lever House had its detractors, it eventually won over a substantial portion of the public, who were otherwise adverse to modern architecture, in part because of its unintimidating scale, its slender proportions, and its street-friendly urban design. In 1982 the New York City Landmark Preservations Committee designated the Lever House a historical landmark, an unusual step at the time for a modern building. The choice of color of the glass curtain wall—a sea green—was not insignificant. These factors helped gain a wider receptive audience than other buildings of the International Style. The Lever House and Philip Johnson's Glass House are considered by many to be the movement's finest accomplishments.

Mies van der Rohe's **860–880 Lakeshore Drive Apartments** (1951) in Chicago are two towers that are not quite twins, with a black curtain wall frame and black glass. Mies's own description of the style of architecture is "skin and bones." For decades, he had sought to build a "pure" expression of form and structure. In his 1922 essay, "Skyscrapers," Mies wrote that architects should "give up the attempt to solve a new task (tall buildings) with traditional forms; rather one should attempt to give form to the new task out of the nature of this task."

The seeds of discontent with the International style were sown in an article by Lewis Mumford called "The Status Quo" (1947). Mumford, who wrote an influential column in the *New Yorker* magazine called "The Sky Line," noted that functionalism, the calling card of architects like Mies, was a "one-sided interpretation of function," and one that Louis Sullivan, one of the true founders of modernism, "never subscribed to." Mumford criticized the current wave of modernism for its "quixotic purities," a stab directly aimed at Mies, its "awkward self-consciousness," and its "assertive dogmatism."

The twin towers of the **World Trade Center** (1972,1973–2001) were not glass boxes, they were just plain boxes. They were among a wave of buildings in the period of the 1960s and 1970s, in which the structural design of skyscrapers played an important role in their

aesthetics, such as the **John Hancock Center** (1970) and the **Willis Tower** (nee **Sears Tower**) (1974), both in Chicago. The unique structural design of the World Trade Center Towers, a "cage" of structural steel on the perimeter in lieu of a skeleton frame, is not considered to be a factor in the collapse of the buildings when they

FIGURE 28.14
Beaubourg Museum. Paris, France.

FIGURE 28.15
Pyramide du Louvre (1985). I.M. Pei. Paris, France.

were struck by commercial airliners hijacked by terrorists in 2001. The consensus is that the excessive heat caused by the burning aviation fuel caused floors in the impact area to fail, and then initiated a "pancake" toppling of the successive floors. It took only ten seconds each for the buildings to implode once the initial floors failed.

The term *postmodern,* introduced in Chapter 26, has also been used to describe other movements in architecture that have come into use after modernism, none of which have much in common with Postmodern Classicism. In *High-tech* architecture, structural and mechanical components of a building, which are normally hidden in traditional buildings, are used as decorative elements, and are often exposed on the building facade. Two such buildings are the **Beaubourg Museum** (1981) in Paris designed by Piano and Rogers and the **HSBC Building** (1985) in Hong Kong by Norman Foster. **The Pyramide du Louvre** (1989) by I.M. Pei was a successful, though initially controversial, solution to the delicate problem of introducing a large-scale entrance lobby to the Louvre Museum in Paris without competing or confusing the original design of the museum, once the home of Louis XIV. It is a true pyramid made of glass.

Sustainable architecture strives for social, economic, and environmental stability, by reducing a building's impact upon those elements in a communal or global context. One aspect is to reduce a building's *ecological footprint,* or its *carbon footprint,* both of which are quantifiable. A *Zero Energy Building* is one that produces as much energy as it uses on an annual basis. The word *green* architecture is often used interchangeably with *sustainable.* Some of the many tools that can be used in green design are: the redevelopment of existing sites,

FIGURE 28.16

The Great Court. British Museum (2000). Foster+Partners. London, England.

rather than placing a building on a site that previously had never been developed; locating a building near public transportation; reusing storm water; recycling wastewater for irrigation; creating buildings that are well insulated; using daylighting and natural ventilation; reusing construction materials; reusing entire buildings; using efficient fixtures and equipment; and using solar, wind, and other renewable energy sources. Solar shading devices were used effectively and dramatically at Norman Foster's **Carre d'Art** (1993) in Nimes, France, adjacent to the Roman temple Maison Carre. Foster and Partners also designed the Great Court addition to the British Museum (2000).

For Further Discussion

Research the name of a modern architect not mentioned in this textbook, and at least three buildings designed by that architect. Briefly describe these works.

CHAPTER
TWENTY-NINE

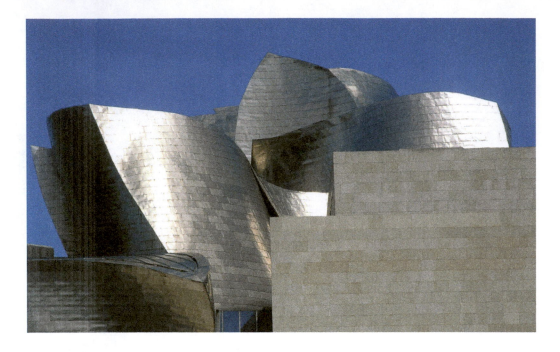

Expressionism

This essential connection between colour and form brings us to the question of the influences of form on colour. Form alone, even though totally abstract and geometrical, has a power of inner suggestion. A triangle (without the accessory consideration of its being acute-or obtuse-angled or equilateral) has a spiritual value of its own. In connection with other forms, this value may be somewhat modified, but remains in quality the same. The case is similar with a circle, a square, or any conceivable geometrical figure. As above, with the red, we have here a subjective substance in an objective shell.

The mutual influence of form and colour now becomes clear. A yellow triangle, a blue circle, a green square, or a green triangle, a yellow circle, a blue square—all these are different and have different spiritual values.

It is evident that many colours are hampered and even nullified in effect by many forms. On the whole, keen colours are well suited by sharp forms (e.g., a yellow triangle), and soft, deep colours by round forms (e.g., a blue circle). But it must be remembered that an unsuitable combination of form and colour is not necessarily discordant, but may, with manipulation, show the way to fresh possibilities of harmony.

Since colours and forms are well-nigh innumerable, their combination and their influences are likewise unending. The material is inexhaustible.

Form, in the narrow sense, is nothing but the separating line between surfaces of colour.[1]

—from Concerning the Spiritual in Art *(1910), by Wassily Kandinsky*

Wassily Kandinsky (1855–1944) was one of the first abstract painters, and one of most influential artists of the twentieth century. He was born in Moscow, but spent much of his life in Germany and France. In 1911 he helped to found Der Blaue Reiter (The Blue Rider), a group of expressionist artists. He later taught at the Bauhaus until it was closed by the Nazis in 1933. Kandinsky and others at the Bauhaus sought to clear collective social and historical predispositions about art and the language used that obfuscated the true nature of the world around us, which consists of empirical elements such as form and color.

For Expressionist artists like Kandinsky and Paul Klee (1879–1940), the abstraction of form, the use of color as an object in a painting, the simplification of objects, the distortion of lines and borders, and, ultimately, and the sub-conscious expression of emotions were important aspects of their paintings. Paul Klee in a plan for theoretical instruction for a course at the Bauhaus, later published as *Pädagogisches Skizzenbuch*, or *Pedagogical Sketchbook* (1953), described a sinuous line as talking a "walk for a walk's sake." These and similar studies explored the essential intonation of Expressionist architecture: it is form and the modifiers of form that ultimately inform the beauty of an object. In architecture, Expressionism rejects traditional language and ideals and substitutes an individualistic aesthetic interpretation that advances

---

1   Wassily Kandinsky, Selection from Concerning the Spiritual in Art, trans. Michael T. H. Sadler. Copyright in the Public Domain.

new ideas, and unlike pure modernism, actively engages sensuality.

In the Russian folk tale *The Firebird*, a young prince by the name of Ivan Tsarevich captures the Firebird, who then convinces the young prince to release him. The bird repays the kindness of the prince with the gift of a magic feather. The prince uses the magic feather to kill the ogre, Kastchei. This triumph allows the prince to win the love of a beautiful princess. The ballet score for *The Firebird* (*l'Oiseau de Feu*) and the subsequent orchestral suite were written by Igor Stravinsky (1882–1971) when he was 28 years old.

In the final section of the suite, the *Berceuse and Finale*, Stravinsky repeats the same motif of four measures 16 times in succession. The theme is introduced by a French horn with a majestic, slower tempo, *lento maestoso*, played softly. In the first repetition, the first note becomes two half notes instead of a whole, and a harp glissando bridges to the next repetition, which transfers to the next higher octave. An ascending counterpoint is introduced. In the next repetition, an incidental bridge appears at the end. The music gradually gets louder.

The fifth playing of the motif is abruptly cut short. Next, the theme is hidden in a transition, and the last tone is held. The seventh playing is louder, grander, and broader. The tempo is accelerated in the eighth playing, and the key briefly changes. The ninth playing is marked with the tempo *allegro non troppo*, lively but not too much, and returns to the original key. The tenth begins with a quarter-rest pause, and so does the eleventh, which also has a key change. The full motif is played in the twelfth, and in the thirteenth, the motif is played in reverse order. The fourteenth playing is marked by the tempo *molto pesante e meno mosso*, very ponderous and less fast. The fifteenth begins with a pause and a verbatim repetition, becoming a little broader. The final repetition returns to the first tempo, becomes very broad, and comes to a spirited conclusion.

The motif of the dramatic finale to *The Firebird* is clearly stated and often repeated, but Stravinsky never allows it to become overly familiar. or tedious; in fact, just the opposite occurs. The listener eagerly anticipates the next repetition. *The Firebird*, like *The Rite of Spring* (1912)

and *Petrushka* (1910–11), challenged the fundamental rhythmic structure of music in a manner that artists such as Picasso and Kandinsky challenged the formal structure of art, and the architects of Expressionism challenged the fundamental forms of architecture.

The fundamental inspiration of Expressionism in architecture is a search for beauty in form itself. In lieu of a limited historical basis for establishing the form of a building, infinite, previously undiscovered possibilities exist. The pre-modern architects began to unravel ties to Classicism; Expressionist and Modernist architects completed the job. The Modernists abandoned decoration completely in favor of function and the purity of form. Art was not relevant. For the Expressionists, the form became art, and art maintained its relevance.

FIGURE 29.2

Monument to the Third International. Vladmir Tatlin. Courtyard of Royal Academy. London, England.

The **Monument to the Third International** (1920) by the Soviet artist and architect Vladimir Tatlin (1885–1953), gained much attention for a project that was never built. It was meant to be erected in St. Petersburg (Petrograd at the time), and rise to 400 meters in height. It was clearly seen as an espousal of modernity and socialism, an antithesis to the values that were defeated by the Bolshevik Revolution of 1917.

One of the earliest Expressionist buildings is the **Einstein Tower** (1919–21), in Potsdam, Germany, by Erich Mendelsohn (1887–1953). Its free-flowing curves are reminiscent of Gaudí's Casa Mila, but without ornament. Le Corbusier's **Notre Dame de Haut** (1955) at Ronchamp, France used curving walls and small irregular window shapes to create a meditative interior space filled with soft light, and gentle forms designed to inspire rather than intimidate.

Unlike Casa Mila, which was integrated into an orthogonal city block in Barcelona, the Einstein Tower and "Ronchamp" are freestanding buildings and that can be viewed like freestanding sculpture, from all around. Architecture that is designed to be a freestanding object creates its own context, and often tacitly or purposefully ignores the tectonic environment in which it is placed. One criticism of contemporary expressionism, sometimes called "star-chitecture" or "wow-factor architecture," is that it can be disruptive to the urban fabric in which it is placed. An occasional disruption to the urban fabric can provide a necessary relief from monotonous forms. However, the openness resulting from the need for "living space" for such buildings can sometimes be unfriendly to pedestrians and thus can create "dead zones" in cities. In other words, a city filled with star-chitecture buildings may be interesting to look at, but may not be as vibrant as ones that are responsive to their urban context.

Eero Saarinen (1910–61), the son of the renowned Finnish architect Eliel Saarinen, became an accomplished architect as well. His most famous design is the **Gateway Arch** (1964) over the Mississippi River in St. Louis. The Gateway Arch is a single, upside-down catenary arch, similar to Gaudí's arches used at La Sagrada Familia. The arch is composed of hollow, tapering, equilateral double-skinned triangles of stainless and carbon steel. The arch

FIGURE 29.3

Einstein Tower. Potsdam, Germany.

FIGURE 29.4

Dulles Airport Terminal. Washington, DC

FIGURE 29.5

Notre Dame du Haut. Ronchamp, France

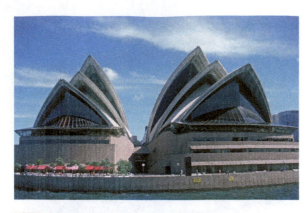

FIGURE 29.6

Sydney Opera House. Sydney, Australia.

was created to be the embodiment of the notion that the city of St. Louis was, and is, the gateway to the West. Saarinen also designed **Dulles Airport Terminal** outside Washington, D.C., and the **TWA Terminal** (1962) at John F. Kennedy Airport in New York City.

In the field of architecture, the three-dimensional graphic software capabilities of the personal computer have affected the manner in which buildings are designed and engineered, allowing architects unlimited creativity in the exploration of complex shapes and structural conditions. One of the earliest uses of computers to analyze complex building structures was for the **Sydney Opera House** (1957–1973), by Jørn Utzon (1918–2008), specifically to work out the engineering of a series of concrete shells that are the centerpiece of the design. The shells are meant to emulate large billowing sails, an acknowledgement of its location at a strategic point in Sydney Harbor. The building complex immediately became a symbol, not only of Sydney, but of the entire country and continent. Despite its epic and notorious cost overruns, the building has proved to be an invaluable asset to the Australian economy.

Utzon was chosen as the winner of a design competition. Eero Saarinen was one of the judges. He arrived late, after the other three judges had begun assessing the 233 entries. Saarinen found Utzon's entry among those the other judges had discarded, and convinced the others to reconsider it. The judges finally concluded that Utzon's opera house was capable of being "one of the great buildings of the world," and ultimately, they were proven to be correct.

The "billowing sails" were made from thin concrete shells, a structural concept developed in the middle part of the twentieth century inspired by the egg shell, which is very thin, but very strong. One of the earliest uses of the concrete shell was Saarinen's TWA. The final shape of the Utzon's shells was created by taking overlapping spheres, which were configured so that a basic curve was repeated, allowing the section of the shell to be made from relatively few concrete forms.

Architectural monuments have attracted tourists for more than two thousand years. Pausanias, a doctor who lived in Asia Minor in the second century CE, wrote a *Guide to Greece* in two volumes, which was a guidebook for tourists, describing the monuments of ancient Greece. The Eiffel Tower was the first modern construction to become a destination for tourists, but Paris had always been a city that had welcomed many travelers. After the Opera House was built, tourists flocked to see it—not to attend a concert or see an opera, but to see the building itself. This was something new for modern architecture. Previously, such pilgrimages were reserved for architects and architectural students fawning over a modernist gem that was unknown to the general public.

The literary critic Harold Bloom, with Paul de Man, Jacques Derrida, and others, put forward an idea in the late twentieth century that the "breaking apart" of form gives poems their "luster." Their theory of *Deconstruction* sought to undermine the rigid foundations of language, and was a self-proclaimed emancipation from the constraints of philosophy, politics, and society. "Freedom, in a poem," wrote Bloom, "must mean freedom of meaning, the freedom to have a meaning of one's own." *Deconstructivism* is an architectural movement of the late twentieth and early twenty-first centuries and is exemplified in the works of the architect Frank Gehry (1929–), Daniel Libeskind, who won the competition to rebuild the World Trade Center; Rem Koolhaas; Peter Eisenman; Zaha Hadid; Coop Himmelblau; and Bernard Tschumi, who were all featured in an exhibition opened at the Museum of Modern Art in New York City in 1988, entitled "Deconstructivist Architecture." The official publication of the exhibition announced that the projects exhibited were of a "different sensibility," disturbing the dream of (modernist) architects to achieve "pure form." "Form has been contaminated," it declared. Deconstruction is *not* the dissimulation of form. It challenges the aesthetic ideals responsible for traditional form. No work of art or architecture can be—or even pretend to be—free from form. If you printed the words "two clothed men, one unclothed woman, and one partially clothed woman lunching in the woods" on a sheet of paper, you would describe the *idea* of Manet's *Le Dejeuner sur l'Herbe*, but idea alone is insufficient. An idea elevates a work of art, but an idea alone is not art, it is merely an idea. Catherine Ingraham, in her review of the exhibition in *Inland Architect*, praised the architecture, but questioned the theoretical premise behind it. A reference to a work's form and style, she wrote, is the "thinnest kind of formal architectural description." Mark Wigley, who wrote the paper for the museum, correctly cited Russian constructivism as an inspiration. Gehry has since distanced himself from the use of the term "Deconstructivist," but the association, so far at least, has not yet "de-congealed."

If such a style does indeed exist, then the **Guggenheim Museum** (1997) in Bilbao, Spain, is its most famous work. Philip Johnson called it the "greatest building of our time." Like the Sidney Opera House, it is a work of architecture that created name recognition for a city, and transformed that city into a destination for tourism. Although Gehry has created other works of similar design, such as the Disney Concert Hall in Los Angeles, the museum at Bilbao seems destined to be his signature work, and a landmark work in the history of architecture.

The building's curving geometric forms are designed to appear arbitrary. The exterior skin of the building is made from sheets of titanium that reflect sunlight at random, so that the building is constantly changing in appearance. The design of the building is thus considered to be *dynamic*, characterized by constant change or activity, as opposed to *static*, constant or unchanging. Titanium (Ti, No. 22), is a high-strength metal named after a generation of gods that preceded Zeus, the Titans. It does not rust, and it is nonallergenic. It is relatively abundant, but is expensive to refine. Until Bilbao, it had

FIGURE 29.7

Guggenheim Museum. Bilbao, Spain.

limited use in buildings, but was used for jet engines, artificial limbs, and golf clubs.

The building has drawn nearly universal rave reviews for its architecture, although some have criticized its *urban design*, how it fits in within the overall context of

FIGURE 29.8

Nationale-Nederlanden Building, or Dancing House. Prague, Czech Republic.

the city. It is an *object building*—that is, one that is meant to be an object of attention from the entire perimeter of its site. From this viewpoint, it is self-centered. It works better as an isolated site than one that is connected to the heart of the city.

The **Nationale-Nederlanden Building** (1996), nicknamed **"Fred and Ginger"** (after Fred Astaire and Ginger Rogers, co-stars in music and dance films of the mid–twentieth century) or the **"Dancing House,"** is an example of an expressionist architectural work that is unfamiliar in its form and detailing yet cohabitates within its urban context very well. As a work of sculpture, it is a work that projects from the orthogonal base fabric of the city block as if a *high-relief*, a molded design that significantly stands out from its surface.

Santiago Calatrava (b. 1951) is an architect, engineer, and sculptor; his works of architecture are expressions of all three disciplines at once. Other late-twentieth-century and early-twenty-first-century architects have explored the use of sculptural forms, and have integrated structure into architectural design, but Calatrava's buildings have achieved a balance among the essential elements of architecture: program and function, urban

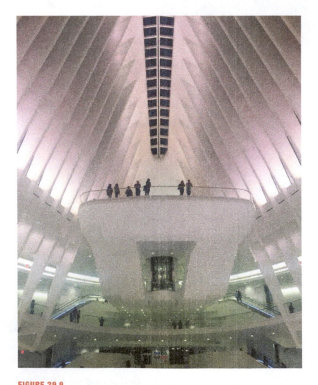

World Trade Center Station. New York City, NY. (Santiago Calatrava).

context, ecological impact, symbolism, expressionism, humanity, and integrity, which, in lesser works, seem to be in conflict. A quite visible illustration of this is the *brise-soleil* of the museum, which is a giant, wing-like sunscreen that opens up to screen the sun. It closes at night, and when it is cloudy. In spite of cost overruns, which have plagued some of Calatrava's other works (and many other "star-chitecture" projects), the **World Trade Center Station** (2016) has been called a spiritual work of architecture, one that addresses the emotions generated by the destruction of the World Trade Center Towers. The statement it makes-the triumph of human imagination and creativity over forces of destruction and hatred-is clearly expressed. Its form is said to be one of a bird being released from the hand of a child.

Beijing National Stadium (2008), nicknamed the *Bird's Nest*, was designed by the Swiss architectural firm Herzog & de Meuron, in conjunction with CADG and the Chinese artist Ai Weiwei. It is a source of great pride for the Chinese people, who, years after the Olympics for which it was built, flock to the site in great numbers to see the building. The stadium has become a national symbol, rivaling, at least temporarily, the Forbidden City and the Great Wall. The distinctive exterior consists of crisscrossing steel beams and columns that are, at once, structural and decorative. They were designed to camouflage the supports of a retractable roof that had been designed for the building that was never built. Like the forms at Guggenheim Bilbao, these were meant to be conceived as random. The namesake of its nickname, bird's nest soup, made from the nests of swifts and other birds, is a delicacy in Chinese cuisine.

Beijing National Stadium. Beijing, China

The Chinese people were given an emblem of their civilization. Jacques Herzog, in an interview in *Der Spiegel* magazine, proclaimed that the building "achieves the maximum of what architecture can achieve." That achievement is no different than any other monument in architectural history, whether Khufu's pyramid, or the great cathedrals at Paris and Chartres. It establishes a permanent place in space and in time for a particular culture. It is not unlike the early human or humanlike hunter, forager, and scavenger who places a stick in the ground, as if to say "this is my place." Like the citizens of Chartres, who saw in their great cathedral a testament to the gloriousness of their city, and that is what the *Bird's Nest* is, except the glory is a people and a nation, not a city. Herzog believes that it does not matter who designed *Bird's Nest*. "It is not really relevant," he says. Architecture, like most other aspects of culture—and life itself—in the twenty-first century, has "gone global."

In the last decades of the twentieth century, and continuing on into the twenty-first century, the form of the skyscraper was again reinvented. The languages of Classicism and Modernity, the Gothic tower and the tall box alike, were discarded. The skyscraper had, at last, found its own form, one that had lost rigidity and dogma. **Burj Khalifa**, or **Khalifa Tower** (2010), in Dubai, United Arab Emirates, by Skidmore, Owings & Merrill, became the world's largest structure upon its completion. It is more than 300 meters taller than the previous tallest building in the world, which is in Taipei, and roughly twice as tall as the Empire State Building. It was inspired by Frank Lloyd Wright's uncompleted project, **The Illinois** (1956), a mile-high skyscraper with 528 stories.

Wright's mile-high skyscraper was designed for up to 130,000 inhabitants. He envisioned it to be "more permanent than the pyramids," referring to its structural integrity, the ability of its materials to endure the forces of nature, and the indefatigability of its design. But it is not just the immensity of scale that creates monumental works of architecture. Skyscrapers are the most visible measures of the creative genius of human civilization. In skyscrapers, more than any other building type, art and science are fused together. In his book *A Testament* (1957), Wright wrote that, in modern architecture, a

FIGURE 29.11

Burj Khalifa. Dubai, United Arab Emirates.

"spiritual integrity" had been attained "for the first time in 500 years," or since the end of the Gothic age. In both ages, architects created buildings that reached to infinity, to heaven, and to the places never before seen. These achievements remind us that architecture, like all the arts, is a mirror of human existence.

For Further Discussion

Select an expressionist work of architecture and identify its predominant shapes. Create a drawing, adding color and/or textures, that presents these shapes as objects of an expressionistic painting. Use any method you are comfortable with, including sketching, tracing, or transforming a digital image.

Frank Lloyd Wright

There were several modern architects who created their own unique, iconoclastic styles, but only one who achieved the reputation of Frank Lloyd Wright (1867–1959), both within and well beyond the insular coterie of architects and architectural critics. In 1991 the American Institute of Architects named Wright the greatest American architect of all time. In spite, or perhaps in debt to, a lifetime filled with personal scandals, professional setbacks, financial irresponsibility, and despite his notorious ego, he was admired by the public as well. Wright's name is still the most recognizable of all architects in America.

The architectural critic Ada Louise Huxtable (b. 1941) wrote in her biography of Wright that his life story would never be invented, because it would seem too melodramatic. After apprenticing at the architectural office of Joseph Lyman Silsbee in Chicago, in 1887 he joined the firm of Adler and Sullivan. Louis Sullivan became his mentor (Wright called him his *Lieber-Meister*, German for "loved master") but the two quarreled over Wright's moonlighting practices, and in 1893 Wright began his own practice. Both Sullivan and Wright are considered the founders of modernism. Both embraced art in architecture, considered anathema to many of the "avant-garde" modernists.

In this regard, Wright's respect for history was more evident than in any other modern architect, with the possible exception of Le Corbusier. He engaged with a mostly silent, but occasionally verbal, feud with the austere modernists, citing differences that were both theoretical and philosophical. At the peak of the success of the International style, Philip Johnson mockingly called him "the greatest architect of the nineteenth century." Of Johnson's glass house, Wright mused, "Here I am, Philip. ... Do I take my hat off or leave it on?" In his book *An American Architecture* (1955), Wright called for the "destruction" of the International style glass box, which he called an inhibition and a restraint. For Wright, modernity was about freedom. Classical architecture had been awash in rules, and modernism allowed the architect to break free from those restrictions. Previously, he wrote:

... all architecture had been the box—a decorated box, or a box with its lid exaggerated, or a box with pilasters, but always a box.

The greatest inspiration for Wright during his career was natural law, which he found fertile, suggestive, and aesthetically helpful. He called this "organic architecture," which seeks a "superior sense of use and finer sense of comfort," and is of, and for, nature.

Wright also believed that the ideas of buildings can be, and should be, expressed by its structure. This is an idea shared with Gothic architecture, but updated and applied differently. Wright was an admirer of John Ruskin, whose *The Nature of Gothic* (1853) was influential in the late nineteenth century. Wright worked a wide palette of materials, and his knowledge of building materials was extensive. He loved all materials, not just concrete and stucco, like many of his contemporaries. He

FIGURE 29.12

Unity Temple. Oak Park, Illinois.

used glass as a material, not a surface, as did Mies van der Rohe, for instance.

In the **Larkin Building** (1904) in Buffalo, New York, Wright designed an interior central court four stories tall, the most daring exploration of space to that date in a skyscraper. Other new innovations included the glass door, wall-hung toilet partitions, air conditioning, steel furniture, and radiant heat. The stair towers became a completely independent block, and also served as air intakes for the ventilation system. The roof was used as a recreation area.

The **Unity Temple** (1906) in Oak Park, Illinois, was one of Wright's most influential buildings. He claimed it was the first building to "come complete as architecture cast from forms." It is considered to be the first completely modern building in the history of architecture. "I thought I was prophetic," Wright would later comment, "and had made a statement bound to re-create the world of architecture." The Universalist Church was formed in 1866 as a nonauthoritarian faith—that is, one that has no formal dogma, and allows for individual spiritual expression. After their church had burned down, the local congregation hired Wright, who lived in Oak Park and was a Unitarian, a faith with similar beliefs. The philosophy of the church, its small size (only 400 persons), and the modest budget all factored into the design of the auditorium area of the temple—a cube, a shape that Wright considered to be noble. The building is designed from the inside out—that is to say, the form of interior space dictates the exterior form. Thus, Unity Temple is the ultimate embodiment of the most famous words of his *Lieber-Meister*—"Form Follows Function." Wright's interpretation of his client's needs was fastidious. The result is that it achieves the two aims of architecture with equilibrium; both art and function are equally served, and they never seem to be in conflict with one other. This aspect of Wright's architecture contributes significantly to his legacy.

The **Johnson Administration Building** (1936) in Racine, Wisconsin, used *dendriform*, or tree-shaped, columns of exposed concrete. The exterior skin is made of alternating ribbons of glass and brick. The ribbon

building style would become common later in the century, particularly in medium-rise suburban office buildings.

In the **Robie House** (1910), also in Oak Park, Wright used strong horizontal lines of brick, a limestone cap, continuous windows, and a copper eave, partly in

FIGURE 29.13
Robie House. Chicago, Illinois.

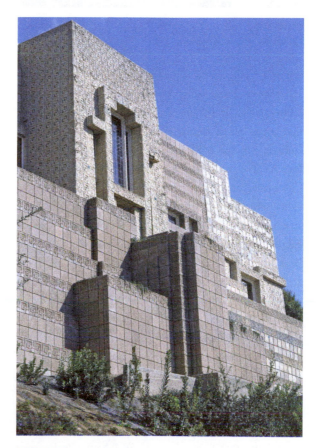

FIGURE 29.14
Ennis House. Los Angeles, California

Expressionism 317

FIGURE 29.15

Fallingwater. Bear Run, Pennsylvania.

FIGURE 29.16

H.C. Price Company Tower. Barttlesville, Oklahoma.

response to the shape of the lot, which was thin, but long. The wide and unusually extensive cantilevers accentuate a low profile. It is one of many houses of that period that critics called *Prairie Style*, a name derived from the landscape of the Midwest. The **Ennis House** (1924) in Los Angeles was one of a series of houses, mostly in California, that used exposed concrete masonry. The individual units were custom-made and had unique patterns, an effect that has been linked to Mayan architecture. The **Edgar J. Kaufmann House** or **Fallingwater** (1939) in Bear Run, Pennsylvania, is dramatically built on top of a creek. Its vertical stone columns, which appear to rise out of the natural rock, are placed in juxtaposition with strong, horizontal stucco parapet walls of balconies that cantilever well beyond their supports, and emphatically the products of human creativity and invention. A poll of its members by the American Institute of Architects cited Fallingwater as the greatest American work of architecture.

The **H.C. Price Company Tower** (1956) in Bartlesville, Oklahoma, was the tallest building designed by Wright that was erected. In startling contrast to the box architecture that was popular at the time, the small skyscraper blends both horizontal and vertical elements, in a manner that gives the building its accessible, humanistic appeal. Wright called the building "the tree that escaped the crowded forest." The floor plan, a rotated square, with a pinwheel spine and an asymmetrical rectangle in one of the four resulting quadrants, was intended to offer "convenient" and "compact" spaces for its users. The concept of the **Solomon R. Guggenheim Museum** (1959) in New York is a "continuous floor." Of the building, Wright wrote that "for the first time architecture appears plastic."

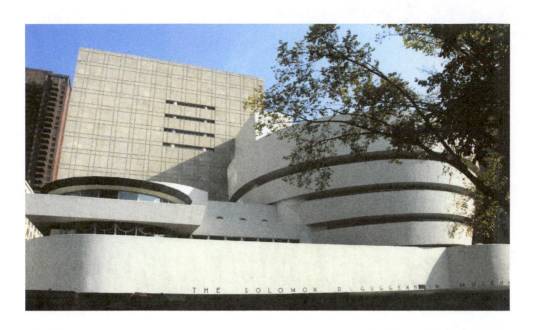

FIGURE 29.17

Guggenheim Museum. New York City, NY.

Credits

Image Credits

All photos in this book, with the exception of those listed below, were taken by the author, Leo Hansen, and may not be used for any reason without prior written permission. The use of photos for educational classroom purposes is specifically allowed without prior permission.

3.6: Photo by Colleen Burke; 4.4: Photo by Leo Hansen & Shannon Lee Brown; 5.5: Photo by Leo Hansen & Shannon Lee Brown; 6.2: Copyright © 2005 by Hardnfast, (CC BY-SA 3.0) at https://commons.wikimedia.org/wiki/File:Ancient_ziggurat_at_Ali_Air_Base_Iraq_2005.jpg; 6.4: copyright © 2014 by Bernard Gagnon, (CC BY-SA 3.0) at https://commons.wikimedia.org/wiki/File:Lion_Gate,_Hattusa_01.jpg; 7.9: Photo by Leo Hansen & Shannon Lee Brown; 11.8: Photo by Leo Hansen & Shannon Lee Brown; 12.9: Photo by Leo Hansen & Shannon Lee Brown; 13.9: Leo Hansen & Shannon Lee Brown; 14.3: Copyright © 2000 by Paul Mannix, (CC BY-SA 2.0) at https://commons.wikimedia.org/wiki/File:Khajuraho_-_Kandariya_Mahadeo_Temple.jpg; 14.11: Photo by Leo Hansen & Shannon Lee Brown; 15.6: Photo by Mark Hansen; 15.10: Photo by Tim Voight; 16.3: Sailko / Copyright in the Public Domain; 16.4: Photo by Leo Hansen & Shannon Lee Brown; 18.6: Photo by Pam Stephany; 18.10: Photo by Arvind Balaraman; 18.11: Photo by Diane Kohlmeyer; 19.5: Photo by Leo Hansen & Shannon Lee Brown; 20.7: Photo by Paul Hansen; 20.9: Photo by Leo Hansen & Shannon Lee Brown; 21.3: Photo by Leo Hansen & Shannon Lee Brown; 21.5: Photo by Paul Hansen; 21.17: Photo by Marie Hansen; 23.5: Photo by Leo Hansen & Shannon Lee Brown; 23.12: Copyright © 2013 by Xiquinho, (CC BY-SA 3.0) at https://commons.wikimedia.org/wiki/File:Potala_Palace_HR.jpg; 24.14: Photo by Leo Hansen & Shannon Lee Brown; 25.5: Photo by Leo Hansen & Shannon Lee Brown; 25.9: Photo by Leo Hansen & Shannon Lee Brown; 27.8: Photo by Robert S. Howard; 28.8: Carol M. Highsmith / Copyright in the Public Domain; 28.9: Copyright © 2013 by Victor Grigas, (CC BY-SA 3.0) at https://commons.wikimedia.org/wiki/File:Approaching_Farnsworth_House_by_Mies_Van_Der_Rohe-3.jpg; 29.3: Copyright © 2006 by Architect, Erich Mendelsohn / Institute for Astrophysics Potsdam. Reprinted with permission; 29.4: Photo by Paul Hansen; 29.14: Photo by Don Zimmer; 29.15: Daderot / Copyright in the Public Domain; 29.16: Photo by Paul Hansen.

Drawing Credits

The drawings in this book were created by Leo Hansen and Shannon Lee Brown.

Title Page Captions

All photos by author.

Chapter One: Crossing of York Minster. England; **Chapter Two:** Flavian Amphitheater, or Colosseum. Rome, Italy; **Chapter Three**: Serifos, Greece; **Chapter Four**: Rouffinac Cave, France; **Chapter Five**: Stonehenge, England; **Chapter Six:** The Pyramids at Giza: Menkaure, Menkaure Queen, Khafre, Khufu; **Chapter Seven:** Temple of Ramesses Ii at Abu Simbel; **Chapter Eight**: Palace of Knossos. Crete; **Chapter Nine**: Temple of Aphaia. Aegina, Greece; **Chapter Ten**: Tholos Temple from the Sanctuary of Athena. Delphi, Greece; **Chapter Eleven**: Bull from Processional Way. Ishtar Gate. Babylon. Istanbul Archaeological Museum; **Chapter Twelve:** The Colosseum; **Chapter Thirteen**: The Treasury. Petra. Jordan. **Chapter Fourteen:** Tectonic Faces of a King or Bodhisattva. Ankgor Thom. Angkor, Cambodia; **Chapter Fifteen**: Pyramid of the Masks. Kohunlich, Mexico; **Chapter Sixteen**: Interior of San Stefano Rotondo. Rome, Italy; **Chapter Seventeen**: Hagia Sophia. Istanbul, Turkey; **Chapter Eighteen:** The Dome of the Rock. Jerusalem, Israel; **Chapter Nineteen**: Eileen Donan Castle, Scotland; **Chapter Twenty**: Speyer Cathedral; **Chapter Twenty-one**: Canterbury Cathedral; **Chapter Twenty-two**: Fresco from Basilica di San Francesco. Arezzo, Italy; **Chapter Twenty-three**: Temple of Heaven, Beijing, China; **Chapter Twenty-four**: Il Duomo, or Santa Maria del Fiore. Florence, Italy; **Chapter Twenty-five**: Cathedral of San Giorgio. Modica, Sicily; **Chapter Twenty-six:** The Apotheosis of George Washington. Interior of Capitol Dome. Washington, DC.; **Chapter Twenty-seven**: La Sagrada Familia. Barcelona, Spain; **Chapter Twenty-eight:** Rietveld Schröder House. Model. Museum of Modern Art. New York City, NY.; **Chapter Twenty-nine**: Guggenheim Museum, Bilbao, Spain.

Appendix

General Architectural Terms

Anthropomorphism The representation of a god, object, or animal with human characteristics; or the or the representation of a god believed to have a human form.

Apse The semicircular end a classical building, Christian church, or a similar space in other works of architecture.

Arcade A series of arches supported by columns.

Arch A curved structural form that spans an opening in which the axial load (the load from above) is transferred to supporting side walls or columns. Prior to the modern era, arches were almost exclusively constructed from stone or brick masonry. A voussoir is a wedge shaped individual unit of masonry which forms the arch. The keystone is the wedge-shaped voussoir at the highest point of the arch; it is often sculpted or decorated. The uppermost part of the column or wall, from which the arch springs is called an impost.

Archaeology The study of human history and prehistory through the excavation of sites and analysis of artifacts and other physical remains.

Architecture The act of creating anything with a complex structure; a complex structure; the act of designing buildings; a body of structures with a commonality of purpose, motif, or methodology; or the style in which a building is designed.

Architrave The lowest part of the entablature in Classical architecture; the molded surround around a door or window.

Archivolt A molding on the face of an arch.

Atlas A column in the form of a male figure, from the Greek god whose task was to hold up the earth.

Balance The state of equilibrium resulting from the arrangement of portions of a building about its apparent axis. Equilibrium is a term of structural mechanics, which means that objects on one side of an equation or fulcrum are equal to those of the opposite side. A common example would be a perfectly balanced seesaw, with different numbers, weights, and distribution of those persons seated on each side. If the seesaw had the exact number of persons, with the exact weight and distribution, then the seesaw would not only be in balance, it would have symmetry. If a building is symmetrical, then all of the components on either side of its central axis are "mirrored" about a central vertical axis.

Balustrade A series of short posts called balusters that support a handrail or coping.

Bas-relief, or low-relief A form of sculpture in which the objects are only slightly projected from the background.

Basilica A Roman public building that served as for courts of law and other public function; A Christian church derived from the Roman basilica with a center nave, colonnades, aisles, and apses at one or both ends; a Roman Catholic church granted special privileges by the pope.

Bay A section of a building created by repeated major structural components of a structure.

Beam A horizontal structural form that spans an opening, transferring the axial load from above to the adjacent walls or columns.

Beton brut Concrete textured by the impressions left by its formwork.

Blind arcade A series of decorative arches and columns projecting from the face of a building.

Brick A man-made building material made of clay formed into a rectangular shape. They can be dried in a kiln or sun-dried; kiln-dried bricks are far more durable. The color of a brick is affected by the color of the clay and the amount of air in the kiln. A building brick, or common brick, is used for structural purposes. A facing brick, whose color and shape are more carefully crafted, is used for visible parts of a facade. A brick wall's coursework refers to the pattern or patterns in which the bricks are laid. A bond is a type of common regular pattern, such as running bond, in which consecutive layers of bricks are staggered. Historically, bricks were used in areas where stone and wood were scarce, such as in the ancient Sumerian, Babylonian, and Persian cultures in what are now Iran and Iraq, or in the southwestern United States.

Bronze A metallic alloy of copper (Cu) and tin (Sn), used for sculptural and decorative purposes in architecture.

Buttress An abutting pier that strengthens a masonry wall.

Campanile An Italian bell-tower.

Caryatid A column in the form of a female figure.

Cathedral A church that contains the cathedra, the seat of the bishop.

Chapel A small church not directly administered by a parish; a private area for worship in a church donated by, and for the use of, a patronage family. Italian: capella.

Chapter-house A room or hall used for meetings in a cathedral or monastery.

Choir The space at eastern end of most cathedrals designated for the clergy; also, chancel. As a related but separate meaning, the part of a church reserved for singers of the liturgy or hymns.

Clerestory, or clearstory A series of windows located above the lower section of adjoining spaces in a building that allows light into the taller space.

Colonnade A row of columns. In Classical architecture, a colonnade of 2 columns is called distyle; 4 columns, tetrastyle; 6 columns, hexastyle; 8 columns, octastyle, 10 columns, decastyle.12 columns, dodecastyle.

Column A vertical structural form that receives axial loading from above. A column that is half-embedded in a wall is called a pilaster. A traditional column consists of a base, the lowest part, the shaft, the main body of the column, and the capital, its uppermost portion directly below the supported structure The capital often has distinguishing characteristics relative to its period, style, or location.

Concept The generalized idea or ideas of a work of art relative to form, symbolism, and/or meaning.

Concrete A building material composed of cement (limestone and clay heated into a powder form), aggregate (pieces of broken or crushed stone), and water. It is placed in forms soon after the water is added, and then hardens. It is used for beams, columns, walls, floor slabs, roofs, arches, vaults, and domes, as well as plastic, or freely-shaped, constructions.

Complexity The use of elements and components in architectural design that involve two or more conceptual matrices in such manner that the wholeness or unity of the building is not compromised. A planned "imperfection," for instance, can break up the monotony of uniformity. An expected repetition can be manipulated or modified to create an alternative theme. Complexity in music is achieved through counterpoint, through changes in rhythm and scales, and other devices. A single theme can be adapted and reused to create an entirely different feeling. In literature, deviations from models of conventional storytelling—flashbacks, alternating narrative perspective, or using devices such as stream of consciousness—can create complexity in a novel or short story.

Content The meaning or significance of a work of art, often through the use of signs or symbols.

Contrast A juxtaposition of objects in such a manner as to highlight their differences or singular values.

Corbel A structural element that supports a projecting wall above

Cornice A continuous projecting decorative feature at the top of a wall or pediment.

Crypt The lower floor of a church or cathedral used for burials, the safekeeping of relics, or as a chapel.

Dissemination The dispersal of ideas or culture by means of communication or direct contact.

Dome A hemispherical structure that is circular in plan and is vaulted for 360 degrees.

Elevation A two-dimensional graphic projection of one horizontal dimension and the vertical dimension. It is used to describe the appearance of a building, its height, the location of doors and windows and other components, and its decoration.

Facade The exterior components of a building that face a particular direction, described either by its orientation, such as front facade or rear facade; by a cardinal point, such as north facade or southeast facade; by its function, such as entrance facade; or by its adjacent public way, such as Central Park facade or Fifth Avenue facade. If a cardinal point is used, the direction refers to the nearest point to the viewer, not the direction the viewer faces. Portions of a building not in the same plane, but facing the same direction, may constitute a single facade. If no orientation is given, then it could be assumed that the reference is to the main, or front, facade. The word elevation is often used interchangeably with facade, but technically refers to a drawing or photograph of a particular facade.

Fenestration The openings in an exterior wall, almost exclusively for the purpose of letting in light. Windows, clear openings, glass bricks or blocks, and glass doors are all components of a building's fenestration. The placement of openings within a facade is called a fenestration pattern. In ancient and historic architecture, the fenestration was often symmetrical, or carefully studied for proportion and balance. Some modern architecture relaxes the approach to fenestration, so that the placement of exterior window components is related more to a building's function and general appearance. The comparative amounts of wall and glass on a particular facade is called solid/void ratio.

Fluting Concave grooves that decorate the surface of a column shaft.

Form is, simply, a particular way in which a thing exists or appears. A work of art's form, consciously or unconsciously, is molded by the political, cultural, economic, and social environments in which it is made. A sonnet or symphony has cultural-based rules of creation. Equally important are unwritten codes: the tonality of music, the symbolic character of images and icons, the patterns of a work's milieu. A green plastic or wooden house used in the popular board game Monopoly is a simplified form of a traditional house. One of the first philosophers to discuss the nature of ειδοσ (form) was Plato, who argued that works of art should seek an ideal form, which is, coincidentally or not, a driving force behind ancient Greek architecture. Aristotle argued that form should be responsive to the audience. A dramatic work should "excite pity and fear," and someone looking at art should find beauty. The 18th c. philosopher Immanuel Kant wrote that "beauty is the form of the purposiveness of an object." Susan Langer wrote in 1953 that "art is the creation of forms symbolic of human feeling." The architect Louis Sullivan, who coined the famous line "form follows function," described form as thus:

Form (is) in everything and anything, everywhere and at every instant. According to their nature, their function, some forms are definite, some indefinite; some are nebulous, others concrete and sharp; some symmetrical, others purely rhythmical. Some are abstract, others material. Some appeal to the eye, some to the ear, some to the touch, some to the sense of smell, some to any one or all or any combination of these. But all, without fail, stand for relationships between the immaterial and the material, between the subjective and the objective, between the Infinite Spirit and the finite mind. Through our sense we know substantially all that we may know. The imagination, intuition, reason are but exalted forms of the physical senses, as we call them.

Foundation The lowest component of a building or structure that transmits the loads of the building to the supporting earth (rock, soil, silt, or sand).

Frame, or Skeleton The structural supporting members of a building.

Fresco A wall painting applied on wet plaster.

Frieze A continuous band of decorative sculpture.

Frontispiece The principal façade of a building.

Hierarchy An arrangement of elements in accordance with their perceived order, based upon status, significance, stature, or form. The hierarchy of a cathedral is related to status: First, there is a vestibule, for those who are impure. There is a font of holy water at the entrance, for purification. Once purified, an individual passes into the next hierarchal level, the nave. The next space, the chancel, is reserved for only those of the highest level, the clergy. A hierarchy can be based upon form. For instance, a triangle is often placed on top of a rectangle, but a rectangle placed upon a triangle would be counter-intuitive, albeit perhaps deliberately so.

Icon A work of art whose subject is a holy figure, such as Christ, a saint, or an angel. In the Eastern Orthodox Church and in some other Christian churches icons are venerated as sacred objects.

indigenous Uniquely associated with a certain people culture or location; innate.

Iron A metallic element (Fe) that becomes hard but ductile when heated at high temperatures. The first iron was produced in the early 1st millennium BCE. Ancient iron was produced by heating the iron ore in wood charcoal furnaces, creating pig iron. The iron was then hammered into shapes, a process known as smelting. In the late 18th c. cast iron, which is melted in blast furnaces, was first used in structures. It is an efficient material for compressive uses, such as columns. Wrought iron is made from puddled pig iron and then rolled into shapes.

Lantern A vertical structure on placed on top of a dome, either circular or polygonal in plan, with windows that allow light to enter into the space below.

Lintel A beam that spans the opening of a door or window.\

Loggia An open gallery, often colonnaded, abutting a public or common area.

Minster A title given to some important churches and cathedrals in England.

Masonry Earthen unitary materials that are bonded together to create a structural or decorative component of a building, usually a wall. The units can be either natural, like quarried stone; manufactured, like concrete block, a mixture of cement (clay and limestone heated to a high temperature), small stones, and water; or configured from nature, such as brick The units can be bonded by mortar (lime and/or cement, sand, and water) or set in place without mortar (called a dry installation). A corbel is a unit of masonry that projects out from the layer below. Corbeling is the process of projecting two or more layers outward, thereby creating a shelf or ledge, or an offset in the wall.

Massing A composition of objects, shapes, or forms that creates a unified whole.

Megaron A hall in an ancient Greek palace complex or citadel.

Monastery A complex of buildings used for a communion of monks, nuns, or others seeking a solitary, devotional lifestyle. In addition to the living quarters, which were typically modest in size and accommodation, a monastery may have a church or temple, a library, a refectory, and agricultural buildings.

Myth A traditional story of the history of a people or culture, or one that explains natural or supernatural phenomena, often involving supernatural beings or events, or heroes with superhuman qualities.

Mythology A collection of myths, particularly one that belongs to a particular culture or religion.

Niche A recess in a wall, often decorated, and sometimes containing a statue or other ornament.

Order The arrangement of the components of a building or part of a building according to a particular sequence, pattern, or method. The Classical orders were systems of architectural design, often called styles, each of which had variations in the components and detailing of buildings.

Parapet A low wall at perimeter of a balcony or at the uppermost floor or roof of a building.

Plan A drawing depicting the two horizontal dimensions of an imaginary horizontal plane cut through the building near or at the floor. It is useful for describing overall layout of the building, its length and width, the location and relationships of its rooms or areas, and its geometry.

Pediment The low-pitched gable end enclosing the attic space of a gabled structure. In Classical architecture it consisted of a cornice, tympanum and a raking cornice.

Plaster A mixture of lime, sand, water, and gypsum applied to masonry surfaces to provide smoothness or decoration. Plaster used for exterior walls is called stucco.

Portico A covered porch or vestibule open or partly open on at least one side.

Proportion The relationship of size or magnitude between one object and another. In mathematics, a ratio is the numeric relationship between two quantities; proportion is the equality of ratios, 1/3 and 3/9, for example. Certain proportions, since the ancient world, have been considered to be more pleasing than others. In music, a perfect fourth interval has a proportion of 4/3. A perfect fifth has a proportion of 3/2. The Greek philosopher Pythagoras recognized the interrelationship between mathematical and musical harmonies in the 6th c. BCE.

Quoin The accentuated masonry at corners of buildings.

Renaissance man A person with multiple talents and pursuits, especially in the humanities.

Rhythm A harmonious arrangement of repeated objects, motifs, or decorative features. Patterns of rhythm, defined as a rhythm scheme are designated by representing each unique pattern with an upper or lower case letter. Examples of rhythm schemes are aaaaa (or AAAA, in which one object is continuously repeated), abab (alternating objects), abba, aaabbbccc, abacaba, etc. Rhythms create a sense of movement in a composition. A simple rhythm is generally more static, having little movement; a complex rhythm is generally more dynamic, having considerable movement.

Roof The uppermost part of a building that shelters the other components of a building and its inhabitants from the weather. Roofs can be flat or sloped; if flat, some pitch or other means is necessary to drain water from its surface. The most common types of sloped roofs are: a gable, which is a continuous triangular shape; a hip, a triangular shaped roof with inclined ends; and a shed roof, which has a single slope. The ridge is the continuous high point at the intersection of two sloping roof surfaces. A valley is the continuous low point at the intersection of two sloping roof surfaces.

Scale The relative size of a building or component of a building with other parts of the same building or with the building as a whole. When these relationships are deemed incompatible, they are considered "out of scale". Human scale is the proportional relationship of a building or site with the human body and the activities of humans. Paul Spreiregen, in his book Urban Design: The Architecture of Towns and Cities, describes successful implementation of human scale as design, in which the parts of a city are "related to people and their abilities to comprehend their surroundings."

Shape The outline of an object as seen in two or three dimensions.

Site The specific plot where the building is placed. A site may contain several buildings, which may be arranged architecturally. A building's orientation is its position on its site in relation to the cardinal directions; to its urban context, such as the grid pattern of streets, a natural element, such as a prevailing wind, or another issue external to the site.

Section A drawing depicting the two dimensions of an imaginary vertical plane cut through any plane of the building. It is useful to describe the interior components of a building, its special characteristics, height, and structure.

Simultaneous or multiple discovery A theory that a new idea, thought, or cultural means of expression can be developed by one or more disconnected sources.

Spire A tapering, conical element on top of a tower.

Steel An alloy of iron and carbon and/or nickel, chromium, titanium, or other metallic elements.

Stone The architectural term for rock that is quarried and used as a building material. There are three basic types of rock—igneous, sedimentary, and metamorphic. Igneous rocks were formed by molten material from the earth's core, either by intrusion (squeezed through the earth's surfaces) or extrusion (spewed from volcanoes), and have cooled and solidified on the surface. Both granite and basalt are igneous rocks used as construction materials, the former intrusive, and the latter extrusive. Sedimentary rock consists of rubble and dust that has consolidated. Limestone is found everywhere on the earth, and is plentiful. A dressed stone is one that has been honed into a particular shape.

Structure A an object assembled from separate parts; a building; a system of components which transfer loads generated by the weight of materials and natural forces (e.g. wind, earthquakes) to the bearing points on the earth's surface. Familiar structural components include columns, beams, arches, vaults, domes, slabs, and trusses. The simplest type of structure is post-and-beam, consisting of two vertical supporting members and a horizontal member spanning between. A frame building consists of multiple post-and-beam components arranged in columns and rows called a structural grid. The term trabeated describes a post-and-beam or frame structure

Symmetry A quality of an object or concept that is balanced by equal components on either side of one or more axes.

Tectonic Of or relating to building or construction; of or relating to the structure of the earth's crust.

Unity A constructed work in which all the components of the building appear as if they were selected and placed by a common theme or concept.

Urban fabric The overall effect of building heights, facade treatments, and massing. Factors that affect a building's relationship with the urban fabric include setback, the distance from the property line, other buildings, or the street; and its orientation.

Use The type of activity of the occupants of the building.

Vault An arch that is extended in the direction perpendicular to its span. A simple, semicircular vault is called a barrel vault. A groin is the line of intersection of the edges of two vaulted surfaces. A groin vault, or cross vault, is a compound vault created by two crossing vaulted surfaces. A rib is an arch-like projection of the edges of a vault that becomes the main supporting member of the vault. A rib vault is supported by diagonal ribs; the web is the non-structural surface framed by the ribs. A fan vault radiates from corner supports in a conoid (resembling a cone) shape.

Vernacular Domestic and functional architecture of a particular country, culture or region, often lacking a particular style

Wood The hard, fibrous material of tree trunks and limbs used for lumber and decorative elements of buildings. The strength of wood used in buildings is affected by the species and age of the tree, and the cross-sectional area of the trunk or limb from which it is made. These characteristics also affect its durability. Wood is subject to decay from fungus and insects, and is more susceptible to fire than most other building materials.

Zoomorphism Representations of animal forms in art, or the representation of a god believed to have an animal form.